2

DIVINE
ENTERPRISE

Divine

GURUS AND THE

THE UNIVERSITY OF CHICAGO PRESS

CHICAGO & LONDON

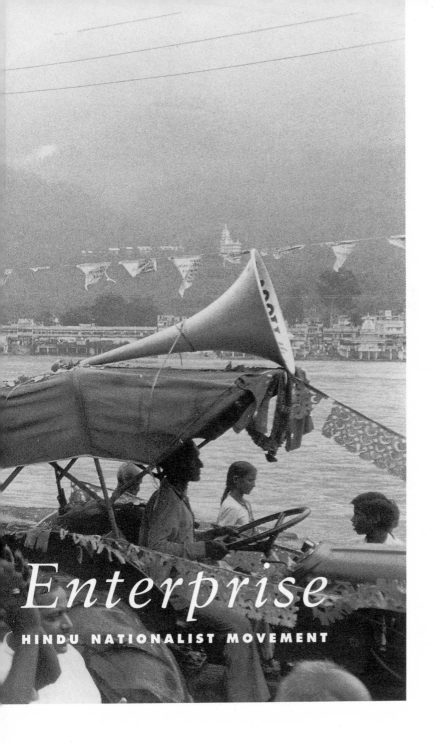

Enterprise

HINDU NATIONALIST MOVEMENT

Lise McKean

Lise McKean is a research associate in the Department of Anthropology at the University of Chicago and managing editor of *Public Culture*.

The University of Chicago Press, Chicago 60637
The University of Chicago Press, Ltd., London
© 1996 by The University of Chicago
All rights reserved. Published 1996
Printed in the United States of America
05 04 03 02 01 00 99 98 97 96   5 4 3 2 1

ISBN (cloth): 0-226-56009-0
ISBN (paper): 0-226-56010-4

Library of Congress Cataloging-in-Publication Data

McKean, Lise.
    Divine enterprise : Gurus and the Hindu Nationalist Movement /
Lise McKean.
        p.   cm.
    Includes bibliographical references and index.
    ISBN 0-226-56009-0. — ISBN 0-226-56010-4 (pbk.)
    1. Hinduism and politics—India.   2. Nationalism—Religious aspects—
Hinduism.   3. Gurus—India.   4. Hinduism—Social aspects—India.
I. Title.
BL1215.P65M35   1996   95-24600
294.5'177'0954—dc20   CIP

For Harry, Lee, and Michael—

a triumvirate of teachers, friends

King: Call back the beaters. And tell the
soldiers to go easy here; this is an ashram and
I'd like to see it respected. Besides, the hermits
are quite unpredictable: quiet on the surface,
but very tense inside. Worrying them is
asking for trouble.

Shakuntala

by Kalidasa

CONTENTS

Many years have passed since first I traveled to India, arriving in Delhi with the itinerary of a wanderer. I had recently completed a B.A. and was ready to learn about the reality underlying the macro-theories and statistics on India's political economy, which were part of my college education. With curiosity whetted by a year's roaming in India, I began an M.A. in South Asian studies at the University of Hawaii, started learning Hindi, and took courses in Indian history, religion, and art. A scholarship from the American Institute of Indian Studies to study Hindi in New Delhi brought me back to New Delhi in 1982.

Like other students on the Hindi program that year, I was dismayed to find that our Indian teachers were as indifferent about teaching us Hindi as they were assiduous about acculturating us to the regimes of New Delhi's literati and bourgeoisie. Indeed, the city's garden of bourgeois delights that I was to find blossoming five years later and in full flower by 1992 was already burgeoning in 1982. Indira Gandhi's government undertook a massive construction program—road improvements, stadiums, five-star hotels—to equip the capital with amenities deemed necessary for hosting the Asian Games and the Non-Aligned Movement Conference. From the roof of my apartment in one direction I could see the domes of emperor Humayun's tomb and in the other the towering lightposts of the newly built Nehru stadium. On daily walks to Hindi class, I passed families of construction workers living alongside the roads and under the flyovers they were building. On the same roads contingents of municipal workers were whitewashing curbs, planting shrubs, and removing dust and debris from one place to another to make the thoroughfares appear attractive and tidy.

Plans for research projects take unexpected turns. While studying Hindi in Delhi, a photo of a woman guru in a neighborhood tea shop prompted me to consider collecting material on her for the M.A. research paper I would have to write on return to Hawaii. After a few trips to her ashram in Agra and always finding her away on tour, I turned my attention to Phoolan Devi, the woman bandit who had become a media sensation. Later I developed the materials I had collected on her into an M.A. paper, "Beauty and the Bandit: Ambiguity and Myth in Indian Journalism."

Two years later when sitting at my desk on a rainy winter day in Sydney and thinking about a field site in north India, memories came to mind of cooling swims in the Ganges at Rishikesh, where mica-flecked waters sparkle in the hot sun. I also recalled the riverside ashrams and temples with their garish statues of gods and mechanical dioramas of scenes from Hindu myths. During an escape from Hindi school in Delhi to the Himalayan foothills of Rishikesh, I had briefly passed through Hardwar. My only memory of it was riding to the Hardwar bus stand in a crowded taxi with a boisterous group of transvestites on pilgrimage.

Another tenacious memory from the Rishikesh trip was the sight of leprous beggars lining the path to the footbridge over the Ganges. Knowing that exchange was an important anthropological theme, and finding that there was little in the literature on beggars in pilgrimage centers, I planned to study this topic and settled on Hardwar as a place to base myself. In March 1987 I returned to Delhi and began to make academic and other social contacts—largely among upper-caste Hindus. Their distaste for my proposed study of beggars was tempered by a prevailing enthusiasm for my selection of Hardwar as a site for fieldwork. A few complained about its greedy brahman priests, but generally Hardwar was highly esteemed and revered as a place where beauty is sanctified by Ganga Ma. Common also were warnings about perils facing visitors to Hardwar: unscrupulous and dangerous persons frequent sacred places, persons with powers they use for malefic purposes.

After surveying Hardwar I decided to focus my research on ashrams, for they seemed to occupy an intriguing and prominent position in the local hierarchy of institutions. Soon after arriving in Hardwar I met Bharati Ma, a woman guru who offered me a room in her ashram. The graciousness of Bharati Ma, her disciples, and devotees made the ashram a home during my stay in Hardwar. I traveled with Bharati Ma on several occasions: to Badrinath with her devotees on pilgrimage from Calcutta; to Gomukh, the spectacular ice cave beyond Gangotri in the high Himalayas, where she initiated three disciples as ascetics; and to Calcutta, her native place where she ministered to the devotees whom she had left behind when she moved to Hardwar twelve years previously.

During the fourteen months that I was based in Hardwar, fieldwork rounds had the regular rhythms and unexpected spectacles of daily life in a pilgrimage town. After preliminary visits to scores of ashrams, I became a frequent visitor at about a dozen, where I became familiar with the presiding guru and residents, local votaries, and habitues. Visits included attendance at rituals and special celebrations as well as informal conversations with whomever would talk with me. Attempts to steer conversations towards sociological or economic questions I had concerning the institution were countered by my interlocutors' vague if not dismissive replies. They insistently directed dialogues towards religious and philosophical topics. Quickly I learned that direct questioning was not effective for procuring information concerning an ashram's cash flow. Conversations with a local lawyer and an accountant proved far more helpful for obtaining a general idea of ashrams' legal and financial affairs.

Delhi provided another site for fieldwork. From Hardwar I made periodic trips there for research on branches of organizations I was studying and to meet with colleagues and friends as a reprieve from the restrictions of ashram life. While in Delhi my rounds were varied: ashram visits, academic seminars, library research, parties, and weddings of friends. Formally and informally I met with people and learned about their work in government bureaucracies and transnational corporations, journalism and law, publishing and cinema, the tourist trade, arts and crafts emporia, small businesses and nongovernmental development agencies. During these visits I grew more familiar with the habitus of Delhi's upper and upper-middle classes, groups whose values and practices I was learning about not only through research on Hindu religious organizations— indeed, many contacts in Delhi or their relatives had ties with some ashram or another—but also through the newspapers and magazines which I was regularly reading. Besides field notes and a hefty collection of religious literature published by ashrams, fieldwork materials also included an extensive clippings file on topics such as gurus and ashrams, political rituals and scandals, dowry deaths and sati, terrorist massacres, communal riots, and the activities of militant Hindu nationalist organizations.

The end of fieldwork in Hardwar coincided with the opening of a new Kali temple at Bharati Ma's ashram. Limited funds frequently brought the project to a standstill, but after a decade of incremental construction, at last the temple was sufficiently completed to consecrate the deity for public worship.

Often during fieldwork I thought things should be worse. The angst of being a novice fieldworker was abated by the many pleasures I found amongst the company I kept in Hardwar and Delhi and from the constant stimulation that accompanies living in the world's second most populous country. When I returned to Australia, I found myself in conditions unfavorable for the project of writing about my field research. The physical and social environment of the isolated, outback town of Derby—flanked by tidal mudflats and glaring desert—offered few pleasures and rendered surreal attempts to occupy myself with intellectual work on Hindu ashrams.

Scorched by a year in the outback, when I returned to Sydney I understood better the dynamics which can prompt people to retreat to an ashram. The library became my retreat. I had formulated many questions concerning Hindu religious organizations in relation to the politics of nationalism and eagerly began to look for clues and answers. The scale of the project daunted me: it had shifted from the seemingly manageable proportions suggested by an ethnography of Hardwar's ashrams to the unwieldy dimensions of the Indian nation-state and the ideologies and activities of nationalists.

When at last I extricated myself from the scholarly archive, I became immersed in the clippings file and spent several months weaving them into thematic essays. These essays concerned the discourse of secularism; the use of Hindu religious imagery in advertising; travel writing on pilgrimage centers; the cults of Mahatma Gandhi and the Nehru family (before Rajiv Gandhi's assassination); public appearances and pronouncements by politicians at events staged by religious organizations. These essays, along with related essays on the ideological content of the concept of sanskritization, on the production of national culture by the Indian state, and on the career and legends of Radhakrishnan—as well as fieldwork and its antecedents in India and elsewhere—underpin the following treatment of the politics of spirituality.

Of the many leads that convinced me of the need to study the involvement of gurus and their organizations in the Hindu nationalist movement, the most powerful impetus was an encounter with Ashok Singhal, the general secretary of the Vishva Hindu Parishad (VHP), during which I witnessed the ferocious determination of Hindu nationalist leadership. This visit to the New Delhi headquarters of the VHP was prompted not only by the attention it was receiving from the media, but also by its own paid-for publicity. For example, the VHP placed a large newspaper advertisement that begins with the headline "Are Hindus Communal?" and summarizes the VHP's arguments concerning the government's failure to solve the communal problem (*Times of India,* February 13, 1988). It blames this failure on opportunistic politicians and Muslim leaders who "go on misguiding their followers into believing that Hindu bodies are communal and enemies of Muslims." It describes Hinduism as *manavdharma* (the religion of mankind); Hinduism is "a parliament of religions and the very antithesis of violence, terrorism and religious intolerance." Reasoning from these tenets, the VHP asserts:

> Thus it can be safely asserted that an enemy of Hinduism is the enemy of human race. To label such a noble Hindu society as communal is the greatest lie in the world. It is a great conspiracy to destroy a noble society for petty gains. Search for Hindu identity and its rejuvenating roots should not be mis-

taken for communalism. . . . All leaders of the world work for the welfare of their own community.

The VHP advises its "Muslim brothers" that if "they want to remove their chronic poverty" they must learn to "live peacefully and fearlessly with Hindus." It closes the advertisement by asking readers to spread the message "to create awakening." The advertisement's last paragraph equates the work of the VHP with national integrity, economic development, and social welfare. To create a sense of urgency and arouse support for the organization, it closes with portents of disaster, a disaster that only the VHP can prevent:

> The birth of the Vishva Hindu Parishad is for the unity and integrity of the country and the moral regeneration of Hindu society, its survival with self respect and uplift of Harijans [untouchables], Girijans [tribals] and other weaker sections. But it cannot continue its work without financial help from each of you. Hope you will not fail us. Only this can save you from disaster.

When I visited the VHP headquarters in February 1988, I was told of my good fortune: Ashok Singhal was present and might agree to see me. After waiting for about an hour I was brought upstairs to Singhal's office. When I told him about my research on ashrams in Hardwar and Rishikesh, he said to me, "Of all nations, India alone has spirituality." Singhal made his declaration in Hindi. Although he used the seemingly English term spirituality, his usage of it was embedded in the ideology of Hindu nationalism with its tenets of the moral and political authority of those who claim to embody and uphold spiritual values.

Singhal's office was adorned with icons of Hindu nationalism: a picture showing an outline of India with Durga inside; a picture of the Rani of Jhansi; a statue of Krishna and Arjuna in their war chariot; a photograph of Jayendra Saraswati, the Shankaracharya of Kanchi; and several images of the sacred syllable *aum*. During most of the time I sat in his office, Singhal directed his attention to his associates. They discussed the VHP's strategies to mobilize mass support and government acquiescence in their drive to take over the Babri mosque and build a Hindu temple on the site in Ayodhya that they claim is Rama's birthplace. The impassioned and violent tone of their discussion about Ayodhya as well as Singhal's hostility to me was unlike the behavior of those speaking about spirituality that I was accustomed to in ashrams. Although I had read numerous newspaper and magazine articles, including interviews with Singhal which explained why Hindus are angry, to witness such belligerence and hatred alerted me to the grave implications of these VHP leaders' determination to fight for political power.

In this study spirituality is conceptualized as a complex of ideas and practices that uses referents to ultimate values to legitimate the authority and self-interested actions of specific political groups and coalitions of groups. The use of anger and hatred to generate particular political identities and mobilize people to fight enemies, evident in the life and work of V. D. Savarkar and witnessed in Singhal, is the other face of spirituality's sentiments concerning the power of selfless love to produce universal peace. This book documents the political uses of spirituality by Hindu nationalists: how it can be used to construct emotional identities for groups and individuals, which can be mobilized for particular political ends; how it provides beliefs and practices for regimes of asymmetrical social relations whereby authority and dominance are generated and legitimated.

ACKNOWLEDGMENTS

Based on my Ph.D. dissertation, the research for *Divine Enterprise* was funded by a four-year post-graduate scholarship from the Australian government and supplemented by funds for fieldwork from the Carlyle-Greenwell Bequest of the Department of Anthropology, University of Sydney. The University of Sydney's Post-graduate Rescue Fund kept me afloat for a few months beyond the expiry of the scholarship.

The sources of intellectual and collegial support for this project are numerous. Michael Allen, my Ph.D. supervisor, generously shared his acumen and enthusiasm. Colleagues and friends in Australia who discussed and read my work include Greg Bailey, Dipesh Chakrabarty, Jean Cooney, Noel Gray, Jacqui McGibbon, Jadran Mimica, Kalpana Ram, and Geoffrey Samuel. In the United States, conversations with Nancy and Robert Foster, Richard Fox, John Kelly, Martha Kaplan, Gananath Obeysekere, and H. L. Seneviratne provided insights into my work. Throughout the long haul, Harry Harootunian encouraged me to persevere.

Affiliation with the Department of Sociology in the Delhi School of Economics at the University of Delhi gave me an entry into academic life in the capital. Professor Jit Singh Uberoi not only agreed to be my "research guide" but also he and Patricia Uberoi shared their formidable intellectual resources with me and often hosted me in their home. Radhika Chopra of the Delhi School familiarized me with the interests of younger scholars and welcomed me into their social world. During visits to Delhi I stayed at times with Sanjay and Sandhya Chatterjee, Shalini Reyes, and Purnima Singh, all of whom contributed friendly and informed interest to my work. Accompanying Lee Siegel in Delhi as he explored the world of conjuring in India refreshed me with the playful side of serious scholarly work.

Foremost among the support I received while in Hardwar came from Bharati Ma, her disciples—Swami Bharati Adyananda, Shobha Ma and

Prema Ma—who live in her ashram, and her devotees who frequent it. Pandit Rajkumar Sharma gave me a guided tour of some of Hardwar's ashrams and he and his family also received me in their home. Suvira Devi of Vedant ashram in Hardwar spoke with me at length about her experiences in ashrams. Mr. and Mrs. Gupta, devotees of Acharya Ram Sharma discussed the teachings of their guru and their active involvement with the Gayatri Parivar. Helen Clapham, a long-term resident in the Hardwar ashram of the Manav Utthan Seva Samiti, assisted in my study of that organization.

Officials at the Divine Life Society in Rishikesh permitted me to stay in the Sivananda ashram on several occasions. Many ashram residents answered my inquiries and I am particularly grateful to Tyagimayi Mata for her keen observations on daily life in the institution. Conversations with Nandini Daly and Devadasi, also residents of Rishikesh, were spiced with witty anecdotes and informed criticisms of the religious institutions and personages around them.

During the years of going and coming back from India, Australia, and the United States, my family has consistently shown interest in and support for my endeavors. Thanks also to Christine De Rosa, Eileen Feibus, and Janet Lynn Kerr for their many years of indulgent friendship. Finally, I am grateful to David Brent and Richard Allen for their editorial expertise.

ONE

Sumptuary Spirituality

Friendliness and curiosity prompted countless people to ask why I had come to India. When I replied that I was living in the pilgrimage town of Hardwar and studying the work of gurus or religious teachers, Hindus typically responded with enthusiastic approval. I was told my topic was well chosen because gurus are teachers of timeless truths and are India's spiritual and social leaders. In the next breath people might caution me about spurious gurus. Yet, they usually followed this warning with assurances that many genuine gurus could be found in Hardwar and nearby Rishikesh.

Gurus—spurious or genuine—are key players in the business and politics of spirituality. The activities of many gurus and their organizations during the 1980s and 1990s are related to the simultaneous expansion of transnational capitalism in India and growing support for Hindu nationalism in India and abroad. These activities produce spirituality's material manifestations and political effects, and can be located within the circuits of commodity production and exchange, i.e., production of use-values for exchange. As producers and purveyors of spiritual commodities, gurus assist in propagating Hindu nationalism, an ideology that relies on referents to Hindu India's unparalleled spiritual prowess and moral authority. Hindu nationalism is an activist ideology: it underpins a movement led by dominant groups to consolidate their political power by mobilizing an array of disaffected social classes.

The nexus of knowledge, power, and wealth in Indian society is inextricable from the authority of gurus, popularly called "godmen" by speakers of Indian English. Godmen may be women. Devotees worship female and male gurus as living gods. By transmitting authoritative spiritual knowledge to worthy followers, a guru acts as a conduit of spiritual power. Integral to a guru's authority and authenticity is membership in a lineage of

1

predecessors and successors who impart eternal spiritual truths and the means to experience them. Many gurus belong to ascetic lineages with regional, pan-Indian, or international networks. Gurus without such ascetic lineages generally claim affiliation with a renowned spiritual predecessor. Many of these more self-styled gurus possess an entrepreneurial flair for building networks of institutions and followers, networks that may grow to rival those of established ascetic lineages.

The importance of lineage is consistent with the conservative political and social orientation which prevails among prominent gurus and their followers. The premise that spiritual power is transcendent and timeless deflects attention from the contingent and often opportunistic economic transactions which underwrite the social power of religious organizations headed by gurus. However much gurus invoke the timelessness of their tradition, they keenly compete to keep their spiritual teachings up to date. In her survey of gurus, Balse admires their fanciful packaging of familiar teachings: "Today's mystics no doubt appeal more to the materialist in man or seek to dazzle with trusted versions of an age old doctrine. Yet they all have a freshness of approach and an enviable ingenuity" (1976, 177).

The guru's death releases portentous forces among followers. Loyalties as well as challenges to gurus and their organizations can be fierce and costly. An interregnum can be a strategic time to adjust the guru's teachings and to attune them to changing political, social, and technological contexts. Property of the organization may be held solely in the guru's name or in a legally established trust society controlled by a board of trustees. Consensus regarding the guru's heir enables an organization to retain intact its property and following. The factional fighting and litigation, the secessions and expulsions associated with succession struggles, diminish an organization's resources and besmirch its reputation. In addition to deploying doctrinal arguments to articulate disputes, followers bitterly fight succession struggles with slander and blackballing, physical intimidation and violence. The incessant litigation of religious organizations pads the pockets of lawyers.

The complex emotional bond between guru and follower encourages passionate involvement in religious organizations headed by a guru. The guru's spiritual superiority makes all exchanges between the guru and follower asymmetrical. Followers demonstrate devotion and gratitude to the guru with offerings and service. However, nothing the devotee gives is as valuable as spiritual gifts from the guru. The social dynamics in the institutional setting of ashrams parallel the hierarchical ranking and asymmetrical exchange relations that permeate other institutions such as family and caste, school and university, small business, corporation and criminal gang, police and military, political party and governmental bureaucracy. The need and benefits of having a guru as well as the best methods of recognizing and serving a spiritual master form recurring themes in Hindu religious literature.[1]

Social psychologist and psychoanalyst Sudhir Kakar argues that the relation between subordinate and superordinate is a dominant model for relationships in Hindu society (1978, 1982, 1985). This model is applicable to the relationship between guru and follower, and renders Kakar's work useful for understanding the psychological dynamics of the guru's authority. He describes the ideal of the superior as "one who acts in such a way that his subordinates either anticipate his wishes or accept them without questioning" (1978, 119). Compliance of the subordinate is achieved through rewards, praise, fear of punishment, and guilt. Kakar maintains that Hindu culture offers a "psychological model of man that emphasizes human dependence and vulnerability to feelings of estrangement and helplessness" (124).

Kakar's model also elaborates the care-taking responsibilities of institutions guided by social and spiritual superiors, responsibilities to protect and provide security for dependents. Such a model of authority generates idealized parental images (130). Gurus and their followers often invoke the parental ideal to describe their own relationship. For example, Bharati Ma, in whose ashram I lived during fieldwork, calls her disciples, devotees, and visitors either son or daughter; they in turn call her mataji (mother). Another guru describes his relation with his followers: "I will never have disciples, only 'children,' because that is the way a real guru should treat a disciple: as a spiritual son or daughter. And the bond between them is far more intense than that between a physical parent and a child" (Svaboda 1986, 41). The idealized parental image also informs the concept of "Ma-Bap," a model of political authority based on the relationship between parents and their child, which can be used to make emotionally charged moral claims for and against legal and institutional forms of authority (Chakrabarty 1989, 163–66).

The guru's authority flows from followers' belief in the guru's proven and potential powers. A guru's reputation for powerful followers attracts more followers (see plate 1). The powers attributed to one's own guru can be as comprehensive as the accusations of fraud made against someone

1. Non-academic books about gurus by sympathetic, skeptical, and critical investigators abound. The following are a selection of such books in English: Brent (1973); Singh (1975b); Balse (1976); Chaubey (1976); Negi (1976); Mangalwadi (1977); and Murray (1980). Jha (1980) and Kovoor (1976) are highly critical of gurus and their credulous devotees. For psychological studies of gurus and their relations with followers, see Kakar (1982, 1985); Caycedo (1966); and Vigne (n.d.a., n.d.b). In his study of mysticism, Staal (1975) examines the role of the guru. In speech and writing, gurus and followers consistently emphasize the need for the guru as well as the ideals and practices structuring the relationship; see, e.g., Sivananda (1981), S. Saraswati (1984), and Narayananda (1972).

else's guru. Devotees believe their guru can heal the sick and materialize objects, foretell events, provide assistance in exams, employment, family and financial matters, and liberate others from the cycle of rebirth. For example, a follower of Sathya Sai Baba describes the divine powers of his guru:

> The Being of Baba and his divine power is beyond our understanding, but there is nothing beyond Him. Innumerable persons have witnessed his divine power: through his will, he can achieve anything, cure cancer, materialise anything, bring about a beneficial change of outlook, make paralysed people discard their crutches. . . . The Being born with divinity uses them [divine powers] to minimise human suffering, and to goad aspirants to the cherished goal of knowing the Reality of the Real, and to make man less matter-bound and more Spirit-bound. (Lal 1975, 3)

Gurus are not alone in recognizing the attractive power of ascribed omnipotence. Packard reports how an advertising agency "found that there is considerable magic in the word power. After many in depth interviews with gasoline buyers the agency perfected an ad strategy that hammered at two words with all letters capitalized: TOTAL POWER" (1975, 72).

Followers' involvement in the life around the guru varies from visits for special festivals to scrupulous attentiveness that anticipates the guru's every move, while support for the organization ranges from modest donations to presentation of a blank check to be filled in by the guru. There is generally a correlation between the amount of time and money expended on devotion and access to the guru, which in turn can enhance a follower's authority over other followers. The more followers and powers the guru has, the more pugnacious the competition for attention. The residences, temples, meeting halls, and gardens of prosperous ashrams can be as colorful and lavish as the pageantry surrounding the guru. Visits to ashrams, devotion to a guru, and participation in celebrations staged by religious organizations provide pleasurable and emotionally satisfying experiences. Such experiences contribute to making spiritual enterprises popular and profitable. They also are means for a guru's followers to build personal and group identities.

The lively, amusement park-like settings of many ashrams present visitors with the spectacle of institutionalized spirituality. Visual representations and verbal testimonials to the guru's spiritual power assure visitors that such power is accessible and abundant. The ashram is the site for the production and consumption of fetish-like commodities, i.e., relationships and objects that have exchange value because they are believed to provide access to the guru's spiritual powers. The dynamics of commodity aesthetics and the power of the commodity's semblance or appearance (Haug 1986, 1987) have parallels with the way that the discourse of spirituality attributes to the guru the capacity to know and fulfill followers' desires. These parallels suggest that spirituality, like commodity aesthetics, can be an instrument of domination:

> The appearance promises more, far more than it can ever deliver. In this respect it is semblance which one falls for. . . . What falls for this semblance is a longing. . . . The semblance offers itself as if it were announcing the satisfaction; it guesses people's nature, reads the wishes in their eyes, and brings the wishes to light on the surface of the commodity. As the semblance in which the commodities come forth deciphers people, it provides them with a language for deciphering themselves and the world. Soon there is no other language than that supplied by the commodities. (Haug 1987, 117)

The interrelations between Hindu religious organizations and the political economy of India are complex and historically variable. The ideological and material profits to be gained from supporting gurus and Hindu religious organizations are today greater than they had been in the first four decades after independence. Formerly, through its interpretation of secularism, India's ruling classes sought to legitimate their power in nonreligious terms and with minimal reliance on the patronage of religious institutions. Nehru's antipathy to Hindu religious leaders and institutions was for many years part of the official Congress platform. However, being neither ignorant of nor indifferent to the political uses of religious ideologues with loyal followings, there were then and there are now even more politicians, bureaucrats, and business and professional groups eager to cultivate working relationships with organizations headed by swamis and gurus (see plate 2).[2]

By the mid-1980s the term "secularism," as used in the Indian press and in political practice, no longer referred to a political system that attempts to distance itself from religious affairs. With the increasing prominence of Hindu nationalist ideology, secularism came to be widely interpreted as the state's obligation to support all religions, with the greatest support going to Hinduism, the religion of a purported majority of Indians. Such a shift in meaning relates to the success of the Hindu nationalist movement's relentless propaganda campaigns and activism. These campaigns malign Nehru's interpretation of secularism and accuse the Con-

2. Sinha (1968, 36) implies that public activities of government officials shortly after independence demonstrated a compromised commitment to secularism, e.g., a government minister participated in the formation of the Bharat Sadhu Samaj (an organization of Hindu ascetics), holding a position on its advisory council, and the president of India and other government officials participated in consecration rituals at the Somnath temple in 1951. Sinha also speculates that "when Rajendra Prasad [first president of India], a devout Hindu took part in so many religious functions or when he dipped in the 'sacred' water of the Ganges, it was difficult for an average Muslim to believe that the Indian state was secular" (35).

gress of being "pseudo-secular." After many decades of steady work, during the 1980s the political agenda of Hindu nationalists began to dominate public debate. Hindu nationalists argued that the Indian state discriminates against the Hindu majority by pandering to non-Hindu groups. Presenting themselves as defenders of democracy, they maintained that the state's discrimination against Hindus threatens democracy. They linked democracy with the stability of Indian society, a stability founded on the spirituality taught by Hindu sages. According to Hindu nationalists, because Hinduism emanates from spiritual values, it is uniquely tolerant of other religions and is the sole basis of an authentically Indian secularism. Such an indigenous secularism, which advocates state support of all religion, is presented as superior to Nehruvian pseudo-secularism, imported from the West, which advocates strict separation of state and religion. Following from these propositions regarding secularism, spirituality, and Hinduism, Hindu nationalists conclude that a Hindu state is necessarily the best guardian of an indigenous Indian secular democracy.

Concurrent with the transformation of the meaning of "secularism" has been the election of a growing number of swamis and sadhus to public office at the local, state, and national levels. The resources available to them as elected officials greatly enlarge their capacity to dispense patronage, which attracts further followers to Hindu religious organizations.

A CLASS JUST ASKING FOR CONSUMPTION

During the 1970s and particularly the 1980s, the private economic sector consisting of Indian and transnational corporations as well as medium- and small-scale industries and services expanded rapidly (Khanna 1987). The Indian state justified changes in policy with explanations based on economic rationalism. At the same time it reduced its reliance on socialism as a populist ideology. These shifts suggest how the bourgeois Indian state adapts its domestic policy to international changes and trends. Pressured by coalitions of ruling-class groups, who wanted to more effectively compete in international markets as well as expand their opportunities to invest capital in potentially profitable private enterprises within India, the state formulated economic policies to support these goals. Khanna argues that the middle classes' turn away from the public sector for employment opportunities "has gradually eroded the social support for the so-called 'socialist' ideology. The strategies to tackle problems of poverty and unemployment have given way to methods of harnessing India's technological and entrepreneurial talent for a capitalist transformation like that witnessed in South Korea" (1987, 59–60). By the late 1980s and early 1990s the globalizing forces associated with the ascendancy of transnational capitalism made redundant many policies of centralized economic planning developed after independence. After four decades of official restrictions on India's involvement in the world economy, the government developed policies enabling the economy to go global and encouraging transnational corporations to invest in India.

Celebrating the capitalist transformation and "consumer revolution" under way in India, newspapers and magazines extolled the virtues of entrepreneurs with cover stories such as *India Today*'s "The New Millionaires and How They Made It" (31 October 1987). In another article, the force behind the expansion of small and medium-sized businesses is identified with neither the desire for wealth nor the greater availability of investment capital but rather with the fact that "young people today prefer work which brings out the entrepreneurial and innovative aspects of their personality" (*Times of India*, 26 July 1987). One journalist asks, "How can India cope with success?" and looks to the new class of affluent consumers as "at once the hope and threat to India's future" (*Hindustan Times*, 7 June 1987). The *Wall Street Journal* reports on this class of consumers with an article entitled: "A Thriving Middle Class is Changing the Face of India in a Land of Poverty: Its Buying Spree Promises Economic Growth" (19 May 1988). The article included a quotation from an executive of a New Delhi advertising agency who regards the middle-class market as "a bottomless pit. . . . Growth is restricted only by a marketer's imagination." In the same article a member of the Government Planning Commission evokes a nationalist identity for middle-class consumers: "It is a class that is just asking for consumption." In his view this class cannot be accused of being parasitic: "You can't charge them as anti-national. They are the products of India."

A magazine cover story entitled "The Power and the Glory" discusses how affluence has transformed the nation's capital: "Meet the new New Delhi. An affluent, sophisticated, modern capital where the country's future is decided. Where there is more conspicuous consumption than Bombay; more culture than Calcutta; and where a new breed of politicians predominate" (*Sunday*, 8 November 1987). The article announces that in the 1980s New Delhi entered "the era of yuppie-style politics where style is all and austerity is yesterday's news." Evidence of affluence could be found in the construction and renovation of luxury residences, burgeoning patronage of five-star hotels, conspicuous consumption of luxury commodities, and in the rush of Indian tourists traveling abroad: " 'After the TV and video boom in Indian households it is now the age of foreign travel,' observes Gautam Chadha, British Airways sales manager" (*India Today*, 31 May 1987). Concurrent with this rush to travel abroad was "The New Gold Rush" (*Sunday*, 13 December 1987). Gold is described as "one of the great subterranean forces in the Indian economy." Buying, selling, and smuggling gold is big business in India and is another link with the international economy. The amount of gold in a woman's dowry is an important factor in marriage negotiations and increases the expense of marriage for women: " 'India buys gold as a necessity for marriage,' " reports a Bombay gold merchant.

The director of the Centre for Policy Research in New Delhi, V. A. Pai Panandiker, analyzes "India's middle class power" (*Hindustan Times*, 25 July 1987). According to his statistics, the top twenty percent of India's population—about 150 million people—have an income share of about fifty percent of the gross domestic product. The black economy, "which is largely meant for the benefit of this group even if all of them do not directly get involved in it," is a source of income that increases their purchasing power by two or three times, making "the income level of this 150 million people a formidable economic power." Assisted by the government's economic policies, India's new entrepreneurs as well as transnational corporations look upon the demand for commodities by middle-class consumers as a profitable and expanding market. Characterizing the political orientation of this new middle class, Panandiker writes: it is a "devotee of the democratic system. It realises that outside the democratic system, its power and influence will be greatly reduced and weakened. The democratic system is ideally suited for its dominance because of the ability of this class to forge continually new coalitions." Upper-caste Hindus "are perhaps the biggest beneficiaries" of policies related to increased middle-class affluence.

Panandiker further characterizes the politics of this class in terms of the "dominance of the Hindus" and the "systematic cooption of others"—Muslim, Sikh, Christian, and scheduled caste groups, who in far lesser numbers are also members of this new middle class. He emphasizes the familial, caste, and class linkages between the rulers of the Indian polity and nonresident Indians (NRIs). The size and influence of the coalition composed of the ruling elites, the new middle class, and affluent NRIs "has become a major phenomenon of the India of the eighties. And this phenomenon is only likely to grow." In Panandiker's opinion, the most "worrisome characteristic" of the new middle class is its indifference to the condition of forty percent of India's population: "If this new class had a choice, this forty per cent would not exist. This lack of concern for the large mass of the poor in India is a serious blight on the socio-political and economic ethos of this class."

Panandiker neglects to analyze the relation between middle-class affluence and entrepreneurial success and mass poverty, which is the structural means for keeping the cost of agricultural and industrial labor and its reproduction extremely low. Instead he considers labor in terms of the "managerial revolution in India" and notes how "India's managerial prowess is now large enough to dwarf the traditional strongholds of the Indian civil service system." In other words, the political influence and social prestige of managers and executives in the private sector has come to match their economic power, diminishing the status of public sector bureaucrats. Like a guru reminding audiences of the need to defend Hindu spirituality from the forces of western materialism, Panandiker reprimands the middle class for showing "every sign of crass materialism and consumerism so often noticed in some of the other civilizations especially of the Western world." After the requisite chastisement, the author concludes his article by affirming the political authority of India's middle class: "More and more economic and political decisions will be dictated by this class. This class will largely determine the nature of the Indian polity and the political economy over the next generation or two. And most important of all, it will lend the country basic political stability."

Economic rationalism is a flexible framework used to explain and justify processes of transnational capitalism. This framework can be adjusted to accommodate a range of political and cultural forms. For example, "Managing for Effectiveness," an article in Indian Airlines' in-flight magazine, describes people's capacity for work according to the Hindu *guna* theory, categorizing people in terms of temperament and personal qualities (*Swagat,* October 1987). It then explains how corporate managers can most profitably use employees of each type. Gurus also use this theory of personal qualities when discussing why various kinds of spiritual disciplines are necessary for different types of persons.

Gurus share with managers and employers the desire to control subordinates. They all rely on the labor of others to secure their profits. Devotees donate money and labor to the guru in the hope of earning the guru's favor and grace. Through deferential behavior and conscientious work, employees hope to earn favors from bosses, favors that might supplement their often inadequate wages. The guru's teachings about disciplined work and simple living complement the interests of employers. Managers and employers may or may not reinforce their authority by demonstrating these virtues in their own lives. However, they rely on references to the virtues of hard work and abstemious habits for moral legitimation of employees' low wages. Through deference and service to superiors, who belong to larger and more powerful social networks, subordinates hope to earn assistance in procuring desired goods and services that may be financially or socially beyond their personal means.

The figure of guru and particularly the ascetic, who supposedly is no longer motivated by desire for personal and material gain, provides a model for relations of asymmetrical exchange. This model is based on the presupposition that persons who exemplify and teach spiritual values reign supreme: the guru always gives more than the disciple or devotee could possibly reciprocate. The ways these exchange relations operate and the language used to describe them are a recurring theme in this book. Moreover, this logic of asymmetrical exchange informs the moral arguments used by persons in positions of authority to represent themselves as disinterested, benevolent superiors. Such arguments support a variety of exchange relationships that can yield handsome profits for gurus.

With a Sanskrit quote concerning the gunas, "You can establish yourself only through your own qualities," a multinational corporation advertises itself and the virtues of its brahman founder. In two double-page advertisements in *India Today*, the Sunflag Group gives transnational capitalism a brahmanic and nationalistic gloss. The advertisements present the capitalist's success as inextricable from his identity as a learned brahman: "Presenting the 400 million dollar business credentials of a Sanskrit scholar"; "The scholar as pioneer and leader." The corporation's founder, Satyadev Bhardwaj is described as a "Corporate Karmayogi." This Sanskrit scholar arrived in Kenya in the 1930s to head a school, "but there his scholastic ability merges with the spirit of enterprise." Fifty years later, Bhardwaj heads a "multinational industrial empire." To this day "the Sanskrit scholar's zeal for philanthropy and enterprise continues unabated. Truly, an example of business and the Gita going hand in hand." Bhardwaj is said to have combined "the best of old world ethics with new wave industry."

What are these old world ethics? Hard work? By whom? For whose profit? Perhaps some of Bhardwaj's old-world ethics are shared by the small industrialists in India whose recent successes are analyzed by Khanna (1987). Not only good education, access to bank loans, and connections with bureaucrats and politicians, but also their "ability to hire workers at very low wages and run 'sweat shops' with low overheads has given them the edge" (Khanna 1987, 56).

The advertisements do not say whether the Sunflag Group has any companies in India. The Indian flag is not among the flags shown. Does Sunflag aim to hoist its flag in India? Whatever the corporation's specific motivation for placing these costly advertisements, through them it represents transnational capitalism with brahmanic and nationalistic imagery. The ads assure upper and middle-class readers of *India Today* that the Sunflag Group is "a modern multinational with its roots in the rich Indian heritage!" The heightened importance of Hindu nationalism and the religious organizations which support it relate to India's political and economic transformation into an aggressive competitor in the marketplace of global capitalism. The expansion of India's private sector has intensified competition in certain economic and political arenas, enriching some groups while leaving others discontent, exploited, uncertain, and resentful (Vanaik 1990).

Hindu nationalism provides an ostensibly populist and highly emotional framework for ambitious and aggrieved groups to articulate political demands. As Hindu nationalist ideology becomes more pervasive and powerful, politicians and bureaucrats rely more heavily on it to legitimate their power and mask their interests. Moreover, the organizations propagating militant and moderate forms of Hindu nationalism present themselves as protectors of spiritual and social values. They also widely publicize their charitable activities. Through its official and unofficial support of religious organizations, the state can present itself as upholding "true secularism," which Hindu nationalists have defined as government support of religion. This support also assists the state in its role as provider of social welfare. Political, business, and religious leaders often describe themselves as "trustees" of Indian society whose duty is to "protect and uplift the weaker sections of society." As the state has decreased its reliance on socialism to represent itself as the benefactor of the masses, religious charity and corporate philanthropy are increasingly important institutional supports for the state's policies favoring the rapid expansion of the private sector, and for the state's patronage of religious institutions.

The increased political importance of religious organizations also relates to investment in them by corporations and businesses. This investment diversifies economic and social networks and provides a means for private sector enterprises to represent themselves as socially responsible and hence worthy of the wealth they command. In turn, leaders of religious organizations propagate beliefs and practices that assist in legitimating the power of ruling-class groups. Gurus construct compliant identities for devotees. They not only train devotees to defer to the authority and knowledge of social superiors—parents and elders, educators and employers, politicians and bureaucrats—but also promise that obedience and devoted service will be rewarded. The authority of major religious leaders' pronouncements on matters spiritual and mundane is strengthened by the social power they derive from the support of wealthy and influential followers.

During the late 1980s the government's economic policies promoted the growth of the private sector, industrialization geared to urban middle-class consumers, and the reduction of transfer payments from rich to poor organized by the state. Vanaik argues that these policies contribute to the creation of two antagonistic nations within India: a privileged nation of affluent consumers and a nation of impoverished masses (*Times of India*, 28 March 1988; 1990). Conflict characterizes the relations between the rural and urban components of the privileged nation as well as the relations between the privileged nation and the masses. The forces of the state are used to police these struggles and protect the interests of the privileged nation. To supplement the state's policing of these conflicts, Vanaik suggests that these two nations must be "connected in some positive way." He is skeptical about the accuracy of the "trickle-down thesis" of free-market economists. Hindu nationalists invoke the two-nation theory but offer a different reading: they accuse Muslims of declaring themselves a separate nation and of trying to split India into two nations. Their solution is a unitary Hindu nation-state.

This study of spirituality as propagated by Hindu religious organizations investigates how spirituality provides ideological and institutional forms for linking in some positive way the various classes and sectors, rich, middle class, and poor, urban and rural. Spirituality is mortar for coalition building among socio-economic classes. It forms part of the magnetic core that attracts individuals and groups to the Hindu nationalist movement. The congenial and compelling face of spirituality attracts and binds supporters into political coalitions that strengthen the movement. Spirituality provides a means for producing identities and mobilizing people. It operates as a populist and democratic facade for the militant and authoritarian infrastructure of the Hindu nationalist movement. Through its embodiment in specific religious organizations, spirituality is Janus-faced in its effects: universalist claims occult the inequalities of class, caste, and gender hierarchies; regimes of interpersonal relationships with the deity or guru (super)naturalize relations of asymmetrical exchange.

The Hindi and Sanskrit terms associated with spirituality *(adhyatmikta)* are numerous and have many shades of meaning. They refer to the individual self *(atm:* pertaining to self; one's own; personal); the individual soul *(atma);* and the supreme soul *(adhyatm; brahma).* The goal of spiritual disciplines *(adhyatatmik sadhana)* and the ultimate spiritual knowledge *(adhyatamjnana; brahma vidya)* as taught by Hindu gurus—most of whom espouse variants of nondualism *(advaita vedanta)*—is merger of the individual soul with the universal, supreme soul. Through such a merger the individual attains liberation *(moksha; mukti)* from the cycle of rebirth *(samsara)* by breaking the bonds forged by one's actions *(karma).* The knowledge *(jnan)* and practices *(sadhana)* taught by the guru, which constitute spirituality, locate an individual's personal life within an encompassing metaphysical totality. The arguments of Hindu theologians and philosophers can be heterogeneous and nuanced. Hindu spiritual teachers, however, uphold an orthodoxy that subordinates the individual's material and social reality to a timeless and transcendental ultimate reality. However, gurus attract followers not simply because they teach about spirituality; followers flock to specific gurus whom they believe possess the power to transform material reality.

Publicity, persons, and institutions promoting spirituality suffuse Indian society. They can be astonishingly flamboyant, particularly in Hindu pilgrimage centers. Ashrams and activities of religious organizations are particularly concentrated in pilgrimage places, sites where visitors avidly encounter institutionalized spirituality (see plates 3 and 4). Over three hundred establishments of gurus and ascetics are located in Hardwar and Rishikesh, the north Indian pilgrimage towns where I conducted fieldwork. The spirituality promoted by gurus and ashrams is part of an array of religious activity associated with pilgrimage—bathing in sacred waters, worshipping in temples, performing life-cycle and mortuary rituals.[3] The abundance of ritual activities and Sanskrit schools earn for brahman *pandas* (pilgrimage priests) and *pandits* (teachers, scholars) a prominent presence in major Hindu pilgrimage centers. Leading gurus, landowning and business families, and representatives of brahman panda and pandit interests are key actors in local affairs. These dominant groups, however, are neither mutually exclusive nor are their goals wholly antagonistic. They all strive to maximize the profits of pilgrim traffic in spirituality and ritual: brahmans own hotels and shops; ashrams earn income like hotels by housing pilgrims; merchants in the bazaar, like gurus in their ashrams, sell religious objects. Writing about Bakeshwar, a Hindu pilgrimage center in West Bengal, Chaudhuri observes that political parties hold regional meetings there and that "the brahmans, the shopowners and even the beggars have abiding interest in the perpetuation of the sacred myth of Bakeshwar which would attract more and more visitors to this sacred area and fetch them more money" (1981, 52).

Many up-and-coming gurus model their organizations after the Divine Life Society, headquartered at the Sivananda Ashram in Rishikesh, or after other establishments that attract sophisticated and wealthy followings and present themselves as promoters of universal religion and true spirituality. Social and economic differences among followings give rise to considerable variation in the size, orientation, and activities of guru-headed institutions. Furthermore, spiritual leaders need not be ascetic initiates or live in an austere manner. However, organizations with ascetic leadership generally attract followings with higher caste and class status than do those headed by nonascetics, who, like ascetics, may live with a minimum, modicum, or full complement of comforts and luxuries.

3. Studies of Hindu pilgrimage centers, particularly by Indian social scientists, frequently evaluate pilgrimage as a tradition which facilitates "national integration." Some works in this genre include: Vidyarthi (1960, 1961); Jha (1971, 1985); Saraswati (1972, 1975); Vidyarthi, Jha, and Saraswati (1979). Examples of non-nationalistic studies of Hindu pilgrimage centers include Morinis (1984) and van der Veer (1988). For studies focusing on pilgrimage see Bharati (1963); Turner (1972); Eck (1981, 1982); and Gold (1988). Also relevant to the study of pilgrimage centers is the historical and anthropological research on Hindu temple complexes such as the collection on Puri edited by Eschmann, Kulke and Tripathi (1978) and work on south Indian temples by Appadurai and Breckenridge (1976), Appadurai (1981), and Fuller (1984).

RENUNCIATION AND THE CREATION OF VALUE

"Is it really too adventurous to say that the agent of development in Indian religion and speculation, the 'creator of values,' has been the renouncer?" (Dumont 1960, 47). Contentious debate surrounds Dumont's theoretical formulations concerning Hindu society. The present discussion redeploys Dumont's ideas about the institution of renunciation, the work of renouncers, and their relation to the role of spirituality in the Indian polity. Dumont suggests that the "secret of Hinduism may be found in the dialogue between the renouncer and the man-in-the-world" (1960, 37). Referring to the renouncer's engagement with speculative pursuits such as liberation, Dumont himself speculates about the ability of the renouncer to act as the "creator of values" and argues that through the institution of renunciation a person can "become to himself his own end" (1970, 231). The renouncer is able to "escape the network of strict interdependence" and "adopts a universal and personal role" (231).

Dumont contrasts the innovations of the renouncer, whose social status "gave him a sort of monopoly for putting everything in question," with the brahman scholar, who conserves and develops knowledge, aggregating it to the requirements of orthodoxy (1960, 47). The innovations of the renouncer do not condemn the religious rituals and social usages of brahmanic orthodoxy but rather place them in a relative and subordinate position to extramundane, ultimate values. Dumont argues that this subordination of the temporal to the spiritual has allowed Indian society "to found itself directly upon the absolute order" (52). The way spirituality represents society as founded on the absolute order has been introduced above and will be taken up again later in the context of pronouncements that Hindu sages and saints are the authoritative teachers of the spiritual values that constitute the foundation of the social order.

Classes and coalitions competing for political legitimacy and social ascendancy require ideologues who depict the emerging social order as synonymous with an absolute order. In India renouncers, brahmans, intellectuals, and politicians vie and ally to define the prevailing terms of the absolute order. Depending on which attributes and activities of the society and of sociality are to be valorized or subordinated, the status of and relations among renouncer, brahman, kshatriya, vaishya, shudra, and untouchable are differently defined (Burghart 1983a). Burghart argues that sociological analysis should not continue to conceptualize Indian society as a total system. Representations of totality are universalizing objectifications by elite groups (including anthropologists) of their own specific frameworks. As an alternative, Burghart suggests that these representations of totality be studied as distinctive and motivated objectifications circulating in an intracultural arena. In this arena the renouncer, the brahman householder, and the martial ruler contest and negotiate the particular schema which secures each group's distinctive status.

The work of Inden (1990) complements Burghart's orientation to a critical sociology of Indian society. Inden presents an incisive critique of indological formulations that employ substantialized essences such as caste or renunciation. This critique points out the limitations of an ethno-sociological approach, an approach that often echoes high-caste apologetics of sociologists and social commentators. The sanksritization model of social change that simultaneously prescribes and describes how lower-status groups relate to higher ones is one example of how positivism and objectivity in the social sciences can support the ideological and political commitments of dominant groups. These ideological commitments are not limited to bourgeois academics and high-caste sociologists. Work by Pollock (1990) and Bailey (1989) indicates how indigenous Sanskrit scholarship as well as western indology objectify and privilege the self-representations of high-status and powerful groups. Pollock contends that many features of orthodox brahmanic tradition or Sanskrit culture are predicated upon the transposition of ritual onto society. Through this transposition "ritual discourse becomes a discourse of social power insofar as it sustains the relations of domination constitutive of traditional Indian society, which are characterized by the systematic exclusion from property, power, and status of three-quarters of the population for more than two millennia" (Pollock 1990, 315).

Like Burghart, Inden challenges analyses that treat Indian society as a closed and totalizing system. Inden is concerned with how human agency—individuals, groups, coalitions of groups—operates to make and unmake the vertically structured groups (ruling societies) that constitute the Indian polity. His treatment highlights activities of ruling societies in terms of their vertical and horizontal, aggregative and combative interrelations. Inden argues that these processes and interrelations are constitutive of the polity. This framework is useful for conceptualizing how the vertical and horizontal coalitions that compose Hindu religious organizations, which in turn are components of the Hindu nationalist movement, relate to larger political and economic processes. In addition to Inden's analysis, Haug's orientation foregrounds class issues for considering the problem of agency and Hindu religious organizations: "When I say that we should look at the actions of real human beings, the real human being is not confined to the individual or the small group, the organization of a class is part of the real human being so the activities of class organizations must be included" (Haug 1987, 247).

Spirituality's emphasis on self-effort, self-realization, and their rewards provides a flexible idiom for expressing the relationships of individuals and groups to the "absolute order" underpinning Indian society. Forty years ago, state controls over the domestic economy were widely regarded as an expression of the timeless Indian values of self-reliance and autonomy. Since the mid-1980s, religious leaders espousing the universalism of Hindu spirituality have come to dominate discussions on the absolute order. This idiom complements the Indian state's commitment to global capitalism and its focus on stimulating foreign and domestic investment in commodity production for India's huge market of middle-class consumers.

Through the renouncer's innovations, and especially the development of *bhakti,* whereby believers conceive of themselves as individuals involved in a personal relation with a particular form of divinity, "an individual religion of choice is added to the religion of the group" (Dumont 1960, 47). As the renouncer's innovations become sedimented in sectarian organizations, individual religion of choice combines with the religion of the group. Dumont's observations can be interpreted to emphasize the economic and political implications of historically variable alliances between the renouncer and the brahman. Analysis of how exponents of spirituality mold strategic political alliances has three principal strands: spirituality's role in the regime of capitalist social relations; its relationship to commodity production and circulation; and its relationship to commodity aesthetics. Dumont's comment that the renouncer is the "creator of values" can also be understood in terms of the social use value and exchange value of the renouncer and guru. Brahmanic orthodoxy, defined here as a malleable ideology and regime of social relations for establishing the hegemony of ruling class coalitions, is a force as political and economic as it is social and religious. It finds in the renouncer a staunch ally, faithful critic, and occasional competitor. There is at once a complementary division of labor between them and mutual encroachments on each other's markets of ideological and material commodities (van der Veer 1988, 41).

Spiritual gurus need be neither renouncers nor brahmans. However, brahmanic ideology, which defers to the spiritual authority of the renouncer while reserving the apex of the social hierarchy for brahmans, also informs the dominant mode in which both renouncers and spiritual gurus are ranked. Through initiation renouncers supposedly rupture their connections with the social world and relinquish their caste status. The high status and social power of brahman ascetics such as the Shankaracharyas, who head important monastic orders and are spokesmen for brahmanic orthodoxy, suggest that within the institution of renunciation, there remains considerable scope for upholding caste hierarchy. Whereas many gurus teach that through spiritual disciplines anyone can become a brahman, no guru has the power to transform followers' caste status. Gurus teach followers how to speak and behave according to the ideal for brahman religious teachers, ritualists, and householders.

Embodiments of divine power in the eyes of their devotees, gurus can themselves become as much a commodity as the goods and services they purvey. Exchanges between devotees and gurus, like those between patrons and brahman ritualists, bear the promise of social use value. It is this promise of use value and the ways in which advertising in capitalist societies presents commodities' semblance of use value and induces people to pursue this promise through consumption of commodities that Haug terms commodity aesthetics (1986, 1987). Those who enter into these circuits of commodity exchange and consumption seek to profit by them. The ideology of spirituality and renunciation makes it possible for gurus and their religious organizations to not only mask the drive for profits that underlies exchanges with followers but also renew the promise of value which they offer to followers. The profits of spirituality enable religious organizations to accumulate economic and political capital. This capital in turn can be reinvested to produce commodities and services that attract more followers and generate more capital, e.g., publications, temples and more guest-rooms in ashrams, conferences and festivals, favors and honors for followers and politicians.

My decision to address the political economy of spirituality relates to the relative neglect this topic has received in the social science literature on Hinduism and Indian society. Work on Hindu topics such as pilgrimage, gurus and their organizations frequently presents expositions of cultural and philosophical materials. The prolific and often critically astute body of Marxian historical and anthropological writing on Indian topics largely eschews analysis of religious institutions and offers no systematic investigation of how Hindu organizations operate within Indian society, how they earn and deploy their wealth, prestige, and followings. This study of institutionalized spirituality draws on a large range of sources concerning Indian religion, history, nationalism, and political economy. Its theoretical orientation draws on ideas associated with critical theory, cultural, and subaltern studies.

ETHNOGRAPHIC AND HISTORICAL MATERIALS ON HINDU RELIGIOUS ORGANIZATIONS

The following discussion reviews work by indologists, historians, and anthropologists which relates to the economics of religious organizations, especially those organizations associated with ascetics and gurus. Like commercial credit, the merit earned through the austerity *(tapas)* and righteousness *(dharma)* of the renouncer and householder and the potency of a ruler *(tejas)* can be accumulated, increased, distributed, snatched away, spent, wasted (Hara 1967, 1970; Inden 1990). The compatibility of these three regimes of exchange is strikingly figured in wealthy ascetic orders such as Shaivite *gosains,* who in the eighteenth century formed cadres of

skilled wayfarers that conducted lucrative long-distance trade in conjunction with sedentary sectarian partners (Cohn 1974). Pilgrimage centers
were important nodes in these commercial networks. Ascetics earned their
wealth as caravan guards and henchmen, as armed pilgrims and mercen-
aries employed by merchants, landlords, and rulers, as well as through taxation, theft, raiding, and moneylending (Kolff 1971; Gordon 1971).

Mercantile *(mahajan)* groups have long patronized religious institutions as a means to advance their business interests and enhance their social prestige (Bayly 1973). With credit as their principle asset to accumulate
and manipulate, mercantile groups share with gurus and brahmans a livelihood highly invested in propagating and enforcing relations of exchange
that are motivated by desire for short- and long-term profits. Donations to
religious establishments and expenditures on ritual and charitable be-
quests are carefully recorded in business and personal account books of
late-nineteenth-century urban mercantile groups (Bayly 1973, 40). Donors
and recipients kept mental and written accounts of forms of social and
financial credit and debt. These exchanges structured relations of dominance, subordination, and partnership within local and regional commercial and marriage networks. In a study of business groups active in Calcutta
in the early decades of the twentieth century, Bagchi's findings (1970) concur with those of Bayly on the support of religious institutions by commercial classes. Bagchi notes that "many of the new trading and banking
groups which emerged into industrial entrepreneurship—the Chettiars,
the Jains and the Hindu baniyas—were much addicted to the building of
temples, dharmshalas, and the endowing of institutions of astrological
learning" (1970, 256).

Late-eighteenth and nineteenth-century ascetic leaders of religious organizations such as the Swaminarayan sect introduced new ideas and practices regarding spirituality and social relations. These innovations related
to changes associated with the British mercantile, military, political, and
missionary presence, and to the rapacity and lechery associated with powerful and wealthy ascetic orders. Like other ascetics intent on proving the
authenticity of their renunciation, Swaminarayan ascetics to this day osten-
tatiously avoid contact with women and money. Hagiographic accounts report that the founder, Swaminarayan, would vomit in revulsion at the
approach of a woman's shadow (Williams 1984, 11). As he became more
established and his resources increased, Swaminarayan's formerly austere
habits gave way to a style that competed in opulence with other wielders of
wealth and power. A legacy of succession rivalries articulated through legal
battles and doctrinal disputes has divided the sect into rival organizations.
Williams reports that strict segregation of the sexes continues to exclude
women from administrative positions. Male management committees control the extensive property and wealth of Swaminarayan organizations,

which are based in Gujarat and have branches elsewhere in India and abroad (Williams 1984, 145).

Although Williams does not systematically examine the economic operations of Swaminarayan organizations, his study has numerous references to their techniques of fund-raising. He notes that during their regular ceremonial tours, Swaminarayan leaders collect gifts and pledges from members (89–91). As with Swaminarayan cadres traveling to urban and rural areas to collect donations, the monastic organization studied by Bradford has "a well-organized collection of donations that takes in large areas of Karnataka" (1985, 97). It is difficult to collect information about the conditions and terms under which these donations are tendered. The researcher's public association with sectarian leaders and administrators limits the scope for discussing with donors the sect's coercive and punitive powers.

Swaminarayan lay members take a vow to respect the personal property and property rights of others (Williams 1984, 139). Other regulations advocate an austere lifestyle and careful business practices, including saving for the future and balancing income and expenditure. One regulation concerns the necessity to formalize business relations with relatives through witnessed and legally binding contracts, a regulation which Williams argues was a response to the expansion of the British legal system and changing mercantile practices. Another regulation requires businessmen to keep daily accounts of income and expenses and to bring new account books to Swaminarayan temples where they are blessed, worshipped with full vedic rites, and signed by the chief ascetic of the temple (123). Williams does not consider the possibility that such ritual activity may be a form of tribute.

Among other methods for raising funds, Swaminarayan lay members are enjoined to donate five to ten percent of their income to the organization. Devotees eager to demonstrate their support and submission to the will of their guru present a blank check and ask the guru to fill in the amount. Outsiders and relatives of members told Williams that active participation in Swaminarayan activities can be a costly commitment. However, active participation has its benefits. It links members with networks of business and social contacts which assist in expanding their businesses and improving their social status. Using the language of spirituality, Swaminarayan businessmen attribute their "self-improvement," their business profits and social climbing, to the divine grace of their guru.

Swaminarayan teachings promise followers that devotion and a prudent lifestyle earn divine blessings of worldly success. Williams notes parallels between the puritanical and commercial orientation of Swaminarayan teachings and Weberian interpretations of the protestant ethic and the spirit of capitalism. However, he found that Swaminarayan "devotees are not comfortable with the comparison because of the negative connotations of the word 'capitalism.' Some leaders prefer to emphasize the use of wealth for social welfare and refer to this as a type of socialism. They quote Swaminarayan: 'Accumulation of wealth is a great danger, distribution of wealth is a blessing' " (41).

Like the teachings of Swaminarayan, the guru eulogized by Kirin Narayan reminds his listeners that "wealth follows worship" and financial ruin ensues when a family neglects its religious and charitable obligations (1989, 241). Narayan reports that this Swamiji uses his social and financial resources to secure employment and favors for disciples (81). Choosing not to interrogate the social power wielded by the guru she studied, Narayan describes renunciation as "an alternative life-style pivoting around spiritual concerns" (77). By treating spiritual concerns as unproblematic and by invoking irony as an explanatory trope, Narayan dismisses critical sociological analysis of renouncers' active engagement in the social world: "Swami R. once told me, dimples deepening as he spoke, 'Though we leave our families look what happens, the entire world becomes our family.' Ironically, the act of renunciation may in fact push an ascetic into more extensive social involvement than if he or she remained a layperson" (79).

In his analysis of three Hindu religious organizations with middle- and upper-middle class urban followings, Babb (1987) depicts a fluid world in which devotees seek to maximize transactions with the guru as a means to advance and ultimately liberate the self. By choosing to privilege continuity and unity over historical specificity and difference, by orienting his study to the "distinctive spiritual disposition" of the Hindu religious imagination as evidenced in the three movements, Babb marginalizes issues relating to the political and economic contexts in which these organizations emerged and operate (1987, 1). He argues that the capacity to "invest the world with religious meaning" characteristic of these movements is a capacity that is universal and dynamic, "endlessly protean and full of creative possibilities" (1).

Babb's deferential attitude to the object of his study, "I have regarded it as a special obligation to treat these movements with all the respect that I deeply feel" (x), limits his ability to examine the sociological and political implications of these movements. He stresses the universalism of Hinduism: "My story also has a moral, which is that cultural distinctiveness should not be mistaken for human uniqueness. If what we find in common between these three belief-systems is profoundly Hindu, it also suggests links between the inner Hindu world and the universals of human experience" (1). Babb defers to the unity-in-diversity conception of Hinduism and claims that the meaning of being a Hindu "goes deeper than mere matters of subcontinental politics or cultural chauvinism" (2). Although I do not share Babb's orientation to Hindus' distinctive spiritual disposition nor his suggestion that this disposition is somehow superior to or deeper than mere matters of politics, his ethnography provides useful materials about how circuits of exchange not only are religiously articulated but also are enacted through the materiality of social relations.

Babb demonstrates in his discussion of Radhasoami sects how their concept of work as worship assists in building prosperous small-scale industries staffed by devotees (27). Radhasoami gurus also relate spiritual practice to employment and teach that the best kind of work requires "submission to authority. This fosters humility and a willingness to accept guidance from superiors" (58). Consistent with their belief that the guru is a supreme being, devotees believe that the guru "cannot be asked to account in any way for his use or management of satsang property" (87). The Radhasoami redemptive economy figures the guru as the source of good fortune (bhag). The devotee's "capital" (punji) is limited. However, through exchanges with the guru which offer a "priceless opportunity to make one's brief human life fruitful (suphal)," devotees can expand their limited capital (59). Devotion and gifts to the guru earn for donors the protection of the guru, yet in certain instances devotees may not be rewarded with the protection they seek. In such cases devotees invoke the belief that the guru's higher purposes are as inscrutable as they are divine.

With a style quite unlike the disciplined routines of the Radhasoamis, Sathya Sai Baba's miracles enchant the material world for his urban devotees (Babb 1987). Sathya Sai Baba attracts rich and powerful followers who are affluent consumers. Babb emphasizes the importance of the guru's charisma in making the organization a "kind of devotional empire, far-flung but totally dependent on the authority of its sovereign" (167). So as not to sully himself by handling money directly, Sathya Sai Baba only accepts donations via his Central Trust. Donations can also be made directly into Sai Baba's account at branches of the Canara Bank. The organization is officially under the control of state councils of management whose members are "distinguished and prominent persons from a variety of backgrounds" (168). Sathya Sai Baba himself is the sole trustee of several of the many trusts which constitute his devotional empire. He makes few demands on devotees to change their religious beliefs, rituals, or daily habits. Like Hindu nationalist ideologues, Sathya Sai Baba emphasizes the need to counter the destructive influence of western culture (172). His many enterprises—schools, hospitals, temples, ashrams—are presented as the means to preserve and promote Hindu cultural and social values that are based on spiritual traditions. In his panegyric of Sathya Sai Baba, Lal notes that the educational institutions of the Central Trust are supervised by "eminent persons" such as a former vice-chancellor of Bangalore University, who "is now retired from government posts, but has been re-tyred by Bhagawan to do a much nobler task" (6).

Sathya Sai Baba's miracles are widely credited with converting numerous skeptics, especially scientists, into loyal devotees. Babb regards accounts of conversion experiences prompted by the guru's miraculous manifestations of sacred ash and other objects to be indicative of how "scientific rationality is fundamentally challenged and in some sense transcended by Sathya Sai Baba's magic" (182). Magic and miracles create an aura of surprise and power, an aura which conditions devotees to suspend disbelief. Balse's description of Sathya Sai Baba's public appearances suggests how their staging communicates power and authority:

> He looked much as a Maharaja of old must have looked except that he wore no crown. The same disparity between the elevated silver crested throne and the cold hard ground, the same supplicating reverence from the masses. There were life-sized portraits of himself flanking both sides of a mounted idol of Sri Krishna behind, half hidden by the throne. (Balse 1976, 42)

Balse states her purpose at the outset of the book: "to separate the spiritual chaff from the genuine grain" (6). She suggests that in Sathya Sai Baba she has found the "genuine grain" but comments derisively on the organization's personnel: "He definitely is a superman possessing some psychic powers above other wonder workers. But his hangers-on which include the officious volunteers with their narrow vision, religious obsession and emphasis on external mores, have made a travesty of spiritualism" (52).

From seemingly nothing but the magnetism of his divine personality, Sathya Sai Baba has built a powerful pan-Indian organization. Through the guru's person and his organization, the increasingly commodity-crowded world becomes for his devotees "a place of wonders to be constantly scrutinized for ever newer marvels. These are people for whom the miraculous has somehow become part of the very furniture of normal existence" (Babb 1987, 199). In Packard's study of how psychological or "motivational research" and social science research was developed in the 1940s and 1950s and was used by the advertising industry in response to the shift from capitalist mass production to mass consumption, he reports that advertising campaigns were designed to convey a sense of permission to indulge oneself, to consume without guilt (1975, 54). Sathya Sai Baba's miracles offer India's monied consumers a self-indulgent, guilt-free experience of the magicality of objects. Involvement with gurus such as Sathya Sai Baba, who preside over devotional empires and charitable institutions, might be further understood as staging noblesse oblige for nouveaux riches consumers whose coveted wealth is a potentially explosive political issue in a society where the majority lives at barely subsistence levels.

The miracles of spirituality and consumer capitalism lie in their capacity to mystify the social relations involved in the production, circulation, and consumption of commodities, and to create individual and group identities that secure the dominance of ruling class groups. As commodities, i.e., complexes of use value and exchange value, the spiritual goods and services associated with gurus and marketed by their organizations are material embodiments of social relations. Through the commodity form, however, these relations assume "the fantastic form of a relation between things" (Marx 1987 [1867], 77). The conception of spirituality being developed here draws on Marx's analogy between the fetishism arising from the commodity form and features of the

> mist-enveloped regions of the religious world. In that world the productions of the human brain appear as independent beings endowed with life and entering into relation with both one another and the human race. This I call Fetishism which attaches itself to the products of labour, so soon as they are produced as commodities, and which is therefore inseparable from the production of commodities.
>
> This Fetishism of commodities has its origin . . . in the peculiar social character of the labour that produces them. (77)

Given the complicated calculations involved in administering a far-flung devotional empire, of paying dividends in prestige and favors to devoted donors, the belief that "unaccountability is an extremely important characteristic of divinity" is extremely useful for justifying the operations of Sathya Sai Baba's and other guru's organizations (Babb 1987, 187). Unaccountability is a powerful force in social relations of domination and exploitation. An Indian sociologist told me that he considered studying the Sathya Sai Baba organization, but decided against it. He feared that his findings would make him an enemy of the organization, and he did not wish to risk incurring the wrath of an organization with so many highly placed and wealthy supporters. Besides being pessimistic about having such research published, he also felt that the enmity of Sathya Sai Baba's organization might jeopardize his academic career as well as the safety of himself and his family. In the process of enchanting the material world for followings of affluent consumers, gurus occult the greed, guile, and violence that secures their status as spiritual leaders.

An incisive analysis of the Shankaracharya of Kanchi discusses specific strategies pursued by this major Hindu leader (Mines and Gaurishankar 1990). The authors argue that the Kanchi Shankaracharya should be understood as an example of the South Indian concept of big man, which is a "notion of individuality and instrumentality that is central to the politics of South India and crucial to an understanding of the dynamic relationship that exists between actions and organization in Indian society" (1990, 761). The world-renouncer as an institutional big man uses strategies similar to those of political leaders. Institutional big men rely on both personal charisma and their satellite organizations, e.g., schools and temples established by the Kanchi Shankaracharya, to attract followers and extend their influence. Their reputations require continued demonstration of generosity and patronage of religious rituals.

Institutional big men bestow honors on businessmen, politicians, and others as a means to distinguish individuals and invest them with authority to act as society's agents (766). The Kanchi Shankaracharya distributes temple rights and confers honors to dramatize his leadership and make alliances. Mines and Gaurishankar use the concept of religious galactic polity to conceptualize how the Shankaracharya's temples and other institutions form a concentric structure that is centered on him. Conflict and competition characterize relations at all levels of the big man's network. Fighting can be particularly intense among lesser big men who represent their own interests and those of different caste, professional, and commercial groups that are involved in the organization's institutions and activities.

Prominent among the Kanchi Shankaracharya's constituency are the high-status *smarta* brahmans for whom he is caste leader and guru. They are organized into the Devotees Society and the Ladies Society. Key management personnel for the Shankaracharya's institutions are smarta brahmans, many of whom are retired from high positions in the government, armed forces, the legal profession, and banking. These and other lay devotees provide linkages with the government and other institutional networks. The Kanchi Shankaracharya's influence and status has increased through the support of his well-placed devotees, including Ramaswamy Venkataraman, former president of India.

The orientation of my analyses of Hindu religious organizations headed by gurus is consonant with Mines and Gaurishankar's findings: "Recognizing the agency of the institutional big-man as a cause of organization profoundly affects how Indian society is conceptualized" (784). Through the institutions they organize as vehicles for their own leadership, institutional big men "create and manage and transform the institutions that give Indian society its corporate frame, while achieving for themselves reputations that distinguish them as instrumental individuals" (784).

Lingayat lay and ascetic religious institutions are similarly structured around institutional big men (Bradford 1985). Bradford provides a detailed account of the relationship between the commercial development of a Karnataka town and its surrounding region and the domination of these institutions by the town's leading mercantile and professional families. Lingayats distinguish between two broad types of participation in religious activities: "innocent" practices such as group singing which foster solidarity among devotees, and "wide awake" practices which require expenditure and heighten distinctions among devotees. Through their "wide awake" devotion, the town's business and professional groups use Lingayat institutions as a "forum for local politics" (Bradford 1985, 97). In many instances, the authority of the swami or institutional big man is not unambiguous. Bradford reports that the town's "little people"—those without land, surplus cash, or influential connections—refer to the swami who heads the organization built up by the wide awake devotion of his wealthy followers as "the dumb swami." They are not honoring this swami for practicing the discipline of silence but rather expressing how the "big people speak for him" (100). This critical evaluation of the Lingayat swami illustrates the tension within the big man role noted by Mines and Gaurishankar, whereby success arouses suspicion about the big man's capacity for sincerity and altruism (1990, 780). This tension between the ideal of the renouncer's detachment from social institutions and the consequences of actual involvement in them is conceptualized by Haug as the contradiction between the ideological powers' predication on transcendent values and the operations of their institutional apparatus: "As the apparatus is first of all a social formation which appropriates the surplus product and seeks to increase its share, there is an incessant internal struggle for advancement, power, privileges, etc. The apparatus of the holy is necessarily unholy" (1987, 76).

Ascetic practices are said to assist an individual in accumulating the merit necessary for liberation from the cycle of rebirth. Asceticism can also extricate a person from the householder's incessant expenditure of merit and incursion of debt. The rewards of withdrawal from the rounds of expenditure that are bound up with the social life of householders are paradigmatically figured in the spiritual powers accumulated by the renouncer. Rare individuals accumulate sufficient merit to achieve liberation during their lifetime, yet innumerable devotees attribute such an accomplishment to their own guru. Devotees believe such a guru is an inexhaustible source of grace and that this grace can be earned and used for achieving desired worldly ends—health and prosperity, sons and employment, success in exams and court cases.

SPIRITUALITY AND THE ANGRY HINDU

Indian industrialist and business groups compete with each other for profits and markets. They also jointly support organizations that lobby for their shared interests, e.g., the Federation of Indian Chambers of Commerce and Industry, or the National Alliance of Young Entrepreneurs. Similarly, religious professionals—ascetics, gurus, brahman ritualists, and pilgrimage priests—not only vie for patrons and consumers of their goods and services but also collaborate by forming and participating in coalitions such as the Vishva Hindu Parishad (World Hindu Council [VHP]). Many of the religious professionals in Hardwar and Rishikesh support the VHP and participate in the conferences and activities it organizes. Heads of leading religious establishments in Hardwar and Rishikesh whose organizations are discussed in the following chapters (the president of the Divine Life Society and the founders of the Bharat Mata temple and of the Gayatri Parivar) all have been associated with the VHP's assembly of religious leaders. As far as I have been able to discern, Satpal of the Manav Utthan Seva Samiti (discussed in chapter 2), has no official position within the VHP. However, his political connections were publicly demonstrated in 1988 when his large Premnagar Ashram in Hardwar was turned over to the Congress Party for a two-week training camp for party workers. Rajiv Gandhi visited Premnagar and addressed its participants during the camp's closing ceremonies.

To trace ideological and organizational antecedents of the VHP, I analyze materials concerning Hindu nationalist ideology as formulated by V. D. Savarkar and its propagation by the Hindu Mahasabha. Work on the Hindu nationalist organization, the Rashtriya Swayamsevak Sangh (RSS), its ideology, and political activities as well as its relations with the Hindu Mahasabha and its role in the formation of the VHP has been instructive for understanding the historical antecedents of the contemporary Hindu nationalist movement (Curran 1951; Andersen 1972; Andersen and Dalme 1987; Basu et al. 1993). Through the VHP, religious professionals have organized themselves into a potent political force, which is a leading protagonist of militant Hindu nationalism in India. Only after I had visited the Delhi headquarters of the VHP in 1988 and reviewed their materials did I come to understand how important its activities are for a study of the socio-political implications of the work of individual gurus and their organizations.

A photograph of the VHP's 1983 All India Sacrifice for Unity (Ekatmata Yajna) accompanied a magazine article entitled, "The Angry Hindu" (*Sunday,* 25 October 1987; see plate 5). The following month other English and Hindu magazines further reported on the political platform and activities of militant Hindu nationalist organizations, with particular attention to the VHP. They all reported that Hindus are angered by government favoritism of minorities and this anger has incited them to support militant Hindu organizations. This characterization of Hindus as angry at the government for disadvantaging them and for neglecting Hindu dharma connotes the avenging and furious powers widely attributed to enraged brahmans and ascetics. In the article, "The Battle Cry of Hindu Extremism," manifestations of Hindu anger are portrayed as the justified means both to express discontent and to pressure the government (*Maya,* November 1987). Photographs accompanying articles about militant Hindus show ascetics brandishing tridents and furious-faced crowds. The power of the angry ascetic and the brahman—and others who claim to be protectors of Hindu dharma—lies in their capacity to arouse indignation and anger in others and lead them to act on it. Das observes that through the powers accumulated through asceticism, the ascetic is believed to have "the power to curse anyone and even forces the gods to fall in with his wishes. The stories of ascetics who were quick to be angered and demanded obeisance are frequent even in the epics" (1985, 206).

Analysis of economic issues is excluded from these emotionally charged articles, which focus on ideological considerations such as cow slaughter, the Ayodhya controversy, and the politicization of religious leadership. Two of these articles, "Will the Hindus Survive?" and "The Battle Cry of Hindu Extremism," include interviews with the VHP's General Secretary Ashok Singhal (*Probe India,* November 1987; *Maya,* November 1987); Singhal's angry face made the cover of this issue of *Probe India* (see plate 6). The VHP general secretary asserted that India "is essentially a country of Hindus and if they are victimised in their own motherland then where will they go to seek justice?" (*Probe India,* November 1987). Singhal talked about the plans of foreign powers to organize an armed revolt against Hindus in India and the need for Hindus to organize and protect themselves from threats posed by anti-Hindu forces in India and abroad. In Singhal's view, "today religious leaders are awake—much more than they ever were."

About the formation of a Hindu state in India the VHP general secretary pronounced that "Hindu consciousness will ultimately culminate in that, and different political parties will ultimately have to keep the Hindu interest in the forefront. No party will exist if it cannot keep the Hindu interests in the forefront." Singhal denied that Hindu nationalism is a form of fundamentalism on the grounds that Hinduism and particularly the Vedas are "interpreted according to the needs of the time. Hindu society is open and dynamic." Certain issues, however are fundamental:

> Take cow slaughter, for instance. Nobody in this country wants cow slaughter. This should be reflected in the Constitution. Why be worried about Muslim Sentiments? But even the government is afraid to do even this. To stop discrimination against Hinduism, a major upheaval may take place. No political party will then escape from this upsurge. And there will be a new Hindu in the 21st century who will not be subdued. (*Probe India,* November 1987)

HINDU NATIONALISM: POLITICAL MOVEMENTS OF IDEOLOGY AND CULTURE

Spirituality's formidable aesthetic and organizational forms contribute to making the Hindu nationalist movement into a powerful political force. Manifestations of Hindu nationalist ideology in national culture are complex and relate to the historical conditions which produce specific forms of national culture (Chatterjee 1986; Appadurai and Breckenridge 1988; Fox 1989, 1990a, 1990b; Vanaik 1990; van der Veer 1994). Nationalism as ideology and political movement is inextricable from domestic and international political and economic struggles between and within classes and nation states (Vanaik 1990; Fox 1989, 1990a, 1990b). Vanaik argues that in India the ideological and political aspects of nationalism have developed in a reciprocal relationship: as an ideology of the nation-state, government-sponsored nationalism uses populist elements from below along with manipulative ones from above; as a political movement, nationalism can be used to articulate not only opposition to the state but also the goals of separation or merger with the nation-state, or reform of state power (1990:116–17).

Spirituality provides referents for the Indian state's claim to uphold ultimate values. Its aesthetic and emotional dimensions communicate forms of socialization from above and produce subjective identities of individuals and groups. This socialization from above is not experienced as domination because of spirituality's ideological effect, which "consists in the turning toward value as the turning away from interest" (Haug 1987, 66). Spirituality assists the state in its construction of itself—especially through nationalist ideology—as an imaginary community, an institution of domination that "must represent an imaginary commonness between rich and poor" (Haug 1987, 137; cf. Anderson 1983). Both in its ideological value form and in its institutionalized aesthetic forms, spirituality is linked with other bourgeois ideological apparatuses to "organize the aggressive silence about capitalist class relations"; together these apparatuses "organize the life and experience of class society as one of classlessness" (Haug 1987, 67). Institutionalized spirituality neither denies nor dwells on the existence or experience of oppression based on economic exploitation. It reframes oppression as a problem amenable to solutions that promise individuals the means to experience transcendent truth.

Partha Chatterjee (1986) examines the emergence of nationalist discourse as an ideology of opposition to British rule in colonial India, and its later transformation into an ideology of the state in independent India. His work provides a historical framework for relating nationalist ideology to both the independence movement and the requirements of a bourgeois nation-state. Although Chatterjee does not focus specifically on Hindu nationalism, he does highlight how the conception of Hinduism as the national religion of India and as the spiritual basis of Indian cultural superiority over western materialism has figured prominently in the discourse of Indian nationalism.[4] Chatterjee schematizes the development of

4. For discussions of orientalism and the contradictions arising within counter-hegemonic discourses as a result of incorporations and inversions of aspects hegemonic discourse, e.g., the opposition of materialistic West and spiritual East, see Bharati (1970); Said (1978, 1985);

nationalist discourse into three moments and associates them with specific political and historical circumstances as well as with leading ideologues: the moment of departure and the work of Bankim Chandra Chatterji; the moment of maneuver and Mahatma Gandhi's success as a populist leader who coopted the masses into the bourgeois nationalist movement while preserving the distance between them and the state; and the moment of arrival associated with Nehru's nationalist ideology based on secular democratic socialism, which suppressed the political contradictions in Indian nationalism and made nationalism the ideology of the state.

The embeddedness of ideas concerning spirituality in Indian nationalism is such that, like the nationalist discourses forged by Bankim Chandra and Mahatma Gandhi, Nehruvian nationalism invoked spiritual values and the cult of Bharat Mata (Chatterjee 1986, 146, 161). Although Chatterjee focuses on these three specific figures, the spiritual and cultural themes that construct nationalism in Hindu religious terms are also evident in the work of other key nationalist ideologues, e.g., Vivekananda, Aurobindo, Tagore, Savarkar, and Golwalkar. Richard Fox emphasizes the importance of the historical specificity of spirituality by asking, "can a cultural construction like spirituality have a progressive character at one historical point and a reified and commodified character at another?" (pers. comm.). Indeed, it is necessary to situate the political uses of spirituality in specific historical contexts. Certainly the scale and pace of spirituality's commodification in recent years is unprecedented. However, I maintain not only that assessing spirituality as progressive depends largely on one's political goals, but also that commodification and reification have been integral to spirituality since its earliest formulations by nationalist ideologues.

In his historical overview of Hindu nationalism, Fox traces its lineage to the 1920s and its institutionalization through organizations such as the RSS (1990b). He argues that Hindu nationalism has burgeoned as a political and cultural force only since the late 1970s, when it enhanced its legitimacy by appropriating Gandhian socialist ideology. In his analysis of Gandhi's nationalist discourse, Chatterjee also notes the usefulness of Gandhianism for articulating the legitimacy of oppositional groups: "Oppositional movements can still claim their moral legitimacy from the message of the Mahatma" (1986, 125). Gandhi had challenged the legitimacy of British rule on moral grounds. Political parties and social movements opposed to the government and striving to augment their political power continue to use moral arguments concerning the greed and corruption of public officials and the grave flaws in the existing socio-political system.

To challenge the ruling party and establish superior moral credentials,

---

Chatterjee (1986); Inden (1986, 1990); Fox (1987, 1989); and Foster (1991). Fox (1989) provides a useful framework for understanding how spirituality figured as an Indian cultural essential in orientalist discourses on India and its role in Hindu nationalist ideology.

opposition leaders emphasize the pernicious effects of government policies. Fox (1990b) and Vanaik (1990) relate the rise of Hindu nationalism since the 1970s to the decline of Nehruvian socialism as a legitimating ideology for the state and to its deployment by specific classes for establishing their claims to political authority and high social status. Fox argues that support for Hindu nationalism comes from the group that has been dominant during the intermediate regime following Indian independence and characterizes this group as "urban forward caste/lower-middle class" ("professionals, teachers, petty manufacturers, traders, civil servants and the like"; 1990b, 71–72).[5] Since the 1970s the status and legitimacy of this group has been reduced by the expanding political and economic power of the large class of rich farmers as well as the restrictions on its employment and educational opportunities resulting from government reservations for other groups.

In Fox's view Hindu nationalism is supported by this "forward caste/lower-middle class" group which includes members of ideological professions such as lawyers, doctors, journalists, and academics. This group propagates Hindu nationalist ideology to legitimate its claims to political dominance. The processes making Hindu nationalism an increasingly powerful ideology and a potent constituent of national culture are situated "within a field of class oppositions and intra-class competitions, often carried forward by caste and sectarian consciousness" (77). Fox's attention to this forward caste/lower-middle class group is relevant to particular aspects of the expansion of Hindu nationalism, but the support of the political and economic elite is certainly no less crucial. Careful examination of the ideology and activities of the VHP and the religious organizations which support various styles of Hindu nationalism provides an avenue for further exploring the issues of class, conflict, and consciousness raised by Fox.

Vanaik's work on Hindu nationalism (1990) complements and extends Fox's analysis. He argues that Hindu nationalism has had a long presence in Indian nationalist thought and that Indian nationhood has been widely conceived in terms of religious rather than linguistic groups:

---

5. For a further discussion of the concept, "intermediate regime," see Fox (1989, 190–92). Fox defines the category "forward caste" as "approximate to the 'educated classes' of Brahmans, Kayasthas, Khatris, and other urbanized high castes who obtained English education and staffed the British colonial enterprise and who have continued to dominate the government and the professions even after independence. It also includes the somewhat lower ranking castes of merchants, money-lenders, and small-scale entrepreneurs, collectively known as 'Vaishyas' or 'Baniyas,' who dominate trade, manufacturing, banking, and other commercial activities" (1990b, 71). For an extended discussion of issues pertaining to class and caste, see Fox's overview of contemporary Hindu nationalism (1989, 235–64 and particularly 249–52).

"Hinduism, not Hindi, became crucial to the formation of nationalist consciousness, leading to the emergence of the Indian nation and nation state and of a pan-Indian nationality" (6). Vanaik characterizes the last two decades in Indian history as a period of transition with the Indian nation-state moving from one variant of bourgeois democracy to another (3). The important political characteristics of the emerging variant are: a continuation of plebiscitary politics at the national level; growth and partial consolidation of Hindu nationalism; growing federalism and decentralization of power; and authoritarian democracy (107). Like Fox, Vanaik maintains that Hindu nationalism is being used by both the bourgeois state and other social groups as the hegemonic ideology to supplant Nehruvian socialism.

Whereas Fox highlights support of Hindu nationalism by the forward caste/lower-middle class, Vanaik focuses on how the state and other groups have come to support Hindu nationalism. He also examines how state support relates to processes of plebiscitary politics that require populist representations of political authority, representations which Hindu religious symbols and ritual activities abundantly provide. Furthermore, the militancy and militarism of Hindu nationalism, with its emotional appeals to strengthen the nation against its internal and foreign foes, assisted the state in justifying its enormous expansion of military expenditure, which during the 1980s increased by 250 percent (Vanaik 1990, 259).

Conflicts arising because the economic integration of India proceeds more rapidly than political integration enhance the usefulness of Hindu nationalism for constructing a broad cultural-ideological consensus for stabilizing the national political order (105). Like the Congress during the independence movement, the Hindu nationalist movement today is a coalition of different class, caste, and sectarian groups. The VHP is a leading organization within the Hindu nationalist movement which mobilizes different groups and coordinates their activities. Supporters of the VHP belong not only to its official political ally, the Bharatiya Janata Party (BJP), but also to the Congress and other political parties. The VHP's leading members include retired officials from upper echelons of the Indian bureaucracy, former director-generals of police, former chief judges, and former government ministers. In its cover story on the involvement of communal organizations in the 1987 Meerut riots, which included attacks by the Provincial Armed Constabulary on Muslims, *India Today* reports that retired senior government officials are involved in the leadership of the VHP (15 June 1987). At the time of the Meerut riots, a former director-general of the state police was the leader of the VHP in Uttar Pradesh.

Involvement in religious organizations is reported as being increasingly respectable and an important means to attain respectability. The terms respectable and respectability camouflage complex political and economic processes whereby persons and social groups invest money and time in religious organizations as a means to expand local, regional, national, and transnational power bases. A Congress (I) politician tells the press, "Suddenly one finds that attachment to a communal organisation is not considered a bad thing" (*India Today*, 15 June 1987). A senior Supreme Court lawyer offers his reasoning for the growth of religious organizations: "Why shouldn't people join communal organisations? It seems to make them instant leaders and gets them important positions in politics and government." Persons with criminal records are reported to be using leadership of religious organizations "as a tool to gain respectability."

India Today reports that the increasing political and economic importance of religious organizations during the 1980s is indicated by the high rate of construction of new religious buildings, many of which illegally encroach on public land (15 June 1987). The number of registered religious buildings in Delhi rose from 560 to 2,000 from 1980 to 1987. In Uttar Pradesh during the same period the number of large religious buildings registered with local municipalities is said to have increased from 4,000 to 6,700. According to a Union Ministry report on communal violence, the rapid increase in the number of religious buildings has multiplied the sites and occasions for communal conflict. Depending on the political and administrative connections of the particular organization and of its opponents, new buildings that illegally encroach on public land are tolerated or destroyed. Every festival and event celebrated at these religious institutions becomes a potential occasion for official intervention relating to conflicts over processions and blaring loudspeakers. The more officials who are members or sympathizers of a religious organization, the more an organization can call upon political and police support in its conflicts with rivals. The VHP's growth during the 1980s is related to its ability to cultivate bureaucratic and police support and financial support from business and other groups, as well as its ability to mobilize large numbers of people to participate in its campaigns and rallies.

Fox suggests that Hindu nationalism finds support among the forward caste/lower-middle class group, which feels threatened by changing political and economic conditions. In Vanaik's analysis, this group is not specifically mentioned. However, this group continues to provide the leadership for the bourgeois political parties which Vanaik argues have turned to Hindu nationalism to assist in solving their legitimacy crisis. Vanaik names the intermediate castes of rural and urban India, i.e., the rural bourgeoisie and the rural and urban petit bourgeois, as the "material driving forces of this cultural expansionism" (1990, 105). He views this group, the "Hindu-community-in-the-making," as constituting more of a cultural and ideological than a political community. Their support for Hindu nationalism relates to their drive for an improved social status consonant with their increased economic and political power: "Assertion of their Hindu identity is the form taken by their aspirations for higher social status and for a cultural upward mobility in keeping with their upward economic and political mobility" (105).

Censuring the political left for an exaggerated fear of Hindu nationalism, which views it as an ominous portent of an emerging Hindu state or Hindu fascism, Vanaik thinks that "the spread of Hindu nationalist appeal and the adoption of a modulated cultural nationalism by mainstream bourgeois parties are not incompatible with the preservation of the broad structures of bourgeois democracy" (108). However, he does regard these trends as making the position of non-Hindus, and particularly those in the lower socio-economic strata, "significantly more insecure" (108). He concludes that a secular Indian state can comfortably coexist with a restrained Hindu nationalism. This coexistence requires the state to cautiously curb the expansion of religious influence.

At numerous points Vanaik suggests types of interventions that could challenge the hegemony of Hindu nationalism. Groups seeking to challenge the desecularization of the Indian polity must form counter-institutions that can successfully compete with institutions having religious affiliations. The power and popularity of religious organizations, in Vanaik's view and which my research supports, largely stem from their "effective and organized insertion into the everyday life of urban neighborhoods. Their ability to mobilize popular communal support is based partly on their capacity to terrorize opponents and protect supporters. It is also partly based on their ability to provide recreation, cultural and genuine welfare services, that is, to meet some of the secular needs of its constituencies" (161).

HINDU NATIONALISM IN THE INTERMEDIATE REGIME

Although I concur with Fox, Vanaik, and van der Veer in dating the expansion of Hindu nationalism in both its ideological and organizational forms to the 1970s and 1980s, in order to analyze this phenomenon I have investigated its antecedents in their more militant forms. Gramsci's observations on the Indian nationalist movement noted the importance of "'underground warfare'" (Chatterjee 1986, 50). During the independence movement, the ideology and activities of underground revolutionary groups propagating hatred and violence complemented the official Gandhian ideology of loving tolerance and nonviolent resistance. After independence, Hindu nationalism itself became an underground presence in the Indian polity, with the state proscribing Hindu organizations at various times, e.g., after the assassination of Mahatma Gandhi and during the Emergency. However, during the period which Fox terms the intermediate regime, supporters of Hindu nationalism—those who fervently wanted to

establish Hindu nationalism as the ideology of the Indian state and to expand the political authority of Hindu religious and cultural leadership—
have been busily at work.

The Swatantra Party was a short-lived political party supported by
capitalist business groups, rural landlords, upper-middle class professionals, and high-ranking government officials who were sympathetic to
Hindu nationalist ideology and active in Hindu religious and cultural institutions. The following discussion of the Swatantra Party briefly introduces
themes which will be taken up in later discussions of the Hindu Mahasabha, Savarkar, and militant Hindu nationalism. Because Savarkar was
for so long marginalized by the dominant nationalist ideologues and academics during the intermediate regime and is now being rehabilitated, his
ideas and activities require careful scrutiny. Attention to Savarkar, no less
than to the Swatantra Party, whose platform in many respects prefigured
policies of the Indian government in its later transition phase, assists in analyzing aspects of both the ideological and organizational potency of
Hindu nationalism in contemporary Indian politics.

In profiles of "Fifty Politicians Who Made All the Difference Since Independence," Chakravarti Rajagopalachari and the Swatantra Party
which he participated in founding receive the following tribute: "The most
visible face of the right in the fifties and sixties, Chakravarti Rajagopalachari believed that if India had to progress, it was imperative that
enterprise was permitted to flourish" (*Illustrated Weekly of India,* 27 December 1987). Rajagopalachari opposed policies of Nehru's government
that limited the growth of the private sector and that fostered what he regarded as spurious socialism. The Swatantra Party, founded by experienced statesmen such as Rajagopalachari and prominent businessmen and
aristocrats, was widely reviled by the Congress Party as an upper-crust club
of tycoons and maharajas with little concern for the poor. However, by the
mid-1980s the Congress Party began to champion policies supporting private enterprise, policies that it had disparaged when advocated by the Swatantra Party three decades earlier: "How times have changed! Much of
what the brilliant statesman then envisaged has been converted into reality
in recent years. By queer legerdemain, private enterprise is no more an abu-
sive concept; it has finally acquired respectability in Rajiv's India" (*Illustrated Weekly of India,* 27 December 1987).

During the intermediate regime, parties with platforms that were explicitly Hindu nationalist, such as the Hindu Mahasabha, the Ram Rajya
Parishad, and the Jana Sangh, could not compete with the Congress. Furthermore, they lacked both the organizational infrastructure and the prestige of the Congress. The Swatantra Party shared the Hindu Mahasabha's
economic agenda and sought to avoid the stigma and marginalization of
Hindu nationalist parties by presenting itself as a secular party. Although

Swatantra spokesman M. R. Masani advocated secularist policies, the party consistently represented secularism in terms ambiguous enough to accommodate a cultural and political Hindu nationalism that might be termed "secularist Hindu nationalism," an ideology aimed to appeal to the cultural preferences of a range of dominant groups. Howard Erdman's study of the Swatantra Party and its relation to the Congress argues that, in post-independence India, strategic concessions made by the Congress to opposition groups made opponents into dependents (1967, 22). Through political compromises the Congress marginalized its opponents and attempted to make them into dependents; it rarely eradicated them (24). Erdman also argues that hostility to Nehruvian socialism was particularly acute among opposition groups. Furthermore, the Congress's platform of socialism obscured the rightist Hindu elements within the party, elements which were strong within the Congress and whose strength limited the implementation of secular and socialist policies.

A review of the ideology of the Swatantra Party is an instructive reminder that the present nexus of capitalism, Hindu nationalism, and an appropriated Gandhianism had been articulated well before the 1970s. The Swatantra Party was formed in 1959 as a non-leftist opposition party to the Congress. Although officially an opposition party, it also enjoyed discreet support from Congress Party members and from capitalists whose investment in the Swatantra Party remained cautious and never approached their levels of investment in the ruling Congress Party (Erdman 1967, 176, 236). Swatantra Party leadership was composed of influential and experienced politicians, bureaucrats, and businessmen, one of whom (Homi Mody) was the chairman of the Central Bank of India owned by the powerful Tata business house. In another leader, K. M. Munshi, the Swatantra Party had an ardent advocate of Hindu nationalism. He had held numerous high offices and was founder and head of the Bharatiya Vidya Bhavan, a pan-Indian cultural organization whose publications glorify Hindu spiritual values, presenting them as necessary for adapting science and technology to benefit Indian society. Munshi's campaign to rebuild the Somnath temple after independence has been praised as an exemplary project by Hindu nationalists campaigning to build a Ram temple in Ayodhya.

Aware of the links between industrial expansion and militarism, the Swatantra Party, like the Congress in the 1980s, found in militant Hinduism a congenial ideology. It used the fear of foreign invasion and internal subversion, propagated so effectively by militant Hindu nationalists such as Savarkar, to legitimate the need for both expanded military production and a highly authoritarian state. Supported by the Forum for Free Enterprise, a body of Bombay corporate heads, and the All India Agriculturalists' Federation, a body representing the interests of rich farmers, the Swatantra Party was conservative, elitist, and capitalist. Its platform was broad: "freedom of property"; opposition to communism, with Hinduism as the most potent means of opposition; opposition to Congress socialism; conservative elitism (Erdman 1967, 148). It appropriated the concept of trusteeship popularized by Mahatma Gandhi to legitimate the elitism of its leadership: "the rich, the wise and the well born must use their advantage for the common good" (37).[6]

The Swatantra Party presented economic and social progress, which would promote the common good, as requiring the restoration of Hindu cultural and spiritual values under the trusteeship of the elite. The Congress government was decried as posing a threat to religion, promoting class hatred, and hence jeopardizing the future of India. The Swatantra Party's definition of secularism as the government's support for all religions has become a definition of secularism widely used by officials and politicians today. Like other bourgeois parties, the Swatantra Party looked to India's "all pervading sense of spirituality" when discussing the relation between the rich and the poor, using spirituality's ideals of unity to mask antagonisms between classes and to endorse the concept of trusteeship by elite groups. Rajagopalachari, who along with Munshi was the party's other principal conservative Hindu leader, claimed that Hindu spirituality honors poverty: "beggars are honored in spite of their obviously unsatisfactory way of life"; "the poor man commands not only respect but a religious status by reason of his poverty" (92). The complementarity of spirituality and capitalism is illustrated in Rajagopalachari's arguments: he uses spirituality to defend capitalist social relations; he uses modernist economic arguments to defend a division of labor based on caste hierarchy.

M. R. Masani, the Swatantra Party's leading spokesman for its liberal capitalist platform, decreed: "Socialism: an Ism that has become a Wasm" (322). However accurate this declaration may have become three decades after it was made, public deference to socialist ideology dominated political rhetoric during the Nehruvian years. Erdman argues that although the Swatantra Party had considerable support from conservative and militant Hindu groups, businessmen, aristocrats, and landlords, its association with capitalism not only impaired its ability to establish its legitimacy but also consistently attracted negative publicity (194). Masani attempted to reverse the terms of the prevailing political discourse. To present Nehruvian socialism as retrograde, he argued that "the controlled free enterprise

6. For a discussion of the the concept of trusteeship in relation to the nationalist movement, whereby urban nationalists claimed to be trustees of peasants' political interests and princes and landlords trustees of peasants' economic interests, see Pandey (1988). The concept of trusteeship and the political groups who have used it in making claims to authority is also examined by Fox (1989).

of Swatantra is progressive, and is, in fact, more representative of the 'spirit of socialism'" (197). He even invoked Marx and Engels to argue that capitalism must be allowed to perform its world-historical task in India. Decrying Nehru as a reactionary, nineteenth-century socialist, Masani heralded the Swatantra Party as the proponent of twentieth-century socialism.

Through its concept of trusteeship, the Swatantra Party represented itself as the protector of the weak. Erdman notes that the party never evinced real concern for strengthening the position of the weak or for addressing economic and social inequality. The basic commitment of trusteeship was to protecting the interests of the strong (199–200). The language of spirituality was used to promote its ideology of responsible individualism and trusteeship. Rajagopalachari combined the language of liberalism with its emphasis on the individual's political and economic freedom with that of brahmanic orthodoxy whereby spiritual values would regulate capitalist social relations: "Properly designed and placed on a spiritual basis, a regulated economy need not be inconsistent with individual satisfaction and individual zeal. The restraints and habits of mind that are required to be developed for altruistic action must flow from faith and inner conviction" (90).

The Swatantra Party also articulated its economic policies in modernist terms, using concepts such as productivity and efficiency. It argued that freedom from excessive state controls and not from the constraints of traditional society, which included traditional forms of philanthropy, were necessary for increasing productivity and efficiency and protecting the weak from the excesses of capitalist competition. Concerning the need for economic planning by the state, the Swatantra Party agreed with the Congress in principle but differed over the extent of state control of planning. One leader thus explained the party's position: "We believe in plan. But our plan is a Gandhian plan, a plan that has for its foundation Dharma" (196). A critic of the Swatantra Party described it as "the forum only of conservative Brahmins and profit minded baniyas" (111). The pro-English language policy of the Party's upper-middle-class English-speaking leaders infuriated its allies from more populist, pro-Hindi, militant Hindu groups and the Jana Sangh. Although its anti-government position on taxation was extremely popular, most of the policies of the Swatantra Party as well as the language and style of its elite leadership remained "relatively remote from popular interests and passions" (207).

Referents to Hinduism and endorsements from Hindu religious leaders were used to popularize the legitimacy of Swatantra Party policies. Party meetings included performance of Hindu rituals. The concept of citizenship promoted by the Swatantra Party was described as consonant with the way of life preached in the *Bhagavad Gita* (94).[7] The Madras Swatantra Party president cited passages from the Vedas and asserted the identity of party doctrines with vedic truths; he also threatened to organize a protest against the inclusion of lands owned by Hindu religious institutions in the Madras land-ceiling legislation (210). At a Swatantra Party convention in Gujarat, a Hindu swami was invited to address the audience. During his speech he condemned the government for not prohibiting cow slaughter and announced that he would begin a fast to protest the government's position on this issue.

Although its national leadership was composed of influential individuals—institutional big men—skilled in the rhetoric and strategies of politics, the party lacked both a regional infrastructure and a popular base. Its coalitionist form was oriented to recruiting regional elites, including aristocrats, former activists in the independence movement, and retired government officials to stand for state and national elections. The Swatantra Party's anti-democratic ethos, which maintained that the masses are unable to inform themselves about issues and that they cannot govern themselves, provided a ready explanation for its poor electoral results. Like other political parties, the Swatantra Party was anxious to manipulate these masses. Erdman notes that the party kept files with detailed information on the caste and religious composition of particular regions and "how communal factors may be exploited in the selection of candidates, in electoral appeals and the like" (210). For example, the party's electoral strategies relied on religious appeals in Gujarat and "rajput war cries" in Rajasthan. In describing the formation and promotion of a new political party and its competition with other parties, Erdman notes, "one Swatantra leader compared the party's position to that of a merchant who seeks to set up a new shop in an old bazaar district. Other merchants view the newcomer with suspicion, if not hostility, as a competitor; they wait to see how business will go; and they will seek some agreements with respect to trade, if circumstances seem to require it" (327). The Swatantra Party made many such agreements with competitors both within the ruling Congress Party and opposition parties, including "some adjustments" with the Communist Party (219).

The Swatantra Party was characterized by the press as having an apex, i.e., leadership and support from ruling class groups, but no base; the Jana Sangh, its political ally, was described as having a base and no apex (224). In his concluding remarks Erdman projects that with the passing of Nehru there would be greater scope for the expansion of moderate and militant

7. Studies of interpretations of the *Bhagavad Gita* by a range of nationalist and religious figures can be found in the collection edited by Minor (1986). Bailey (1988) critically examines the continual return to the *Bhagavad Gita* by scholars of Hindu religion.

rightist groups. Although conflict within these groups has fragmented them, they have remained active throughout Indian society. He suggests that a "renaissance of more 'Indian' ideas could come increasingly to permeate public life" if the policies associated with Nehru are condemned as having failed because they were western (259). Moreover, Erdman links this renaissance with militant Hindu nationalism, and envisions that it would have negative consequences for Hindu-Muslim relations but could facilitate social and industrial advance if it led to a stronger, more centralized nation-state.

Vanaik censures leftists for their phobic attitudes to militant Hindu nationalism because such attitudes impede critical analysis and effective intervention. Twenty-five years earlier, Erdman faulted commentators on Indian politics for "steadfastly ignoring the substantial, if often latent or untapped or disorganized reservoirs of right-wing strength in India. . . . Neither in intellectual nor in practical terms will the many problems posed by the Indian right be solved by denying that they exist" (260). Since Erdman wrote these words, Hindu nationalism in militant and modulated forms has become a major ideological weapon and political strategy for consolidating the power of India's ruling classes. It has become a movement with both apex and base.

The activities of gurus and their organizations introduced in this chapter are relocated in chapter 2 in the context where I initially encountered them, in the north Indian pilgrimage town of Hardwar. Analysis of government tourist and pilgrim literature delineates connections among pilgrimage, spirituality, and national identity, and highlights the language and imagery associated with Hindu Hardwar. This literature also suggests how the government provides ideological and infrastructural support for religious professionals and pilgrimage businesses. The next portion of chapter 2 relates Hardwar to the history of political activism associated with Hindu organizations formed before independence, with particular attention to the Hindu Mahasabha. The drive of the religious and political leadership of these organizations was then and continues to be the prosecution of claims to be protectors and organizers of all Hindus and authoritative interpreters of Hindu spiritual and social values.

Founded in Hardwar in 1915, the Hindu Mahasabha selected V. D. Savarkar as its president in 1937. Chapter 3 concerns Savarkar's life and work—as underground revolutionary and propagandist, imprisoned freedom fighter, and militant Hindu nationalist. A study of Savarkar is instructive for understanding the ideology and activities of contemporary Hindu nationalist organizations. It is also necessary to competently argue against Hindu nationalist revisions which attempt to rehabilitate Savarkar, whose rallying cry was "Hinduise all politics and militarise all Hindudom."

Chapter 3 also examines Savarkar's key texts, in which he systematized the ideology of Hindu nationalism and formulated policies of Hindu Sangathan (organization) concerning the political mobilization not only of caste Hindus but also of untouchables, tribals, Indian Muslims, and Christians. During frequent tours Savarkar recruited support from Hindu aristocrats, capitalists, and urban educated groups for a movement with the goal of Hindu political, economic, and cultural dominance backed by the force of a sympathetic military and police establishment.

Chapter 4 opens with an overview of the institutional and ideological linkages among political parties whose platforms support Hindu nationalism and which are predecessors of the Vishva Hindu Parishad. Founded in 1964 by religious leaders, the VHP defines itself as a nonsectarian Hindu religious, cultural, and social organization concerned with advancing the cause of Hinduism and the welfare of all Hindus. Building on themes treated in the chapter on Savarkar, I discuss the VHP's policies and programs concerning tribals, untouchables, Indian Muslims and Christians, and overseas Hindus. The second part of chapter 4 focuses on the ritualization of Hindu nationalism through the VHP's 1983 Sacrifice for Unity. Through the Sacrifice, which traveled throughout India as a pilgrimage of and sacrifice to the Hindu deities Bharat Mata and Ganga Mata, the VHP involved large numbers of Indians in its activities and raised money for its projects. As in the discussion of the VHP's promotional materials, here too I examine the linkages between religious leadership, politicians, and government officials who supported the execution of the Sacrifice.

Chapter 5 charts the career of a prominent VHP leader, the brahman ascetic Swami Satyamitranand. His association with the VHP is mentioned in chapter 4 in the context of his involvement with the Sacrifice for Unity ceremonies in Hardwar. This association is further studied through analysis of biographic and hagiographic materials. The analysis addresses both the conventions structuring the story of "the divine pilgrimage of an ascetic," and the processes whereby a guru inherits and builds up a following, and expands and establishes religious and educational institutions within India and abroad. The chapter includes a reading of Satyamitranand's instructions concerning "spiritual advancement" of the individual. He asks, "how much of affluence is desirable; at what stage it appears extravagance?" and promises that Hindu scriptures and gurus provide the answers.

Chapter 6 concerns Satyamitranand's crowning achievement, the founding of the Bharat Mata mandir (Mother India temple) in Hardwar. The conception of India as a Hindu holy land, consecrated by the deeds of deities and saints, is discussed in earlier chapters in connection with pilgrimage, Savarkar's formulations of Hindu nationalism, and the ideology of the VHP. Through an analysis of Satyamitranand's Bharat Mata temple in Hardwar, a temple dedicated to the same goddess whom the VHP sent on tour of India, I explore in depth this cultic formulation of national identity. The temple, however, is not simply dedicated to Bharat Mata. Its eight levels assemble and enshrine deities, warriors and martyrs, satis, gurus and saints, all of whom signify history, religion, and culture in images consonant with the ideology of Hindu nationalism.

The Divine Life Society (DLS) founded by the Tamil brahman ascetic Sivananda is introduced in chapter 7. Primarily a Hindu religious organization, the DLS has had considerable success in convincing both Hindus and non-Hindus that Sivananda's teachings constitute a universal religion. Unlike Satyamitranand, the DLS is discreet about its Hindu nationalist sympathies. However, there has been explicit use of Sivananda's teachings by contemporary Hindu nationalists, and there are formal and informal ties between the DLS and the VHP. Having established the contemporary connections between the DLS and Hindu nationalism, I then move back in time to examine the career and teachings of Sivananda and the formation and expansion of the DLS. The discussion highlights Sivananda's formulations of a universal religion based on Hindu spirituality as well as the publications, charitable activities, publicity, and fund-raising tours whereby the organization has attracted powerful and wealthy supporters.

The facilities and activities of the Sivananda ashram, the headquarters of the DLS in Rishikesh, are described in chapter 8. Discussion of the public audiences given by DLS General Secretary Krishnananda considers how these sessions disclose the social power wielded by those who command the discourse of spirituality. As much of my research in the ashram was assisted by women residents, the chapter concludes with profiles of women's work and lives in the ashram.

The DLS is also the focus of chapter 9. During 1987 it celebrated the birth centenary of its founder. Through its many centenary activities, the DLS publicized itself and the support it receives from politicians, bureaucrats, and other prominent persons. Using both DLS publications and my fieldwork materials, I discuss the different phases of the centenary campaign and examine how the DLS promotes its status as a premier Hindu religious organization and propagates in a modulated form the ideology of Hindu nationalism.

Chapter 10 further develops themes articulated in the previous chapters, and elaborates issues related to spirituality's political economy. Then I turn to how violence informs configurations and worship of Hindu goddesses—shakti—who constitute the composite deity of Bharat Mata. By examining uses of spiritual referents in advertisements selling consumer goods and commemorating dead capitalists as well as newspaper reports of fatal cases of gurus' manipulations of their followers and incidents of human sacrifice to shakti, the chapter illustrates spirituality's pervasive power in contemporary Indian society.

The epilogue briefly recounts subsequent events which further indicate the Hindu nationalist movement's political momentum and successes. It discusses the VHP's leading role in destruction of the Babri mosque and its relentless drive to build the Ram temple in Ayodhya.

TWO

Hardwar and Rishikesh: Gateway to Gods and Godmen

CENTERS OF SUMPTUARY SPIRITUALITY

The Hindu nationalist movement uses emotive religious imagery to popularize its political agenda and attract support for rallies, mass rituals, and electoral campaigns. With their concentration of producers and consumers of religious goods and services, Hindu pilgrimage centers are important places where activists publicize Hindu nationalist ideology and organize support for the movement. Politicians pilgrimage to Hardwar—only five hours by road from Delhi—to stage launches and comebacks; their platform need not be explicitly Hindu nationalist. When former Indian prime minister V. P. Singh launched his political party in July 1987 with a rally in Hardwar, speakers prophesied the importance of the event by recalling that Indira Gandhi had commenced her successful comeback against the Janata Party from these very same banks of Ganga Ma in Hardwar. One article about militant Hinduism comments that "in 1982 Indira Gandhi attended the consecration of the VHP's Bharat Mata Mandir in Hardwar. Today the same VHP is leading the movement for Ram Janma Bhoomi and for this reason is being condemned" (*Maya*, November 1987). As a major Hindu pilgrimage center, Hardwar is revered as a place with physical, social, and spiritual powers. Sources of these powers include the sacred waters of the Ganges; ayurvedic medicines made locally from Himalayan herbs; the miraculous capabilities attributed to Hardwar's yogis, swamis, and gurus; and the acts of brahman pilgrimage guides and priests who propitiate ancestors, promise boons, and keep current records concerning networks of lineage, kin, caste, and regional groups and gifts to brahmans (see plate 7).

Hardwar has long been used as a site by groups and individuals who are attempting to organize and strengthen the potency of their political profile and actions. The Hindu Mahasabha, an early Hindu nationalist organization, held its initial meetings in Hardwar. Its founder, Pandit Malaviya, assisted brahman pandas (pilgrimage priests) working in Hardwar and elsewhere to organize themselves and effectively promote their interests, particularly through affiliation with larger networks such as the Hindu Mahasabha. Many of Hardwar's currently prominent gurus and swamis, pandas and pandits actively support the VHP and publicly participate in VHP processions, rallies, and assemblies held in Hardwar and elsewhere.

During fieldwork I visited and studied dozens of gurus and their ashrams while residing in the small ashram of Bharati Ma, a woman guru. Analysis of materials on these many different ashrams—visits and conversations with gurus and devotees, observation of daily routines, rituals and special celebrations, and devotional literature—informs my understanding of aspects of the more intimate dynamics of involvement with gurus and their organizations. Because this book primarily concerns macro-relationships among Hindu organizations, Hindu nationalism, and political and economic processes, I focus on two powerful international organizations which are headed by ascetic leaders: the Samanvaya Parivar (Family of Harmony) with its Bharat Mata temple in Hardwar and the Divine Life Society with its headquarters at the Sivananda ashram in Rishikesh.

There are also numerous Hindu organizations in Hardwar, some of them with branches throughout India and overseas, which were founded and are led by gurus who are not renouncers but are married men with families. Of these organizations headed by non-ascetics, the Gayatri Parivar (Gayatri Family) and the Manav Utthan Seva Samiti (Humanity Uplift Service Society) are particularly prominent in Hardwar. Although either of these organizations could be the topic of an entire book, both are briefly sketched in this section to illustrate gurus and organizations which contrast with those that are examined in depth in later chapters. Ethnographic and textual materials describing the environs of Hardwar and Rishikesh further develop themes from the previous chapter that concern the constellation of spirituality, commerce, and politics. The third part of the chapter outlines the history of Hardwar as a center of pilgrimage, trade, and Hindu activism.

Depending on the social status of the leader and the cultural preferences of its following, a religious organization variously emphasizes ascetic, brahmanic, and/or royal imagery of authority. These cultural models of authority and dominance occur in different combinations and are not mutually exclusive. They are a means of distinguishing religious organizations and defining their relative status. Deference to the superior status of religious organizations headed by ascetics enables gurus and devotees to distinguish their own organizations as being oriented to spiritual goals and hence superior to other types of organizations, e.g., political, caste, business, professional. As the preceding discussion of institutional big men suggests, in practice the distinction between spiritual and other organizations is blurred. For example, an ascetic may be the organizational focus for a particular caste group. Ascetics may establish or participate in explicitly political organizations and be elected to public office. However, the distinctions relating to ascetic, brahmanic, and regal styles of authority, between spiritual power and worldly power, provide means to differentiate religious organizations from other corporate groups headed by big men. The existence of a large market for spiritual goods and services further encourages gurus and their organizations to maintain an identity that keeps them distinct from other corporate groups.

THE GAYATRI PARIVAR

Named after the Gayatri mantra, a mantra that was once exclusively the possession of upper-caste Hindu men, the Gayatri Parivar (Gayatri Family) was founded by brahman guru Acharya Shri Ram Sharma. His wife, Mata Bhagwati Devi Sharma, who assisted her husband in managing the international Family from its Hardwar headquarters, succeeded her husband as head after his death in 1991. In its promotional literature the Gayatri Parivar refers to the tradition of the brahman sage or *rishi* to authorize Sharma in his role as spiritual leader. It portrays Sharma and his wife as possessing the attributes of hoary rishi couples: ashram-dwelling brahmans; teachers of spiritual science; and guardians of morality and the social order. This modern rishi couple teach that chanting the Gayatri mantra and performing the vedic fire sacrifice are imperative for the individual and society to advance spiritually and materially (see plate 9). In *The New Age Force: Gayatri* (Rawal 1981) a book written by a devotee of Sharma and published by the Bharatiya Vidya Bhavan, the Gayatri mantra is heralded as the means to create a new Ram Rajya and as the mother of the Vedas and "the soul of Hindu Civilization. Hindu Civilization is a divine civilization and can fittingly be called the civilization of mankind" (Rawal 1981, 53). The Gayatri Parivar is not the first organization to emphasize the Gayatri mantra as a devotional practice. Cow protection societies of Gorakhpur in the late-nineteenth century instructed upper-caste male members to chant this mantra three times daily (Amin 1988, 295).

Whereas the Gayatri mantra is described as the mother of divine culture, *yajna* (vedic fire sacrifice) is said to be the father. A booklet published by the Gayatri Parivar, *Tested Experiments of Fruitful Gayatri Sadhana* (B. Sharma, n.d.b), describes yajna as "an audiovisual method to instill moral and spiritual values in the hearts of men and women" (16). It is hailed as the "key to the revival of Divine Culture." Signifying "piety, austerity and generosity," yajna is a "discipline to check an individual's animal instincts and to divert to higher purpose any degenerate tendencies in society" (9). In ancient times spiritual and political conferences are said to have been in the form of yajnas that involved "huge populations and thereby influenced at one and the same time the environment throughout the length and breadth of many nation states" (17). All the benefits of the different types of yajnas organized in the past "can now be achieved through Gayatri Yajna. . . . Those who have concern for Indian traditions should put in their effort to propagate Gayatri Yajna on the widest possible scale" (17).

Members of the Gayatri Parivar sponsor yajnas to mark important occasions and Hindu holidays. For example, a Hardwar building contractor sponsored a two-day Gayatri yajna after completing construction of an ashram complex commissioned by an organization of wealthy, high-status south Indian saraswat brahmans which is headed by a brahman ascetic. The yajna proceedings commenced with a procession of about fifty local women and girls to the Ganges. At the riverside and under the supervision of male officiants of the Gayatri Parivar, the women worshipped the bright yellow pots that they had filled with Ganges water. In a boisterous procession directed by the Gayatri Parivar men, the women carried the pots on their heads back to the contractor's house. The following day fire sacrifices were performed by about one hundred people. On both days, tea, snacks, and meals were served to ascetic and lay guests. Personnel deputed by the Gayatri Parivar to conduct the yajna proceedings reminded the audience of their duty to make a donation. As will be seen later in the discussion of the pan-Indian Sacrifice for Unity sponsored by the VHP, the Gayatri Parivar is one of many groups that use yajna as a means of publicizing its organization, attracting supporters, and raising money.

Accounts of Sharma's life claim that his divine guru, a 4,500-year-old yogi living in "sublime form" in the Himalayas, has guided all his actions. When Sharma was fifteen years old this guru began to instruct him on how to "amass spiritual power to discharge greater responsibilities" in the service of mankind (R. Sharma n.d.b, 3; hereafter, *Deeds*). To establish his nationalist credentials, these accounts emphasize that Sharma had been a disciple of Mahatma Gandhi and was imprisoned during the freedom movement. After independence he is said to have sold his "vast ancestral property" and used the money first to build a school and then an ashram in the pilgrimage town of Mathura. Sharma's enterprises are described as having been designed to complement the efforts of the secular government of newly independent India: "The task of eradicating individual, social and mental backwardness and of setting into motion reformatory social action would have to be taken up by selfless social activists supported by the masses. For this, he felt that the powerful religious establishment which held sway over the hearts of people should be pressed into service" (Parihar n.d., 1; hereafter, *Shantikunj*). Sharma conceives of his work as striving to make the religious establishment "as useful as the welfare state of today." The Gayatri Parivar claims to successfully answer the question, "In what ways should the existing religious establishment be modified so that it may acquire the capacity and capability to mould mass consciousness to make it pure and receptive to the winds of change?" (7). Moreover, through its success, the Gayatri Parivar asserts that it has proven how "the present indifference and indignation felt for religion could be diverted into constructive channels" (7).

The Gayatri Parivar represents itself as a mass-based organization which does not rely on contributions from the rich. It claims to be wholly funded by the small donations—"daily collection of handful of foodgrains by women and ten paisa per day by men"—and voluntary labor of its many members and by the sales of its publications (Pandya n.d., 8; hereafter, *Unique Heritage*). The Gayatri Parivar suggests that the religious establishment, as manifest in Hindu organizations such as itself, has the capacity to supplant the welfare state. It blames poverty on the sloth of the poor: "lethargy and poverty live together as bosom friends." Wealth is portrayed as inevitably ensuing from hard work and partnership with God. This ideology of wealth and poverty presents no challenge to existing property relations nor does it allow inquiry into the socio-economic structures associated with mass poverty. For this organization as well as others which institutionalize spirituality, welfare—of individuals, groups, the nation, and the world—is a commodity whose promise of use value attracts members and naturalizes both the status and interests of ruling-class groups.

In the 1970s the Gayatri Parivar built its enormous Shantikunj ashram in Hardwar to house the Sharma couple, visitors, and about a hundred families of devotees. Resident devotees live in their own nuclear family units within the ashram compound. Children attend the ashram school, women tend to their domestic duties and staff the ashram kitchen, and the men tend to ashram business, which includes office work and the thousand-letter-a-day correspondence with members of the organization's 2,400 branches. Gayatri Parivar men also make publicity tours during which they sell publications and conduct rituals, recruit members, and instruct people about the boons of belonging to the Parivar. These workers are extolled for having "given up bright careers to toil day and night for a pittance" (*Shantikunj*, 3). Some ashram residents told me that they rely on income from family property, investments, and pensions to supplement this "pittance." The official literature presents the situation thus: "some have chosen to depend on their past savings but are working happily and dedicatedly day and night." Sharma's adult son oversees the operations of the Mathura ashram.

Occasionally the Gayatri Parivar cannot silence voices of those who have had a falling out with the family. The Gayatri Parivar attracted press attention after former disciple Swami Prayagananda wrote a letter to the president of India denouncing Sharma as a "fake guru" and a "fraud." The disappointed disciple also returned the doctorate Meerut University had awarded for his dissertation, "Shri Ram Sharma: The Man, His Life and Mission" (*Times of India*, 16 November 1987). In its statement to the press the Gayatri Parivar described Swami Prayagananda as having been "disowned and expelled" by Sharma for his "anti-guru activities." It maintained that "the inside truth" was that Prayagananda "had an eye on the huge assets of Acharyaji's trust establishments at Hardwar and Mathura and expected to be throned as the heir of the ageing Acharyaji."

Sharma's prolific pen and the Parivar's busy printing presses are instrumental in popularizing his teachings. He wrote Hindi abridgments and commentaries on numerous religious texts. Some of the many other topics he has written about concern: the importance of Hindu pilgrimage; women's duties as wives and mothers; the proper education of children; the need to base society on the spiritual values of India's ancient and divine culture; how this divine culture should be propagated among and by emigrant Indians and should form the basis of world culture.

Sharma attributes his achievements to the blessings of his guru, blessings that he earned through his own hard work. His explanation of this exchange relation parallels his own relations with members of the Gayatri Parivar:

> God behaves in such a way that he does not give anything to anyone without receiving from him. . . . I also gave whatever was demanded of me. This contribution was instantaneously rewarded. . . . I have loved and in return, been profusely loved. About 24 lakh [2.4 million] of persons have been contributing their valuable time, day and night in the work of building a new era on my suggestion. (*Deeds*, 6)

This theme of devoted service *(seva)* and its rewards is elaborated in the booklet, *Make God Your Partner in Day-to-Day Life* (R. Sharma n.d.d; hereafter, *Make God*). Sharma instructs readers that success in life "requires the cooperation of others at every step" (1). He describes life as a business, an industry in which "there is no possibility of loss, failure or distress if partnership with God is strengthened" (3–4).

Like other Hindu organizations, the Gayatri Parivar acknowledges the need to emulate successful strategies of Christian missions. In addition to strategies of proselytization shared with Christian missions, Sharma's mass marketing of spiritual science (the science pertaining to the formation and transformation of consciousness) has parallels with "motivational research" used in advertising and public relations (Packard 1975). Packard refers to an article published in the *Public Relations Journal* reporting on how "smart preachers" were using public relations techniques to "fill up pews and maintain a 'strong financial condition'" (1975, 178). Packard notes, however, that the report acknowledged that an

> "obstacle" to a really hard-hitting use of P.R. in sacred activities was that a "dignified approach" is demanded. Another obstacle is "the problem of showing the practical worth of some religious values." But it added: "If we are to pattern our techniques on those of the Master, we must bring the truth down where people can understand it . . . talk about common things . . . speak the language of the people." . . . The report detailed how the smart preacher can use TV and other mass media, and how to cope with "Mr. Back-slider." (He is wooed back by "psychological influences.") The final tip to preachers was to check results carefully to find just "what clicked." (179)

As a "smart preacher," Sharma uses a variety of explanations—psychological, economic, and spiritual—to elaborate his central point: self-improvement requires partnership with a superior, and "if man today is poor and miserable, the sole reason is that he is devoid of partnership with God" (*Make God,* 3). Love of God transmutes "iron-like desires into gold." Ascetic practices inculcate true devotion and perseverance; they are the "real spiritual disciplines by which God is pleased and He grants de-sired boon" (7). Moreover, those persons who practice these spiritual disci-plines develop virtues and powers and become saints. With these virtues and powers such persons *(tapasvi)* "do what they want and get all which they like. Those who want to attain leadership, public service, wealth, re-spect, worldly enjoyments should in the first instance make themselves a tapasvi" (8).

Sharma concludes his discussion of the need to enter into partnership with God (and guru) by returning to his economic model:

> Gifts and boons can be obtained by making God a partner in life business. Most of the partnership firms function by borrowing capital from others. Similarly several persons inherit property from their father and by making careful and appropriate use of it, they make immense material progress. God is also ready to invest capital in your life. You are getting these riches in inher-itance. Just be careful in properly planning and utilising this wealth appro-priately. (8)

He stresses that after "self-building" one must use the fruits of one's achievements for "self-enlargement" and "benevolent" purposes (R. Sharma n.d.e, 5; hereafter, *Spiritual Training*). Using one's resources in such a manner requires cautious calculation: "it will be a costly affair if they are misused." The subtext of Sharma's teachings is that participation in the Gayatri Parivar is a safe and sure method whereby the individual first builds up spiritual and material resources through hard work and self-restraint, and then invests these resources in the benevolent activities of the organization.

In another booklet, *Basic Concepts of Material Achievements* (R. Sharma n.d.a; hereafter, *Basic Concepts*), Sharma relates the importance of spiritual disciplines to the development of self-confidence. He prescribes the behavior that distinguishes possessors of self-confidence and the training necessary for the practice of this "high-class virtue":

> A smile on the lips with lustre of hope in the eyes is the only external identity of self-confidence, firm determination and genuine character. Those leading successful life are never seen disappointed, sad, serious or in a confused state of mind. . . . It is therefore essential for everyone to try to bring a smile on the lips and lustre of hope in eyes to convince others of one's superiority. If this has not been brought into practice, one should take the help of a mirror and practice this by acting. Anyone can see how ugly the face looks while one remains sad. It is a symbol of inefficiency. (*Basic Concepts*, 4–5)

In this context Packard's observations are suggestive for understanding the commercial aspects of Sharma's exhortations concerning the practiced smile and the aura of confidence and superiority. Packard discusses how advertising firms consider an atmosphere which promotes confidence and positive thinking as necessary for high levels of consumption and how they have found that a "cheerful atmosphere" encourages consumers to spend money (1975, 185–86).

Besides its "man-making mission" within India, the Gayatri Parivar also conceives of its mission in global terms. A booklet attributed to Sharma's wife and translated into English by an officer in the Indian Administrative Service, *Divine Culture Shall Expand, Not Remain Confined* (B. Sharma n.d.a; hereafter, *Divine Culture*), outlines a method for bringing "the treasure house of our ancestors" to the "international mart" which would result in "our great cultural values gaining currency" (14). Worldwide adoption of these great cultural values is posited as the only alternative to "total annihilation of the human race through mass suicide" (15). The text asserts that "India may be backward in acquiring wealth but she can still export her cultural heritage, spiritual outlook and civilised traditions to the outside world" (15).

The Gayatri Parivar offers its services to emigrant Indians. These include tourist facilities and training courses at its Hardwar ashram, and spiritual and social services organized by its overseas branches (e.g., assisting emigrant Indians to arrange the marriages for their children). References to emigrant Indians and overseas operations also carry with them a promise that membership in the Gayatri Parivar offers an opportunity for establishing useful international connections. By the early 1990s the Gayatri Parivar successfully joined the "international mart" of overseas Hindu organizations. Its branches in the United States and Canada sponsored large yajnas in Toronto and Los Angeles in 1993 and another in Chicago in 1995. The slogan on the emblem that appeared both on advertisements for these yajnas and on the cover of the yajna souvenir volumes reads: "Cultural Conquest of Whole Universe."

Ritual discipline and a voluntarily abstemious lifestyle form the ethos of the Gayatri Parivar. These practices are said to be rooted in the ancient and unparalleled science of Hindu spirituality. Sharma teaches that modern science and its technological products are merely material supplements to spiritual science. They are subordinate but useful for substantiating the findings of spiritual sciences. Whereas economic problems and their solutions are "an area mainly dominated by physical scientists and capitalists who invest money," spiritual scientists attend to "the work of refining the personality of man. The sphere of spiritual consciousness is more important than the material sphere" (R. Sharma, n.d.c, 5; hereafter, *Spiritual Science*). Only spiritual scientists like Sharma are capable of using the knowledge gained from physical sciences for human good: "The trend and atmosphere which is capable of uplifting humanity at large can be achieved only by advancement of spiritual science." The work of spiritual scientists, "experiments conducted in the name of brainwashing are the need of the day" (6). In the interests of the "public good" spiritual scientists "train the masses to adopt sublime thinking and dutifulness" (6).

Brahmavarchas is the Gayatri Parivar's laboratory of spiritual science in Hardwar. It is an edifice for displaying modern science as encompassed within the frames of spirituality and brahmanic ritualism (see plate 10). The ground floor houses twenty-four shrines to different forms of the goddess, one shrine for each syllable of the Gayatri mantra. On the level above these shrines visitors are told that the displays they see are scientific laboratories. On about a dozen visits I never saw anyone doing anything behind the glass windows of laboratory dioramas marked with labels such as pulmonary, cardio-vascular, neurological, and psychological chambers. Adorned with hand-drawn posters, test tubes, and other basic pieces of laboratory equipment, the displays seem a cross between a high school science lab and an exhibit at a historical museum. A description of Brahmavarchas in a Gayatri Parivar publication presents a different view: "Visitors are often heard saying that they have never seen such a sophisticated laboratory. Naturally enough, where the objects of research are so totally different from conventional research, the equipment required would have to be extraordinary" (*Spiritual Science*, 6).

A fast-talking guide explains to visitors how in these laboratories the Gayatri Parivar's spiritual scientists conduct experiments, diagnose the psychic causes of physical maladies, and prescribe the appropriate spiritual remedy. In the middle of the courtyard and surrounded by the goddess's shrines is another shrine encased in dark glass. It contains books by Sharma, a picture of him and his wife, and an object that looks like a computer. The guide assured me it is in fact a computer and that it is used to record and analyze the results of tens of thousands of spiritual experiments. Like the laboratories upstairs, I never saw anyone working at the computer inside the shrine.

This cultic treatment of science and technology suggests how institutionalized spirituality appropriates signifiers of status and power. Journalists described India in the 1980s as in the midst of not only consumer and managerial revolutions but also a computer revolution: "Computers a Quiet Revolution" (*India Today*, 31 December 1987). Hindustan Computer Limited advertised for marketing trainees and electronic engineers with the headline, "Minds Are Not Created Equal. Neither Are Careers" (*Indian Express*, 13 January 1988). An advertisement for a private training course in computers advises parents, "You sent him to the best school. The best college. Gave him the best that you could buy. This year he will graduate. Or perhaps he has graduated already. It's time to think of his career. Why not computers? It's a growing industry" (*Times of India*, 12 September 1988). Another article reports that "the computer revolution is on in the country" and it promises to make jobs in "lower order services more exciting which in turn would result in respectability for these jobs. For example secretaries, nurses, janitors, sales clerks and cashiers are going to become more 'respectable' once computers are introduced in their fields and they take over the 'dirty' part of their jobs" (*Times of India*, 26 July 1987).

The exhibits of the Gayatri Parivar need be situated in this larger context of technological change, with its promise of secure and respectable employment for the middle and lower-middle classes. Like the solar energy panel and windmill on display at Gayatri Parivar's sprawling Shantikunj ashram, where groups of government school teachers are among the thousands who come every year for moral and spiritual training courses, the scientific laboratories and the enshrined computer present to viewers a particular ideology of science. This ideology accords with that promoted by conservative popular science movements throughout India which sponsor exhibits and dramatic shows. *India Today* reports on a "unique science show," a "month long road show" traveling with five convoys across 25,000 kilometers and performing at 525 towns and villages (15 November 1987). The show is said to depict science as a means for meeting "basic needs, self-reliance and national integration." In his discussion of popular science movements, Vanaik discerns conservative and radicalized trends (1990, 196–97). The conservative trend aims to "disseminate a scientific temper and outlook," i.e., to educate the masses to view science as a force which is as beneficial to them as it is to the ruling classes. The other is a more radicalized trend which regards popular science movements as "an integral part of the struggle for dramatic social change," for example, the popular science movement in Kerala whose slogan is "Science for Social Revolution" (196).

Unlike the organizations studied in depth in later chapters, the Gayatri Parivar in India does not have a sizeable elite, English-speaking following. However, as it continues to grow in North America, its prestige in India may increase and it may attract more affluent followers. At present, however, the style of the Gayatri Parivar remains populist rather than elitist. Though its leaders and preachers seem more rustic than urbane, they have been extremely successful in expanding their base of support both in India and overseas. The Indian Government issued a postage stamp to honor Acharya Sharma, and high-ranking officials—including Indian president Shankar Dayal Sharma—attend Parivar yajnas. This suggests that the Parivar has well-placed allies. Perhaps these influential allies find in the Parivar a large and populist front organization for the Hindu nationalist movement: Sharma's teachings resonate with the tenets of Hindu nationalism, and the Gayatri Parivar has had a long association with the VHP. Acharya Sharma had been a member of the VHP's Central Margdarshak Mandal, an advisory body of religious leaders.

MAHARAJI AND THE HOLY FAMILY

With its iconic treatment of scientific instruments, the Gayatri Parivar represents science as a force at once complementary and subordinate to institutionalized spirituality. A few kilometers away from Shantikunj and Brahmavarchas, the Manav Utthan Seva Samiti at its Premnagar ashram adapts science for other uses. Built largely by a group of former bonded laborers from Madhya Pradesh who have become devotees of the guru and serve him as the organization's mobile construction crew, a twin tower of toilets connected to a biogas plant is this ashram's unique monument to the scientific age. These monumental facilities are meant to meet the needs of the ashram's visitors when they gather in crowds numbering over 100,000 for various celebrations throughout the year. At their New Delhi ashram, the organization's headquarters, devotees work on computers and modern printing equipment to produce monthly journals and other publications in several languages including English.

The somber and restrained atmosphere at the premises of the Gayatri Parivar, where armed guards sat outside the late Acharya Sharma residence, contrasts with the more festive and informal ambiance of the Manav Utthan Seva Samiti. Both organizations are far less exclusive than the Divine Life Society and claim to have millions of followers throughout India.

The Manav Utthan Seva Samiti is currently headed by Satpal Rawat, eldest son of its founder, Hans Rawat. (See appendix 1 for official statements by the Manav Utthan Seva Samiti concerning its teachings and activities.)[1]

The present organization is a portion of a previously larger one that had split into two after Satpal's younger brother, Balyogeshwar—the wondrous boy guru Maharaji—became both an international success and scandal in the 1970s. Balyogeshwar had been supported by a faction within the organization, a faction that after the death of the founding father had wanted to capitalize on the fashion for gurus prevailing in Europe and North America.[2] Khushwant Singh reports an interview during which Balyogeshwar explained in the following terms the assets of being a guru: "Divine knowledge is like money in the bank. It is my money. I have the cheque book. But only after I write the cheque and sign it can you draw the money" (1975a, 70).

Satpal now heads the Manav Utthan Seva Samiti in India and spearheads its rapid expansion. The Samiti owns property in the United States and has followers there and in other foreign countries, but its principal operations and property holdings as well as the bulk of its supporters are in India. The Samiti's published accounts of its history report Satpal's smooth succession to his father's position. The Samiti is silent about Satpal's brother, Balyogeshwar, and the scandalous family feud.

Satpal, his wife, and two sons as well as another brother, this brother's wife, and three daughters constitute the focus of the Manav Utthan Seva Samiti's cult of the holy family. Devotees worship the holy family and regard Satpal and his relatives as divine beings with spiritual powers (see

1. For a brief discussion of the Manav Utthan Seva Samiti, see Hoens (1979).

2. For background material on the international commercial operations of Balyogeshwar's Divine Light Movement, see Cameron (1973). Refuting allegations against Balyogeshwar of smuggling, being involved in politics, and making "anti-India statements," a large newspaper advertisement placed by his organization in 1987 claims that the controversy surrounding him has persisted over the years (*Times of India*, 4 December 1987). He is described as having married only once, thus "it is quite baseless to say that he is a polygamist [his father had two wives]. He is a respectable householder having four children." It describes Balyogeshwar's mission as involving international tours during which he explains to "people in general without any distinction of caste, colour, race, stature or wealth that the source of happiness, peace and contentment lies within one's own self. He also provides practical techniques to get united with it in order to enable a person to have an access to that treasure which is full of joy, tranquillity, satisfaction and love. He is trying to prepare humanity to face and overcome the present day tussle and turmoil prevailing in the world in the name of achieving world peace, on individual basis. In fact, what Guru Maharaj Ji is trying to do is not being comprehended by most of the people, with the result that he is included in the category of those persons who have become mere machines to collect wealth, while Maharaj Ji has taken a pledge to complete this huge task without any monetary consideration" (*Times of India*, 4 December 1987).

plate 11). Like the multiplicity of deities in the Hindu pantheon, the various members of the holy family multiply the symbolic forms through which devotees can experience their relationships with divinity. The use of Satpal's extended family for attracting a range of devotees is similar to the use of complexes of images by advertisers for particular products in order to diversify the types of consumers the products can attract (Packard 1975). To illustrate his point Packard quotes from a market research report on car owners written by social scientists: "A car can sell itself to different people by presenting different facets of its personality. . . . Advertising is a multiplier of symbols. Like a prism, it can present many different facets of the car's character so that many fundamentally different people see it as their car" (1975, 53). Until her death in 1991, Satpal's mother, the second wife of the founder, was actively involved in the work of the Samiti. She and her deceased husband, along with the living members of the holy family, are worshipped by devotees with rituals similar to those performed for a Hindu deity in a domestic shrine or temple.

As are many other gurus, Satpal is usually called Maharaji by his devotees, an appellation suited to his regal style of pomp and ceremony and his rajput caste status. The Samiti expresses the authority of Satpal with cultural imagery related to ideals concerning righteous Hindu kings, especially as elaborated in the *Ramayana*. As his father was before him, Satpal is likened to Janaka, the father of Sita. He is believed to share with that righteous Hindu king not only paternal concern for his devoted and loving subjects but also spiritual knowledge and power. Devotees' contact with Satpal and his family is generally limited to public appearances at celebrations marking the birthdays of holy family members or Hindu holidays. During these appearances devotees gaze upon the holy family, listen to their sermons, and line up—sometimes waiting hours under the scorching summer sun—to momentarily touch their feet, make offerings, and receive their blessings (see plate 12).

Folksy paintings of a king sitting atop an elephant on parade before his subjects decorate walls at the Premnagar ashram. When crowds throng the ashram for a three-day celebration of Satpal's birthday, his sons and nieces are sent forth on an elephant for a royal progress through the ashram grounds. Devotees enthusiastically join in the procession. The social distance between Satpal and his mass of followers, who are largely drawn from the urban lower and lower-middle classes and rural artisans and small landholders, is like that between a politician and electoral masses, a factory owner and factory workers, a corporate manager and clerical workers, or a rural landlord and landless laborers. Satpal's sons and nieces are enrolled in some of the country's most elite and expensive private schools in Dehra Dun. This social distance contributes to the charisma of the holy family. It is mediated by initiated disciples, who work full time to maintain constant and direct contact with followers at the organization's branches throughout India.

Satpal's Premnagar ashram in Hardwar, with its spacious gardens, swimming pool reserved for members of the holy family, and carefully maintained buildings, offers visitors an experience of proximity to the lovely delights of wealth. Devotees who have donated the requisite funds for building a room in the ashram are housed in well-appointed residential buildings. During major celebrations, however, most devotees camp on the ashram's grounds. A woman employed by the Delhi Municipal Corporation as a street sweeper once told me that she and her family are followers of Maharaji and regularly attend celebrations at the Premnagar ashram. She explained that Maharaji teaches the equality of all castes and that even sweeper families like hers are allowed to sit and dine with the "big people." Most devotees are indeed fed en masse during large gatherings. However, during crowded celebrations the really big "big people" dine separately, often from five-star style buffets laden with delicacies prepared by professional chefs. During one such epicurean luncheon, I noticed that the women of the holy family had changed out of glitzy costumes that sparkle under the spotlights and into heavy brocade saris, the attire favored by wealthy women for weddings and other important social occasions.

During the holy family's frequent tours of Samiti branches, devotees have opportunities for more intimate contact with them. Private audiences with family members and particularly with Satpal, the institutional big man, are considered a special privilege. Devotees who have had private audiences proudly recount to others their experience of proximity to divinity. Besides these public encounters, the blessings and protection of the holy family are believed to be bestowed upon devotees who meditate privately upon them.

Several hundred full-time workers live as ascetics in the Samiti's branches and ashrams throughout India. These men and women link the devotees with the guru, and they are the organization's preachers and administrators at the local level. Mangalwadi describes the relation between lay devotees and the guru's ascetic intermediaries, who are known as mahatmas: "serving the Sadguru in practice means obeying orders from the Mahatmas and propagating the knowledge" (1977, 196). He also notes that many of the mahatmas require lay devotees to demonstrate intense desire for the secret divine knowledge, which can involve begging them for initiation. About the secret knowledge obtained during initiation, Mangalwadi reports that an ex-disciple described it as entailing instruction in specific meditation techniques through which physical manipulation of eyes, tongue, and ears produced effects interpreted as divine light, divine nectar, and divine sound. During my many visits to the Samiti's ashrams in

Hardwar and Delhi, mahatmas and devotees often asked me when I would "take knowledge" and why I had not yet done so. When I generally replied that my research did not require that I be initiated, many assured me that I would eventually experience the desire for divine knowledge so intensely that I would request initiation.

The holy family attracts followers from a range of class and caste backgrounds. It regularly stages events that draw over 100,000 people to its Hardwar ashram and draws even larger crowds to its annual celebration of the founder's birthday in Delhi. Although most of its followers are from the lower range of the socio-economic spectrum, the organization's recent expansion in south India and particularly in Bangalore is attracting a more educated and wealthier group of devotees. To an even greater extent than the Gayatri Parivar, the Manav Utthan Seva Samiti has a populist appeal. Social groups such as sweepers that are often shunned by other religious institutions are accepted as devotees of the holy family and participate in Samiti activities.

FIRST CAME THE SEERS THEN THE SOLDIERS

The literature of the Gayatri Parivar and the Manav Utthan Seva Samiti beckons devotees to visit their guru's ashram in Hardwar. Government tourist literature, advertisements, and travel articles in newspapers and magazines also invite visitors to Hardwar. This literature shares the idiom of gurus and pandas—professional hosts in pilgrimage centers—that extols Hardwar as "Gateway to the gods" (*Times of India Travel Supplement*, 27 September 1987).[3] One guidebook describes Hardwar as a "godly gift to the Godfearing. A sincere call to the Mateshwari, or a dip in the sacred water, is sufficient to lodge one into the Heavens. All his sins are washed away and he gets fully purified; totally a new purified soul" (N. Singh, n.d., 26). Pilgrims find in Hardwar an array of ritual and sectarian forms characteristic of contemporary Hinduism. Even its name adapts itself to sectarian preferences: for Vaishnavite devotees it is Haridwar, for Shaivites it is Hardwar; it is synonymous with the flowing presence of the goddess Ganga Mata.

There are many possible reasons for a pilgrimage to Hardwar. After arrival, pilgrims quickly learn from pandas, gurus, shopkeepers, and guidebooks that the reasons to visit Hardwar are even more numerous than

3. For a description of Hardwar composed by Rajkumar Sharma, a prominent panda, see appendix 2. In it he prefers to use the term "purohit" instead of panda. Jameson notes that Hardwar pilgrimage priests are known as "tirtha purohit" as well as panda and that they define panda as "literally" meaning "the ability to distinguish good and evil" (1976, xvii). Pandas are also called "Gangaguru," particularly by pilgrims from Rajasthan (Jameson 1976, xvii).

they imagined. They might perform Hindu life-cycle rituals; wash away sins with a bath in the Ganges; search for or visit a guru; celebrate festivals; worship at shrines of deities; donate money to feed brahmans and sadhus, widows and beggars; buy religious goods and literature. Depending on their status and personal preferences, pilgrims stay in government and private hotels, in rooms owned by pandas and ashrams, and in guest houses *(dharmshala)* owned by wealthy families and caste groups, or they may camp by the riverside.

Just as pilgrims come to Hardwar from villages, towns, and cities throughout India, so too religious organizations and sects with followings from all over India have branches or headquarters in Hardwar. Its proximity to New Delhi, the hub of national politics, renders Hardwar an important site for Hindu leaders to articulate their demands and demonstrate their solidarity. The formation in 1989 of a new district with Hardwar as its headquarters indicates the government's concern to enlarge its own power base in the pilgrimage center. Through the expansion of government offices in Hardwar, politicians, and bureaucrats extend their local patronage networks. This in turn strengthens their position for negotiating with leaders of religious organizations active in Hardwar.

The official reason for forming the new district relates to the Kumbh Mela, a huge bathing festival held periodically in Hardwar: it would enable government departments to better coordinate the arrangements for hygiene and public safety necessary during the festival (*India Today*, 15 November 1987). Although police and district officials deployed over 10,000 people to control the crowds gathered for Hardwar's 1986 Kumbh Mela, their efforts were not entirely successful. Forty-six people were trampled to death by pilgrims surging to the river for their bath on the most auspicious day of the festival. The Government of India tourist brochure describes the Kumbh Mela held in Hardwar every twelve years as the "world's largest religious fair." The procession of orders of sadhus is named as the "prime attraction." At this time "religious leaders of many of the sects of Hinduism also establish their own camps here, making the Kumbh a massive reassertion of an ancient faith."

Government tourist literature presents an official interpretation of pilgrimage which treats it as an important component and desirable commodity of Indian national culture. The Government of India's highly produced tourist literature arouses the desire to purchase emporia arts and crafts. This tourist literature also celebrates pilgrimage with photos and commentary depicting pilgrimage centers as exuding robust piety and timeless mystical attraction. These lustrous publications are largely directed to foreign tourists and nonresident Indians visiting from overseas. They treat pilgrimage as a fundamental expression of the vibrant unity of India, a view reverently espoused by producers of India's national and transnational culture and echoed in English-language newspapers and magazines.[4]

The Government of India Department of Tourism's brochure for Hardwar and nearby Rishikesh, Mussoorie, and Dehra Dun (1987) opens with: "First came the seers. Then the soldiers." The brochure pictures Rishikesh and Hardwar as realms of religion and spirituality. Color photos show crowds of pilgrims gathered for bathing and evening Ganges worship *(arti)* as well as solitary sadhus with either matted hair, turbans, or shaved heads. The text complements the photos: in Himalayan caves ancient rishis "sat in motionless solitude" until their efforts were rewarded by "flashes of intuition" which brought "the answers to the secrets of the soul." Such seers are said to live today in the ashrams of Rishikesh, and in nearby Hardwar "schools of ancient wisdom still research and teach the timeless wisdom gleaned from the Himalayas."

Juxtaposed with the spiritual attractions of Hardwar and Rishikesh are the worldly places of interest in Dehra Dun and Mussoorie. The brochure attributes the origins of Dehra Dun and Mussoorie to British soldiers. They drove back "tough Gurkha fighters" and built hill resorts for the "families of the guardians and rulers of the Raj." Befitting this legacy, the text emphasizes the pleasures these resorts offer: scenic picnic spots, cable car rides, wooded municipal gardens, roller skating, and pony riding on the Mall. Whereas the text highlights the religious institutions of Hardwar and Rishikesh which attract "solace-seekers from all over the world," it enumerates Dehra Dun's prestigious governmental institutions: "the giant Oil and Natural Gas Commission, the world-renowned Forest Research Institute, the famed Indian Military Academy and the Survey of India." In Mussoorie, "residential schools like Woodstock, Waverly and King George's, and the Central Services' Lal Bahadur Shastri National Academy inculcate a sense of discipline and pride." Citizen groups of Dehra Dun and Mussoorie are acclaimed as being "in the forefront of India's heritage and ecological preservation movements." The brochure thus presents an image of a national culture that is balanced between the modern secular institutions and amenities of Dehra Dun and Mussoorie and the religious institutions in the spiritually salubrious environs of Hardwar and Rishikesh.

The section on Hardwar begins with a factual tone, and then recounts its legendary origins. It proceeds to describe the religious institutions of Hardwar and concludes with a few facts about the Kumbh Mela. Readers first learn that Hardwar's altitude is 292 meters and its name is derived from "Hari (God) and Dwar (door)." Hardwar is built on the site where

---

4. For discussions concerning the study of national culture and its processes of production, see Appadurai and Breckenridge (1988); Fox (1990a, 1990b); Foster (1991).

the Ganges emerges from the mountains. It is "a pilgrim town whose antiquity is difficult to establish." This ambiguous statement about antiquity is followed by an account of the myth of Hardwar's origin.

"Legend has it" that the rage of an ancient sage initiated events leading to Hardwar's appearance. Purification by the Ganges was the only means to cleanse the souls tormented by the sage's curse. When the river descended from the mountains, the "fury was so great that it threatened to inundate the entire world." The world was saved by Shiva, the "Great Lord of the Mountains," who restrained the river in the locks of his matted hair. His intervention tamed the Ganges so that "only as much water as would wash away the sins of the dead" would flow through Hardwar.

The sage's anger had the benign result of occasioning the descent of the Ganges and the foundation of Hardwar; British soldiers are celebrated as founders of hill resorts. N. Singh's account of Hardwar starts with the curse of the sage but does not mention British or Gurkha soldiers. Instead, Muslim invaders are remembered for their destructive fury. In a section entitled "Historic Ravages," his guidebook reminds readers that the region has been "incessantly invaded, devastated and looted by the barbarism of racial grudge and greed for power and pelf of Moslems" (N. Singh n.d., 14–15). Readers are told where in Hardwar they can find Hindu temples which had been damaged or destroyed when "sometimes in the fourteenth and eighteenth century, Moslems invaded it and satisfied their racial wrath with their atrocious activities devastating the temples, plundering the people and burning their homes" (15). Najib-udduala of Najibabad is named as one particularly rapacious Muslim invader who "raided the place any time when he willed . . . burning and plundering the villages" (15).

Press coverage of militant Hindu organizations emphasizes Hindus' anger and rage against aggressive Muslims and the Indian state, whose secularism is said to advantage non-Hindus and oppress Hindus. These organizations keep alive hatred for Muslims and the desire for vengeance by promulgating accounts of past Muslim attacks on Hindus. They also encourage Hindus to participate in militant activities as the means to defend themselves against further attacks on their religion, their honor, and their motherland. Many of Hardwar's pandas and ascetic orders publicize and participate in militant Hindu activities.

Militant organizations like the Vishva Hindu Parishad (VHP) and the Rashtriya Swayamsevak Sangh (RSS) are also supported by Hardwar's religious leaders, who according to the Government of India tourist brochure, have "established their ashrams here." Indeed, some of Hardwar's biggest ashrams are sites for Hindu nationalist activism. Hardwar Swami Paramanand is a leading VHP ideologue, and in 1982 the heads of seven ascetic institutions in Hardwar initiated 150 VHP preachers (Jaffrelot 1993, 420).

The VHP often holds rallies in Hardwar as well as periodic meetings of its assembly of religious leaders. One such assembly in 1990 led to the formation of the Shri Ram Kar Seva Samiti, a militant group whose activities contributed to the destruction of the Babri mosque in Ayodhya. This government brochure, however, describes Hardwar's ashrams as "centres where work, precept, example and discussion help self-realisation in a non-dogmatic, very Indian way." Statements such as this as well as the conspicuous absence of the term Hindu and only a single reference to Hinduism in the brochure are consistent with an official national culture in which Hindu and Hinduism are suppressed but necessary referents. However, as the quotations from the brochure and guidebook as well as its religious topography suggest, Hardwar accommodates a range of dogmatic and politicized interpretations of Hinduism and history.

The text of the government brochure inscribes in generically Indian terms particular tenets of Hindu nationalism. Deeds of Hindu deities define the landscape of Hardwar and Rishikesh. These deeds are commemorated by "eyecatching" shrines such as the Daksh Temple and Sati Kund. About this particular religious complex the text explains: Sati "burnt herself in the sacrificial hearth" because she was "very insulted at her father's rudeness" toward her husband Shiva. Hindu tolerance, another nationalist tenet, is inscribed as the "non-dogmatic" character of Hardwar's religious teachers. "Self-realisation" suggests a popular configuration of national culture that claims proprietorship of spiritual knowledge and transcendent unity.

The depiction of Hardwar as quintessentially Indian receives a livelier and lighter treatment from Khushwant Singh (*Sunday*, 10 January 1988). His article expresses the critical yet reverential attitude frequently disclosed by academics and other Delhi residents when they learned I was doing fieldwork in Hardwar. This attitude is also infused with a sense of proprietorship which presumes the knowledge of and authority to judge all forms of Indian culture. Singh decries Hardwar's commercialism and pestering pandas and laments a landscape disfigured by architectural eyesores. Identifying himself as not Hindu but Sikh and atheist, he claims to come to Hardwar "as a pilgrim bent on ancestor worship." By likening himself to a previous pilgrim, Allama Iqbal—"scion of a Brahmin family turned Muslim"—Singh embeds in his article an increasingly marginalized strand of nationalist ideology which stresses cultural synthesis as the determining feature of Indian identity. He thus suggests that Muslims, Sikhs, and Hindus all come to Hardwar to worship ancestors; they are coparceners of a single patrimony. To the question, " 'What does India mean to you,' " Singh offers the reply: "The one thing that evokes all that is Indian in me is the worship of the Ganga at the hour of sunset. Every time I watch the aarti at Har-Ki-Pauri [in Hardwar] something happens to me and I feel like one transfixed to the spot where I stand. Buried deep in my psyche are chords that stir to some elemental music. For me it is a five-minute-long spiritual orgasm" (*Sunday,* 10 January 1988).

To conjure the scene Singh summons Bengali girls with "bewitching eyes"; his lascivious glance catches them putting afloat leaf boats with flickering flames. At Har-ki-Pairi, six priests "bearing salvers of oil lamps" worship the river. The sounds of conch, temple bells, and the chant, "Ganga Ma ki Jai," combine with the sight of the flames to induce a "five-minute hypnotic trance." The jocund tone defers to sober piety with Singh's final remarks: "There are no words to explain the experience. It haunts you for the rest of your days."

With its blurred black-and-white photos and pages of text crammed full of information, the Uttar Pradesh Tourism Department's brochure for Hardwar and Rishikesh has a provincial appearance when compared to the Government of India's glossy, four-color literature. Its text more explicitly beckons the Hindu pilgrim. The language is a less sophisticated Indian English and the text is replete with lexical errors. Printed before Hardwar had become a separate administrative district, it opens with a brisk account of Hardwar's origins:

> Haridwar lies under District Saharanpur and is situated on the right bank of holy river Ganga at the foot of Shivalik mountains. Haridwar has been a sacred place for pilgrimage since Pauranik age. In the age of Puran it was named as Mayapuri. The Chinese traveller Huien Tsang has mentioned about this place in his memoirs. It was also known as Gangadwar and Tapovan. More ancient than these names is Kapilasthan, as it is said that the ancestors of Raja Bhagirath were burnt at this place by the curse of sage Kapila. For their salvation, he performed Tapa and brought down Ganga from Heaven.

Below this introductory sketch, the brochure sets out "General Informations." Readers learn that Hardwar's population in 1981 was 114,415; its area is 12,032 square kilometers. Seasonal temperatures and rainfall are given. The "best season" to visit is "throughout the year." Visitors are advised to bring woolen clothing for winter and cotton and tropical clothing for summer. Hindi, Punjabi, and English are listed as the languages spoken in Hardwar.

The brochure is filled with lists of hotels and "important dharmshalas," travel agencies, conducted tours, and distances to other pilgrimage and tourist centers. Prominent temples and ashrams of Hardwar and Rishikesh are described in the text and marked on maps. Among the sights evaluated as "worth seeing" are: sunset arti of the Ganges at Har-ki-Pairi, Hardwar's "most sacred bathing ghat"; the Hanuman temple of the Pawan Dham ashram "built with pieces of glasses"; the Ved Mandir Museum; and the Pharmacy of Gurukul Kangri University. At Beauty Point visitors can "have wide angled view of Hardwar." Other places of interest around Hardwar include the industrial and residential complex of Bharat Heavy Electricals Ltd., a Government of India undertaking, and a government antibiotics factory. Shoppers are advised under the heading "Local Handicrafts" that the "bamboo baskets of Haridwar are famous." The brochure's contents and tone reassures the reader that Hardwar and Rishikesh are filled with sights "worth seeing" and that there are ample facilities for making the pilgrim's visit comfortable and convenient. The pantheon of Hindu gods is accommodated in Hardwar's many temples and sacred sites. Similarly, a single temple may itself be the abode of the many forms of god, as in the case of the Manav Kalyan Ashram: "All twenty four avatars of God have been depected [sic] in this ashram which can be easily seen by the visitors. The image of Lord Shiva and Lord Krishna have been dipected [sic] in the shape of Ardhnarishwar [androgyne] in this Ashram."

The Uttar Pradesh government brochure encourages visitors to plan an excursion to Rishikesh, twenty-five kilometers north of Hardwar: "The yoga centers of Rishikesh have enhanced the significance of the place, home tourists and foreign tourists from all over the world visit this place to have lessons in yoga and meditation." Rishikesh's origin is attributed to Raibhya Rishi, who performed "hard penances" here. He was rewarded when God appeared and took the name "Hrishikesh." Deploying the rhetoric of indirect discourse by using phrases such as "it is said" and "the mythological story is," the brochure combines a factual tone with the religious idiom shared by pandas and pilgrims. The following passage illustrates this narrative technique and gives another version of the origin of Daksh Mahdev temple and Sati Kund. They are "located about 3.5 kms from Tourist Office, Haridwar. The mythological story about this place is that Daksh Prajapati, father of Sati (Lord Shiva's first wife) performed Yagna at this place. Daksh Prajapati did not invite Lord Shiva and Sati felt insulted. Sati burned herself in Yagna kund." The passage's closing returns to direct discourse but continues without interruption in the indicative mood and declarative voice of the preceding sentences: "Kankhal is one of the five sacred places (Panch Tirth) around Hardwar. The five tirthas are Ganga, Kushwat, Bilwa Tirtha, Neel Parvat and Kankhal." The brochure has a note in bold type reminding readers that the establishments mentioned in this publication are not exhaustive and their inclusion does not "necessarily signify official approval or recognition." The whole brochure, however, signifies government patronage of Hindu pilgrimage.

These government brochures suggest particular contours of official culture not only by how they depict Hardwar as a pilgrimage center but also by what they omit. They are silent about the important historical links between commercial activity and pilgrimage and their present forms in Hardwar. The press and popular opinion criticize Hardwar and other pilgrimage centers as places where the pious are the prey of greedy operators. Such critiques lament present conditions and idealize a past when pilgrimage was not yet synonymous with rapacious commercialism.

Hardwar owes its emergence as an important pilgrimage center to an escalation of commercial activity. Before the eighteenth century, Hardwar was a quiet spot where people primarily came for a ritual bath in the Ganges. Its flow of pilgrims swelled in the mid-1700s, when the spring bathing festival became the occasion for a major north Indian trading fair (Lochtefeld 1992, 118). Besides increasing the numbers of pilgrims, the spring fair attracted merchants, traders, and agents of large banking and credit houses from throughout the subcontinent. It also attracted Hindu ascetics and orders. Some acted as armed guards for merchant caravans; others were themselves merchants who accumulated substantial property and capital and became leading landowners and powerbrokers in Hardwar. Once such ascetic was Shravan Nath. He spent Rs. 100,000—an enormous sum of money in 1820—on a temple endowment and feast for brahmans (Lochtefeld 1992, 124). When the railway altered trading patterns in the 1880s, Hardwar lost its position as an important market center and fewer people attended the spring bathing-trading fair. Although the numbers coming for the spring fair declined, the railway made Hardwar more accessible for pilgrims throughout the year.

In Hardwar pilgrimage is business. From arrival to departure pilgrims spend money on transport, food, lodging, and rituals; they make donations to brahmans and gurus; they purchase religious articles and souvenirs. Religion is not only good for business; in the opinion of one former businessman who lives in Hardwar as an ascetic, religion is "the best business of all: start-up costs were low, there were never any problems with supply or inventory, and one received tangible goods for intangible ones" (Lochtefeld 1992, 219–20).

HARDWAR AND PAN-HINDU MOVEMENTS

The convergence of business, religion, and politics in Hardwar makes it an important site for institutional formations of Hinduism and national culture. It is also an important site for Hindu leaders and their followers to gather and organize themselves for political action. In a travel article on Hardwar, which reads like a synthesis of the brochures published by the tourism departments of the Government of India and Uttar Pradesh, the author asserts that "today" Hardwar is "a must on every devoted Hindu's pilgrimage itinerary" (*Times of India Travel Supplement,* 27 September 1987). The pilgrim and tourist materials discussed above introduce contemporary representations of Hardwar that highlight its attractions as a place of Hindu pilgrimage.

Hardwar also attracts religious and political leaders; it provides them with a prestigious place to assemble to formulate issues, propagate ideologies, and establish institutions that produce a politicized Hindu identity. Such an identity can be used by leaders to mobilize different class, caste, and sectarian groups to support specific political projects. The discussion begins by providing historical examples of how Hindu leaders came to Hardwar to espouse ideologies and form organizations with social and political agendas. The treatment of these examples highlights sociological processes. It does not subordinate historical rupture and change to a presumed historical continuity, but rather uses accounts of past events as tools for conceptualizing and analyzing the operations of Hindu organizations in contemporary India.

Of the leading nineteenth-century proselytizers and reformers of Hinduism, perhaps none was as incendiary as Dayananda Saraswati, the founder of the Arya Samaj, a Hindu sect which condemned brahmanic ritualism and considered the Vedas to be the basis of religious and spiritual truth. During his visit to Hardwar in 1866 as part of a preaching tour, he enraged brahmans and others with his denouncements of Hindu practices such as pilgrimage, bathing in the Ganges, and idol worship. Prevailing forms of Hindu ritualism, he claimed, were not sanctioned by the Vedas and hence were without religious value (Farquhar 1967, 108). Later Arya Samaji leaders no longer found Hardwar so thoroughly reprehensible. In 1902 the Arya Samaj opened the Gurukul Kangri, its premier educational institution, in Hardwar.

In 1895, however, opponents of the Arya Samaj gathered in Hardwar to establish the Sanatan Dharma Sabha under the leadership of Din Dayal Sharma. A powerful public speaker and effective organizer, Sharma attracted the support of brahman pandits and titled men with a platform that united them in opposition to the missionary activities of Christians and Arya Samajis. He had also worked with Swami Gyanananda of Mathura to establish the Bharat Dharma Mahamandala in 1887. Farquhar describes its formation as a "bold attempt" by its founders "to gather together the whole of the Hindu people in a single organization, partly in self-defence, partly for religious instruction" (316).

The Mahamandala consisted of a national body, provincial associations, 600 local societies in towns and villages, and 400 affiliated institutions. It not only adapted strategies of Christian and Arya Samaji missionaries for propagating its message but also modeled its support of Sanskritic learning after institutions supporting orientalist-indological scholarship. Mahamandala activities were under the direction of five separate departments: preaching, religious endowments, sacred learning, publications, and libraries and research.

The Bharat Dharma Mahamandala published its own research journal, a monthly English-language magazine, and provincial magazines in vernacular languages. Like the Bharatiya Vidya Bhavan, the Gita Press of Gorakhpur, and numerous Hindu religious organizations today, the Mahamandala sold an extensive range of books about Hindu religion and philosophy. It also published booklets for free distribution. To recruit and train preachers, the Mahamandala established its own school. Farquhar comments that like other religious movements of its time "even the superlatively orthodox Bharat Dharma Mahamandala makes the claim of universalism, and offers to sell to anyone the books, which according to Hindu law, must be seen by no woman and by no man outside the three twice born castes" (437).

The first annual meeting of the Mahamandala was convened in Hardwar. Jones notes that elaborate religious rituals and the passing of resolutions consonant with the interests of Hindu orthodoxy characterized its annual meetings (1981b, 449). He also likens the style of these meetings to that of the Indian National Congress. With the retirement of Swami Gyanananda, internal fighting led to the Mahamandala's decline, and the organization "faded from view in the early years of the twentieth century" (Jones 1981b, 449). A former justice of the Calcutta High Court assumed formal leadership, and the Maharaja of Dharbanga, in the honorary office of General President, contributed to the organization the wealth and prestige of royal patronage. Pandit Madan Mohan Malaviya succeeded Swami Gyanananda as the Mahamandala's leading publicist. Malaviya was also a prime mover in the Hindu University Society, which drew together new and existing Hindu sabhas and raised most of its funds through patrons of the Sanatan Dharma movement (Gordon 1975, 56).

Every twelve years, when Hardwar hosts the Kumbh Mela, millions of pilgrims gather for an auspicious and purifying bath in the Ganges. One journalist described the 1986 Kumbh Mela in Hardwar as a "cosmic galaxy of ants crawling to the vibrations of a central sensor"; a pilgrim compared bathing in the Ganges to "drinking at your mother's breast" (*India Today*, 15 May 1986). The spectacle of the Kumbh includes processions of naked, trident-wielding sadhus and swamis bedecked in gold brocade sitting atop elephants. During the Kumbh Mela, Hindu religious organizations and monastic orders vie among themselves to display their ritual status, wealth, and official connections. Organizations earn prestige and followers through their patronage of Kumbh events: feasts for sadhus and pilgrims, elaborate rituals, musical and dramatic performances, discourses by scholars and popular preachers. The Kumbh also provides an occasion for religious and political leaders to form and consolidate alliances among themselves and to impress the public with displays of solidarity.

During Hardwar's 1915 Kumbh Mela, the Maharaja of Darbhanga revived the dormant Sanatan Dharma movement by forming an All India

Sanatan Dharma Sammelan, which two years later amalgamated with the Bharat Dharma Mahamandala (Gordon 1975, 155). The All-India Conference of Hindus was also convened in Hardwar at this time. The resolution to convene this Conference had been passed by the Punjab Hindu Conference. Arya Samaji and other Hindu leaders in the Punjab opposed the secular nationalism of the Congress because it allowed for the possibility of domination by Muslims in the Punjab where Muslims outnumbered Hindus. Punjabi Hindus had social and economic ties with Hardwar through pilgrimage and patronage of Hardwar's pandas and ascetic orders. They chose it as the site for convening the Conference to form a Hindu organization that might help to strengthen their own position in the Punjab. The Conference brought together representatives of provincial Sanatan Dharma sabhas, the Arya Samaj, caste associations, cow protection societies, and groups supporting Hindi in the Devanagari script. Delegates to the All-India Conference of Hindus in Hardwar formed the Sarvadeshak Hindu Sabha, later renamed the Hindu Mahasabha.

The establishment of the Hindu Mahasabha in 1915 was the realization of a long-standing goal of Hindu leaders. Five years earlier at the Allahabad Congress Conference a prominent Kanpur banker and president of the Vaish caste association had unsuccessfully attempted to establish an all-India Hindu organization in response to the newly formed Muslim League. Hindu Sangathan became the name for the ideology espousing that Hindus of different caste and sectarian groups must organize themselves into a unified front for effective political action. *Hindu Sangathan: Saviour of the Dying Race* by Arya Samaji leader Swami Shraddhananda propounded the ideology of Hindu Sangathan—the organization of Hindus—and celebrated the founding of the Hindu Mahasabha. Among the many Hindu leaders who have promoted and interpreted Hindu Sangathan, V. D. Savarkar figures as perhaps the most influential. His Sangathanist writings and activities are discussed in the following chapter.

With its broad platform of Hindu organization and unity, the Hindu Mahasabha initially avoided controversial issues such as widow remarriage and untouchability. Swami Shraddhananda and Mahatma Gandhi were among the speakers at the 1915 Kumbh Mela in Hardwar who supported the Conference's proposal to form the All-India Hindu Mahasabha. Motilal Nehru had opposed the formation of the Hindu Mahasabha in 1910 but by 1915 was a member of the board of the United Provinces Hindu Sabha.

Hindu Mahasabha leaders, like those of the All-India Congress of the same period, were largely based in the major trading cities of the United Provinces. They were involved in a range of Hindu revivalist and reformist movements. Gordon argues that because this political context was dominated by Hindus, there was little distinction between secular political association and involvement in religious or caste organizations (1975, 151). In a speech to the All-India Congress Conference in 1926, Motilal Nehru recommended that the Hindu Mahasabha join the Congress because "there is no concealing the fact that the Indian National Congress is predominantly a Hindu organisation. It started and developed as such and whatever accession of strength it received from the Muslims from time to time is fast decreasing due to the revival of Indian Muslim organisations" (quoted in Gordon 1975, 186).

With its stress on consensus issues such as cow protection and promotion of Sanskritic Hindi in the devanagari script, the Hindu Mahasabha provided a means for the "further development of existing social and commercial links and connexions between groups and individuals in the leading cities of north India" (149). The executive committee of the Hindu Sabha in the United Provinces formed a coalition of wealthy and socially powerful upper-caste men. It included members of rich banking and landholding families, the most successful lawyers in Allahabad High Court, and a well-known journalist.

The Hindu Mahasabha, Pandit Malaviya, and the Maharajas of Benares, Gwalior, Jaipur, and Bikaner supported Hardwar's pandas in their dispute with the government over the rechannelling of Ganges water associated with canal construction (Jameson 1976). With the leadership and guidance of Malaviya, Hardwar's pandas, who formed the local brahman elite with a livelihood dependent on pilgrimage and brahmanic ritualism, organized themselves into the Ganga Sabha in 1916. The Ganga Sabha belonged to the Hindu Mahasabha and contributed both publicists and funds to its causes of cow protection and the prohibition of alcohol. In her dissertation on Hardwar's panda community, Jameson describes the records of the Ganga Sabha as evincing "fierce concern—both spiritual and economic—for the sacred places of the city" (1976, 46). Membership in the Hindu Mahasabha linked the Ganga Sabha with powerful, influential allies such as Malaviya who could support the pandas in local Hardwar issues. In turn Hardwar's pandas cooperated with Mahasabha leadership by promoting locally and among visitors to Hardwar the programs of the Hindu Mahasabha.

As priests and professional hosts of pilgrims, pandas have had and continue to have contact with people from a range of social classes, regions, and castes. Important pandas also travel to visit their pilgrim clients at their homes. During such tours they collect pledged donations and encourage pilgrimage to Hardwar. Thus, panda leaders have access to information and public opinion concerning local conditions and relationships among prominent families and caste groups in diverse parts of India. Their knowledge and range of contacts has many uses for leaders of political and religious movements who require such information when formulating their policies and strategies. Hardwar's panda community itself has provided candidates for local and state elections. For example, Rajkumar Sharma was elected to the Uttar Pradesh Legislative Assembly when the Janata Party came to power after the Emergency.[5]

The Hindu Mahasabha held its 1916, 1917, and 1921 annual meetings in Hardwar and had its headquarters there until 1925. During the 1920s Malaviya worked for the expansion of the Hindu Mahasabha in rural areas by establishing the Kisan Sangha, an organization of farmers in name but in form an organization dominated and funded by wealthy landowners (Gordon 1975, 179). After 1923 the support of English-educated urban professionals decreased and the Hindu Mahasabha became increasingly dominated by large landowners of Agra and Oudh and banking and landowning magnates of larger north Indian cities.

Arya Samaj and Sanatan Dharm factions within the Hindu Mahasabha fought over the issue of *shuddhi,* the movement promoted by the Arya Samaj and other reformist groups to proselytize Hinduism among Indian Christians and Muslims and "purify" untouchables. In his presidential address to the 1922 annual meeting of the Hindu Mahasabha, Malaviya argued that shuddhi was necessary for raising up the depressed classes by imparting religious instruction and teaching them to improve their sanitary and social habits. In response to the resolution passed by the Hindu Mahasabha in support of shuddhi, orthodox pandits "broke into rage extolling Brahmin supremacy" (quoted in Gordon 1975, 71). Malaviya assured the assembly that the shuddhi resolution "did not force them to eat with them or enter into marriage with them [untouchables, Muslims, Christians], but to recognize them as one of them, to love them" (169).

Under the militant leadership of B. S. Moonje, Bhai Parmanand, and

---

5. Sharma commemorates the participation of members of the panda community in the cow protection movement and the independence movement (appendix 2). Jameson briefly discusses the involvement of Hardwar's panda community in the independence movement (1976, 41–42). Although most pandas "gradually" came to support Gandhi's campaign against the British, "they disapproved of many of his internal policies (the ending of caste restrictions, etc.). Those who were political sufferers were regarded with reverence, and even today, they possess a very high status" (42). After independence, pandas, including supporters of the Congress, opposed the secularism and social policies of the government and "regarded themselves as the voice of protesting sanatanis all over India" (42). As an example Jameson catalogues events in the political career of Rajkumar Sharma: he was imprisoned in 1948 for protesting against the ban on the RSS after the assassination of Mahatma Gandhi; in 1952 he was imprisoned for demonstrating over the political status given to Kashmir; and while imprisoned in 1956 for protesting against cow slaughter, he went on a hunger strike (42). Many Hardwar pandas continue to be active in movements associated with specifically sanatani causes—national prohibition of alcohol and cow slaughter and the construction of cow shelters—and their professional organization, the Ganga Sabha, "supports these causes morally and financially" (42–43).

V. D. Savarkar, the Hindu Mahasabha lost the support of comparatively moderate Hindu leaders such as Malaviya and Lala Lajpat Rai. These militant leaders, and particularly Savarkar, transformed the Hindu Mahasabha from a religious and social movement into a political force of Hindu nationalist opposition to the Congress Party and the Muslim League. They advocated hatred of Muslims and groups opposed to their cause of establishing a Hindu nation-state. They inveighed against the policies and activities of both the Congress and the Muslim League. In 1932 the Hindu Mahasabha passed a resolution at its annual conference endorsing the formation of the Rashtriya Swayamsevak Sangh (RSS) and encouraging members of provincial Hindu sabhas to support the expansion of the RSS and to assist in making it a "strong organization of Hindus" (quoted in Jones 1981b, 460).

Hardwar has been and remains a site where Hindu leaders articulate political projects and identities suffused with religious symbolism. The following chapter focuses on V. D. Savarkar, who became president of the Hindu Mahasabha in 1937. It analyzes his work, which propagated ideological and organizational forms of militant Hindu nationalism. Savarkar began his political career in the early twentieth century as a revolutionary terrorist. His skillfully crafted polemics inform those of contemporary Hindu nationalists which circulate in spoken and written discourse. Savarkar's voice echoed in Hardwar panda Rajkumar Sharma's narratives of Indian history and in denunciations of Muslims recited by a Hardwar lawyer, who is an active member of the RSS and legal counsel to numerous Hindu organizations. With echoes of Savarkar resounding in the narratives and reasoned arguments of publicists and supporters of Hindu nationalism, critical attention to his work contributes to debates concerning the ideology of Hindu nationalism and the discourses that define and produce national culture.

THREE

Savarkar: Nationalist Ideologue and Organizer of Hindus

HINDUISE ALL POLITICS AND MILITARISE ALL HINDUDOM

Through his writings and speeches V. D. Savarkar systematized and popularized Hindutva, the principles that underlie the ideology of Hindu nationalism (Hindu *rashtravad*). During the late 1980s Hindutva became the most common referent for ideological and organizational forms of the Hindu nationalist movement (VHP, RSS, Shiv Sena, Bajrang Dal). Savarkar defined as Hindu those inhabitants of Hindustan who considered it both their holy land *(punyabhoomi)* and the land of their ancestors *(matribhoomi; pitribhoomi)*. In Savarkar's formulation only Hindus are the legitimate "sons" of India; Hindus are entitled by birthright to rule India. Savarkar posited this concept of Hindu patrimony and proprietorship: "What the Hindu Mahasabha can never tolerate is to despoil the Hindus of anything which is justly and equitably and nationally theirs. Simply because they constitute the overwhelming majority in Hindustan their own Fatherland and Holyland" (n.d., 192).

In his "Essentials of Hindutva" written in 1922, Savarkar systematically defined the principles of Hindu nationalism (1964). His later writings and speeches repeat the principles of Hindutva and apply them to specific political issues. As president of the Hindu Mahasabha from 1937 to 1944, Savarkar traveled throughout India to promote Hindu Sangathan—a campaign to organize and mobilize support for upper-caste Hindu political leaders who opposed Congress and Muslim leaders. During the years preceding independence the Hindu Mahasabha ceaselessly denounced Muslims as antinational. It fiercely opposed the demand for Pakistan and condemned the Congress as pro-Muslim, anti-Hindu, and antinational.

In his fifty-ninth birthday message in 1941 Savarkar raised as the rallying cry of Hindu nationalism, "Hinduise all politics and militarise all Hindudom." Savarkar's call to militarize Hindus was also part of an ongoing

71

campaign of the Hindu Mahasabha to increase the number of Hindus in the military through supporting Hindu Militarization Boards which encouraged the enlistment of Hindus in the armed forces and assisted upper-caste Hindu men in obtaining commissions. British recruitment of Indians during World War II provided an opportunity for Hindus to enlist in large numbers, which was a goal of Hindu nationalists who wanted to reduce the high proportion of Muslims and Sikhs in the military. This rallying cry of Hindu nationalists is quoted in the introduction to *Hindudhwaj* (Hindu flag), a collection of statements made by Savarkar while president of the Hindu Mahasabha. The editors of *Hindudhwaj* describe Savarkar's rallying cry as the best summation of the ideology and practical application of the pan-Hindu movement. Savarkar's attacks on the policies of the Congress government, his diatribes against Muslims, and the charges brought against him concerning involvement in the assassination of Mahatma Gandhi, of which he was acquitted, earned for him and his supporters the enmity of the Nehruvian faction that dominated the Congress government in independent India.

Today, with the increasing respectability and power of organizations that champion Hindutva and claim to defend the interests of a Hindu majority, Savarkar's reputation is being rehabilitated. For example, an article entitled "Fifty Politicians Who Made All the Difference in the Four Decades Since Independence" introduces Savarkar with the honorific Veer (the heroic, brave, strong) and the epithet "The Militant Hindu" (*Illustrated Weekly of India,* 27 December 1987). The article describes Savarkar as "the patrician, who had a distinguished record of opposition to the British and was even sentenced to two consecutive 25-year-life transportations, had turned to his faith during his decade-long incarceration in the Andaman jail." The article asserts that Savarkar "is acknowledged as the precursor of today's Hindu revivalist movement." It does not specify who constitutes the movement that today reveres Savarkar as its precursor. Instead it states that "his impressive record in the freedom movement and his aggressive social reform" has made him more influential than Hedgewar and Golwalkar, the "founding fathers" of the RSS.

In his early political career Savarkar was involved in underground revolutionary groups in India and in Europe whose goal was liberation of India from British rule. After M. L. Dhingra assassinated Sir Curzon Wyllie of the India Office in 1909, the press accused Savarkar as being responsible for the murder but he was not arrested at that time (Trehan 1991, 22). However, in 1910 a warrant was issued by the Government of Bombay for conspiring to wage war against His Majesty the King and Emperor of India, and Savarkar was arrested in London. During his journey to India, he escaped from his guards when the ship stopped in Marseilles. He was immediately apprehended by French police and returned to the British, but his daring attempted escape was widely publicized. Savarkar's supporters challenged the legality of his arrest in France, and the case was brought before an international tribunal in The Hague. After eight days of hearings the tribunal decided in favor of the British, conceding that "an irregularity had been committed in the arrest of Savarkar and in his being handed over to the British police" (quoted in Anand 1967, 41). On return to Bombay, Savarker faced three separate trials by tribunals and in December 1910 was sentenced to transportation for life and forfeiture of his property (Trehan 1991, 26). His imprisonment in the Andaman Islands from 1910 until 1922 and his confinement by the British to Ratnagiri district in Maharashtra from 1922 until 1937 earned for Savarkar the status of a freedom fighter. A broad spectrum of Hindus today—from militant Hindu nationalists to liberal secular nationalists—count Savarkar among those heroes who dedicated their lives to the cause of national liberation. Savarkar's caustic and incendiary writings constitute important primary texts for understanding the ideology promoted by Hindu activists in contemporary India. His texts formulate a history of Hindus as a race and chart their emergence as a nation. Savarkar's writings also concern the glorious destiny of the pan-Hindu movement. Like other political manifestos, his texts can inspire dogmatism and prompt adherents to organized action.

When the British rescinded the order restricting Savarkar to Ratnagiri in 1937, he became president of the Hindu Mahasabha and traveled throughout India. His campaign, known as Hindu Sangathan, aimed at organizing Hindus into a powerful political force. He also tried to influence the policies of British officials and rulers of Hindu states. Owners of newspapers and presses sympathetic to the Sangathan movement printed his attacks on the Congress, the Muslim League, and the British Government as well as his writings on the objectives and programs of the Hindu Sangathanist movement.

While in Europe from 1906 to 1910, Savarkar met other revolutionaries who were working to overthrow imperialist regimes. His meeting with Lenin figures prominently in accounts of his life. Hindu ascetic orders have *naga* cadres (martial ascetics), the Indian state has the military and police, politicians and underworld bosses have their *goondas* (henchmen). The Indian independence movement involved not only Gandhian strategies of nonviolent protest and civil disobedience but also acts and threats of violence by revolutionary groups. Keer prefaces his biography, *Veer Savarkar,* by contrasting him with Gandhi and installing the Veer high in the pantheon of freedom fighters:

> There are sometimes two types of great men working for the good of society at one and the same time. The first type prefers to be pained for the welfare of society while the second whips it to betterment. Gandhi typifies the first and

Savarkar represents the second. Savarkar had the light of a man of mission, the insight of a statesman and the foresight of a political prophet. His life removes the wrong impression created in the minds of non-Indians that the Indian Freedom Movement started with Gandhi and Nehru. (1966, viii)

A critical study of nationalism in India requires attention to Savarkar's writings and activities. His voice is muted if not ignored in much of the scholarly writing on the freedom movement, which emphasizes the contributions of Gandhi and Nehru. This reading of Savarkar does not argue that his ideas and activities have inevitably led to the increasingly hegemonic status of Hindu nationalism. Instead, it attempts to provide historical background for understanding the discourse and activities employed by Hindu organizations such as the RSS and VHP that have established such a powerful presence in contemporary India.

Savarkar asked to be remembered not as a heroic freedom fighter *(Swatantryveer)* but as "Savarkar, the organizer of Hindus," for a life devoted to the cause of Hindu Sangathan (Keer 1966, 499). Attention to his life and work assists in conceptualizing how Hindu organizations operate within Indian society. Conforming to the official Congress disdain for Savarkar, influential Indian and western social scientists since independence have largely ignored him. However, he had an influential voice which generated emotional involvement in the freedom movement. No less than the words of Vivekananda and Aurobindo, of Gandhi and Nehru, Savarkar's militant idiom has become embedded in popular and social scientific discourses concerning national identity and social change.

THE MAKING OF A MILITANT HINDU

Keer's biography of Savarkar introduces its subject with the conventional references to characteristics which presage great destiny—prestigious lineage and precocity, courage and intelligence. Keer often reminds readers that Savarkar personally did not observe caste regulations, but he stresses that Savarkar was born into the high-ranking caste of "Chitpavan Brahmans that produced Nanasahib of 1857 fame, Vasudeo Balwant and Lokmanya Tilak" (2). His ancestors included scholars and landlords. His parents are said to have been pious and steeped in the traditions of the epics and myths. They taught their son popular ballads commemorating the heroic deeds of Maratha warriors.

Savarkar was no ordinary child. As a young boy he "showed signs of his inborn genius" (3). His capacity for martial leadership was no less precocious. When only eight years old Savarkar responded to news of Hindu-Muslim riots in north India and Bombay by leading school boys to attack a mosque with stones: "The Muslim school boys gave battle to Vinayak, the Hindu Generalissimo"; he also organized Hindu boys in military drills and mock fights (4). When Savarkar was ten years old his mother died of cholera. Keer stresses the son's passionate devotion to his mother and his intense grief at her loss. His father is described as a stern disciplinarian, undemonstrative and distant; he died of plague in 1899.

Savarkar and his elder brother were sent to Nasik for high school, where he belonged to and recruited members to the Mitra Mela (later named the Abhinava Bharat Society), a secret society of revolutionaries active in western and central India. Its objective was armed revolt to liberate the motherland from British rule. Members greeted each other by saying, "Bande Mataram—salutations to the Mother." The Mitra Mela, like other political groups, organized public religious festivals and made them into "political and national functions" (9). To demonstrate their courage and public service Mitra Mela members in Nasik not only carried plague corpses to cremation grounds, but also "chastised the tyrannical elements and browbeat the bully" (10).

Just before matriculation Savarkar was married to the eldest daughter of a man who "wielded much influence" in the state of Jawhar. Such a marital alliance would prove useful for Savarkar's later campaigns to involve rulers and officials of Hindu states in the pan-Hindu movement. With financial support from his father-in-law, Savarkar entered Fergusson College in Poona in 1902. He attracted around himself a group whose motto was "survival of the fittest." They studied texts of European revolutionaries, debated political problems and strategies, dressed alike, and used *swadeshi* (handmade Indian) goods (14). Like the young *brahmacharis* that they were—disciplined and abstemious students—"they believed in energy and endurance and not in enjoyment" (16). They opposed the 1905 Partition of Bengal by supporting the boycott of foreign goods and by burning foreign cloth.

For his involvement in antigovernment activities and for his speeches expressing hatred for British rule, Savarkar was expelled from residency in the college. However, he successfully passed his B.A. exams and proceeded to Bombay where he studied law and continued to recruit members for the Abhinava Bharat Society. At this time he also wrote prose and poems in English and Marathi, including revolutionary ballads, a poem decrying the cruel treatment of Hindu widows, and an essay which claimed that "Hindus are responsible for the poverty and disorganisation of Hindustan. But if they ever desire to attain prosperity, they must remain Hindus" (22–23).

In 1906 Savarkar went to London on a scholarship from Shyam Krishnavarma. Savarkar's patron was a wealthy Indian living in London, who was himself actively promoting Indian independence through the India Home Rule Society and his journal, the *Indian Sociologist* (Fox 1989, 122–23). Keer reports that Krishnavarma was an associate of Swami

Dayananda Saraswati and originally had come to England as an assistant to the Sanskritist, Monier-Williams. He received an M.A. from Oxford, studied law, and was called to the bar in London. Krishnavarma also studied with Herbert Spencer, whose ideas concerning the evolutionary importance of struggle and the survival of the fittest he used to argue that revolution was the natural outcome of suppressed forces of national evolution. Krishnavarma later worked as an official in three Indian princely states. Although in 1906–7 his writings supported passive and peaceful civil disobedience, by 1909 his *Indian Sociologist* advocated violent revolution (Fox 1989, 123).

As a protege of Krishnavarma, Savarkar developed and promoted revolutionary ideas and activities among other Indians studying in Britain. Savarkar studied law but he was never called to the bar because he refused to renounce his political activities. Keer argues that Savarkar had a greater mission than amassing wealth by arguing petty cases: Savarkar was destined to become the "nation's barrister" (Keer 1966, 52). Instead of devoting himself to courtroom battles, Savarkar used his barrister's skills in oratory and argumentation for "feeding and fanning the wrath of Indian revolutionaries" (42). About Savarkar's leadership Keer enthuses: "The members of the Abhinava Bharat were all intellectual giants, Savarkar gave them light and literature. He told them that whosoever wanted to live a deathless life should die for the freedom of his country" (36).

The Abhinava Bharat Society used the Free India Society as a front organization to recruit and test potential members before they were used in clandestine operations. The Free India Society also organized celebrations of festivals for Indian students in Britain but "of course there were those like Pandit Jawarhalal Nehru who did not join" (33). Like a barrister's mind which strives to anticipate and outwit the opponent's strategies, the mind of an underground revolutionary is honed by endless intrigue: "Savarkar's resourceful brain knew all the types and twists of the revolutionary business" (49).

Savarkar's ideas were influenced by contemporaneous currents of European political and social thought. In 1907 his Marathi translation of Giuseppe Mazzini's autobiography was published by his brother in Nasik, where the volume was taken out in a procession by "young and old devotees" (34). Savarkar's introduction to the translation applied Mazzini's ideas to the Indian context. The book sold out within three months and was proscribed by the government.

SAVARKAR'S IDEOLOGY OF HINDU NATIONALISM

Savarkar's monumental *Indian War of Independence, 1857* was published in 1908, the year after publication of his translation of Mazzini's autobiography. The text offers itself as a scientific history that refutes British accounts which treat the of events of 1857 as a failed mutiny. Savarkar wrote that his undertaking was also the "holy work of the historian" (1970, 1). He referred to Mazzini when asserting that every revolution has an "all-moving principle" that inspires men to fight and die. Savarkar named *swadharma* (one's own duty/religion) and *swaraj* (self-rule) as the motivating forces of the War of 1857.

Savarkar's *Indian War of Independence, 1857* was immediately pro-scribed, but like the Mazzini autobiography it circulated widely and stealthily. Another biographer of Savarkar describes the impact this work had for Indian revolutionaries: "The *Indian War of Independence* stood for nearly half a century as the Indian revolutionaries' handbook or gospel. It is almost impossible to exaggerate the wide and profound influence exercised by its militant propaganda for future Indian freedom" (Anand 1967, 78). While Indian moderates were advocating legal evolution towards a politically independent India, Indian revolutionaries—also known as extremists—disdained gradualist approaches and demanded immediate and violent action. Savarkar and members of the Abhinava Bharat Society advocated making and stockpiling weapons and translated and distributed a Russian bomb-making manual. They emphasized the need to propagate revolutionary ideas among the Indian army and in Indian princely states. In a pamphlet entitled *Bande Mataram,* Savarkar asserted that assassination of British officials is the first stage of revolution and the "best conceivable method of paralyzing the bureaucracy and rousing the people" (quoted in Keer 1966, 90).

In the *Indian War of Independence,* Savarkar depicts the revolutionary principles of swadharma and swaraj as being shared by Hindus and Muslims, who fought as "Hindi Brethren" against the British (9). The text highlights the capacity of Indians—Hindus and Muslims—to unite and fight together against British rule. It also discusses the obstacles impeding the success of the 1857 revolution and the brutality of British domination and retaliation. Savarkar's epic and magisterial explication of battles and strategies, alliances and betrayals, victories and defeats produces a work capable of inciting passion for revenge while simultaneously instructing readers on how to organize a revolution.

The chapter entitled "Secret Organisation" delineates strategies to prepare for and engage in revolutionary warfare. Clandestine negotiations among political and religious leaders figure prominently in this chapter. Savarkar admitted that it is difficult to determine the facts concerning secretive operations and negotiations, but he maintains that "one cannot but admire the skill of the organizers" (77). The text includes instructions on how religious personages—pandits, sadhus, sannyasis, swamis, fakirs, and maulvis—can be used by revolutionaries as publicists of the cause. They are given the responsibility for secretly and openly promoting violent hatred of the enemy and fervent desire for freedom:

> While itinerant Sannyasis and itinerant preachers preached in the villages
> and the bigger country towns, local preachers were being sent to the bigger
> towns. In all the important places of pilgrimage where thousands of people
> congregated, the ever-existing dumb dislike of the usurping Feringhi [foreign]
> rule was intensified into active hatred by the Revolutionary preachers. (83)

"Women gypsies" should also be used to spread the revolutionary message. With their persuasive soothsaying, these fortunetellers could popularize—particularly among women—belief in the impending downfall of the British, "depict the evil machinations of the alien rule and prescribe revolution as the only remedy and spell which could and would get rid of this evil which had possessed their motherland" (85). Through these and other means the revolutionary message was widely disseminated: "The war was preached in temples and Tirthas, in Kshetras, Jatras [pilgrimage places] and in festivals, on the road and in the house, amongst the sepoys and citizens, in Natakas and Tamashas [street theatre and spectacle], to men as well as women" (85).

In the *Indian War of Independence* Savarkar stressed the cooperation between Hindus and Muslims against their common foe, the British. The text highlights the heroic deeds of Muslims and Hindus and acknowledges that Muslims are noble sons of mother India. About Ahmad Shah, a Muslim who was betrayed by a Hindu raja, Savarkar wrote:

> The life of the brave Mohammedan shows that a rational faith in the doc
> trines of Islam is in no way inconsistent with or antagonistic to a deep and all
> powerful love of the Indian soil, and that the true believer in Islam will feel it
> proud to belong to and a privilege to die for his mother-country. (456)

The increasing antagonism between Hindus and Muslims after the 1921 Moplah uprising of Muslims against Hindus is reflected in Savarkar's later work, *Hindu Pad-Padashahi* (Hindudom and Hindu Kingship [1925]), where Muslims replace the British as the enemy of Hindus. Here the heroes are the valiant Marathas who fought to avenge Hindu honor and to restore Hindu dharma to its rightful power and glory. In this work Savarkar depicted Muslim attacks on Hindu temples, brahmans, cows, and the rape of Hindu women in relentlessly gory detail.

Hindu Pad-Padashahi, like the *Indian War of Independence,* is a didactic text, a manual for planning and executing a revolution. It also concerns the strategies whereby the Marathas created and consolidated a Hindu empire. It emphasizes Maratha patronage of Hindu institutions and brahmanic learning; through patronage of Sanskrit scholars, the sacred language of the Hindus "received a great impetus under the Maratha rule"

(1925, 266). Maratha rulers convened assemblies of scholars in Poona which conducted examinations and distributed honors and prizes. Under the "protection of Maratha arms" Hindu religious teachers traveled freely throughout India "from Rameshwar to Hardwar, from Dwarka to Puri" (major pilgrimage centers and brahmanic strongholds) and their efforts insured that the "moral education of the people was not neglected" (226). As arms of imperial policy, monastic institutions received the patronage of the Marathas and their allies: "Great and organised agencies like the one founded by Ramdas had spread out a regular network of Mathas and convents throughout India, were financed by the Empire and served as so many centres not only of religious but also of political propaganda" (226). Maratha rulers built bathing ghats and temples in important pilgrimage centers and "freed Hardwar and Kurukhsetra."

Both these works by Savarkar are full of imagery drawn from Hindu ritual and metaphysics, particularly vedic fire sacrifice (yajna) and spiritual liberation (moksha). This imagery valorizes death in battle as the sacrificial means to propitiate the war god and to purify and liberate oneself and one's holy land. The *Indian War of Independence* has chapters entitled "Adding Fuel to Fire" and "Lit Up the Sacrificial Fire." The following passage exemplifies this imagery of religious sacrifice: "Far more profitable is death through the attempt to establish Swaraj than life in slavery. The sacred fuel burning in the sacrificial fire is a thousand times more life-giving than the log of wood burning in the funeral pyre" (1970, 388).

Savarkar intensified this equation of martial and religious values in his exaltation of Ramdas, the guru of Shivaji who inspired Marathas to fight against Muslim rule. When positing that swaraj and swadharma formed the "mental science" of the 1857 revolution, Savarkar attributed to Ramdas the following words: "Die for your Dharma, kill the enemies of your Dharma while you are dying, in this way fight and kill and take back your kingdom" (11). Elsewhere Savarkar extolled Ramdas as the "high priest and prophet of Hindu Revival and the war of Hindu Liberation" (1964, 31). Perhaps he even modeled himself on Ramdas, the militant guru of the Marathas.

Hindu militarization was a prominent item on Savarkar's and the Hindu Mahasabha's agenda and was related to the principles of Hindutva. Savarkar wrote his "Essentials of Hindutva" after he was transferred from prison in the Andaman Islands to a jail in Ratnagiri in 1922. In his etymological discussion of the word Hindu, Savarkar disclosed his keen understanding of the politics of naming: "the name seems to matter as much as the thing itself" (1). He named Hindutva as that which "embraces all the departments of thought and activity of the whole being of our Hindu race" (3). Hindu and Hindutva are defined by residence in Hindustan, love for and worship of its land. Hindus share a common blood and culture, laws

and rites, feasts and festivals. However, Savarkar asserted that his definition of Hindutva is open for continued expansion: "This definition of
Hindutva is compatible with any conceivable expansion of our Hindu
people. . . . The only geographical limit of Hindutva are the limits of our
earth" (74).

In order to prosecute his case, Savarkar used the imagery of lineage and
ritual to discuss the emergence of the Hindu nation. He equated the expansion of the Hindu nation through the subcontinent with the spread of vedic
fire sacrifice, which acted as the force defending Hindus from attacks by
sacrilegious non-Hindus (7). He proclaimed Rama as the founder of a new
political institution, the *chakravartin,* or world conqueror-ruler. Rama's
return to Ayodhya after his diplomatic and martial successes in the south
and in Lanka marks the birth of the Hindu nation (8). Buddhist teachings
are described as "mealy mouthed formulas of ahimsa and spiritual brotherhood" that weakened the Hindu nation (13). This reference to ahimsa
could also be understood as an attack on Mahatma Gandhi's strategy of
nonviolence. For Savarkar the world was not evolved enough for nonviolence to be a prudent policy. Like other nationalist ideologues, however, he piously reverenced the Buddha as a spiritual son of the holy
motherland.

Savarkar emphasized the role of struggle and domination in the formation of the Hindu nation. He described the process through which Aryans
established their supremacy in the subcontinent:

> By an admirable process of assimilation, elimination and consolidation, po-
> litical, racial and cultural, they welded all other non-Aryan peoples whom
> they came in contact with or conflict with through this process of their ex-
> pansion in this land from the Indus to the Eastern sea and from the Hima-
> layas to the Southern sea into a National unity. (1949, 38)

In "Essentials of Hindutva," Savarkar stated that Hindu national identity
had been formed through conflict with "non-self" as embodied by Muslim
and British invaders: "Nothing can weld peoples into a nation and nations
into a state as the presence of a common foe" (1964, 27). The Hindu nation
emerged as a result of prolonged and furious conflict, by a process of elim-
ination and assimilation, a process also characterized as "organic growth"
(1949, 41). In a rebuttal to a statement by Jinnah concerning Pakistan, Savarkar described the process whereby the Hindu people came to constitute
the nation and polity he names Hindudom:

> During the course of the last 5,000 years of its continuous growth and con-
> solidation, this gigantic Octopus of Hindudom has clutched and crushed
> within the formidable grips of its mighty arms a number of Shakasthans,
> Hunsthans, the Marathas swallowed and gulped down your very Empire en-
> tirely and altogether before it knew what was happening. (n.d., 374)

Contemporary Hindu nationalists have incorporated the universalism that had informed orientalist and advaita vedantin discourses about Hindu tolerance. In "The Essentials of Hindutva," however, Savarkar vigorously condemned universalism. He associated it with nonviolence and attacked both for being opiates which delude and weaken Hindus. Universalism, he asserted is inimical to the most urgent political task facing the Hindus: "the necessity of creating a bitter sense of wrong and invoking a power of undying resistance" (1964, 16).

Essentialism underpins both universalism and Savarkar's rejection of it. Universalism valorizes an essential identity which transcends differences among individuals and groups. Savarkar's Hindutva offers an ideology which essentializes racial, cultural, and national differences. Yet a type of universalism operates within Savarkar's Hindutva, one which posits a transcendent and homogeneous Hindu nation: "One God, one goal, one language, one country, one Nation" (Keer 1966, 193).

According to Savarkar, a Hindu loves and worships India for being the land of one's ancestors as well as being sanctified by the blood of Hindu martyrs and the presence of Hindu gods. He stressed that although Muslims may be born in India, they are not Hindus because they do not worship India: "We would be straining the usage of the words too much—we fear to the point of breaking—if we call a Mohammedan a Hindu because of his being a resident of India" (1964, 54).

Hindus not only form a nation (rashtra) but also a race (jati) with a common origin and blood. Savarkar considered the presence of castes as "standing testimony to a common flow of blood from a brahman to a chandala," noting that the untouchable chandala is a Hindu born of a brahman mother and a shudra father (55). He evaluated caste as a way "to fertilise and enrich all that was barren and poor, without famishing and debasing all that was flourishing and nobly endowed" (56). Savarkar relied on an imperialistic royal we to assert the existence of the Hindu race: "We feel we are a jati, a race bound together by the dearest ties of blood—and therefore it must be so" (58). Through their "iron actions" individual Hindus may lose the caste status assigned to them at birth and be relegated to a lower caste. No action, however, can forfeit a Hindu's Hindutva.

Savarkar argued at length for the indigenous origin of the term "Hindu," whose referent expanded with the expansion of the Hindu nation. He claimed that "Hindu" even made its way into the vocabulary of the ancient Jews, for whom it meant strength and vigour because "these were the qualities associated with our land and nation" (49). However, although "Hindu" may be a laudable verbal export, the term "Hinduism" is a suspicious foreign import: "If there be any word of alien growth it is this word Hinduism and so we should not allow our thoughts to get confused by this new fangled term" (53). For Savarkar "Hinduism" refers to religious belief and practices. It forms only a small part of the totality of Hindutva. Jains, for example, he counted as Hindu even if they do not practice Hinduism or believe in the Vedas. Whereas Hindutva denotes the historical, racial, and cultural totality constituting the Hindu nation, Hinduism is the totality of all religious beliefs held by different communities of Hindus.

Sanatan Dharm is said to be the religion practiced by the majority of Hindus, yet non-sanatanis such as Sikhs, Jains, and Arya Samajis are racially, culturally, and nationally Hindu. The term "Hinduism" creates confusion when it is wrongly conflated with Sanatan Dharm. Savarkar equated Hinduism with the generic term "Hindu Dharm." This term encompasses Sanatan Dharm, the religion of the "majority of Hindus" as well as the "religions of the remaining Hindus, Sikh, Arya, Jain and Buddh dharm" (68–69).

Savarkar offered his own definition of Hinduism as "a system of beliefs found common amongst the Hindu people" (66). He discussed neither the systematizers nor the principles of systematization. Instead he asserted that Hinduism is the "conclusion of the conclusions arrived at by harmonizing the detailed experience of all the schools of religious thought" (70). In order to appease non-brahman castes and Hindu modernists, Savarkar suggested that certification not caste status be the criterion for priesthood (190). He did not say how or by whom priests would be certified.[1]

Hindutva further defines Hindus as a people with a common culture. Hindus are bound together "by the tie of a common homage we pay to our great civilization—our Hindu culture" (59). Savarkar named this common culture "sanskriti" and argued that Sanskrit is the language that expresses

---

1. Cf. G. S. Ghurye, the prominent Indian sociologist, who wrote that opening up the priesthood to "anyone with minimum education . . . would provide Hindu society with its old bond of a common priesthood, based not on hereditary right but on liking and capacity. It would at the same time take the edge off the non-brahmin clamour against Brahmin priests" (1961, 326). Elsewhere in the same text Ghurye argued that the threat through legislation to brahmans' monopoly on priestly occupations is tantamount to threatening the group responsible for national solidarity and integration. He claimed that legal interference with brahmans' rights to act as priests will ultimately lead to "the dissolution of the only bond holding together the diverse castes, viz., the employment of a common priesthood" (181). In a slightly different register Srinivas describes Hinduism as a "loose confederation of innumerable cults, the connecting threads of which are found in Sanskritization, and in the last resort, Brahmins" (1967, 69).

Savarkar's influence on Indian sociological discourse has not yet been thoroughly examined. It is relevant to understanding the ideological agenda of Ghurye's work, e.g., his deployment of the concept of Hinduization, and is present in more muted tones in the work of those trained by Ghurye at Bombay, including M. N. Srinivas, e.g., his concept of sanskritization. A study of these issues might proceed by examining the relation between form and content of work by brahman ideologues, contextualizing and contrasting the aggressive and acerbic Savarkar and Ghurye with the mellifluous Radhakrishnan and Srinivas.

and preserves this culture. He equated sanskriti with civilization and defined civilization in idealist and religious terms as "the expression of the mind of man. At its best it is the perfect triumph of the soul of man over matter and man alike" (59).[2] The *Ramayana* and *Mahabharata* are the cornerstones of this shared Hindu culture. These two epics have the power to "bring us together and weld us into a race even if we be scattered to all the four winds like a handful of sand" (61). Hindus may look elsewhere, but they can find sources in their own culture for patriotic inspiration: "I read the life of Mazzini and I exclaim, 'how patriotic they are.' I read the life of Madhavacharya and exclaim, 'how patriotic we are'!" (64).

Sanskrit and Hindi figure prominently in Savarkar's discussion of culture. He glorified Sanskrit as the language in which "our Gods" spoke, "our sages" thought, and "our poets" wrote. It is "our mother tongue." Extending the maternal metaphor, Savarkar asserted that Sanskrit is the language "which the mothers of our race spoke and which has given birth to all our present tongues" (61). All that is best in Hindus seeks "instinctively to clothe itself in Sanskrit" (61). Savarkar not only was arguing implicitly for increased patronage of groups, usually brahmans, whose livelihood involved knowledge of Sanskrit, but also he was warning that their neglect threatened the vitality of Hindu culture.

Hindi is given the status of "eldest daughter" of Sanskrit. Hindi provides a "safe and sure passport to the rajasabhas [ruling assemblies] as well as to the bazaars" (26). Before the Muslims and British invaded and imposed their foreign languages, Hindi was the pan-Indian language used by "the Hindu pilgrim, the tradesman, the tourist, the soldier, the Pandit" (107). Savarkar advocated that Hindi should again become the pan-Indian language and viewed the movement for Hindi as the national language as neither new nor forced. Savarkar well understood that like cow protection, the promotion of Sanskritic Hindi in devanagari script was a consensus issue for upper-caste Hindu Sangathanists. It could unite Hindu groups such as Sanatanis and Arya Samajis, groups that were divided by disputes over doctrine, ritual, and social reform. Included in the Hindu Sangathanist movement were local associations devoted to promoting Sanskritic Hindi

---

2. Although the urbane idealist philosopher, educationalist, and statesman Radhakrishnan did not share Savarkar's vehement style, there are parallels between their representations of Hindu civilization and society. In the introduction to the first edition of the encyclopaedic *Cultural Heritage of India* published by the Ramakrishna Mission in 1937, the chairman of its board of editors, Radhakrishnan, writes: "The civilization which is inspired by the spiritual insight of our sages is marked by a certain moral integrity, a fundamental loyalty, a fine balance of individual desires and social demands, and it is these that are responsible for its vitality and continuity. To a departure from the ideals can be traced the present weakness and disorder of the Hindu civilization" (1970, xxiii).

and Marathi. Like his policy on Sanskritic Hindi, Savarkar wanted to re-move Urdu and Persian words from Marathi and replace them with words derived from Sanskrit.

Common laws and rites as well as common feasts and festivals contrib-ute to Hindus' shared culture. Savarkar claimed Hindus' common laws are founded upon "underlying principles of Hindu jurisprudence" (63). He neither suggested nor specified what these principles might be. However, he was more specific about the festivals shared by Hindus and lists them as Dassera, Diwali, Rakhibandhan, and Holi. He included the Kumbh Mela, the Jagganath Puri festival, and pilgrimage as other elements of Hindus' common culture. Savarkar's suggestion that Hindu festivals and rituals have social functions which do not require religious belief implicitly ap-peased reformers and modernists who criticized popular Hinduism as irra-tional and superstitious. Savarkar admitted a plurality of individual motivation but insisted a true Hindu participates in Hindu festivals and rituals: "The quaint customs and ceremonies and sacraments they involve observed by some as religious duty, by others as social amenities, impress upon each individual that he can live best only through the common and corporate life of the Hindu race" (64). Savarkar's discussion of Hindu cul-ture concludes with references to the spirituality that infuses it and is insep-arable from it. Just as Hindus owe their physical being to the land and blood of their forefathers, "Hindus inherit sanskriti, owe their spiritual be-ing to it" (65).

SAVARKAR ON HINDU SANGATHANIST ISSUES:
UNTOUCHABILITY, TRIBALS, AND CONVERSION

Like numerous other social reformers, Savarkar criticized the practice of untouchability. For Savarkar untouchables are Hindus. The Hindu San-gathanist movement regarded its policy on untouchables as necessary for countering attempts by Muslim and Christian missionaries to convert them. Savarkar praised Hindu rulers of Akkalkot and Indore for issuing orders to "banish" untouchability from their realms and encouraged them to enforce this policy (n.d., 37, 89). However, the editors of *Hindudhwaj*, who record these statements, offer readers an apologetic concerning Sav-arkar's policy on untouchability. They maintain that Savarkar acts in a pri-vate capacity when dining with untouchables and he "never means any affront to his Sanatanist co-religionists" (xii).

The campaign against untouchability was part of Savarkar's larger goal of organizing a range of social groups into a cohesive unit made up of members who identified themselves as Hindus. The divisiveness among Hindus caused by untouchability contradicted Hindutva and impeded Hindu Sangathan. In its early stages, Savarkar publicly supported Dr. B. R.

Ambedkar, the important untouchable politician and leader of the movement against untouchability. He presided over a conference of untouchables and distributed sacred threads to them. Savarkar, however, also
blamed untouchables for untouchability. He reasoned that like the upper
castes they too were guilty of treating certain groups as untouchable (1949,
147).

To institutionally incorporate untouchables into the Hindu Sangathan
movement, Savarkar established a pan-Hindu temple in Ratnagiri and encouraged others to build and open temples to untouchables. He organized
and attended pan-Hindu dinners and festivals. At one such festival a
sweeper appeared before the crowd singing vedic hymns and chanting the
Gayatri mantra (Keer 1966, 184). "Savarkar's workers" engaged in missionary work among untouchables which included studying their living
conditions, teaching them cleanliness, guiding and worshipping them
(196). However, despite these policies concerning untouchability, Savarkar
remained resolutely silent on the economic situation of untouchables and
their systematic exploitation by upper castes.

According to the principles of Hindutva, tribals, like untouchables, belong to the Hindu nation. They too have inherited Hindu blood and culture
and regard Hindustan as their fatherland and holy land. For Savarkar what
distinguishes tribals from other Hindus is that they have not yet come
"fully under the influence of any orthodox sect" (1964, 77). Hindu Sangathanist missionaries, therefore, were sent to work among tribals and integrate them into the Hindu nation. Such missionary work was heralded as
necessary to counter the "denationalization" Savarkar associated with
tribals' conversion to Christianity (Keer 1966, 458).

As president of the Hindu Mahasabha, Savarkar promoted *shuddhi*,
the practice whereby untouchables, Christians, and Muslims publicly embraced Hinduism. He presided over public functions during which non-
Hindus and untouchables were ceremonially proclaimed to be converted
into caste Hindus. Shuddhi campaigns were linked institutionally with the
establishment of pan-Hindu temples. Income from these temples was used
to pay the expenses for shuddhi ceremonies, like the one during which Savarkar advocated the shuddhi of all Muslims in Kashmir (n.d., 427–28). In
its early days shuddhi, as promoted by the Arya Samaj and other social reformers, was strongly opposed by representatives of conservative upper-
caste groups. However, through the efforts of Savarkar and others, shuddhi
became the "mainspring of Sangathanism" and a "war" to defend the
Hindu nation against attacks by Christian and Muslim missionaries (Keer
1966, 179–80). After independence Savarkar continued to denounce
Christian missionaries as enemies who were working to denationalize
Hindu tribals. Following his speech on this issue in Poona in 1953, "Hindu
Sangathanists drove out missionaries from Poona" (458).

FEMININE IMAGERY AND WOMEN FOLLOWERS:
HIS COUNTRY WAS HIS ONLY SWEETHEART

Like other patriarchal ideologues, Savarkar celebrated woman as mother. He considered a woman's beauty to be given to her in trust so that it might be increased in her children. Familial and domestic duties structure the life of the Hindu woman: "Kitchen and children were the main duties of women. For a woman to suckle a baby at her breast was according to him [Savarkar], her greatest pleasure" (Keer 1966, 230). The maternal image also dominates Savarkar's vision of nature and relates to his belief in struggle and the survival of the fittest: "A lioness besmeared with a deer's blood suckling her cubs at her breast was his Nature's picture" (275). Savarkar had many uses for the maternal figure. Mothers must teach their children—especially sons—the lore of warriors, which instills the desire to sacrifice their blood and lives to destroy enemies of the motherland. In the *Indian War of Independence* he concluded his account of Mangal Pandey, a brahman warrior, by interpolating, "Let every mother teach her son the story of this hero with pride" (1970, 106).

Women demonstrate their devotion to the holy motherland not only by cultivating heroic qualities in their sons but also by engaging in battle. During the battle against the British in Kanpur, all the women "left their Zenanas and jumped into the battlefield" (227). Foremost among courageous women is the Rani of Jhansi. Savarkar commemorated her as a fearless military leader, who on the battlefield was "found everywhere inspiring heroism even in the coldest hearts" (464). In his foreword to the 1970 edition of the *Indian War of Independence,* G. M. Joshi praises Savarkar's "gifted intuitions" for reviving the memory of this heroic Hindu warrior-queen and adds that "humble I and a thousand other Indians have named our dear daughters after Laxmibai, Rani of Jhansi" (1970, xxiii). Women also prove their virtue and courage through sati. Savarkar lauds the 150 royal women who killed themselves after the defeat of Kumar Singh's army (438). In some circumstances, however, women can be impediments to the efforts of strategists and warriors. Savarkar blames women for the premature and failed Sepoy rising in Meerut.

Savarkar's writings accord women a role in the fight for independence. Accounts of his life suggest that he attracted women followers to the cause of militant Hindu nationalism. On the occasion of his fifty-ninth birthday, women's sections of Hindu Sangathan organizations held meetings "where their faith in the president's message of 'Hinduising politics and militarising Hindudom' was reiterated" (n.d., 421). When he arrived at the railway station in Poona, representatives of 150 different organizations garlanded him and women worshipped him (659). Biographers variously depict Savarkar as surrounding himself with women and as disdaining them. Keer notes that Savarkar excluded his wife from his public life and reports that when she was ill and departing for the hospital Savarkar was "not in the mood" to say farewell (1966, 529). After her death he donated money in her name to select organizations. Keer maintains that Savarkar enjoyed meeting with women followers and spent much of his time in their company. He refers to an occasion when Savarkar refused to meet with Bhai Parmanand, his predecessor as president of the Hindu Mahasabha, contrasting that with the fact that "some women visitors had free access. This unfortunate diversion consumed much of his energy and time" (477).

Others refute this view that Savarkar fancied the company of women admirers. In response to a rumor that an affair with an English woman led to his arrest in London in 1910, Anand maintains that "no companion of Savarkar, or even anti-companion, ever saw him mixing with women" (1967, 214). He quotes Gyanchand Verma, an associate of Savarkar as having said, "If Savarkar had any sweetheart, his country was the only sweetheart he had" (214). Whatever his relations with his wife, other women, and men may have been, as a political organizer and strategist Savarkar well understood the necessity for the Hindu Sangathanist movement to inculcate its ideals among women and involve them in its activities and campaigns.

HINDU MILITARIZATION AND THE "ISLAMITE PERIL"

The anti-Muslim theme in *Hindu Pad-Padashahi* forms a prelude for Savarkar's later denunciations of Muslims before and after independence. Although not addressed in this discussion, when considering Savarkar's ferocious attacks on Muslims, readers should keep in mind that these were partly directed at Muslim leaders, who themselves were making contemptuous charges against Hindus. The Sangathanist movement contended that the Hindu people constituted a nation and a majority in India, and the strength of their numbers entitled them to politically and culturally dominate minority communities: "Let all Hindus once and for all declare that the Moslems have not obliged the Hindus by being in the minority and the Hindus are in majority because they proved themselves fit to struggle for national existence" (n.d., 233). In his assessment of the Muslim League as advocates of a regressively theological concept of statehood, Savarkar implicitly invoked Nazism when threatening Hindu vengeance: "if we Hindus in India grow stronger in time these Moslem friends of the league will have to play the part of German-Jews" (1949, 65).

Riots between Hindus and Muslims were one form of this "struggle for national existence." Savarkar often referred to them when reiterating his belief in the undying animosity between Hindus and Muslims. He described riots in Bombay and Ahmedabad as premeditated attacks by Muslims which demonstrated that the two ideologies "have come to grips and mean to fight with each other to the finish" (n.d., 397). In his biography of Savarkar Anand complies with the prevailing norm of secular nationalism and describes how British rule disrupted the amicable relations between Hindus and Muslims, "The communal strifes were unknown on the subcontinent and were never seen or heard before the advent of British rule" (1967, 55). Savarkar, however, attacked those who attribute the origins of Hindu-Muslim conflict to British rule. He accused them of propounding the fallacious position that "the history of the last ten centuries of perpetual war between the Hindus and Moslems was an interpolation and a myth" (1949, 133).

To mobilize Hindu opposition to partition, in 1944 Savarkar and the Hindu Mahasabha convened the Akhand Hindustan Leaders Conference. For Savarkar the Conference provided the means "to organize this whirlwind of protest against these sinful designs to break up the integrity of Hindustan as a nation and a state" (1964, 548). The Conference contributed to Hindu Sangathan by bringing together religious leaders of different sects to speak unanimously against partition and against the ongoing negotiations of the Congress, the Muslim League, and the British. In a speech publicizing the Conference, Savarkar announced the sources of support who stood united in their fight against "political matricide": "The prominent leaders of our Sikh brotherhood, the Mahantas of different Mathas and Ashrams, His Holiness Shankaracharya of Puri, the Sanatani, the Arya Samaji, the Sangathanist leaders and their personalties occupying prominent position in the social and political life of the country have already consented to attending the Conference" (550).

The violence of partition intensified Savarkar's attacks on Muslims and the Congress. He condemned the Congress and the Indian state for not protecting its citizens. While Hindus and Sikhs were being massacred by Muslims, "ministers of the Indian state were literally feasting and fiddling to celebrate their bloodless revolution" (552). He reviled "Puny Pandit" Nehru and his "Carpet Knights" for betraying the Hindu nation: they consented to the formation of Pakistan, a Muslim Raj, but denied Hindus the right to form a Hindu Raj in India (552, 555). Savarkar maintained that in the treacherous aftermath of partition, during which Delhi was nearly captured by "Moslem hordes," it was legitimate that "millions of Hindu-Sikhs prompted by the instinct of self-preservation and animated by the spirit of pan-Hindu consolidation rose in arms" (552). Moreover, he accused Nehru of not fulfilling his duty to retaliate against Muslims after having demanded that "the people should leave right of retaliation" to the government. He concluded this attack, entitled "Nero Nehru," by presenting Nehru and his associates as indebted to the prowess of Hindu Sangathanists: "If Panditji and his Congressite comrades are still safe and secure in their seats, they owe it to this brave fight which the Hindu Sangathanist and Sikh forces gave in the nick of time" (552).

Savarkar celebrated Hindu Sangathanists as the vanguard of the independence struggle. The sufferings and sacrifices of each of them exceeded those of "all the Gandhist ministers totalled together" (555). These courageous Sangathanists "cannot be terrorised by the threat of such Carpet Knights as the pandit and his clan" (555). Savarkar's bitter words suggest the enormous anger and disappointment of Hindu Sangathanists in response to their marginalization from political power and the ascendancy of the Congress under Nehru's leadership in independent India.

After independence Savarkar contended that Muslims in India, Kashmir, Hyderabad, and Pakistan were a threat to the Indian state. He claimed that "Muslims have tacitly declared war on Hindustan" and were likely to sabotage the state from within as well as attack from outside (553). He branded Muslims in the Indian police and military as potential traitors whose assistance would enable Pakistan to defeat India. To counter this Muslim threat, Savarkar again advocated Hindu militarization: "to forestall and counteract this Islamite peril our state must raise a mighty force exclusively constituted by Hindus alone, must open arms and munitions factories exclusively manned by Hindus alone and mobilize everything on a war scale" (1964, 553).

Savarkar and other Hindu leaders promoted an ideology of militarization and associated it with the need to defend Hindu interests: "Relative non-violence is our creed, and therefore we worship the defensive sword as the first saviour of man" (Savarkar 1949, 201). They also linked Hindu militarization with the need to increase the role of Hindu capitalists and workers in the production of military hardware. In order to defend the Hindu nation and the Indian state against Muslim onslaughts, it was necessary to reduce the numbers of Muslims in the military, police, and public service and to exclude Muslims from owning or working in munitions factories.

As necessary elements of militarization, Savarkar encouraged Hindus to support science, technology, and industrialization; he condemned Mahatma Gandhi's opposition to industrialization. In Savarkar's plan for India's industrialization, "science would lead all material progress and would annihilate superstition" (Keer 1966, 84). In a speech to high school students in 1953 Savarkar exhorted the audience to bring the "secret and science of the atom bomb to India and make it a mighty nation" (457). Addressing an audience in Poona in 1960, Savarkar placed military power as the foremost goal of a nation and subordinated all else to it: "He said military power was the only criterion of greatness of a nation. He would prefer Hitler to the Democracy that was cowardly and yielding to every aggressor" (522). His birthday in 1963 was celebrated in conjunction with

Militarization Week. In a speech at a meeting to honor Savarkar and to support militarization, RSS head Golwalkar praised Savarkar's "Essentials of Hindutva" as a "text-book, a scientific-book" (527). Poona University honored Savarkar by establishing the Veer Savarkar Military Studies Chair to "train military thinkers" (532).

As a publicist for militarization and capitalist industrialization, Savarkar attracted the support of Indian capitalists. When recuperating from a heart attack in 1949, Savarkar was the guest of Seth Walchand Hirchand, who owned an airplane factory and shipyard. However much Savarkar highlighted struggle as the force behind social and political evolution, he argued that "national coordination of class interests" must be the basis of India's economic progress (Savarkar 1949, 141). Savarkar never indicated what constitutes this coordination of class interests. The following statement suggests that Savarkar associated poverty with weakness and sided with the rich and powerful: "Those who have not, let them delight in exerting to have. But those who have—may be allowed to derive pleasure from the very fact of having" (n.d., 85). Rather than admit that Savarkar had no sympathy for the burgeoning millions of impoverished Indians, Keer obliquely concedes that Savarkar was not involved in movements aimed at improving the living conditions of industrial or rural laborers and adds, "there was no urge in his ideology for economic equality" (1966, 552).

Under Savarkar's leadership the Hindu Mahasabha promoted an economic platform that posited as its goal the advance of the Hindu nation. Its platform welcomed the "machine age," maintained that there was no community of economic interest of Hindus and Muslims, and declared private property to be inviolate. It advocated policies which would protect Indian companies from foreign competition and would provide special protection for Hindu economic interests (1949, 41–42). Any concern for addressing issues of poverty and exploitation was absent from this economic agenda. Instead, Savarkar repeatedly asserted that class interests could and should be "coordinated."

Hindu Sangathanist leaders promoted a policy of militarization and industrialization that advocated the expansion and protection of capitalist enterprises owned by Hindus. Savarkar's pronouncements concerning Hindu princely states indicates that Hindu Sangathanists endorsed the autocratic powers wielded by Hindu rulers and zamindars and solicited support from them. Savarkar described Hindu states as "citadels of organized Hindu powers" (1949, 344). He specified these organized powers to be martial and administrative and viewed these states as being models of Hindu government. He even suggested that the King of Nepal should become the emperor of Hindu India. His 1937 presidential address to the Hindu Mahasabha opened with "homage to the Independent kingdom of Nepal" and greetings to Hindus in "greater Hindustan"—Africa, America, Mauritius, and Bali (n.d., 252–53; 1949, 3). As will be discussed in later chapters, the Vishva Hindu Parishad involves the King of Nepal and descendants of Hindu maharajas in their activities and recruits support from overseas Hindus.

Savarkar prophesied the importance of Hindu princely states to the future of the Hindu nation and claimed that "the Pan-Hindu movement animates the Hindu Princes too" (1949, 171). He condemned Congress's attacks on the policies of Hindu states and extolled Mysore, Travancore, Oudh, and Baroda as examples of progressive Hindu states. Invoking the opposition of aristocratic-commoner, he pronounced Hindu princes to be fully capable of patriotic leadership: "History abounds with instances which show that great patriotic leaders come out of the princes also as out of the commoners" (n.d., 80). Savarkar also worked to unify rulers of Hindu states through their support for the Hindu Mahasabha, and in 1945 he presided over the All India Hindu States Conference held in Baroda.

CAMPAIGNS AND TOURS BY THE "SUPREME DICTATOR" OF HINDU SANGATHAN

In describing Savarkar on tour, one newspaper reported: "He came, he saw, he conquered." Like other public figures in India, as president of the Hindu Mahasabha and a leading figure of the Hindu Sangathanist movement, Savarkar continuously traveled throughout India. Through such tours he publicized various Sangathanist campaigns by addressing audiences and collected money for himself and for Sangathanist organizations. He made local issues into pan-Hindu causes and popularized pan-Hindu causes before local audiences. Elections too figured as occasions to promote pan-Hindu issues: "There is a Pan-Hindu Issue involved in every electoral contest" (Savarkar 1949, 240).

When Hindu ascetics organized to protest the demolition of a Shiva temple in Delhi, Savarkar spoke publicly in their support. Capitalizing on the political potential of the issue, in his 1939 presidential address to the Hindu Mahasabha he discussed it along with the Hyderabad civil resistance movement:

> The splendid and sustained struggle the Hindus have carried on at Delhi in connection with the Shiva Mandir affair, deserves also an all-India homage. It too sounds the same warning that the Congress does not and will not and cannot defend a Hindu cause against an anti-Hindu aggression. . . . On the site where stood the tiny mudhut which has been so high-handedly destroyed, I already see rising before my mind's eye a magnificent Temple of Shiva and thousands of pilgrims crowding to worship at it before a decade passes away. (1949, 95)

In regard to the Shahid Ganj case, which provoked controversy over legislation providing for the return of a religious property to Muslims, Savarkar warned that such legislation would set a dangerous precedent because it "would force the Hindus on a similar principle of 'once a temple, always a temple' to claim back their temples too, converted into mosques, in days gone by. It is wise for us all to bury the past" (n.d., 41) Savarkar's words are ingenuous: he relentlessly reminded Hindus of the need to remember the past in terms of Muslim's affronts to Hindus and the need for retribution. Violence between Hindu and Muslim groups over disputed religious properties demonstrate that the past remains today a political site for excavation, destruction, and construction.

Named "supreme dictator" of Hindu Sangathan in the 1938–39 Hyderabad civil resistance movement, Savarkar condemned the Nizam for the ill-treatment of Hindus within his realm and for his "mad Pan-Islamic ambitions" (64). He claimed that educational institutions established by the Nizam "aim to humiliate Hindu Culture and Hindu Honor" (88). The Nizam's rule posed a grave danger: "Hindu preachers" have been assassinated and under the Nizam Hindus are "threatened with extermination as a race" (49).

Assessing the success of the Hyderabad civil resistance movement, Savarkar noted that the Hindu Mahasabha had sent 3,700 members to participate and Hindu Sangathanists had contributed 70,000 rupees to meet expenses. He claimed that the movement had pressured the Nizam to reform anti-Hindu practices. Moreover, through this movement, Hindu Sangathanists had unified the constituents of the Hindu nation and had roused Hindu consciousness. Fighting together "under a common Hindu banner in defense of Hindu rights and in vindication of Hindu honour," Hindu Sangathanists had defeated the Muslims, whom they believed were covertly supported by the British and by the treachery of the Congress (116). Savarkar extolled the glorious victory and honored the courage and sacrifices of Hindu Sangathanists with a "worshipful tribute" to the martyrs who laid down their lives in the righteous war *(dharma yuddh)* against the anti-Hindu forces of the Nizam. On behalf of all Hindus Savarkar expressed "abiding gratitude towards all those Hindu Sangathanists who had gone to the front and braving tortures, deadly assaults and imprisonments, fought in defence of the Hindu cause" (118).

A survey of Savarkar's public engagements during his years as president of the Hindu Mahasabha indicates the range of organizations whose membership honored him and supported Hindu Sangathan. During his 1937 visit to Nagpur he met with women at a Seva Sadan, opened the Marathi Literary Conference, attended a meeting of the cow-protection society, and gave a speech at the RSS headquarters. While on tour he conferred with leaders of local Sanatan Dharm sabhas and addressed audiences at ayurvedic, Arya Samaj, and Sanskrit schools. Newspaper offices, libraries, women's groups, RSS branches, and merchants' associations also welcomed Savarkar and listened to his speeches about Hindutva and Hindu Sangathan. He also visited Sikh gurudwaras where he advocated Sikh militarization.

Crowds often gathered at train stations to welcome his arrival. Hindu Sangathanist organizations also arranged processions through towns and cities to honor him and display the strength of their numbers. During his visit to Madurai, Savarkar appeared before crowds in a carriage drawn by eight white horses. At Madurai's Meenakshi temple priests conferred on Savarkar the honors usually reserved for Maharajas and "heads amongst priests" (636). About Savarkar's activities as a publicist, Keer notes that he "used platform, press, examination centres, theatres, circus tents, festivals, fares [sic] and functions for popularizing the movement and whipped the people into revolt" (1966, 195). In recognition of his unceasing efforts to promote Hindu Sangathan, Savarkar was known as "Sangathanacharya—master-brain at organization—and others described him as their new Shankaracharya, the supreme head of new Hinduism" (187). Just as devotees worship their guru as God, Savarkar inspired worshipful displays: "To thousands of Hindus Savarkar appeared as an incarnation of God. . . . Thousands touched his feet with devotion and kissed his hands in spite of his fervent disapproval of these things" (317).

Devotees of temple deities, of gurus, and of Savarkar the Sangathanacharya express their devotion not only with ritual acts but also with cash donations. During his tours Savarkar raised funds for Hindu Sangathan projects and for use at his own discretion. In 1951 Savarkar began collecting money to build a shrine dedicated to revolutionary martyrs. In 1952 he presided over a three-day celebration that honored the memory of the martyrs and the official dissolution of the Abhinava Bharat Society. The following year Hindu Sangathanists collected 13,000 rupees toward the purchase of buildings for an Abhinava Bharat Society Memorial in Nasik. A group in Poona presented Savarkar with 127,000 rupees for his sixtieth birthday, and at his seventy-fifth birthday celebration in Bombay, his supporters gave him 11,111 rupees. A Delhi daily newspaper, the *Vir Arjun,* raised 51,000 rupees to present to Savarkar (534). These accounts, however, do not discuss how Savarkar spent these large sums of money.

Support for Savarkar's militant Hindu ideology and the Hindu Mahasabha was particularly strong among Marathi brahmans. Among these supporters were some who opposed Golwalkar's policy of keeping the RSS out of overt political activity. Many of them left the RSS in 1942 and formed the Hindu Rashtra Dal under the leadership of Nathuram Godse. Keer describes the Dal as a "new semi-volunteer organization aimed at the spread of and propagation of unalloyed Savarkarism . . . which could not be principally preached by any other organization" (363). In Godse's final statement during his trial for Mahatma Gandhi's assassination, he proclaimed that he was one of millions of Hindu Sangathanists who revered Savarkar as their leader and hero (Andersen and Dalme 1987, 40). Godse was convicted of assassinating Mahatma Gandhi and sentenced to death.

After Gandhi's assassination angry crowds attacked the house in Bombay which Savarkar's supporters had given him. Because of his close association with Godse, Savarkar was arrested and tried for conspiring to assassinate Gandhi. Although the court found him innocent, many believed that Savarkar had inspired or instructed Godse to assassinate Gandhi. These events turned popular opinion against Savarkar, yet they also strenghtened the commitment of his dedicated following. After his acquittal, his militant Hindu nationalist speeches led to his arrest on charges of creating ill will between Hindus and Muslims. He was released after agreeing to discontinue his political activities. He continued to give speeches and publish books promoting social and cultural elements of Hindutva ideology (434). Two years later, the government lifted restrictions on Savarkar's political activity and his speeches again became overtly political.

Through the 1950s until his death in 1966, ill health limited Savarkar's public appearances. However, he maintained a devoted following who presented him with honors, money, and who, after his death, continue to propagate his ideology of Hindutva. In 1957 Bombay Hindu Sabha members collected 30,000 rupees to fund the propagation and publication of Savarkar's ideology. The following year in Poona his supporters built a hall and named it Swatantryveer Savarkar Sabhagriha. When Savarkar died in 1966, over 100,000 people are said to have come to pay their last respects. An honor guard of 2,000 RSS workers lined the procession route to the cremation ground.

During most of his career, public antipathy characterized relations between Savarkar and the Congress Party. Yet some Congress politicians favored an alliance. Soon after independence Vallabhbhai Patel and C. D. Deshmukh unsuccessfully tried to induce Savarkar and the Hindu Mahasabha to join forces with their conservative faction within the Congress (Keer 1966, 390). Public functions honoring Savarkar were off-limits for Congress politicians. Nehru refused to share the stage with Savarkar at a centenary celebration of the 1857 revolution in Delhi. Keer notes that no Congress minister attended celebrations for Savarkar's seventy-fifth birthday and none came to his cremation. However, when Lal Bahadur Shastri became prime minister after Nehru's death, the Congress government began paying a monthly honorarium to Savarkar. Keer describes this as an indication that the "government began reconciling to Savarkar" (533).

As the national organization of Hindudom, Savarkar maintained that the Hindu Mahasabha concerned itself not simply with religion but with all aspects of life. Its importance would not diminish after independence, and Savarkar instructed the Hindu Mahasabha to "continue its mission even after Hindustan is politically free" (1949, 112). He opposed suggestions that the Hindu Mahasabha admit non-Hindus as members, arguing that Hindu solidarity and power required an exclusively Hindu organization. He bequeathed to the next generation the "true ambition of rendering the Hindu Mahasabha itself, the National Parliament of Hindustan" (1964, 561).

This ambition, in Savarkar's view, would be realized through relentless and ubiquitous work to promote Hindu Sangathan and through continued involvement in electoral contests. He advised Hindu Mahasabha candidates not to be discouraged if they lost elections: "Even the most powerful parties of today, the Nazis or the Fascists or the Bolsheviks or the Democrats did not sweep the polls at a bound" (1949, 62). Before independence Savarkar counted many Hindu Congress members as sympathetic to Hindu Sangathan, claiming they supported the Congress only because it "affords them the guarantee of being elected at any polls whether to the local bodies or the legislature, or assures them of some post or profit here or there" (1949, 183).

Like Savarkar, the Hindu Mahasabha's reputation was damaged by accusations of involvement with Mahatma Gandhi's assassination. Its leaders and workers were arrested and the organization was banned; the Mahasabha was later cleared of responsibility for the assassination (Jones 1981b, 473). After the ban was lifted, Mahasabha leaders disagreed over the future of the organization in independent India. Shyama Prasad Mookerjee, who succeeded Savarkar as Mahasabha president in 1944 and was vice president in 1948, argued that the Mahasabha should withdraw from politics and a new political party should be formed that would be open to all religious communities, "using the broadest possible definition of Hindu" (473). Other Mahasabha leaders disagreed with Mookerjee, who resigned and later founded a new political party, the Bharatiya Jana Sangh.

The Hindu Mahasabha entered the 1952, 1957, and 1962 general elections and in each succeeding election steadily lost the little electoral support it enjoyed. In 1952 it fielded thirty-one candidates for the Lok Sabha, won four seats and .95 per cent of the vote; by 1962 it fielded thirty-two candidates and won only one seat and .44 per cent of the vote (474). Although the Mahasabha failed miserably at winning elections, it remained a prominent voice of militant Hindu nationalism. Its political role was later more successfully adopted by the Bharatiya Janata Party (BJP) and its religious and cultural activism by the Vishva Hindu Parishad (VHP). In the wake of Indian politics in the 1980s and early 1990s, Savarkar's prophesy of the future success of the Sangathan movement when the Congress would have to compete with Hindu political parties to prove their pro-Hindu credentials sounds uncannily apt:

> If the Hindu party persists in contesting elections, a day will come when the Congressite Hindus shall have to go to the polls with a conspicuous "bandhan" besmeared on their foreheads and the Tulsi rosary in their hands to prove to the Hindu electorate that it was they, the Congressites, who were Hindus of a purer ray serene than the Hindu Sangathanist heretics. (163)

Using the terms of the dominant political idiom of the 1960s, Keer celebrates Savarkar as modern and secular: "Savarkar was the first Indian leader to give India the message of secularism and modernism before the advent of Nehru and Roy on the political front of India" (1966, 551). He does not define modern or secular but associates them with Savarkar's support for science. Elsewhere, however, Keer refers to Savarkar's 1949 speech that proclaims the flag and symbols of the Indian state to be Hindu. Such symbols demonstrated that India was not a secular but a Hindu state: "Savarkar affirmed that India was after all now a Hindu State established under a Hindu flag with the Dharma Chakra of the Hindu Race as its state symbol" (1966, 425). Savarkar espoused a Hindu national identity based on pride and on contempt for British rule, the secular Congress, and Muslims. His teachings provided an attractive alternative for groups who considered their interests jeopardized or constricted by Gandhi's teachings, Nehru's secularism and socialism, and by Communists.

Savarkar is said to have lacked the qualities necessary for leading a mass movement—he is described as moody and erratic, stingy, dictatorial in conversation, and unable to negotiate with other leaders (Keer 1964). His powerful Hindutva polemics, however, led the way for people to conceptualize and articulate their political and cultural identity in Hindu nationalist terms. This identity presumes Hindus are unified by their common enemies and common interests. Hindus are counted as a majority who have the right to political and economic supremacy. In their drive to consolidate and legitimate their power and authority, ruling-class groups in contemporary India build on Savarkar's legacy. They have adopted Hindutva polemics and Hindu nationalist ideology to politicize religious and social organizations and mobilize them to fight against common foes— Muslims, Gandhians and Congress pseudo-secularists, godless communists, and any number of other political opponents.

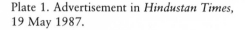

Plate 1. Advertisement in *Hindustan Times*, 19 May 1987.

Sant Devraha Baba, who sits atop his raised platform in his hut at Vrindaban, blessing the Lok Sabha Speaker, Mr. Balram Jakhar, who places his head at the foot of the Sant on Friday.—PANA.

Plate 2. Photograph and caption in *Times of India*, 14 September 1987.

A child born at Gorgama village in Khagaul near Patna is being worshipped because of the growth below the nose which is believed to be the beginning of a trunk like that of Lord Ganapati. — TOI photo.

Plate 3. Photograph and caption in *Times of India*, 15 September 1987.

Plate 4. Advertisement in *Hindustan Times*, 17 August 1987.

Plate 5. Cover of *Sunday* magazine, 25 October 1987.

Plate 6. Cover of *Probe* magazine, November 1987.

Plate 7. Postcard of Har-ki-Pairi, the main bathing area in Hardwar.

Plate 8. The Jai Ram ashram in Hardwar. The large sculpture portrays a popular story about Shiva. Mechanical dioramas underneath the sculpture (not shown) depict other stories about Hindu deities and heroes.

Plate 9. Postcard of Gayatri Parivar founder, Acharya Ram Sharma and his wife Bhagwati Devi with his 4,500-year-old guru and the goddess Gayatri.

Plate 10. Visitors on a guided tour of the Gayatri Parivar's Brahmavarchas in Hardwar. It has shrines to Gayatri Devi on the main
floor and the laboratory of Spiritual Science on the second floor.
The Bharat Mata temple rises in the background.

Plate 11. Widow crouching to touch the feet of Satpal's brother's daughter, on the roof of Premnagar ashram in Hardwar.

Plate 12. Devotees waiting in line at Premnagar ashram to touch Satpal's feet and receive his blessings.

Plate 13. Cover of the Vishva Hindu Parishad's Ekatmata Yajna souvenir volume showing the goddess Durga, sacrificial fire, ritual pot, and masses of participants.

Plate 14. Billboard for the Bharat Mata temple at the Hardwar railway station.

Plate 15. Bharat Mata statue at the Bharat Mata temple in Hardwar (from set of post-cards sold at the temple).

Plate 16. Freedom fighter Chandra Shekhar Azad in the Shrine of Heroes at the Bharat Mata temple (from set of postcards).

Plate 17. Sati Padmini, one of two statues of women in flames in the Sati Shrine at the Bharat Mata temple (from set of postcards).

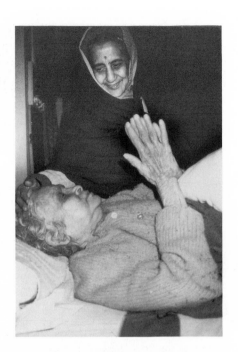

Plate 18.
Devasharanananda with
Tyagimayi at the Divine
Life Society's hospital,
Sivananda ashram.

Plate 19. Two woman ascetics at the Sivananda ghat, Sivananda ashram. Stairs lead up to the renovated Sivananda residence-museum and down to the Ganges.

Plate 20. Disciples on stage speaking about their Gurudev, Sivananda, during the final week of celebrations at the Sivananda ashram commemorating the centenary of Sivananda's birth.

Plate 21. Sivananda ashram personnel leading the crowd in chanting and singing during the Centenary Procession to Rishikesh. The Ganges, temples, and ashrams are in background.

Plate 22. Statue showing the goddess slaying a demon, under construction at the Santoshi Ma ashram in Hardwar.

Plate 23. Sign on the wall next to the entry gate of the Shakti ashram in Hardwar.

Plate 24. Bharati Ma (on left) and her disciples consecrating the Kali temple at the Bharati Ma ashram in Hardwar.

FOUR

Hindu Sangathan after Savarkar: The Vishva Hindu Parishad

ASSESSING EVERYTHING FROM THE VIEWPOINT OF SPIRITUALISM

In 1944, on the grounds of poor health, Savarkar declined requests that he accept another term as president of the Hindu Mahasabha. However, he continued touring India to promote Hindu Sangathan and Hindu nationalism. The Hindu Mahasabha had been the leading political forum for religious and social leaders who supported Hindu nationalism before and following independence. Its dominance as an opposition party representing conservative, anti-communist Hindu interests was later challenged by other political parties, such as the Swatantra Party and the Bharatiya Jana Sangh. Since the 1980s the Bharatiya Janata Party (BJP) has become the leading champion of Hindutva and Hindu nationalism and an increasingly formidable challenger to the Congress Party. Its allied organization, the Vishva Hindu Parishad (VHP) is the focus of this chapter.

Before introducing materials concerning the formation and operations of the VHP, I examine the Hindu Mahasabha's 1952 and 1962 election manifestos to indicate how the ideology developed by Savarkar became incorporated into the political discourse of independent India. Following this, extracts from the 1957 and 1962 election manifestos of the Bharatiya Jana Sangh are presented, which show a further and more populist transformation of Hindu nationalism. Although I emphasize continuities in ideological orientation, the many institutional and informal linkages among these organizations over time should also be kept in mind. For example, prior to founding the Bharatiya Jana Sangh in 1951, S. P. Mookherjee was a leader of the Hindu Mahasabha, was elected as a Mahasabha member of Parliament, and served in Nehru's cabinet. Furthermore, the Rashtriya Swayamsevak Sangh (RSS) provided leaders and workers both for the Jana Sangh and its successor the BJP as well as for the VHP (Andersen and Dalme 1987; Brass 1990).

In the 1952 election the Hindu Mahasabha declared:

> [The Party] stands for reestablishment of a Hindu Raj in Bharat with a form of Government in accordance with the Hindu conception of polity and economy. The Hindu Mahasabha intends to develop Bharat as a National home for Hindus where the sublime qualities of Hindu ideology can find a place for self-fulfillment.
>
> The Hindus possess a characteristic outlook on life, a well-defined cultural background, distinct historical traditions and are thus easily distinguishable from others. The misconceived notion of secular democracy cannot inspire the masses. It is the ideal of Hindu Rashtra alone which can make people residing all over Bharat and speaking different tongues united in common purpose, strong in combined action and capable of making India a powerful nation. Hindu Rashtravad is a dynamic and progressive conception capable of absorbing all modern scientific inventions and modern social and economic thoughts. (J. Sharma 1964, 786)

In this manifesto the Hindu Mahasabha continued to espouse its earlier position on militarization—in accordance with Savarkar's famous dictum, "Hinduise all politics and militarise all Hindudom"—asserting that its goal was to "develop the country as a first rate military power in order to make its voice felt in the United Nations" (787). The Hindu Mahasabha gave top priority to the development of "industries connected with war machines and materials of all types" and supported a policy of compulsory military education for men aged eighteen to twenty-five. Its economic platform advocated "maximum freedom in trade and commerce" and the reduction of taxes on "petty shopkeepers and small industrialists" (789–90). (This platform was later adopted by the Swatantra Party, which was formed in 1959.) The 1952 manifesto stated its opposition to both communism and socialism in the following terms:

> The Hindu Mahasabha is not wedded to any ism. It does not believe that classless society is ever possible. So long as society is based on division of labor, existence of classes with varying interests is inevitable. The Hindu Mahasabha does not believe in class war. It believes in the national coordination of class interests to the mutual benefit of all. (792)

Concerning its position on education and culture, the manifesto declared that "moral and religious education not sectarian but based on broad principles of Hindutva will be imparted in all educational institutions and suitable arrangements for teaching Sanskrit in advanced schools will be made on a large scale" (790). Although Savarkar was not specifically mentioned, the Hindu Mahasabha adapted his formulation and systematic elaboration of the principles of Hindutva. Echoes of Savarkar's voice also resound in a statement of goals made by the Hindu Mahasabha in 1950: "To organise and consolidate all sections of the people into one organic whole" (793). Another of its goals was "to revive and promote ancient Indian ideals of plain living and high thinking and the glorious ideals of Aryan womanhood" (793). The 1952 manifesto concluded by reiterating the position set forth in its opening, the transformation of the Indian state into a Hindu state: "The Hindu Mahasabha believes that Hindus have a right to live as Hindus and rule, legislate and govern themselves in accordance with Hindu ideals. Hindu Rashtra has to be established and a Hindu ideology must have a homeland for its unfoldment" (792).

Ten years later in its 1962 election manifesto, the Hindu Mahasabha accused the Congress Party of betraying the nation while hypocritically shouting "Bharat Mata ki Jai" (Victory to Mother India). It denounced Urdu as a foreign language and demanded that Sanskrit be the language of official oaths and the Constitution. Other issues addressed by the manifesto included the expulsion of foreign Christian missionaries and the support of ayurvedic medicine. Its position on establishing a Hindu state remained unaltered, although articulated differently than ten years previously: "The Hindu Mahasabha intends to develop Hindustan into a State based on Hindu ideology, which possesses a characteristic catholic outlook on life, with a well-defined cultural background, easily distinguishable from the cultures of all other nations" (796). The manifesto closes with the mantra favored by Hindu nationalists: "Bharat Mata ki Jai, Hindu Rashtra ki Jai, Hindi, Hindu, Hindustan ki Jai. Vande Mataram" (810).

In his presidential address at the 1968 Hindu Mahasabha Conference, N. N. Banerjee propounded Savarkar's principles of class coordination. Like Swatantra Party leader M. R. Masani, who invoked Marx when making his argument about the historical mission of capitalism, Banerjee also invoked Marx when claiming that Hinduism has "all the sympathy for the have nots" (quoted in Jones 1981b, 475). But unlike Marx's "pure materialism," Hinduism "assesses everything from the viewpoint of Spiritualism." The Mahasabha president associated this spiritualism with Hindutva, which "demands economic uplift and social equality" through class coordination. A "collective dictatorship"—rule by a group of five—is presented as the political solution to a "corrupt democracy."

Banerjee elaborated the platform of the Hindu Mahasabha. It supported decreased state controls over the private economic sector, Hinduism as the official religion of India, and the prohibition of cow slaughter and family planning. Its platform advocated the expansion of India's power in the international arena and reiterated its hostility to Pakistan. These policies are represented as necessary to the main goal of the Hindu Mahasabha: "to establish Hindu Rashtra in Bharat by all legal means." This entails the defeat of the "false concept of secularism introduced by Congress." The Mahasabha continued to assert that Hindus constitute a nation and not a community; hence, they are entitled to a "homeland for their own religion, culture and philosophy": "We repeat we want to establish a State in Bharat which will be based on principles of Hinduism."

As a contrast to the nationalist idiom of the Hindu Mahasabha, a brief consideration of the 1957 election manifesto of the Bharatiya Jana Sangh is instructive. Notice its shift from the Hindu-exclusivist position of the Mahasabha to one which represents itself as concerned with the interests of Hindus and non-Hindus alike. Bharat is the Sanskritic Hindi term for India and the official name used for India on currency and stamps. Bharatiya is the adjectival form of Bharat which means Indian; it also has strong ideological connotations related to brahmanic norms of social and religious behavior. This new party replaced the concept of Hindutva propagated by the Mahasabha and Savarkar with that of Bharatiya culture:[1]

> For the preservation of national unity, without which neither the hard won freedom can be preserved nor the big plans for economic development and social reconstruction be executed, Jana Sangh will take the following steps:
>
> 1. Creating a feeling of equality and oneness in the Hindu Society by liquidating untouchability and casteism.
> 2. Nationalising all non-Hindus by inculcating in them the ideals of Bharatiya culture. (J. Sharma 1964, 611)

Like other noncommunist opposition parties, the Jana Sangh opposed the centralization of economic power by the state and chastised the government for its corruption. It condemned "government interference" in cultural, social, and religious spheres, in education, literature, arts, and sciences. Furthermore, it opposed government measures which restrict the economic autonomy of religious institutions: "The covetous eyes of the government are fixed on the temples and religious seats as well as on saints and sadhus" (610).

The Jana Sangh manifesto advocated expanded support for ayurveda, a system of medical education and treatment suffused with brahmanic concepts about the body, mind, and soul. It promised that ayurveda would be developed "as the national system of medicine and it will be made the vehicle of improvement for health" (621). Such a development, i.e., government support for ayurvedic training and production of ayurvedic medicines, would also be a vehicle providing employment for upper-caste Hindu practitioners and teachers of ayurveda.

Consonant with other items on its platform, the Jana Sangh supported prohibition of cow slaughter. It also promised to repeal the Hindu Marriage

---

1. For a discussion of the concept of bharatiya in Hindu nationalist discourse, see Fox (1990b).

and Hindu Succession Acts. It maintained that because the joint family and indissoluble marriage form the basis of Hindu society, "laws that alter this basis will ultimately lead to the disintegration of the society" (622). Conservative, patriarchal Hindus condemned this legislation particularly because it gave women legal rights to inherit property and to divorce.

The concept of Bharatiya figured prominently in the Jana Sangh's 1962 election manifesto. Although it had opposed government interference in cultural and religious life, it asserted that the party is the means "to reinforce ideals of Bharatiya Sanskriti and Maryada," in other words, upper-caste Hindu cultural, ethical, and moral ideals (625). It promised that for strengthening "national unity," special measures would be taken for "inculcating in all Bharatiya citizens an abiding faith in Bharatiya culture" (628).

STEPS TO CONSOLIDATE AND STRENGTHEN HINDU SOCIETY

Different stories about the origin of the VHP circulate. One version says that Golwalkar, the head of the RSS, was dismayed by the lack of unity among Hindu religious leaders and convened a meeting with them in Bombay in 1964 to address this problem (Andersen and Dalme 1987, 133). Other versions relate that in 1964, Swami Chinmayananda hosted 150 religious leaders at his Bombay ashram (Patchen 1989, x, 219; van der Veer 1994, 130). The different versions concur on the outcome of this Bombay gathering: the formation of the Vishva Hindu Parishad (World Hindu Council) with Swami Chinmayanda as president and S. S. Apte, a high-ranking RSS official, as general secretary. As with the Hindu Mahasabha, the Bharatiya Jana Sangh, and the Swatantra Party, the concepts of Hindutva, Hindu Sangathan, and Hindu nationalism were to be the cornerstones of the new organization. It advocated the ideology of militant Hindu nationalism systematized by Savarkar and promoted by the RSS under the leadership of its founder, K. B. Hedgewar, his successor, M. S. Golwalkar, and its highly disciplined cadre of workers. However, like other powerful organizations, the VHP speaks with many tongues, and not all of them are militant.

Chinmayananda gave his own account of founding the VHP shortly before his death in 1993, when giving darshan to devotees at a spiritual camp on the campus of Grand Valley State University in rural Michigan. His assistant introduced me as a Hindi-speaking anthropologist from Chicago. The audience asked the usual questions that devotees ask a guru. My question was anomalous and unwelcome. Prefacing it with, "I read in your biography that you were the founding president of the Vishva Hindu Parishad," I asked Chinmayananda about the VHP's activities in India. He immediately tried to dismiss my question by asserting that he did not authorize the biography. I challenged his rebuff by saying that official VHP records also state that he was its founding president. He paused, sighed, and began to lecture:

> When *your* pope came to India [Paul VI in December 1964], he said he was going to convert 125 people to Christianity. Public opinion made him withdraw his plan but I was in Bombay and announced that I would convert 200 people to Hinduism and I did. Then I had the idea to start a group to work for conversions. I didn't have enough people of my own so I asked the RSS for their help. Guruji [RSS head, Golwalkar] liked the idea and had thousands of workers everywhere. The VHP has grown into a mighty force. It is all over the world. After I started the VHP, I returned to my own mission as spiritual teacher of vedanta. Anyone can do the work of the VHP. I have been invited to the VHP's Conference in Washington as the keynote speaker and will be given an award. Awards are good because they mean a press conference and publicity. Later in August I will speak at the Parliament of the World's Religions in Chicago.

One spiritual camper assured me that Chinmayananda was a present-day Vivekananda, a truly great spiritual leader. For four decades Chinmayananda had traveled throughout the world building a network of institutions which propagates nationalistic Hinduism among well-educated, affluent, upper-caste Hindus. Chinmayananda received his award at the VHP of America's Conference in Washington. But just two weeks before he was to follow Vivekananda's footsteps to Chicago and the 1993 Parliament of the World's Religions, he died in California. He lived long enough to say with the pride of certainty that the organization which he helped to establish, the VHP, had "grown into a mighty force."

In its literature the VHP describes itself as a religious, cultural, and social organization for 600 million Hindus living in eighty countries. It claims to favor no specific Hindu sect or doctrine. Its stated aim is to unite an array of religious sects which identify themselves as Hindu, i.e., those that reverence the central tenet of Hindu nationalism: India is their holy land. The founding members of the VHP included prominent leaders representing brahmanic ritualism or sanatan dharm, reformist, Jain, Buddhist, and Sikh groups.

Golwalkar supported the formation of the VHP as an organization which would link the RSS with Hindu religious leadership. A high-ranking RSS leader, Shivram Shankar Apte, was selected as the first general secretary of the VHP, and RSS workers were instrumental in establishing the VHP's organizational network. K. M. Munshi, founder of the Bharatiya Vidya Bhavan (an important institution popularizing Hindu cultural nationalism) and a leader of the Swatantra Party, was also a VHP founder.

Complementing its patriarchal ideology, the VHP's founders were exclusively male.

"To take steps to consolidate and strengthen Hindu society" appears as the first item in the VHP's nine-point statement of aims and objectives (*The Hindu Awakening: Retrospect and Promise [HARP]*, 9). The other points in its platform elaborate this primary objective and outline the means to achieve it. The VHP undertakes to "protect, develop and spread" Hindu ethical and spiritual values; to establish contacts with and help all Hindus living abroad; to found an order of lay and initiate missionaries and open centers to train them for propagating "dynamic Hinduism." It also aims to promote activities and research in cultural, scientific, literary, social, religious, and charitable fields. For infrastructural support of these activities, the VHP is resolved to "found, maintain, take over or render assistance to" not only charitable institutions such as schools, medical clinics, libraries, orphanages, and widow's homes but also religious institutions such as "temples, maths, and other centers for preaching and teaching the principles of Hindu Dharma and Culture." This policy of forming new institutions as well as taking over and assisting existing ones articulates the VHP's strategy of corporate expansion throughout India and abroad.

Building on the work of prior propagandists who advocated Hindu spirituality as a necessary force in the modern world, the VHP describes its mission as global and humanitarian. Such an image attempts to procure for the organization an international respectability which complements its aim to involve overseas Hindus in its activities. Hence the ninth and final point in its list of aims and objectives: "To diffuse knowledge of, and preach ethical and spiritual principles and practices of Hinduism suited to modern times in all parts of the world so as to be conducive to the welfare of humanity as a whole."

This position is reiterated in the booklet's last section, entitled "Religion is a Science," a statement by VHP president Maharana Bhagwat Singh Mewar. He is described as a "dynamic, traditional leader from an illustrious dynasty of the 1,400 years long time *[sic]* of the Great Maharanas of Mewar" (44). Maharana Bhagwat Singh maintains that the code of conduct to be found in the Vedas, Upanishads, and other scriptures is named Manava Dharma, the religion of mankind. This true religion recognizes no "social levels" and does not discriminate according to class or creed. The world is indebted to Bharat for its gift of Manava Dharma: "Bharat-Khand is the birth place of 'Manava Dharma' and hence, popularly known as Hindu Dharma and the Bharatiya people are the custodians of 'Manava Dharma,' the adherence to which places Bharat, at one time, in the position of 'Guru' (teacher) of the world, but of love, respect and devotion" (44). Sufferings arise from personal faults, neglect of vedic injunctions, and the "misinterpretation and disapplication of Religion." The Maharana, who is extolled as seventy-fifth in a lineage which includes great warriors as well as the Hindu saint "Bhaktimata Meerabai," summarizes the purpose of the Vishva Hindu Parishad: "to help man to rediscover himself, to realise himself of Nature (Truth) and to overcome being made a fool of and trodden upon" (45).

Two years after its founding the VHP convened a "momentous and mammoth World Hindu Conference" during the Kumbh Mela in Allahabad. This conference is celebrated as the first such gathering of all the sects of Hindu Dharma since the "reign of Samrat Harsha Vardhan 1,300 years ago." Of the many "inspiring messages and appreciations from dignitaries" sent to the Conference from all over the world, the VHP records three: from the King of Nepal; from J. K. Birla, a king of corporate capitalism; and from President Radhakrishnan. The president of India's message reads: "I am glad to know that there will be a conference of Hindu religion. Incessant self-renewal from the Vedas to the Upanishads, to the Geeta, to the Acharyas and the modern Bhaktas has been assuming different emphasis. The same process of renewal is happening today and Hinduism is getting modified from within" (10). In one publication the VHP states that 25,000 Hindus from twenty countries participated in this conference; the figure is inflated to 75,000 in a later publication.

A similar inflation of participants from 100,000 to 200,000 occurs in the VHP's accounts of its second World Hindu Conference, held in 1979 in Allahabad. The highlight of this conference was the meeting on the same platform "after a lapse of more than a thousand years" of the Shankaracharya of Jyotishpeeth and the Dalai Lama. These "two great spiritual leaders" proclaimed together the "glory of true Dharma" (11). "For the first time in history" pandits from Varanasi welcomed the Dalai Lama by chanting vedic mantras; "in reciprocation" the Dalai Lama "publicly honoured these Pandits in the traditional Buddhist way." Whatever his political motivation, the Dalai Lama's appearance on this platform supports the VHP's assertions concerning its embrace of Jain, Sikh, and Buddhist groups.

The VHP does not specify the sources of funds used to mount these conferences, but support from powerful, prominent capitalists is suggested by references to them. "Industrialist" D. Khatau is thanked for his efforts to make the 1966 Conference a success. V. H. Dalmia, "industrialist and philanthropist" is named as the chairman of the reception committee of the 1979 conference, who gave a "warm welcome to all Hindu leaders and delegates." Also recorded are the messages to the 1979 conference from Prime Minister Moraji Desai and the King of Nepal. The obsequious message of Sir Seosagar Ram Gulam, Prime Minister of Mauritius, conforms to the VHP's ideology of Hindu India's global mission: "In matters of religious faith, social beliefs and cultural relations, the Hindus living in other countries look to India for dynamic guidance. I hope this conference will not only find ways to preserve the eternal values in our ancient culture but also contribute to the uplift of entire humanity" (12).

In addition to its World Hindu Conferences, the VHP regularly organizes state and district conferences throughout India. These conferences are said to aim at "mass contacts to arouse consciousness in Hindu Society" (13). The confidence and self-reliance which such conferences inspire among Hindus are described as indicators of their success. In its account of these regional conferences, the VHP enumerates the numbers of participants: of the eighteen conferences listed for the years 1969–82, three are said to have attracted a half million participants; one million people are said to have attended the 1981 conference in Delhi. The accuracy of these figures may be questioned. However, they do indicate how the VHP strives to prove its claims to lead a pan-Hindu mass movement.

MANY HAVE SET EXAMPLES BY ACTUALLY PRACTICING WHAT THEY PROFESS

The VHP's platform of social reform focuses on the "weaker sections" of Hindu society, particularly untouchables and tribals. Like Savarkar, the VHP denounces untouchability because it fragments Hindu society. The "true view" of dharma opposes untouchability and promotes "self respect and solidarity among Hindus" (*HARP*, 14). Following their true dharma, Hindus throughout the world "should maintain the spirit of unity and equality in their mutual intercourse." Its campaign against untouchability is said to be in the tradition of past sages, saints, and acharyas. The successor to Golwalkar as head of the RSS, Balasahib Deoras, is invoked as one who has "provided a great social incentive" to fight untouchability. Accordingly, the religious teachers or "Dharmacharyas" associated with the VHP "have issued directions in unequivocal terms condemning untouchability and many have set examples by actually practicing what they profess."

Savarkar advocated that Hindu Sangathan would be strengthened by making Hindus of all castes—presumably male—eligible for standardized training as priests. The VHP has implemented such a project for untouchables. With the assistance of "learned Brahmin Pandits" from the fabulously wealthy Tirupati temple, the VHP sponsored a month-long camp to train untouchables as temple priests (*Vishva Hindu Parishad: Message and Activities [MA]*, 3). The untouchables were also taught the fundamentals of Hindu dharma and the procedures for performing marriage and funeral rituals. The VHP plans to conduct such training camps "in every district in due course." Such camps enable the VHP to selectively recruit untouchables into its organization. These untouchable priests and the temples and clients who employ them provide a means for the VHP to extend its formal and informal networks of patronage among untouchable communities. Its literature, however, does not specify the extent to which untouchable groups are involved in its activities.

Prefacing the discussion of its projects among "weaker sections," the VHP asserts that "to come to the aid of poor and needy is an ancient Hindu tradition" (*HARP*, 14). Being children of the same Mother India makes tribals or Girivasis and Vanavasis "brethren" of caste Hindus. Millions of them "urgently" require the medical and educational assistance that the VHP offers. In this context, the VHP articulates in a more muted tone the antipathy to Christian missionaries so stridently enunciated by Savarkar and the Hindu Mahasabha. Because of a lack of Hindu institutions, 20,000 Hindu orphans are being brought up in Christian orphanages. Hindu nationalist arguments concerning the "denationalization" of tribals by Christian missionaries are implied with the assertion that "projects taken up by the VHP are producing nationalist leadership among the Tribals" (16).

The VHP also targets Hindus "nearer to home" who require their attention: the growing population of slum dwellers, who "as Hindus deserve all our help and sympathy." The VHP's social service projects to aid Hindu society's weaker sections are said to number 867. They include hundreds of Bal Sanskar Kendras, which "mould the character of the younger generation from childhood"; schools and students' hostels; hospitals and dispensaries; food and clothes distribution centers (14–16).

"Shuddhi" was the term used by Savarkar and Hindu Sangathanists for the movement and ceremonies which "reconverted" Muslims and Christians to Hinduism. The rationale for the movement was that conversion to Christianity and Islam threatened to make Hindus a minority within India. It presumed that such converts were in fact Hindus who needed to be brought back into their ancestral faith. The VHP has renamed this movement *paravartan* and translates it as "homecoming." Like advocates of shuddhi, the VHP relates its homecoming campaign to a decreasing Hindu population and offers as proof census figures which show a decline in the Hindu population. It asserts that "even after partition" the Hindu population has declined to a minority in nineteen districts and that thirteen more districts "face the danger of losing their Hindu majority" (20).

As if the shuddhi movement never existed, paravartan or homecoming is depicted as a wholly new phenomenon within Hinduism. The VHP asserts that those brethren who were lost to alien faiths in the last 1,000 years had not been "welcomed back" by Hindus. However, this is no longer the case: "now our Acharyas have changed their stand in this respect and bless all who return to their original fold." It claims that paravartan does not entail conversion because it is simply the return of groups to their ancestral Hindu dharma. As elsewhere, statistics are given to indicate the scope of this VHP project: by 1983 there have been nearly 75,000 paravartans, and "the process is gaining momentum" (21). Although the initiative for paravartan is attributed to Hindu religious teachers or acharyas, the VHP assigns to Hindu society the task to "welcome more and more of them with due honour and help their rehabilitation and integration" (22). The VHP does not specify the processes involved in their "rehabilitation and integration." Their "rehabilitation" may well entail an "integration" which demands deference to and dependence on upper-caste VHP leaders and supporters.

In response to the "conspiracy to convert eighty million Hindus to Islam particularly from the backward classes, which was designed by Pan Islamic Fundamentalists and financed by petro-dollars," the VHP has organized specific campaigns to awaken the masses (Jana Jagaran) and to protect Hindu culture (Sanskriti Raksha Yojana) (35). These campaigns mobilize thousands of VHP volunteers for "door to door contacts with the masses." They also involve the establishment of 1,000 social service centers in "backward and inaccessible" areas by VHP workers. This missionary activity is said to achieve "the vision of Swami Vivekananda." Hindus who are already "awakened" are reported as having contributed large sums of money for these projects.

In 1981 a group of Tamil untouchables, whose improved economic status could not offset the stigma of being untouchable, converted to Islam. This embrace of Islam and rejection of Hinduism and untouchability infuriated Hindu nationalists and disturbed caste Hindus. These conversions in Meenakshipuram prompted the VHP to organize its Jana Jagaran and Sanskriti Raksha campaigns.[2] It claims that "remedial measures" were quickly devised whereby "large numbers of so-called converts returned to their original faith" (35). The Gnana Ratham or "chariot of wisdom" is another response to the Meenakshipuram conversions. The VHP describes it as a "prudently thought of religious device to bring the message of Hindu religion to the doors of rural masses and help to eradicate untouchability." The chariot of wisdom is a mobile propaganda unit. A van is equipped with audio-visual equipment and a "powerful public address system." Traveling with the Gnana Ratham is a "learned individual" who preaches "in the most simple and appealing manner." He is accompanied by VHP workers;

2. Matthew (1982) and Mujahid (1989) analyze the political implications of the Meenakshipuram conversions. Cf. Gordon on the Molplah uprising in 1921: "For months the Hindu press in North India was obsessed with the forced conversions and with the means of reclaiming their lost brethren. The full horror of the rebellion was made the more immediate through the distribution of newsreels in the commercial cinema" (1975, 163).

their mission is "to promote the tenets of Hinduism and to prove its superiority over any other religion or faith" (*MA, 5*).

The Gnana Ratham is also a mobile Hindu temple. The chariot is "sanctified by an idol, Lord Muruga." Its route is publicized in advance so that villagers can prepare and assemble for its arrival. The program includes singing devotional hymns, a lecture "on any dharmic subject," and a feast for the poor. The VHP considers the most important item in the Ratham's program to be that "any individual irrespective of any caste could perform the Abhishek of the Deity by him or herself" (*MA, 5*).

Over 200,000 people are said to have participated in the Ratham's programs during its progress through 110 villages of Tamil Nadu. Funding for the Ratham "venture" came from industrialist K. K. Birla, Lakshmi Mills, Aruna Sugar, Hivelm Industries, Sundran Charities, and *The Hindu* newspaper (*HARP, 36*). The VHP also sponsored two Dharma Rathams to travel through Kerala. It reports plans "to undertake a similar venture for propagating Hindu Dharma" among tribals in Bihar. Through these Rathams the VHP popularizes its ideology and recruits followers from rural and remote areas. They also assist in establishing local networks of VHP supporters which can be used for mobilizing people not only to participate in larger scale VHP activities—the 1983 Sacrifice for Unity (Ekatmata Yajna), the 1984 Sacrifice to Liberate Ram's Birthplace (Ram Janmabhoomi Mukti Yajna), and the later attacks by Hindu militants (kar sevaks) on the Babri Masjid—but also to vote for VHP-endorsed candidates in elections.[3]

The VHP refers to its activities which exclusively involve women as Matri Shakti (42). Unlike the long passages concerning work among untouchables and tribals, the VHP only briefly refers to its Matri Shakti program. Thousands of Matri Mandals (women's centers) are reported as having been formed throughout the country. A Matri Sammelan or women's assembly is convened during every Hindu conference, but the proceedings are not reported on in these two VHP texts. Women's participation in mass rituals are the only activities of Matri Mandals that the VHP reports: 600,000 women performed the Var Lakshmi puja in Andhra Pradesh; 1,008 women, "including some from Harijan localities," performed Vilukku puja in Madras, Bombay and Kanyakumari district.

Besides its missionary activities among the "weaker sections" of Hindu society, the VHP also ministers to pilgrims at major Hindu pilgrimage centers during festivals such as the Puri rath yatra and the Kumbh Mela (*HARP, 16*). By offering these services to pilgrims, VHP officials involve themselves with local administrative apparatus in pilgrimage centers. This involvement gives them the opportunity to participate in decision-

---

3. For another discussion of the Ekatmata Yajna and the Ram Janmabhoomi Muktiyajana, see van der Veer (1994).

making processes during which they can make demands for resources and privileges for themselves and their member organizations. For example, the VHP pressures officials who allocate the sites for camps during the Kumbh Mela to grant good sites to swamis and gurus favored by the VHP. By locating its favored publicists in high-status sites near the hub of activity, the VHP strategically positions itself for recruiting new members from among pilgrims, sadhus, gurus, and politicians.

Like governmental agencies and other voluntary groups, the VHP involves itself in relief work among victims of natural disasters. In its discussion of "relief and rehabilitation" work, the VHP quotes "Guruji" Golwalkar, former head of the RSS: "In the field of human service, no distinction should be made between man and man. We have to serve all, be he a Christian, a Muslim or a human being of any other persuasion [sic]; for calamities, distress and misfortunes make no such distinction but afflict all alike" (16). Through such work, the VHP can establish or further contacts among disaster victims as well as the local administration. Expansion of its influence into local affairs is also the means whereby the VHP contributes to conditions leading to human-made calamities like communal riots. Relief work among Hindus in the aftermath of such riots provides the VHP with a sympathetic audience for its militant Hindu nationalist ideology.[4] Furthermore, the expenditure of funds raised by the VHP for disaster relief is difficult to trace; fund-raising in India and overseas for disaster relief might offer a pretext to bankroll campaigns of Hindu nationalists.

REESTABLISHING THE SCIENTIFIC STRUCTURE OF OUR AGE-OLD SOCIETY

In addition to its numerous and varied "reformatory efforts," the VHP concerns itself with "social transformation" (18). Besides its work to counter untouchability and "indifferences towards the downtrodden," the VHP

---

4. Andersen and Dalme discuss how the RSS "earned enormous goodwill" for their work among Hindu refugees during the upheavals of partition (1987, 48–50). In *Basic Concepts of Material Achievements*, Acharya Sharma of the Gayatri Parivar advises his followers on how to capitalize on solicitude offered to persons in distress: "The affection and cooperation of others is needed in even the smallest work. The way to achieve this is give and take. We get only when we give and a beginning should always be made from one's own side. One should not sit doing nothing and wait in the hope that without taking any initiative on his part others will favour him with affection and cooperation of their own accord. It is necessary to become courteous, have a sweet tongue, give respect and extend cooperation. It is not necessary to be overzealous or affluent in this respect. One of the ways to extend cooperation is to participate in all small or big matters, in matters of happiness and sorrow and enquire about service which can be rendered to others. It does not cost a pie in extending a helping hand to a person involved in some calamity and assist him as far as possible. This is a way by which several persons can be befriended and by their contribution, cooperation can be sought from time to time in our march towards progress without making any demand, just by giving a hint of our need."

wants to eliminate "outmoded rituals and superstitions." This goal requires that the VHP work towards "re-establishing the scientific structure of our age-old society." The VHP presumes that its cadres of sectarian leaders are fully authorized to define and supervise this process of homogenization and modernization of Hinduism and Hindu society.

This process is articulated in the form of an eleven-point program. Rituals should be shortened and reduced to a minimum; they should be performed by families themselves. Temple priests "from all regions" should be trained. Temples should be efficiently managed; temple "wealth" should be used for "upholding Dharma and benefit to all Hindus"; and new temples should be built "in Harijan localities." In other words, the VHP works to involve itself in temple administration: profits should be reinvested to expand religious institutions and to employ and reward personnel who support the VHP. The remaining three points encode the VHP's strategy for involving members of different economic classes in its activities. It claims to work for "equal social status for all" and strives to involve the "well-to-do for the upliftment of the weaker sections of our society." Like Savarkar and the Hindu Mahasabha before it, the VHP never analyzes or challenges the processes whereby the "well-to-do" produce and protect their wealth.

Just as the VHP appropriates for itself the role of protecting all Hindus, it ascribes to the wealthy the duty of assisting the "weaker sections" of Hindu society—especially through donations to the VHP. Agency and benevolence belong to the VHP and the well-to-do. Untouchables, tribals, and the impoverished are indebted recipients of charity. Uplift by upper-caste Hindu benefactors, like the "trickle-down effect" invoked by some capitalist economists and apologists, is posed as the solution to poverty and deprivation.

The VHP requires loyal workers to execute its projects. Positioned between the points on equal social status and upliftment by the well-to-do, is a point exhorting "well educated and talented youth to becons [sic] self-reliant and to serve the motherland." The VHP uses the tenet of Hindu nationalism which equates holy motherland with nation to recruit young Hindus as devoted and patriotic workers. Youthful devotees are implicitly promised the rewards that devoted service earns. Besides its schools and libraries, its *Ramayana* and *Mahabharata* examinations and *Gita* recitation competitions are further channels through which the VHP inculcates its ideology among young Hindus and rewards and recruits them.

At its 1979 World Conference, the VHP decreed a new code of conduct, the "six do's for every Hindu" (18-19). The code was formulated to "suit the modern conditions of life" and to rectify the "various anomalies which have crept into our social customs during the long period of our decay." All Hindus are enjoined to believe that the "Sun is Eternal God" and to worship the sun every morning "at the crack of dawn." The VHP decrees "aum" to be the "celestial replica of God." It instructs all Hindus to wear the symbol around their neck—like Chandra Swami who sports a gold ingot engraved with aum—and to inscribe aum on "books, diaries, exercise books, visiting cards, letterheads, purses, vehicles, etc."[5]

The VHP code teaches that regardless of sectarian affiliation Hindus share the sun as their god and aum as their symbol. Hindus also have a shared "sacred book." If Christians have the Bible and Muslims the Koran, the VHP declares that "Shrimad Bhagavad Gita the sacred book of the Hindus, irrespective of various Sampradays [sects], contains the essence of Hindu philosophy and way of life. Every Hindu must keep a copy of the Gita in his home" (19). This estimation of the *Gita* is not new. Many Hindu leaders, including Mahatma Gandhi and Radhakrishnan, had previously popularized such a view of the *Gita* and countless Hindu teachers continue to do so.

The last three "do's" of the VHP code of conduct for all Hindus explicitly concern the religious duties incumbent upon Hindus as a family unit. The code addresses the male head of the household as the person who is responsible for the observance of these injunctions. Hindus must keep an image of their family deity in their homes and worship it daily. They must also grow *tulsi,* a plant "well-known for its religious importance and medicinal qualities." Finally "every Hindu along with his family members" must go regularly to "his centre of faith like temple, Math, Gurudwara, Prayer Hall etc., for seeking inspiration" (19). The VHP thus creates for Hindus a codified form of Hinduism. It requires Hindus to define themselves in terms of specific beliefs, symbols, and practices. At the same time it permits Hindus to elaborate on this basic Hinduism in accordance with their own needs and desires.

The VHP propagates its ideology and publicizes its activities through

5. Concurrent with press attention to the rise of militant Hindu nationalist organizations was its coverage of Chandra Swami, a guru whose international circuit included connections in the Middle East, Beverly Hills, and Paris (color photos of Chandra Swami appeared on the covers of *Surya India,* August 1987, and *Maya,* December 1987; *Sunday,* 13 December 1987, introduced an excerpt from a book on Adnan Khashoggi with, "Adnan Khashoggi and godman Chandra Swami must be the oddest couple in the Iranscam scandal"). Chandra Swami's association with the VHP, although never explicitly stated in these press reports, was suggested by an interview with one of his devotees, movie star Raj Babbar, who is also active in politics (*Illustrated Weekly of India,* 20 September 1987). This devotee recalled that he first met Chandra Swami during an assembly of religious leaders at the Kumbh Mela in Hardwar. Chandra Swami was introduced by VHP leader and Bharat Mata Mandir founder Swami Satyamitranand as having "donated a large amount of money" to the temple. "Impressed" by the "beautiful marble temple" with its statue of Bharat Mata and portraits of the martyrs and "great leaders who have done a lot for the country" and by Chandra Swami's "description of Hinduism as a religion that defies definition, that is all-encompassing and one that had given him peace and contentment," Babbar was "inspired" to introduce himself to Chandra Swami and invite him to be his guest whenever he visited Bombay (*Illustrated Weekly of India,* 20 September 1987).

its various journals. Eight centers publish monthly journals in regional languages. The central office in Delhi publishes a Hindi and English monthly journal, *Hindu Vishva,* which "places before the Hindus of the World their glorious heritage as well as their present problems and solutions. It also contains the report of the activities of the Vishva Hindu Parishad" (40). The VHP also publishes a monthly English-language journal in Britain and the United States. In addition to official VHP publications are countless others in English and Indian languages whose news coverage and features support and complement the VHP's Hindu nationalist agenda.

Besides its journals, the VHP publishes and distributes "cultural and religious literature." Most publications are in Hindi but titles are also given for English, Sanskrit, Gujarati, and Marathi publications. The following Hindi titles indicate the idiom through which the VHP codifies Hindu religion and culture and constructs it as an object of devotion and the means to spiritual liberation: *Hindu Sanskriti ke Pramukh Granth* (The Principal Book of Hindu Culture); *Hindu Dharma ki Mahima* (In Praise of Hindu Dharma); *Mukti-Dwar* (The Gateway of Liberation). The title, *Hindu Shabda ki Utpati aur Itihas* (The Origin and History of the Word Hindu), recalls Savarkar's polemical etymology which linked development of the term Hindu with the emergence of Hindus as a race and nation. The VHP's volume on Mahatma Gandhi indicates that this past foe of militant Hindu nationalists has been appropriated by the VHP to enhance its respectability.

THE VHP'S ORGANIZATIONAL STRUCTURE: THE OFFICIAL VERSION

Although the VHP's published representations of its organizational structure do not address how the VHP actually operates, they do indicate that the central and regional executive bodies of the VHP provide leadership for its branches and for a confederacy of affiliated organizations whose support is integral to the execution of its projects and campaigns. In 1982 the VHP claimed to have extended its operations to 302 districts within India and twenty-three foreign countries. At that time it had a total of 3,000 active units and planned to establish at least 1,000 more during 1983 (*MA,* 1). It also planned to "mobilise" 1,000 full-time workers by the end of 1983, which would have doubled the then present number. It counted 118,522 persons as members of the VHP and had 315,500 as its target for 1983 (2).

The VHP also reports on its work among overseas Hindus. In 1971 S. S. Apte, the RSS leader serving as the VHP's general secretary, visited twenty-one countries to build the "edifice of Vishva Hindu Parishad organization abroad" (*HARP,* 32). It has divided the world into five zones. It appoints zone coordinators who "contact Vishva Hindu Parishad workers and sympathizers in all the countries in their zone and make efforts to establish Vishva Hindu Parishad units in those countries and to get them affiliated to the Vishva Hindu Parishad in India" (*MA*, 7). Through quarterly reports to the VHP's central office and attendance at meetings of the Governing Council and the Board of Trustees, these zone coordinators ensure that "a proper liaison" exists between the work of the VHP in India and abroad. Through his foreign tours Apte built the edifice for the VHP's work abroad; member and affiliate organizations multiply the edifices by building temples in "Trinidad, Leeds, Boston, Bolton and other places." At eighty-eight Veda Mandirs in twenty countries, the VHP has consecrated the "Ved Bhagwan (A book weighing eleven kilograms and containing the text of all the four Vedas)."

The VHP records the names of politicians and other public figures who attend their Indian conferences or send messages to them. Similarly, it commemorates the ninth conference of the VHP of America: "Mayor Tom Bradley of Los Angeles inaugurated the conference, and President Ronald Reagan of U.S.A., Pujya Swami Chinmayanandjee Maharaja and President of Vishva Hindu Parishad, India, Maharana of Mewar sent messages" (8). It also records a passage from the conference's valedictory speech by Swami Tilak who reminded the audience that they must go on struggling and they must observe their dharma. The Swami also warned that miracles and mystery are not reasons to follow dharma. Vedanta is not for the "passive man." It is the means to attain a "peaceful mind in a strong body." He concluded with a summation of the VHP's interpretation of the personal and social mission of Hinduism: "Unlike capitalism where the individual exploits society, or socialism, where the State exploits the individual, Hinduism believes that everything belongs to God and no one may exploit any one. However, action is the need of the hour. Do not count on possession of anything. We must create the necessary self-confidence and self-reliance to achieve this goal" (8). Through its repudiation of capitalism and socialism, the VHP suggests the moral supremacy of Hinduism, of Hindus, and of India.

The personnel listed as constituting the VHP's formal organizational structure consists of sixteen patrons, fifteen life trustees, forty-five ordinary trustees, and twenty overseas trustees. The Governing Council consists of twenty-four office holders (*HARP*, 23–27). Industrialists and jurists, maharanas and maharanis, swamis and pandits figure among the names listed for these high-ranking VHP officials. The VHP counts among its achievements the fact that "many Hindus belonging to various political parties have increasingly started identifying themselves as Hindus and in many cases have joined the Parishad" (*MA*, 2). In addition to this success, the VHP also asserts that "Government Servants, Officers of High Rank, High

Court Judges, Industrialists, Businessmen, Educationists and Intellectuals are joining us everyday to promote the unity of the vast Hindu Nation" (2).

In a section called "Glimpses of Vishva Hindu Parishad Activities," the VHP documents with twenty pages of photographs the involvement of important public figures in its activities (*HARP*). With the caption, "The underlying Hindu spirit surfaced and Hindu politicians also adorned the dias," a photo shows the Governors of Uttar Pradesh, West Bengal, and Bihar sitting with the Prime Minster of Nepal on stage at a VHP conference. Another photo shows two of the VHP's "architects of Hindu unity," S. S. Apte, the first general secretary, "discussing problems of Hindu Society" with Justice R. P. Mukherjee, the first working president. "Philanthropist-industrialist" Jaidayal Dalmia is pictured with Sant Prabhudutt Brahmachari; they are described as "two veterans of Hindu cause." Standing before a VHP banner that has an aum in its center, A. P. Divan, chief justice of the Gujarat High Court, addresses a VHP district conference in Gujarat. A photo of a "massive" Jan Jagaran meeting in Poona shows V. R. Thorat, a "Congress (I) leader," addressing the crowd.

The VHP involves religious leaders in its activities by appointing them as patrons and trustees. Religious leaders also constitute the VHP's Central Margdarshak Mandal (Advisory Committee), which consists of thirty-nine (later expanded to 200) "Acharyas of several sects who will conduct and guide the religious, moral and ethical functions of Hindu Society" (*HARP*, 28). Like the VHP's assembly of religious authorities which formulated the "minimum code of conduct for every Hindu," the Mandal also makes pronouncements on Hindu dharma (*MA*, 8).

Mandal members along with other VHP officials attend the VHP's many conferences and preach to assemblies. Through state level Mandals the VHP involves regional and local religious leaders and their followings in its activities. Members of these Mandals are also delegated the responsibility of implementing the policies of the Dharma Sansad (7). Along with photos of public officials appearing on stage at VHP gatherings, "Glimpses of Vishva Hindu Parishad Activities" includes numerous photos of prominent religious personages. At these public events, they are given the seats of honor; their high status is affirmed by the deferential behavior of lay dignitaries.

In order to further involve leaders of religious sects in its activities, the VHP established a Dharma Sansad (Parliament of Religion). In its description of the purpose of the Dharma Sansad, the VHP relates it to "Sadhu Shakti [Ascetic Power], a mobile thought Bank" that was a "perennial source of strength to millions" (*HARP*, 30). Through the Dharma Sansad, the VHP hopes to "revive the tradition of Sadhu Shakti" and make it "play a greater role in nation building activities." Members of the Dharma Sansad meet regularly to deliberate on issues of "public importance in religious and social fields." The VHP considers the Dharma Sansad to be an important means for strengthening Sadhu Shakti and for "increasing the traditional strength of Dharma." The Sansad also convenes periodic Sadhu Sammelans during which VHP and monastic leaders discuss current VHP campaigns and solicit support from the thousands of assembled sadhus.

The VHP also sponsors a program whereby sixteen districts in India are "adopted" by fourteen religious leaders and two industrialists. The "targets" in adopted districts replicate the VHP's program of social reform and uplift of weaker sections discussed above. Through this program, the VHP encourages leading members to operate in specific areas as extensively as the local conditions and their means allow. The VHP further articulates its aggressively expansionist policy, which requires ever more personnel and resources, as responding to the need to strengthen Hindu society so that it can defend itself against attacks. The texts of both the *Hindu Awakening: Retrospect and Promise* and *Vishva Hindu Parishad: Messages and Activities* conclude with "An Appeal." Hindu society is "under attack from several quarters." It is no longer sufficient to merely be a Hindu by birth: "one has to be a conscious and convinced Hindu to meet and survive that attack" (*MA*, 11). The VHP has "taken up this heavy task" of removing the problems which have accumulated over the ages (*HARP*, 46).

Their removal is necessary for strengthening Hindu society to "face the modern world" and to "hold up India's head as one of the leading nations of the world" (46). The VHP works to create a common platform for organizations to come together "and mobilise their resources for the renaissance and consolidation of Hindu society" (*MA*, 11). To meet this "great challenge" the VHP stresses the need for a "large band of dedicated workers" and for "material and monetary support" (*HARP*, 46). Contributions have been "heartening." However, the VHP reminds readers that the "need is ever growing": "The Vishva Hindu Parishad appeals to all our Hindu brethren to join the organisation in large numbers and give it every support in thought and action; in men and money" (46).

RITUALIZING NATIONALISM: THE VHP'S SACRIFICE FOR UNITY

The escalation of the VHP's activities throughout India intensified in 1983 when it mounted the Sacrifice for Unity (Ekatmata Yajna). "Ekatmata" connotes identity or oneness of the group as opposed to individuality (Sanskaran 1981, 307). The Sacrifice might also be understood as the VHP's attempt to achieve for itself and for its reigning president, Maharana Bhagwat Singh Mewar, the status as the nation's chakravartin: Bharat's preeminent protector and promoter of Hindu dharma. In the following discussion, I examine the Sacrifice as a strategy—refined for subsequent VHP campaigns—to publicize its ideology of Hindu nationalism through popular symbolic and ritual forms. I also investigate how mass participation in the Sacrifice extended the VHP's reputation, infrastructure, and field of operations throughout India. Materials for this discussion are drawn from the VHP's 160 page book, *Ekatmata Yajna (EY)*, and supplemented by van der Veer's analysis (1994). Except for a two-page English summary of the Sacrifice (13–14), the text of *Ekatmata Yajna* is in highly Sanskritic Hindi (see plate 13).

Lasting over one month, the Sacrifice consisted of processions, rituals, and rallies which were held throughout India and in Nepal. The Sacrifice extended to an all-India level publicity techniques the VHP developed through its Gnana Ratham project in Tamil Nadu. Unlike the more local Tamil deity worshipped during the Gnana Ratham procession, the Sacrifice raths carried shrines which allowed participants to have darshan of and worship the pan-Indian goddesses Bharat Mata and Ganga Mata. Van der Veer notes that the Sacrifice used broad and noncontroversial Hindu symbols to maximize participation and minimize the potential for conflict among different sects and doctrines (1994). Bearing a statue of Bharat Mata and an enormous ritual pot filled with the sacred water of Ganga Mata, the raths symbolize the promise of power and auspicious abundance associated with the mother goddess. Besides her benevolent attributes, the mother goddess also embodies furious and destructive powers in her form as Durga and Kali. The chariot or rath itself bears martial connotations and symbolizes the VHP's "sacred book," the *Bhagavad Gita*.

The Sacrifice procession *(yatra)* involved the movement of three principal raths along pilgrimage routes through India. One route went from the Pashupatinath temple in Kathmandu to Rameshwaram in Tamil Nadu, and another went from Ganga Sagar in West Bengal to the Somnath temple in Gujarat. The third route, which will be the focus of this discussion, began in Hardwar, proceeded to Delhi, and terminated at the tip of India in Kanyakumari. About mid-point in their journeys the three main yatras met in Nagpur, headquarters of the RSS. As part of the proceedings in Nagpur, RSS leader Deoras publicly honored the manufacturer of the statues of Bharat Mata and the giant ritual pots mounted on the raths. In addition to these principal yatras, the Sacrifice also included three hundred smaller, regional yatras. Like tributaries to the river Ganges, these yatras added to the volume of participants in the main yatras.

The VHP maintains that over sixty million people participated in the Sacrifice. Of *Ekatmata Yajna*'s over one hundred photographs, about half show scenes of huge crowds. The reader sees photos of people, especially women and girls, carrying ritual water pots on their heads. Many of the pots are decorated with flowers and a large aum. Other photos show VHP volunteers restraining crowds which are pushing towards the raths to view Bharat Mata and to receive prasad. Like government travel brochures and Festivals of India, the VHP too presents the official version of tribal culture which celebrates its festive vitality. Several photos show the raths being welcomed by dancing tribals.[6]

In their statements about the Sacrifice, VHP officials and supporters repeatedly assert that the sole purpose of the Sacrifice is the promotion of national unity or integration. They insist that the Sacrifice has no relation to politics. Although there are references to opposition from some Congress politicians, they maintain that such opposition could not deter Bharat Mata's devotees from participating in the Sacrifice and making it a "success beyond all expectation." A full-page color photo shows VHP officials meeting with Indian president Zail Singh. They also met with the home minister. Both the president and the home minister are said to have been very interested in the Sacrifice and supported its goal of national integration. In addition to the "grace of God, blessings of Saints and cooperation of the public," the success of the Sacrifice is attributed to the "full cooperation" of the government and bureaucracy (*EY*, 13–14).

Ekatmata Yajna reports that at many places district magistrates and high-ranking police officials presided over Sacrifice ceremonies. The deputy chief minister of Manipur was the chief guest at Sacrifice functions in Imphal. In Uttar Pradesh a district magistrate lifted curfew for six hours so that people could participate in the Sacrifice; this official and his wife led the worship of Bharat Mata and Ganga Mata. The VHP's desire to remind readers that it receives the support from the highest quarters is suggested in

6. Another example of how tribal groups have been recruited to participate in Hindu yajnas is reported by *India Today* in "The Tribal Godman," an article about guru Biharidas and his activities among "the superstitious and simple minded tribals of Bastar" (30 June 1987). Claiming to be the reincarnation of the "legendary and popular" maharaja of Bastar who was killed by police in 1966, Biharidas is the institutional big man of the region: "he has emerged as the single most significant force in the tribal heartland of Madhya Pradesh." The article reports on a three-day yajna held at his ashram which attracted about 20,000 tribals from Bastar district and from nearby areas of Orissa and Maharashtra. The chief minister of Madhya Pradesh was scheduled to attend but did not. However, "at least half-a-dozen MLAs and an MP of the ruling Congress (I) Party showed up to the occasion to support Baba Biharidas's efforts for national integration through the yagna." He is said to have charged one-hundred rupees from each yajna participant: "it is a business that is rapidly becoming an industry with powerful political overtones." The article discusses the complicated affairs of Biharidas: his links with the Congress (I) Party; raids on his ashram by the Income Tax Department to claim arrears in taxes; and court battles concerning his ashram's alleged encroachment on government land. In their drive to "expose" Biharidas, government officials "traced his antecedents to a Harijan family in Orissa and discovered a deserted wife in the village" and published these findings in pamphlet written in a tribal dialect. Undeterred by these charges, his followers continue "gazing at him with awe and child-like devotion. 'When these people come to me for help, how can I deny them?' asks the baba" (*India Today*, 30 June 1987).

its report of the following incident. When a deputy commissioner attempted to halt the yatra's progress through a district in Assam, the "foresight of the Home Secretary" countermanded the local official's order and
permitted the yatra to proceed.

In terms similar to those used by the Gayatri Parivar discussed in chapter 2, the Sacrifice for Unity is described as a sacrifice in the "Vedic sense":
"through its medium, young and old, male and female, all of them forget-
ting their own identities and differences gathered for Archan and Pujan of
Bharat Mata and Holy Ganga Mata" (13). Participants do not simply
forget their identities and differences. The Sacrifice explicitly fashions them
according to the VHP's ideology of Hindu cultural and political identity
and instructs people in the appropriate expression of this identity. Addressing an audience gathered at opening ceremonies in Hardwar, VHP president Maharana Bhagwat Singh Mewar explained that the Sacrifice's
purpose is to instill the feeling of unity and devotion to the nation (19).

The construction of this Hindu identity draws on the idiom used in
past and present nationalist discourses, which figures the processes of liberating and consolidating the nation in terms of religious and particularly
vedic sacrifice (yajna). A sacrifice is performed with a particular goal in
mind, e.g., to conquer enemies, to have a son, to give thanks, to earn a favorable rebirth or a long, heavenly respite before being reborn. While the
sacrifice of freedom fighters is commonly figured as earning the boon of
political liberation, the VHP asserts that the purpose of the Sacrifice is to
restore the unity of Bharat and to earn the honor of being called the prog-
eny of Ganga Mata and Bharat Mata (4). The VHP regards this Sacrifice as
perpetuating an ancient Hindu tradition and claims that it is the first occasion since the time of King Yudhishthira, leader of the Pandavas in the *Mahabharata,* that such a sacrifice has been performed. The Vedas are said to
teach that sacrifice should be at the center of life. Sacrifice yields the best
and purest things in life; it ensures not merely the welfare of individual participants but also the welfare of society (8). Through sacrifice both the individual and the society affirm their Hindu identity.

The Hindu identity promoted by the VHP relates to its platform on
social reform and transformation. The VHP's report describes the tens of
millions of Sacrifice participants as Hindu brethren. They belong to different sects and have different customs but all share the same "pure attitude"
which maintains that "we are one. Our happiness and sufferings are one.
There is no inequality, no untouchability, no reservations, no high and
low" (4). Sanatanis, Arya Samajis, Jains, Buddhists, and Sikhs are likened
to the five Pandava brothers: they are Hindu brethren. Untouchables and
tribals, Muslims and Christians are also embraced as Hindu brethren. The
report notes that in many places "Christian and Muslim friends" participated in the Sacrifice and "proved that irrespective of their mode of worship

all of them are Hindus culturally and nationally" (13). According to the VHP, whoever cooperated with the Yatra attested to their essential Hindu identity: "whether Vanavasi or Girivasi, Communist or Congressite all of them as Hindus gave full cooperation to the Yatras."

The text gives numerous examples of incidents to substantiate the existence of this Hindu cultural and national identity. A government minister in Orissa, whose name—Haribullah Khan—is invoked to signify that he is Muslim, was "so much overwhelmed by emotion" upon seeing the Bharat Mata and Ganga Mata raths that he offered flowers and fifty-one rupees. The Sirajuddin Seva Samiti, a Muslim organization in Bihar, assisted in Sacrifice preparations and "Muslims of Prayag did not lag behind." In Bombay girls from Muslim College participated, and in Kerala a "Christian professor felt pride in declaring that 'Panths [paths or sects] may be different but Dharma is one' and that originally all of them were Hindus."

The Sacrifice was widely publicized through the media. *Ekatmata Yajna* mentions that over 150 press conferences were held before and during the Sacrifice. On its first day alone, national radio and television made fourteen announcements concerning the Sacrifice. An article from *India Today* is cited for reporting that politicians could learn a lesson from the VHP's Sacrifice: in Gorakhpur a high-caste Thakur woman and an untouchable woman worshipped "side by side." Elsewhere a sweeper and a member of a "so called backward community" were selected to perform special rituals.

Through the Sacrifice, the VHP furthered many of its projects, particularly popularizing the worship of Bharat Mata, a goddess central to the cult of Hindu nationalists. The VHP welcomed all to spend their time and money on the rituals of Hindu nationalism that it promotes. In the field of Dharma, all are equal: "all worshippers are one and the same in His eyes" (13). The VHP resolutely denies that it has a political agenda and readily acknowledges social distinctions when targeting groups for uplift and rehabilitation. However, it maintains that "the seeming differences between so called high caste and low caste Hindus are the creation of contemporary politics."

Like other political and religious organizations striving to expand their popularity and authority, the VHP presents its credentials as an organization concerned with the needy masses: "The VHP is a dedicated organization for serving the masses. This is its strength and inspiration. The VHP bows to the masses" (8). Poverty and the masses are closely linked in political discourses on Indian society. To demonstrate its status as Bharat's preeminent protector of Hindu dharma, the VHP must express a paternal concern for the poor. In his statement about the Sacrifice, VHP official Ashok Singhal refers to the organization's interest in India's impoverished masses. His discussion of poverty opens with a quote from Vivekananda:

"If your neighbor is hungry and unclothed, your life is worthless" (9). Singhal asserts that sixty percent of India's population is poor. In such circumstances "social unity" is impossible to achieve. Hence the VHP works to ameliorate the conditions of the impoverished masses by going to slums, villages, and remote places. Its projects help the poor and downtrodden to "stand on their own feet" (9). Here as elsewhere, the VHP castigates "class conflict" as unnecessary and detrimental to social unity. The VHP attributes the Sacrifice's success to the ability of its leaders to mobilize the support of diverse religious groups and of the rich and poor:

> Whereas on the one hand to make the Yajna a success the Parishad President Adaraniya Shri Maharana Bhagwat Singh Mewar was making all out efforts, on the other hand the whole hearted co-operation and blessings were available of Jagadguru Shankaracharya Pujya Shantanandji Maharaj, Pujya Swami Chinmayandandji Maharaj, Pujya Kanchi Kamkoti Shankaracharya, Jain Munis, Boudh Bhikshus, Sikh Saints, Kabir Panthi Mahant, Mahamandaleshwars and other Dharmacharyas. The weak and downtrodden depressed classes and the industrialists all had shown their keenness to make their bit of contribution in this Dharma Yajna. In reality it was a Yajna in which all had joined with a spirit of dedication and oneness. (14)

Although the VHP advocates equal social and ritual status for all Hindus, Singhal asserts that it is impossible to abolish the differences between the rich and poor (10). It is possible, however, to feed and clothe the poor. Singhal relates poverty to the intensely politicized issue of conversion. Poverty renders the weaker sections of Hindu society vulnerable to the "foreign powers of Islam and Christianity." With their greater economic resources, these foreign powers threaten to break up Hindu society (10). Through the Sacrifice, the VHP aims to "create the feeling of brotherhood necessary for social welfare." Singhal considers economic solutions as central for resolving social problems. The VHP promises to provide solutions to such problems with its charitable activities. Hence, Singhal closes his assessment of the poverty problem by soliciting funds for the VHP: "In our society sacrifice is very important, but after the sacrifice one must make a donation." Elsewhere an example of a generous donor is given: the priest in Somnath who was assigned the prestigious duty of performing the final ceremonies donated 10,001 rupees to the VHP. The pageantry of these Somnath ceremonies is illustrated with a color drawing on the back cover of *Ekatmata Yajna*. While Shiva was being worshipped inside, flowers were being showered down upon the Somnath temple from a hovering helicopter.

Islam and Christianity are used to signify threats to the unity of Hindu society and the Indian nation. The VHP's projects and activities are presented as the necessary defense against these threats. References to the participation of foreign countries in the Sacrifice connote India's status as the origin and hub of Hindu culture and religion. The VHP expresses its ambition to make India a Hindu state by honoring the King and Queen of Nepal as rulers of a Hindu state. The rath that set out on its 5,500 kilometer route from Kathmandu after rituals performed by the king and queen carried a sign with a portrait of the king. It read, "I Want to Keep Nepal an Ideal Land of Hindus." The king and his supporters were not merely passively coopted by the VHP. They too used the Sacrifice to further their own political purposes both within Nepal and abroad.

Besides the Nepali participation in the Sacrifice, delegations from Burma and Bhutan joined the rath yatra in Calcutta. The VHP describes this participation as demonstrating that the three countries "may be politically separate from Bharat but the cultural soul of all these countries is one within" (13). Like tribute to an imperial capital, water from rivers considered sacred by Hindus in Mauritius, Pakistan, and Bangladesh as well as Lake Manasrovar in Tibet were brought to the Sacrifice in Delhi.

By staging the Sacrifice in Delhi at India Gate, the VHP occupied the epicenter of the national capital for one day. The VHP recounts the heroic efforts necessary for organizing the event. Preparations began four months in advance. Despite all the cooperation the VHP claimed to have received, the government did not give formal permission to hold the Sacrifice in Delhi until just before the date. Hence VHP workers labored "night and day" to construct the stage and prepare for the Sacrifice. The event included the convergence at India Gate of the main yatra from Hardwar with 261 local yatras. The VHP thanked leaders of Delhi's large and small temples, maths, and Sikh gurudwaras for publicizing the Sacrifice and encouraging people to attend.

A crowd of 200,000 people is said to have gathered on the grounds adjacent to India Gate, where 125 shrines with pots of Ganges water were set up to enable people to worship Ganga Mata. Hindus widely believe that the sanctity of Ganges water makes it a potent and desirable possession. Representatives of 2,100 religious establishments brought pots to be filled with Ganges water; it was also "distributed" to 35,000 people. The Sacrifice filled the coffers of the VHP not only with the donations incumbent upon Sacrifice participants but also through mass sales of small pots of Ganges water.[7]

After the rituals were performed at this Delhi rally, VHP and religious leaders delivered speeches from a twelve-foot-high stage adorned with a

---

7. Biharidas, the "tribal godman" discussed above, also capitalizes on popular belief in the efficacy of sacred water. He is said to have "invented ingenious methods for making money. Once, he earned lakhs of rupees by selling water from a nearby nullah [tap] as holy water" (*India Today*, 30 June 1987).

huge backdrop of Bharat Mata, Ganga Mata, and the ritual water pot. VHP officials repeated the claim that the Sacrifice had no political purpose and that the VHP has no connection with politics. Religious leaders representing Jain, Sikh, Buddhist, Sanatani, and Arya Samaji groups "gave blessings for the success of the Yajna." They praised the "holy work" of the Yajna from which would come the "organization and unity of Hindu society," or in Savarkar's words, Hindu Sangathan (85).

LAUNCHING THE SACRIFICE FOR UNITY FROM HARDWAR

Through its text and photos, maps and statistics, the *Ekatmata Yajna* documents state by state the progress of the raths throughout India. Besides the crowd, the principal characters parading throughout the text are VHP officials and prominent leaders of religious sects. Indeed, the ubiquity of religious leaders in Sacrifice events further indicates their importance to the structure of the VHP. Not only are they VHP ideologues and publicists but also they embody its claim to represent the unity and totality of Hindu society. The VHP notes that over 50,000 sadhus gathered at assemblies of the Sadhu Samaj and the Akharda Council of Uttarkhand held in Hardwar to make arrangements for the Sacrifice.

Processions set out from pilgrimage places high in the Himalayas and converged in Hardwar, the starting point for one of the three main routes. An examination of the Sacrifice for Unity ceremonies in Hardwar suggests how the VHP uses popular lore of Hardwar for embroidering the Sacrifice with emotive religious and cultural significations. The ceremonies commenced in Hardwar at dawn, the time that the VHP prescribes for all Hindus to worship their shared god, the sun. At this initial ceremony VHP president Maharana Bhagwat Singh Mewar filled the enormous ritual pot with Ganges water from Brahma Kund, a famous bathing site in Hardwar. Next came the blessing of the rath yatra with rituals at the Daksha temple. The text reports that "it appeared as if Daksha Prajapati was atoning for his previous sin" when waters brought from Himalayan shrines were used by the priest of Daksha mandir to worship Shiva and bless the raths (13). Readers are reminded that this ritual was performed at the site where Sati killed herself because her father Daksha refused to invite her husband Shiva to his sacrifice.

After these ceremonies, ascetic orders and religious leaders along with "thousands of their devotees" formed a procession three kilometers long. It brought them from Daksha temple to Har-ki-Pairi, Hardwar's most renowned spot for bathing and evening worship of Ganga Mata. At Har-ki-Pairi VHP officials joined religious leaders to perform a vedic fire sacrifice. The ceremony is commemorated with a color photo of men adorned with ritual regalia sitting around a sacrificial fire; wives of lay participants sit behind the men.

When the sacrifice was completed and afternoon was darkening, a "special Ganga arti" was performed. A large color photo of a priest holding a lamp with leaping flames records the VHP's performance of this popular Hardwar ritual. The text notes that the former mayor of Delhi participated in the Sacrifice and evening arti along with religious leaders and VHP and RSS officials. Furthermore, despite the fact that just the previous day the Congress plastered Hardwar with posters opposing the Sacrifice, the Uttar Pradesh Congress government deputed a former minister to attend the ceremonies.

The following day Swami Satyamitranand Giri, a prominent member of the VHP and founder of Hardwar's Bharat Mata temple, presided over Sacrifice ceremonies. He performed puja of the Bharat Mata and Ganga Mata raths before they set out on their six week yatra to Kanyakumari at the southern tip of India. A profile of the career of Swami Satyamitranand and a discussion of the Bharat Mata temple are the focus the next two chapters. They address Swami Satyamitranand's involvement with the VHP and how his eight-story Bharat Mata temple monumentally consecrates and publicizes the tenets of Hindu nationalism.

Through the Sacrifice the VHP extended its organizational apparatus and strengthened its structure for mounting future local, regional, and national campaigns. The VHP considered the conclusion of the Sacrifice as a new beginning: it resolved to keep aflame the spirit of unity with further programs and projects. Such projects include the celebration of an annual Unity month throughout India, the establishment of Centres of Awakening, and the construction of a World Hindu Brotherhood Centre in Delhi. Through these and other projects the VHP capitalized on the monetary, institutional, and symbolic profits it earned as organizer and patron of the Sacrifice for Unity. These profits and projects enabled the VHP to more aggressively and effectively mobilize people and resources for the takeover of the Babri mosque and the construction of a Ram Janmabhoomi temple in Ayodhya.

FIVE

Swami Satyamitranand: VHP Leader and Founder of Hardwar's Bharat Mata Temple

Religious leaders with establishments in Hardwar and in nearby Rishikesh hold important positions within the VHP. Of the thirty-nine members of the Central Margdarshak Mandal, the VHP's council of religious leaders, four have their headquarters in Hardwar and Rishikesh. Many other members have ashrams and temples in these pilgrimage centers. Swami Satyamitranand Giri is a member of the VHP's council of religious leaders and the founder of the Bharat Mata temple in Hardwar. Satyamitranand's name and photograph can be found on numerous pages of the VHP literature discussed in the previous chapter. Along with the Dalai Lama, three Shankaracharyas, and two ex-vice chancellors of Benares Hindu University, the VHP names Satyamitranand as one who supported "the idea of the world Hindu forum," i.e., the formation of the VHP (*The Hindu Awakening: Retrospect and Promise [HARP]*, 7–8). In its other information booklet, *Vishva Hindu Parishad: Messages and Activities (MA)*, Satyamitranand's name appears on the first page with the names of ten other founders of the VHP. He is also a trustee of the VHP and a member of its Council of Religion (Dharma Sansad), which is noted as having held one of its meetings in Hardwar.

Like thirteen other religious leaders and two industrialists, Satyamitranand has "adopted" a district. His district is Ajmer, Rajasthan; adoption involves establishing institutions that support VHP goals and distributing patronage. The purpose of these institutions is "upliftment" of backward sections, promotion of Sanskrit, banning of cow slaughter, renovation of temples, and construction of schools. Foremost among the duties of those who adopt districts is to stop the conversion of Hindus to "alien faiths" and "to integrate those returning to their ancestral faith" (*HARP*, 37). In a discussion entitled "Bridging the Gap," Satyamitranand's name appears once again. The text refers to events sponsored by the VHP which "strengthen the bonds of oneness" among Hindus. Satyamitranand is also mentioned as having participated in an assembly of VHP leaders which passed a resolution condemning untouchability; later members of the assembly visited "Harijan [untouchable] Localities under the inspiring leadership of Pujya Swami Satyamitranandji" (*MA*, 6). Among the photos in "Glimpses of Vishva Hindu Parishad Activities" is one of Satyamitranand. Justice H. Mahapatra, central vice president of the VHP, is shown "presenting an art piece" to Satyamitranand. With a stern expression he accepts "a humble present to a great Swami."

When I met Satyamitranand at his Hardwar headquarters in November 1987, he told me of his trips around the world to visit his devotees. He also spoke of having resigned his post as Shankaracharya of Bhanpura Math in Madhya Pradesh because it restricted his activities, particularly his travel abroad. I was not given the opportunity to ask the numerous questions I had about his organization, the Bharat Mata temple, and his involvement with the VHP. After a brief exchange Satyamitranand dismissed me, saying that he was busy preparing for another trip abroad. Most of my attempts to engage personnel at his ashram and the Bharat Mata temple in conversation were also rebuffed. One lay disciple who was sitting in the temple early one morning, however, was more talkative. He had come for a long visit to Hardwar from Ahmedabad. His said that he had retired, that his children were grown and settled, and that he only wanted to serve his guru, Satyamitranand. His service entails sitting in the temple for four hours a day: he chants mantras and keeps an eye on visitors. For his services he receives food and accommodation from Satyamitranand's ashram, which is adjacent to the temple. This devotee lamented that even when he came to Hardwar, he rarely had a chance to meet with his guru because Satyamitranand was usually away. Rubbing his fingers together, he said that Satyamitranand often travels to the United States and Canada to raise money for the temple. He explained that Satyamitranand had a particularly strong following among Gujarati Patels in India and overseas. He too pointed out that Satyamitranand had to give up his post as Shankaracharya in order to "do more seva" (religious service).

Before I had learned about Satyamitranand's involvement in the VHP through reading its literature, I had inquired at the local newspaper about the location of the offices of the Hardwar branches of the VHP and the Rashtriya Swayamsevak Sangh (RSS). The editor directed me to Satyamitranand's Bharat Mata temple. Later when visiting the VHP's headquarters in New Delhi, I asked Ashok Singhal, the general secretary, about Satyamitranand and his relation to the VHP. He vaguely replied that Satyamitranand had ties with the organization. Only later, after studying the VHP literature, did I learn just how extensive these ties are. The manager of a small ashram near the Bharat Mata temple told me that when Satyamitranand's links with the RSS had earned him the disfavor of Indira Gandhi's government, he sponsored a big sacrifice in Hardwar during which prominent swamis and politicians spoke approvingly of Indira Gandhi. Later, his relations with Indira Gandhi became even more cordial: in 1983 she attended the ceremonies for the consecration of the Bharat Mata temple.

Satyamitranand has allies and foes in Hardwar and beyond. During the 1986 Kumbh Mela he was allocated a site next to a swami who was a bitter rival. The two are said to have competed fiercely in the attempt to upstage each other. When Satyamitranand procured the most prestigious Ram Lila troupe, his rival had to settle for the second best. Throughout the weeks of Kumbh festivities, their rivalry escalated and their duelling loudspeakers created a deafening noise. Satyamitranand, however, has local allies. For example, while visiting the Hardwar ashram of Santoshi Ma, a young woman guru whose supporters have helped her secure the prestigious title and position in the ecclesiastical hierarchy of mahamandaleshwar, I was shown not only the Durga statue and temple under construction but also a Hindi article about Santoshi Ma. Satyamitranand had written the article. Like a reference for a protégé, it lavished praise upon Santoshi Ma.

When I asked Rajkumar Sharma, Hardwar's leading publicist for its brahman priests and a former Janata Party member of the Uttar Pradesh legislative assembly, about the VHP, he responded by estimating that its assets are worth at least 50 million rupees. He also said that he is a VHP member and knows Ashok Singhal, and added that in July 1988 he attended the VHP's Sadhu Sammelan (Assembly of Ascetics) in Hardwar. Satyamitranand's ashram helped organize the Assembly and housed many of its participants. According to Sharma, the principal issues discussed at this VHP gathering included cow protection, the liberation of Rama's birthplace in Ayodhya, and the conversion of Hindus to Christianity and Islam. He said that in order to counter foreign influences that threaten the culture of Bharat, the Assembly decreed that if Indians regard Rama and Krishna as "national heroes" and touch India's sacred ground three times with their head while saying "Bharat Mata ki Jai" (Hail, Mother India), then they may belong to "any religion."

No one in Hardwar, either at the ashrams or my other contacts, ever volunteered information about the VHP. Only after visiting the New Delhi office and reading through its literature did I become aware of its structure and its linkages with religious establishments throughout India, and begin asking direct questions. Sharma's guided tour of ashrams soon after my arrival in Hardwar, however, may have inadvertently set me on the trail. One of the ashrams that Sharma had brought me to was Sant Mandal, the headquarters of an organization headed by Jagdish Muni, an ascetic belonging to the Udasain sect. Both the woman disciple managing the ashram and Jagdish Muni—when he was not on his frequent tours outside of Hardwar—always found time to talk with me and cordially invited me to the ashram's various special functions. During these celebrations, which often included feasts for sadhus, brahmans, Hardwar notables, and the guru's lay devotees, the audience would join together in boisterous yet pious rounds of "Bharat Mata ki Jai, Ganga Ma ki Jai, Sanatan Dharm ki Jai, Adharm Nash Ho" (Victory to Bharat Mata, Victory to Ganga Ma, Victory to Sanatan Dharm, Destruction to Opponents of Dharma).

Once I stopped by Sant Mandal after a visit to the nearby Bharat Mata temple. When I showed Jagdish Muni the postcard of a sati shrine in the Bharat Mata temple depicting a woman in flames, he smiled. From my tone of voice, he probably detected that the sati shrine had upset me. At that time sati was a particularly charged subject of public debate: the previous month the widely publicized and highly controversial sati of Roop Kanwar had occurred in Rajasthan (Vaid and Sangari 1991; Hawley 1994; Hawley, ed. 1994). Jagdish Muni asserted that sati was part of dharma; it was a form of devoted service to the husband. According to him, women should be permitted—but not forced—to kill themselves after their husband's death. Women who chose sati should be worshipped.

The sight of Jagdish Muni sitting on a stage and preaching to an audience had become familiar, yet I was startled when I saw a photograph of him doing so in the VHP's *Ekatmata Yajna*. The photograph shows him on a stage with a row of laymen sitting one level beneath and in front of him. A VHP banner hangs behind him. The photograph's caption explains that Jagdish Muni is addressing an audience gathered for the Sacrifice for Unity in Naraul, Harayana. Along with two other swamis, Jagdish Muni traveled with the procession through Harayana. The text also records that politicians from the Lok Dal, Congress (I), Akali Dal, and Janata parties joined sectarian leaders in Dharma Sammelans held in fifty places throughout Harayana in conjunction with the Sacrifice. Besides his Sacrifice duties in Harayana, where many of his followers reside, Jagdish Muni was also a member of the Sacrifice reception committee in Roorkee, a town near Hardwar. He joined with VHP officials and other religious leaders in ceremonies at Roorkee's Nehru stadium where, after a fire sacrifice, arti, and speeches, the crowd "took an oath in Sanskrit."

At Jagdish Muni's Hardwar ashram I witnessed several displays of the violence underlying authority and challenges to it. Once some ascetics and pandits severely questioned and then verbally and physically punished the ashram's senior Sanskrit student for his alleged role in attacking an old sadhu living in the neighborhood. On another occasion when both Jagdish Muni and his disciple-deputy Radha Ma were away, the young male ascetic in charge during their absence aggressively flaunted his power. He ordered me out of a chair, which I was normally given to sit in, and onto the floor at his feet. I promptly departed rather than comply with his command. On another occasion my conversation with Radha Ma and Jagdish Muni was interrupted when a local tradesman came to collect payment for materials and labor. Jagdish Muni berated him but the man persisted in making his claim. Finally, peeling a few bills off a large roll, Jagdish Muni threw them on the ground. He continued his verbal abuse while the tradesman bent down to collect the scattered cash. With his wad of bills and his intimidating style, Jagdish Muni is an institutional big man, a cruder and smaller big man than Satyamitranand, whose nearby temple towers over Hardwar.

SATYAMITRANAND: THE DIVINE PILGRIMAGE OF AN ASCETIC

Published materials concerning Satyamitranand are structured by hagiographical and biographical details common in accounts of a guru's life written by devotees. These accounts portray Satyamitranand as a spiritual hero who endured and overcame numerous hardships. They also provide information concerning his family and educational background as well as the processes whereby he attained his position as leader and founder of religious and educational institutions. The following discussion uses materials from a thirty-page Hindi booklet, *Divyalok: Parivrajak ki Divya Yatra* (Chaturvedi and Sharma 1986 [Heaven: The Divine Pilgrimage of an Ascetic]; hereafter *D*), written by Satyamitranand's devotees Brahmajeet Sharma and Krishnakant Chaturvedi, the latter of whom is the head of the Sanskrit Department at the University of Jabalpur in Madhya Pradesh.

The booklet's foreword names the two devotees whose donation funded publication. It was first published in May 1983 for the opening of the Bharat Mata temple. A second edition was published in March 1986, in time for the Kumbh Mela. Other publications used for discussing Satyamitranand's career as a guru and VHP leader include a special issue of a Hindi magazine *Ekatm Saptahik* about the Bharat Mata temple and Satyamitranand, and the section entitled, "A Brief Life Sketch" in the English guidebook to the temple which opens, "It seems frivolous to try to introduce Swamiji: millions of Indians, both in India and overseas, already know him very well and hold him in high esteem and reverence. For almost four decades, he has been continuously striving to raise the quality and dignity of his fellow human beings" (*Bharat Mata Mandir [BMM]* 1986, 21).

With heavy jowls, folded hands, fringed shawl, and tulsi beads, Satyamitranand's photograph fills the cover of *Divyalok*. The preface assures readers that through associating with saints and reading their life stories, man increases his purity and procures residence in *divyalok* (heaven). To help men in this undertaking, Satyamitranand was born in 1932 in the "historic city" of Agra into a noble and religious brahman family which visited ashrams and hosted gurus and swamis at home. As usual in this genre, readers are told that Satyamitranand's greatness was prophesied when he was but a child. Perceiving the boy's luminous *(tejsvi)* qualities, a sadhu declared that Satyamitranand would never be happy as a house-holder. This exceptional boy, predicted the sadhu, would become an ascetic and "serve society."

Shiv Shankar Pandey, Satyamitranand's father, taught in a government school. The father was rewarded for his commitment to teaching by India's famous educator and statesman, Sarvepalli Radhakrishnan: "For his faith, devotion and complete dedication in upholding educational ideals, his con-temporary President Radhakrishnan awarded him presidential honors" (*D*, 4). At the age of six, Satyamitranand was sent away from Agra to attend a village school and live with the teacher. The reader's sympathy for the boy is evoked with references to how much he missed his mother and how his father was unable to send him money. To endure these sufferings he began to visit temples and attend spiritual discourses: "slowly but surely, he was tak-ing his first steps on his spiritual pilgrimage" (5). Satyamitranand was a spiritual and literary prodigy. He went into trances and had visions of God, who comforted him and blessed his spiritual pilgrimage. When he was only eleven, he wrote a devotional poem based on these visions; a Kanpur maga-zine published it and awarded Satyamitranand a prize for being the maga-zine's youngest published poet.

Satyamitranand's ardent devotion to Bharat Mata also began at a young age. While a schoolboy during the years 1942–47, "the whole coun-try was awakened by Mahatma Gandhi, Vir Savarkar and other revolution-aries and influential individuals" (6). This awakening had a profound effect on Satyamitranand and filled him with devotion for his country. Although he was too young to understand all the issues discussed by the leaders, "when people saluted the flag and proclaimed 'Bharat Mata ki Jai,' he went into rapture and with his young voice, he shouted with all his strength 'Bharat Mata ki Jai.' Carrying a small flag, he ran to join in the proces-sions" (6).

When he was older, Satyamitranand was sent to study Sanskrit at a traditional school (gurukul) in Nagpur. Later he attended an Arya Samaj college in Kanpur. As a student in these different educational institutions Satyamitranand would have been exposed to a variety of religious and na-tionalistic idioms and practices that were then current in north and central India. Along with students from all over India, Satyamitranand sat for Hindi and Sanskrit examinations in Allahabad. These examinations were sponsored by the Hindi Literature Conference, which was meeting in con-junction with the Indian National Congress Conference. "Being a natural teacher," Satyamitranand helped other students prepare for the exams. The text notes that Satyamitranand's father was again unable to send him money. *Divyalok* does not detail Satyamitranand's educational qualifications; however, readers of English are informed in a "Brief Life Sketch" that "along with modern education leading to the M.A. degree, he studied our scriptures and continued his regular practice of meditation and self-discipline, in search of the Ultimate Knowledge and Truth. He accomplished the designations of Sahitya Ratna, Shastri, and M.A. but his quest continued" (*BMM,* 19).

IN SEARCH OF THE ULTIMATE KNOWLEDGE AND TRUTH

Despite his protests, Satyamitranand's family continued to pressure him to marry. He recounted to them the story of Ramdas, who did not want to marry and ran away from his family. Later, Satyamitranand too ran away, traveling to pilgrimage places. Having left home, he worried because he felt that he could not return if he was unsuccessful in his spiritual journey. After renunciation, tradition enjoins the sannyasi to never again speak of family members; after Satyamitranand's departure from home, the text has no further references to his family. Following his arrival in Hardwar Satyamitranand spent his days meditating beside Ganga Ma and making the rounds of ashrams and gurus. One day a sadhu stopped to talk with him and suggested that because he was educated, he should go to the Divine Life Society's Sivananda ashram in Rishikesh. There he would be able to serve a guru who could show him the true path. Satyamitranand felt great joy when he met Sivananda. He was told that he could stay and work in the ashram if he wished. But Satyamitranand wanted to devote all his time to his sadhana or spiritual practice. He reasoned that life in the ashram would be too much like being a householder.

Accordingly, he decline Sivananda's offer and headed to Swargashram across the river, where he faced further tribulations. As a new sadhu in the ashram, at mealtime he was sent to the back of the line. Even after waiting in line, he did not receive any food. This harsh treatment disheartened him and he went to Ganga Ma to pray for help. His prayer was answered when suddenly the manager of the nearby Kali Kamaliwali ashram approached him and offered room and board at the ashram.

Satyamitranand then made the arduous pilgrimage to the Himalayan shrine of Badrinath, where he vowed to continue his life as a sadhu. Soon after this he found the guru he was searching for and was initiated by Mahamandaleshwar Vedvyasanand, an ascetic famous in Hardwar and Rishikesh for his austerities. During this next phase of his ascetic life, Satyamitranand's daily routine involved twelve hours of chanting the name of god, four hours of self-reflection, and four hours of performing service for his guru. His dedication and devotion pleased his guru and Satyamitranand took a vow to remain silent for eleven months. Impressed by the young ascetic, a Calcutta merchant donated money to feed him.

After completing his vow, Satyamitranand pilgrimaged from the Himalayas to Kanyakumari for "darshan of Bharat's holy places." During his pilgrimage, he is said to have met and helped many poor people. After returning to Hardwar, his guru ordered him to work on the ashram's monthly Hindi magazine. Later, when asked to become the head of a math in Bhanpura, Madhya Pradesh, the twenty-seven-year-old Satyamitranand initially refused. He wanted to remain near his guru and Ganga Ma. The following year, however, he agreed and in 1960 he was initiated as a sannyasi and as Shankaracharya of Bhanpura math by the Shankaracharya of Jyotirmath at Rishikesh's prestigious Sannyas Ashram. With this initiation Satyamitranand "was installed as a world teacher in the field of dharma" (D, 13).

SATYAMITRANAND THE SHANKARACHARYA

As Shankaracharya of Bhanpura math, a "position of great honour and prestige," Satyamitranand's "many sided personality came into being in the spiritual and social service of humanity" (BMM, 20). Soon after his installation he set out on a tour of Gujarat. Like the press report on Savarkar's tour of Sindh—he came, he saw, he conquered—Divyalok recounts Satyamitranand's impact on a Gujarati village. He arrived unannounced and no one met him at the station. However, the villagers were immediately attracted by the youthful yet distinguished sannyasi. News of this new Bhanpura Shankaracharya spread among villagers "like a jungle on fire." Villagers arranged a big procession, and he stayed for twelve days lecturing to them.

During these lectures, Satyamitranand spoke about the need for a school in the village. Factional disputes had hindered past efforts to build a school. Satyamitranand reprimanded the villagers and encouraged them to work together. He is portrayed as an able fund-raiser. Villagers presented him with 1,500 rupees which he in turn donated for building the school. They then raised another 1,800 rupees for the building fund, and Satyamitranand undertook to raise more money from the surrounding villages. Without any further information about the funds or the school's management, the reader is told that a building was constructed and named after Satyamitranand (D, 13–14).

During this tour of Gujarat, Satyamitranand revealed his powers to remedy both social and individual problems. A childless Mr. Patel requested that Satyamitranand perform a yajna "like in ancient times." He hoped that this ritual might ensure that he become a father. When his wife gave birth after the yajna, Patel acclaimed Satyamitranand a great man (*mahapurush*). Satyamitranand's fame spread quickly among Gujaratis. Patel's younger brother, who lived in Africa, invited Satyamitranand to visit him. In order to maintain the ritual purity incumbent upon him as a brahman shankaracharya, Satyamitranand traveled with a brahman cook. During this first foreign tour he spent three months in East Africa. Initially people were surprised to see such a young man as shankaracharya but soon they were rushing to him for his blessings. Large crowds attended his lectures in Nairobi, where he stayed for three weeks.

During one of his lectures, he recited a couplet which advised India to be on guard against an attack by the Chinese. The text explains that at this time relations between India and China were good. The Indian ambassador reprimanded Satyamitranand for his statement. Two years later when China and India went to war, this same ambassador is said to have apologized to Satyamitranand and declared him to be an accomplished sannyasi whose spiritual powers enable him to foresee the future (15). Thus, the text uses this incident to portray Satyamitranand as one whose spiritual accomplishments give him insight into worldly affairs and authority to make pronouncements on them.

When Satyamitranand returned to India, he traveled to Rajasthan, where he met with old and new devotees. He even attracted the attention of the chief minister of Rajasthan and the maharaja of Jhalawar, who both came to hear him preach. The chief minister was so impressed that after the lecture he asked if he could be of service to Satyamitranand. The sannyasi "wanted nothing for himself" but suggested that the government might donate land for a religious school or gurukul. The chief minister complied by ordering the government to donate sixty-eight acres of land for the school. The account concludes that Satyamitranand's inspiration and initiative was responsible for the establishment of the school. As in the case of the village school in Gujarat, Satyamitranand is portrayed as a heroic prime mover.

To establish Satyamitranand's credentials as a noncommunalist Hindu leader, the text introduces a Muslim devotee. While touring in Rajasthan, a Muslim man approached Satyamitranand and told him that children were suffering because there was no school bus. Satyamitranand replied that he had several buses and that he would donate one to the school. Thanking him for his generosity, the Muslim said, "I am a devotee of Swamiji and am deeply influenced by his message that teaches respect for all religions" (16).

Satyamitranand's appearances at important religious conferences as well as his tours "awakened the desire" in the people of Madhya Pradesh, Gujarat, Rajasthan, and Uttar Pradesh to see and listen to him. If as a boy Satyamitranand ran to join processions in support of Indian independence, the text intimates that Satyamitranand earned for himself the status of a great nationalist. Processions now honored him. When he visited Bardoli in Gujarat—noted as a place where the conservative Hindu stalwart and Congress leader Sadar Vallabhbhai Patel had been active—Satyamitranand was seated in the same vehicle that had taken Subash Chandra Bose on a procession. The chairman of the municipal committee counted Satyamitranand with Subash Chandra Bose and Mahatma Gandhi as the three great men who had visited Bardoli. He said that Satyamitranand harmonized the ethics and purity of Mahatma Gandhi with the fiery brilliance of Subhash Chandra Bose. As in the VHP literature, references to the Mahatma connote work for the spiritual and material welfare of the nation. References to Bose, like those to Savarkar, connote militant nationalism.

During the years 1965–68, Satyamitranand continued to tour in India and abroad. Like a marketing report charting his successes, the text says he traveled to eight countries on this second foreign tour. During his visit to Mauritius, he was received by the prime minister and appeared on television. By 1986 Satyamitranand had lectured to followers in "over forty countries in Asia, Africa, Europe, N. America and the Far East. He eloquently interprets the teachings of ancient vedic scriptures, to propagate the sacred ideals of Sanatan Dharma, and instills in us Bhakti devotion that bestows mental peace, serenity and sublimity to us" (BMM, 20).

RELINQUISHING A LIFE OF SPIRITUAL PRESTIGE AND PROMINENCE

Satyamitranand's successes abroad were not entirely well received in India. After his return from the first foreign tour, he went to a yajna but the sadhu organizing it ordered him to leave. Because Satyamitranand had been overseas, the sadhu maintained that his participation would pollute the yajna and render it unacceptable to the gods. This incident is used to introduce Satyamitranand's decision to resign his post as Shankaracharya. It can also be read as an example of how religious leaders use ritual to publicly express rivalry and conflicts. The official account of the resignation, however, relates it to Satyamitranand's commitment to serve humanity:

> Swamiji is one of those rare souls who has relinquished a life of spiritual prestige and prominence by resigning from his Gadi [throne] as Jagatguru Shankaracharya. In doing this he has opted to follow his inner calling to serve the needy and suffering of all faiths both in the East and West. Through untiring and selfless efforts, he has established permanent assets like Samanvaya Seva Trust, Samanvaya Kutir ashram, and Bharat Mata Mandir at Haridwar and Samanvaya Parivar in many parts of the world. (BMM, 20–21)

Although Satyamitranand resigned his position in June 1969, he did not lose the supporters he had gathered around him during his nine years as

Shankaracharya. *Divyalok* notes that, although many of his disciples and devotees did not want him to give up his high position, they remained his loyal followers after he did so.

The year after his resignation as the head of Bhanpura math, Satyamitranand participated in the founding of the VHP. His service to the VHP and attendance at its gatherings are said to have contributed to the success of the nascent organization (D, 18–19). At this time Satyamitranand also lectured at various universities and schools, particularly in Jaipur, Jodhpur, Ahmedabad, and Gwalior: "Wherever Swamiji went, groups of young students gathered around him. His lectures had great influence on the students" (19). By preaching to students, Satyamitranand was strengthening the foundation of the VHP in these cities.

Passages referring to students emphasize Satyamitranand's popularity among youth. Repeated name-dropping emphasizes his close contacts with VVIPs. In 1969 Satyamitranand visited England. The next sentence informs readers that India's ambassador to England, Jivraj Mehta, and his wife Hansaben Mehta, former vice-chancellor of Baroda University, were working with "great love and devotion to advance Satyamitranand's work" (19). The London branch of the Bharatiya Vidya Bhavan organized a formal reception for Satyamitranand. From England he traveled to Germany, France, Switzerland, and other countries to acquaint people with the "true form" of Hindu life. Immediately following this account of his 1969 European tour, readers are told that Satyamitranand traveled through Asia in 1973. He visited Japan, Thailand, Malaysia, Singapore, the Philippines, and other countries. He lectured for thirteen days in Hong Kong. When he arrived in the Philippines only one person greeted him at the airport. However, by the time he departed thousands of devotees bade him farewell. In Thailand he lectured on the "holy life of Rama." Readers are assured that as a result of this tour Satyamitranand's influence spread among many more "important people" (19).

Satyamitranand's next triumph was at the Maidan in Bombay, where pivotal rallies of the independence movement had taken place. The first day's turnout was disappointing, but by the second day newspapers had publicized his visit and more people came to hear him. On subsequent visits to Bombay more and more people gathered for Satyamitranand's lectures. In 1982 organizers of the annual event in conjunction with the National Book Trust began to sell audio cassettes of these lectures (19–20).

References to the Meenakshipuram conversions of untouchables to Islam and the VHP's Hindu homecoming (paravartan) movement introduce the passage extolling Satyamitranand's "very great revolutionary work" against untouchability (20). Resignation from the post of Shankaracharya brought an easing of strictures regarding ritual purity, and Satyamitranand is said to have become a "universal mahatma." In this new capacity he led a procession of 5,000 people to a slum of untouchables in Jodhpur. When he reached the slum, women were cleaning the streets for him with the ends of their saris. He tried to stop them, but they persisted, saying that it was the first time a saint had come to visit them. One woman performed arti before Satyamitranand and asked if she might also perform *rakshabandhan* to bind him to her as a brotherly protector. He replied that as a sannyasi he is bound to everyone. However, he let her perform the ritual, promised to share in the joys and sufferings of this woman and her family, and then left the untouchables' slum (20–21).

As in the passages concerning his visits with villagers and tribals, Satyamitranand is depicted as the saintly benefactor of untouchables. Wherever he went he spoke against untouchability: it was his "mantra for awakening the Hindu people" (21). At a Virat Hindu Sammelan organized by Karan Singh, heir to the defunct throne of Kashmir, Satyamitranand addressed a crowd of one million people in New Delhi. His success was such that after this appearance, he was in even greater demand. Organizers of other Hindu rallies invited him to speak at their gatherings. On these occasions, Satyamitranand reminded Hindus that they should honor and feel pride for their religion but they should not despise any other god or religion.

Vivekananda is said to have inspired not only Satyamitranand's religious teachings but also his decision to establish his own organization, formally named the Samanvaya Parivar (Family of Harmony). The stated aim of the organization is to promote Bharatiya culture within India and abroad. The Samanvaya Parivar emphasizes religious aspects of Bharatiya culture; its branches sponsor Hindu rituals as well as discourses on the *Gita* and the *Ramayana* (22). The Samanvaya Parivar also stresses service to the poor and needy and calls such service a form of worship that pleases god. This definition of service complements the ideology of the VHP and provides a rationale for recruiting workers and funds for projects which purportedly "uplift the weaker sections" of Hindu society.

Branches of the Samanvaya Parivar were established in places where Satyamitranand already had toured as Shankaracharya and later as a VHP leader. His ashram in Hardwar became the Samanvaya Parivar's headquarters. Followers in London, Thailand, Nairobi, Canada, Mauritius, and other foreign countries quickly responded to Satyamitranand's call to establish branches of the Samanvaya Parivar abroad. Like other religious organizations, soon after its founding the Samanvaya Parivar began to publish a monthly magazine. It included excerpts from Satyamitranand's discourses and kept devotees informed about the activities of their guru and his organization.

Divyalok provides detailed accounts of Satyamitranand's foreign tours. Devotees in England invited him to attend a Guru Purnima celebration in 1985. Of all annual ritual occasions, Guru Purnima is perhaps the most lucrative for a religious leader: on this day disciples and devotees demonstrate their love and gratitude to their guru with generous donations. Satyamitranand remained in England for two months and then traveled to Vancouver. During his three-week visit to Vancouver the consul general of India invited him to attend an Independence Day gathering. On this occasion Satyamitranand and his disciples "honored the Bharatiya flag and Bharat Mata." After mentioning Satyamitranand's participation in Independence Day celebrations at the Indian Consulate, the account of his visit to Canada concludes with a reference to a Vancouver newspaper article. It is said to have reported Satyamitranand's visit with the headline, "Swami Satyamitranandji Maharaj—Symbol of Secularism" (28).

From Vancouver Satyamitranand traveled to Copenhagen to attend a VHP conference. Delegates from Hindu organizations in twelve countries also attended. They are said to have been so impressed by Satyamitranand that they gave him "open invitations" to visit their countries. Similarly, numerous invitations from various religious organizations awaited Satyamitranand on his return to India. The last pages of *Divyalok* are an itinerary of a man with a mission. After touring northern India and before setting off for Gwalior, Bombay, Goa, Karnataka, Calcutta, and another round in Gujarat, Satyamitranand visited the nation's capital. *Divyalok* reports that President Zail Singh invited him to attend a "family satsang" at the president's palatial residence. Like references to his contacts with Indira Gandhi and other politicians, mention of this invitation from the Indian president signifies Satyamitranand's success and prestige. The spiritual power which he is believed to embody is inextricably bound to his connections with secular power.

Divyalok presents a hagiographic account of Satyamitranand's life. It claims to be an inspirational text for spiritual seekers. At both the outset and conclusion the authors assert that Satyamitranand's devotion to God and Bharat Mata are as exemplary as his teachings and deeds. Those who follow his teachings, which show the path of love and compassion, are sure to obtain "good fortune."

SATYAMITRANAND AND HIS SUPPORTERS: THE DECREE OF HIGH ESTEEM AND DEVOTION TOWARDS ME

Compared with *Divyalok*, the special issue of *Ekatm Saptahik (ES)*, published to commemorate the consecration of the Bharat Mata temple, is less hagiographic. It presents Satyamitranand as a guru who is as devoted to his followers as they are to him. Here, as in *Divyalok*, itineraries of tours in India and abroad are provided. However, the special issue gives particular attention to his involvement with the VHP. This emphasis on the VHP is illustrated by photographs of Satyamitranand on stage at VHP district conferences in Rajasthan. The pages of photographs and numerous other pages are embellished by the VHP's emblem, aum. Excerpts from Satyamitranand's speeches in *Ekatm Saptahik* set forth the Hindu nationalist tenets of the VHP. For example, the following is a passage from a Hindi speech which Satyamitranand is said to have delivered four times in one day at a VHP district conference in Kota:

> Hindus are not a community. Inhabitants of Hindustan are Hindu. It is our duty to practice dharm. The meaning of Hindu dharm is the method of Hindu life. It is Hindu culture or Arya culture. Our dharm is sanatan dharm which is described in the Manusmriti. The term Hindu and the duties of a Hindu were explained and demonstrated by Vir Savarkar and the Hindu Mahasabha. (*ES*, 8)

Following these words of Satyamitranand's are those of Maharani Shivrani Devi of Kota. As president of the Women's Sammelan which met in conjunction with the VHP's Sammelan in Kota, the Maharani reminded the women in the audience that their duties as mothers and sisters were more important than any other. Hindu religion would provide them with honor and peace; it had no place for fighting and dissension. Women should consider trees as their mother and worship them as a manifestation of god. Women should reverence the Rani of Jhansi, Mirabai, Sita, and the mothers of Ram, Krishna, and Shivaji as their own mothers. The passage closes with the Maharani telling women to observe their duties as wives and householders (8).

Much of this publication consists of letters written by Satyamitranand to devotees, including Solanki, the publisher and editor of *Ekatm Saptahik*. Solanki introduces these letters as evidence of Satyamitranand's loving concern for his devotees in India even when he is as far away as England or Canada. Through these letters Solanki publicizes not only his devotion for his guru but also the intimacy he enjoys with him. In these letters Satyamitranand reminds his followers of the importance of his mission abroad. Although most of the letters are in Hindi, the following is taken from a letter published in English that Satyamitranand sent to Gajendra Singh Solanki from England in 1973:

> By Grace of God, I have arrived in London on the 13th of this month, I believe that I have been sent to this universe by Almighty God for specific mission of spreading His sacred literature and Bhagwatam through religious discourses in different corners of the world. By His Grace, through my limited capabilities, I am endeavouring to fulfill this mission even by travelling.
>
> The occasion of Guru Purnima was celebrated with greatest of zeal and enthusiasm and hundred of our Hindu brethren and sisters participated in

the Pujan performed with Veda-mantras at Vivian Hall in Wembley. In a country like England where the western culture is at its climax, this ceremony of Guru Purnima was creating a realistic impression of some Ashram on the Banks of the sacred Ganges.

Here in London, I remember the decree of high esteem and devotion towards me by you all in India and I feel deeply touched by your co-operation and good-will. May Almighty God continue to bestow upon you His choicest blessings and may your family prosper.

[signed] Your ownself, Swami Satyamitranand. (*ES,* 17)

A full-page photograph documents the principal event of Satyamitranand's subsequent visit to England in 1981. It shows him presiding at an assembly of 6,000 devotees. The two-day event included worship, discourses on the *Gita,* and a feast. It was sponsored by the London branch of the Samanvaya Parivar.

Like Savarkar as president of the Hindu Mahasabha, as a publicist for the VHP and fund-raiser for the Samanvaya Parivar and the Bharat Mata temple, Satyamitranand campaigns from a range of podiums—religious, cultural, educational. Besides his presence at VHP gatherings, his other public appearances in Kota and its environs recorded by the photographs and text of *Ekatm Saptahik* include: visiting a Hanuman temple during which he extolled Hanuman's devotion to Rama; lecturing at a High School in Kota after which women donated gold and jewelry in response to his call for Hindu workers and funds for charitable work among tribals to counter the activities of Christian missionaries; attending a function sponsored by the VHP for raising funds to build a Ram temple, yajna enclosure, and bookshop; addressing a poetry conference at the Cow Protection Bhavan in Kota whose theme was "Protection of the Nation"; and sitting on stage with other swamis at Gita Satsang Bhavan for a celebration of Gita Jayanti (birthday of the *Bhagavad Gita*).

The *Ekatm Saptahik* special issue provides an overview of various institutional and organizational networks through which Satyamitranand publicizes his causes and solicits funds. It also provides evidence of the support which he enjoys from large and small businesses. Compiled and published by Satyamitranand's supporters in Kota, thirty advertisements fill ten of its thirty-nine pages. These advertisements range from full-page ads such as one placed by Shri Ram Enterprises, a major Indian corporation, to smaller ads placed by local businesses—Raj Radios, the Kota Sari Shop, Trishul Electricals, Kota Rice Mills Association. Advertisers might have varying degrees of personal commitment to Satyamitranand. Their advertisements, however, publicly announce at least nominal support for Satyamitranand, which in Kota seems to be synonymous with the VHP. Four years after its publication, this special edition of *Ekatm Saptahik* was on sale at the Bharat Mata temple bookstall in Hardwar. It may not have been a best-seller, but advertisements in it provide regional businesses with a record of past support for Satyamitranand. Furthermore it also provides regional businesses with a channel to publicize their goods and services to a wider audience.

IN SEARCH OF A PATRONAGE

Like other gurus, Satyamitranand attracts people to serve him. This service earns the guru's patronage or grace, which devotees regard as integral to the success of worldly and spiritual endeavors. Gurus may publicly acclaim the donations and service of devotees, but the value of their contributions is never acknowledged as exceeding the transcendental value of the guru's grace. This circuit of exchange requires that gurus command and purvey a body of spiritual knowledge and practices and assure people of its profitability.

Based on translated transcripts of tape recordings of Hindi discourses, the English booklet *Sadhana* introduces Satyamitranand's spiritual teachings by asserting that "there are large areas where modern scientific thought and Rishi's ideas have common ground" (1987, 2). The Preamble opens with quotes from the *Bhagavad Gita* and Mahatma Gandhi, a "Rishi of our own age," and then turns to Satyamitranand:

> This book is yet another addition to the already vast literature on sadhana. But, the abstruse thoughts and statements of philosophy cannot be grasped without the guidance of a person whose life is devoted to sadhana, who has grasped the essence, the meaning inherent in the words used to define the undefinable. There is bound to be repetition: nothing is said that is not already in our tradition. These are gems of inspiration from Swamiji during his various discourses on sadhana, upasana, bhakti. (2)

The authenticity of Satyamitranand's teachings is attributed to their conformity to tradition and to Satyamitranand's own spiritual accomplishments. *Sadhana* is replete with quotes from Hindu texts and references to saints: the *Bhagavad Gita,* the *Ramayana,* and puranas; ancient rishis, Adi Shankaracharya, the Buddha, and Mahavira; Mahatma Gandhi, Ramana Maharshi, and Aurobindo. The compiler and translator reminds readers that this text cannot communicate Satyamitranand's extraordinary presence: "The tape recorder also misses out" on the "atmosphere of devotion" that pervades audiences listening to him (2).

Satyamitranand's "pithy yet enigmatic" words convey his knowledge of a "vast literature"; Hindi and Sanskrit verses are "intermingled with interesting and homely anecdotes of lucid depth" (2). His discourses are "delivered at a prolific speed." These features, as well as his "highly cultured poetic language," create "an intimate setting in which simple truths and values, the Wisdom of vedanta is presented for easy reception, digestion and assimilation" (2). The compiler and translator completes the Preamble by thanking Satyamitranand for his grace in assigning him the task of translating and compiling *Sadhana*. He describes the task as a "rewarding spiritual experience" and with "utter humility" dedicates the book at his guru's "feet in a true spirit of self-effacement" (3).

Sadhana's initial chapter, "In Search of a Patronage," sets forth why devotees need God. All creation "hinges on some support." The material world presents "opportunities and incentives for efforts." Effort is rewarded with "progress in wealth, prosperity and affluence, in comforts, happiness" (4). However, circumstances "do not always favour us" and situations arise causing disappointment and grief. Although family and friends may provide solace, "the true bond of intimacy can only exist between us and our creator." The solution to our problems lies in our relation to the "invisible, unmanifest creator." Hence "we need to establish the relation, intimacy and unison with Him to tackle our situations, plan our future and make our life auspicious and fruitful" (4).

Having defined the problem and the goal, Satyamitranand, like other gurus, claims to know and teach the means to attain the stated goal. The disciple must "fall at the feet of the Guru, serve him, the one who has grasped the essence of Vidya (knowledge of self). The 'Service' of the Guru implies opportunity for proximity, for close contact. It is then possible to know the guru, to visualize his unusual qualities to catch his inspiration to mature into the essence, the gist of Reality" (36). The booklet's thirty short chapters chart the course whereby Satyamitranand instructs and encourages the disciple. The following chapter titles suggest how the concepts of need, method, progress, and goal structure Satyamitranand's teachings: "What is the Good of Human Existence?"; "Towards Success in Sadhana"; "The Fruit of Upasana"; "Some Do's and Dont's"; "Why Sadhana?"; "Methods in Sadhana"; "The Measure of Progress"; "Experience in Sadhana"; "Assurance to Sadhak"; "The Goal is in Sight."

Unlike the materials concerning Satyamitranand discussed earlier, *Sadhana* restricts itself to the guru's spiritual teachings. There are no accounts of Satyamitranand's success as a fund-raiser, his tours in India and abroad, his involvement in the VHP, his contacts with Indira Gandhi and other politicians. Issues such as untouchability, conversion, tribals, and poverty are also absent. In *Sadhana* society is not the focus of concern. Emphasis is on the individual's quest to achieve the merger of one's immanent self with the transcendent Self, to realize the truth that atman is brahman. Like other gurus, Satyamitranand claims to impart this spiritual knowledge, this knowledge of the self. He enjoins his followers to be "self-dependent." With the guru as teacher of knowledge concerning the identity and means of realizing the self, dependence on the guru implicitly informs the devotee's self-dependence cultivated through sadhana and seva.

WE NEED TO DESERVE WHAT WE DESIRE

Spiritual discipline or sadhana should structure all aspects of the devotee's or sadhak's life. Diet should be pure, i.e., the sadhak should not eat meat or drink alcohol. Satyamitranand asserts that people are "responsible for their own woes." Past and present actions produce the "thorns of karma" that cause suffering (33). "More intensive devotion to Him" is inspired by hardship and suffering: "we ought to stipulate in our prayers that He give us more pain and grief." True devotion requires "emotional involvement to get inner strength to progress. We need to deserve what we desire" (35). Satyamitranand's teachings espouse a spiritual attitude to social obligations and secular employment. The sadhak "has his duties as per his station in life." Devotion to duty and work is described as the "whole hearted involvement in our secular duties in the spirit of a long-enduring worship" (57). According to Satyamitranand, dishonesty and hypocrisy in social life arise from fear of social boycott; yet, "there is not sufficient fear of God." By becoming "truly God-fearing," sadhaks perform all actions in accord with God's wishes and "there appears a spiritual quality in our secular work" (58). Satyamitranand's pronouncements regarding devotion to and fear of God implicitly refer to his own authority: disciples and devotees commonly believe that the guru is God.

Worshipful work promises the rewards of material success. However, it is necessary to "control our greed, our craze for 'grabbing and hoarding'" (58). Satyamitranand asks "how much of affluence is desirable; at what stage it appears extravagance?" He elaborates the problem: "Often, there is the tendency to look down upon persons who are poorly equipped. We live in a world surrounded by various items of hardware designed to give us cosy comforts in life. The items of luxury of today turn into necessities tomorrow! This difficult enigma and imitation of neighbor evolves endless desires and leads to greed and grab" (59). The sadhak should live simply and contentedly. Through secular work, the sadhak produces wealth; whatever is "not needed" should be donated "to support worthy causes."

Contentment and charity are further means for the sadhak's spiritual advancement. Satyamitranand advises that it is more difficult to renounce wealth than to amass it. However, the generous individual who shares wealth with others is amply rewarded: "The use of wealth is for altruistic purposes, the motive is of sharing it with others to help the needy so that the giver experiences bliss. There is experience of bliss, of grace of the Lord, through blessings of the Lord who resides in the hearts of the needy" (48). Satyamitranand's spiritual teachings admit no questions concerning social relations whereby the rich amass wealth and the poor live in deprivation. The charity of the rich is rewarded with blessings and bliss. Like suffering, poverty is figured as an advantage for spiritual seekers, as it facilitates "rapid progress in sadhana": "Simple persons who are used to living with contentment with minimum requirements, can easily develop an equipoise in miseries and happiness. They have fewer attachments, less malice, grudge or hatred and soon learn to live contentedly with the turn of fortunes. This helps them develop the virtue of equanimity in joy or gloom" (60).

Social and economic distinctions are simultaneously acknowledged and transcended in Satyamitranand's teachings. Sadhaks work in accordance with their "station in life," but their work is unified by a single goal—desire for peace. Satyamitranand asks, "Why do we work? A labourer works in a factory, an industrialist establishes a big industrial estate, a sannyasi lectures, a sadhak meditates in a lonely cave in the Himalayas, a poet composes poems. . . . They are all looking for peace" (26). Spiritual interests are immanent and transcendent; economic interests are ephemeral and epiphenomonal. The quest for spiritual peace unifies industrialists and factory workers. The social relations that underpin the industrialist's profits and the hardship of factory workers' lives are ignored in Satyamitranand's spiritual teachings. Sannyasis lecture because they seek peace: what about their fund-raising lecture tours, such as Satyamitranand's efforts as VHP leader and founder of the Bharat Mata temple?

The spiritual disciplines expounded by Satyamitranand in *Sadhana* are not novel. Publications providing similar spiritual instruction are available at ashrams and bookshops throughout India and abroad. Like other Hindu gurus whose speeches and writings present vedanta "for easy reception, digestion and assimilation," Satyamitranand preaches palatable and familiar prescriptions. He exhorts aspirants to meditate, chant mantras, recite the name of God, worship God, keep company with other sadhaks (*satsang*), read scriptures and the lives of saints, and listen to and reflect on spiritual discourses.

Satyamitranand's authority as a spiritual teacher relies on his use of widely accepted idioms and images relating to spiritual and devotional practices. His authority is further strengthened not only by his status as a brahman ascetic and former Shankaracharya, but also by his association with the VHP and the Bharat Mata temple. Through teachings such as those recorded in *Sadhana*, Satyamitranand provides disciples and devotees with idioms for defining their individual and social identities and methods for conducting their lives in accordance with these identities. Devotees are not simply passive recipients of the guru's knowledge and grace. By adhering to the guru's precepts and by offering the guru obedient service, they actively construct their own identities. These identities are not only spiritual, individual, and idiosyncratic but also social and shared with the guru's other followers. Furthermore, depending on the political import of the guru's teachings and activities, followers construct personal and social identities infused with complacency, acquiescence, or militancy.

SIX

The Bharat Mata Temple:
Satyamitranand's Candid Appraisal

BHARAT MATA AND HER MILITANT MATRIOTS

In 1983 the VHP's Sacrifice for Unity sent a mobile Bharat Mata temple forth from Hardwar. Mounted on a truck, it traveled as part of a procession through cities, towns, and villages from Hardwar in the north to the southern tip of India at Kanyakumari. Satyamitranand, the founder of Hardwar's Bharat Mata temple, conducted the rituals prior to the procession's departure. In 1978 he had presided over the ground-breaking ceremonies for the monumental eight-story Bharat Mata temple in Hardwar. Six months before the Sacrifice for Unity, the temple's "Opening Ceremony was performed by Rt. Hon. Smt. Indira Gandhi, the Prime Minister" (*Bharat Mata Mandir [BMM]* 1986, 13). The temple is estimated to have cost ten million rupees.

To understand what it meant to build a huge temple to Bharat Mata in the early 1980s requires backtracking to Bengal in 1882, and to the publication of a novel. Bankim Chandra Chatterji's novel, *Anandamath* (Monastery of Bliss), marks the invention of the tradition of Bharat Mata. The literary style of *Anandamath* more closely approximates Hindu epics than the nineteenth-century British novel. Characters, their relationships and actions serve to evoke a range of emotions in the audience: sorrow and anger, fear, disgust and revenge. Bankim Chandra's expressive powers reach their greatest intensity in his elaboration of the religious devotion of Bharat Mata's children, a devotion so powerful that it purifies and liberates the mother and her children.

The rapacious British have enslaved Bengal; they have brought famine and despair. Under the leadership of the ascetic Mahatma Satya, the Order of the Children protects the good and punishes the wicked British and their collaborators. The audience visualizes Bharat Mata when the Mahatma leads Mahendra, a potential disciple, to three rooms, each containing a different form of Bharat Mata. In the first room is Bharat Mata before British conquest: "a gigantic, imposing, resplendent, yes, almost a living map of India." In the second room, a tearful Bharat Mata wears rags and a sword hangs over her head. The Mahatma explains, "She is in the gloom of famine, disease, death, humiliation and destruction," and the sword signifies how the British keep India in subjection and how Bharat Mata will be freed. In the third room a heavenly light radiates from "the map of a golden India—bright, beautiful, full of glory and dignity!" The Mahatma says, "This is our mother as she is destined to be." Mahendra excitedly asks when Bharat Mata will be so radiant and cheerful again. The Mahatma replies, "Only when all the children of the Motherland shall call her Mother in all sincerity" (Bankim Chandra Chatterji 1992, 43).

After testing his devotion, the Mahatma initiates Mahendra, whose property and wealth are used to build an iron storehouse for the Order's treasury and a factory to make weapons. The Mahatma explains that two types of Children join the Order. Those like Mahendra are few; they are chosen and given a secret, higher initiation by Mahatma Satya and become leaders of the Order. They vow to give up wealth, pleasure, and personal attachments until they achieve their goal of purifying Bharat Mata from the pollution of alien domination. Death is the penalty for breaking this vow. The Order's second type of member consists of householders and beggars who present themselves when summoned for warfare and receive a share of the spoils. Their leaders' speeches quicken their devotion to Bharat Mata, which in turn inspires ferocity in battle: "the fire of anger was in their eyes, and the passion of stern determination on their lips, and one could hear brave words of revenge from their mouths" (63). In addition to the main plot which culminates in the victory of the Children over the British, there are two important subplots, involving two women whose husbands are leaders of the Order. They combine their duties as virtuous wives with active devotion to Bharat Mata, inspiring and reinforcing their husbands' heroism. One waits patiently for her husband to return; the other in the guise of a male ascetic joins her husband in the Order. The story reveals that only self-sacrificing devotion to Bharat Mata brings the questing heart what it desires: a liberation that is at once political and spiritual.

The 1992 English edition of *Anandamath* includes the dedication that was made by the translator, B.K. Roy, to Benjamin Franklin and Aurobindo in 1941, together with his seven-page preface (Roy 1992). Roy declares that Bankim Chandra's "great achievement for India was that he made patriotism a religion and his writings have become the gospel of India's struggle for political independence" (18). He refers to the song "Bande Mataram" that Bankim Chandra wrote for the novel and explains how it became the nationalists' call to duty, the freedom fighters' anthem. Its lyrics and particularly its chorus, "Bande Mataram" (Hail to the Mother), inspired both Gandhian pacifists, who suffered atrocities in British jails, and Aurobindo revolutionaries who were sent to the gallows for "loving their own country" and died with the "sacred mantra of Bande Mataram on their lips" (13). In Roy's opinion, *Anandamath* "set forth the principle of unselfish militancy as taught by Krishna in the Bhagavat Gita, the Bible of the Hindus" (13). The translator celebrates Bankim Chandra for founding a lineage of revolutionaries, a lineage that militant Hindu nationalists have extended to the present and claim as their own.

The identity of the patriarchal Indian nation-state and its citizenry has been and continues to be expressed in terms of devotion to the goddess Bharat Mata, Mother India. Partha Chatterjee's work emphasizes the complementarities between nationalist discourse and the cultural identity of the middle class under British rule (1986, 1990). Analysts of contemporary Hindu nationalism highlight the interrelations among support for the movement, global and domestic economic transformations, and changes in middle-class identity and practices (Vanaik 1990; Fox 1990a, 1990b). Work by feminists demonstrates how nationalist discourse, first during British rule and later in the postcolonial nation-state, articulated the "woman question" in terms of the requirements of changing cultural and economic practices of the upper and middle classes (Sangari and Vaid 1990). Under colonial rule, the emergent Hindu patriarchy's differentiation of social space into public and private spheres required a new ideal woman.

This ideal woman should be a wife and mother. She should be as frugal and fastidious in her housekeeping as she is devout and knowledgeable about religious traditions. She should be sweetly subordinate to her husband, yet sufficiently educated and informed to provide satisfying companionship. The welfare of her family, and particularly her husband, depends upon her spiritual powers, which are earned through the performance of rituals, scrupulous chastity, and incessant self-sacrifice. The ideal attributes to virtuous wives and mothers the capacity to inspire husbands and sons to become heroic nationalists. Sangari and Vaid argue that this particular ideal woman is ideological because from a diverse array of possibilities, specific gender roles have been selected and universalized; through this process "the formation of desired notions of spirituality and womanhood is thus part of the formation of the middle class itself, wherein hierarchies and patriarchies are sought to be maintained on both material and spiritual grounds (Sangari and Vaid 1990, 10). Reminding readers of the importance of caste and class inequalities to the study of gender in India, Sangari and Vaid argue that the current politicization of religious identities "has given a new lease of life to patriarchal practices under 'religious' sanction" (2). In short, patriarchal projects are embedded in the Hindu nationalist movement.

The discourse and practices of Hindu nationalism create specific subjectivities and contest others. The promoted subjectivities are commonly articulated in terms of the duties of Bharat Mata's children and are differentiated according to age, gender, socio-economic and caste status. Matriots are Bharat Mata's devoted and dutiful children who constitute an ideal, loyal citizenery. Militant matriots are those who, ever eager to assert their devotion, readily construe events as offences against Bharat Mata. The narrative of militant matriotism might be read as an oedipal drama of the patriarchal nation-state. The nation is figured as a loving Mother and her devoted children; the secular state and Muslims (as heirs of Muslim invaders) figure as the tyrannical Father. Either celibate or supported by their devoted wives, Bharat Mata's sons are valiant protagonists whose struggle is a righteous patricide, a conquest that simultaneously liberates the nation—the Mother and her children—and enables her sons to enjoy the power and riches they wrested from the malevolent Father.

Bharat Mata's apotheosis in her present form at the Bharat Mata temple dates back to this Bengali novel in which she inspires her children, under the leadership of the male Hindu ascetic Mahatma Satya, to vanquish the British and restore peace and prosperity. *Anandamath* marks the invention of a tradition. It is a tradition of matriotism that combines European political concepts of the nation-state, progress, order, and patriotism with a complex tradition of mythological elaboration and ritual worship of Hindu goddesses *(devi, shakti)* that is particularly strong in Bengal. However, as the burgeoning literature on nationalist ideologies and national cultures demonstrates, invented traditions are not static. They are continually reinvented in specific contexts to produce and challenge dominant constructions of class, religious, and gender identities. In India diverse groups—bourgeois social reformers, Hindu and secular nationalists, peasant leaders, feminists, and even Nehru himself—have fashioned for their own purposes this invented tradition of imagining India as a Hindu goddess.

The Bharat Mata cult propagated by contemporary Hindu nationalists combines the devotional and heroic imagery of *Anandamath* with a set of elements defining Hinduness (Hindutva) formulated in 1922 by Savarkar. He defined as Hindu those who consider India not only their holy land, a land sanctified by the presence of Hindu gods and the blood of its heroic martyrs, but also the land of their ancestors. Hindus are a race and a nation with a common origin and blood, culture, and civilization. Savarkar stressed the importance of struggle against Muslim and British enemies to the formation of the Hindu national identity. The Bharat Mata temple enshrines these very deities and national martyrs.

WE ARE ALL CHILDREN OF BHARAT MATA

Satyamitranand's hagiography, *Divyalok* (Chaturvedi and Sharma 1986) discusses at length his devotion to Bharat Mata and how it compelled him to build the Bharat Mata temple where Hindus could worship her and learn about Bharat's spiritual culture. Like Savarkar and other Hindu nationalists, Satyamitranand teaches that Bharat has the oldest culture in the world and is the land where God has repeatedly chosen to be incarnated. Sages and saints are born in Bharat to teach the path of devotion. Although there was already a Bharat Mata temple in Benares, Satyamitranand wanted to build one in Hardwar to acquaint visitors with Bharat Mata's "cultural, spiritual and divine glory" (*D*, 22). Temples to many other gods fill Hardwar, but there was no temple for Bharat Mata. Thus, Satyamitranand decided to build a temple where visitors could worship not only Bharat Mata but also Bharat's other gods, great saints, heroes, and satis (see plate 14).

Having resolved to build such a temple, Satyamitranand and his world-wide organization, the Samanvaya Parivar (Family of Harmony), worked to raise money for its construction. According to *Divyalok*, Satyamitranand was disheartened when funds were not immediately forthcoming. He prayed for help, and soon his devotees in India and abroad as well as the VHP were organizing rallies and yajnas to raise money. This account of the fund-raising campaign records the various places where Satyamitranand spoke and how much money he collected. On a previous visit to Bardoli, Satyamitranand had been installed in a pantheon of nationalist heroes with Subash Chandra Bose and Mahatma Gandhi. When he came again during his Bharat Mata Temple fund-raising tour, he was presented with nearly four million rupees (*D*, 24).

Satyamitranand chose May 15, 1983, the birth anniversary of the first Shankaracharya, as the date for consecrating the Bharat Mata temple. Announcements were published in newspapers throughout India inviting "all citizens" to attend. Invitations were also sent to heads of religious sects and to politicians. People began arriving several days in advance to attend the many events leading up to the consecration. On May 14, Satyamitranand led a procession through Hardwar to the temple. One Hardwar resident who witnessed the kilometer-long procession is reported as saying that he had not seen such a huge and grand procession in fifty years. He likened it to the Kumbh Mela, which features Hardwar's most spectacular parade of Hindu religious leaders and ascetics (26). Satyamitranand brought five hundred Vedic brahmans to perform a Vishnu yajna. The festivities included recitations of sacred texts, a Ram Lila performance, lectures by religious leaders, banquets for ascetics, and numerous other ritual activities. Prime Minister Indira Gandhi arrived punctually at the time appointed for the consecration. The principal consecration rituals were conducted by the Shankaracharya of Dvaraka; Indira Gandhi participated by performing *arti* before the statue of Bharat Mata. After worshiping Bharat Mata, she sat on stage with religious leaders and addressed the audience. Over 100,000 people are said to have attended.

The following year Satyamitranand's devotees from India and abroad were invited to Hardwar to attend a five-day spiritual camp. Five hundred people gathered to receive his blessings and be honored for their assistance in building the Bharat Mata temple. The camp was inaugurated by Swami Chidananda, a VHP member and head of the Divine Life Society (cf. chapters 7, 8, and 9); several other religious leaders also addressed this select gathering of Bharat Mata's devotees and Satyamitranand's followers. One week after the conclusion of this camp, the procession for the VHP's Sacrifice for Unity arrived in Hardwar. *Divyalok* is silent about Satyamitranand's involvement in the Yajna, but VHP sources say he figured prominently in ceremonies held in Hardwar and elsewhere in northern India.

While the devotional tone is more pronounced in the temple's Hindi guidebook, the English guidebook is printed on better quality paper and has glossy color photographs of the temple and the Bharat Mata statue on its front and back covers. The Hindi guidebook's front cover has a drawing of the temple with the orange Hindu flag flying above it and an aum above that—insignia of the VHP. Its back cover shows a photo of Satyamitranand. The first paragraph below the photo reads like a précis of Savarkar's "Essentials of Hindutva": "We are all children of Bharat Mata. Our country is one, our society is one, our civilization is one, our culture is one, our relations are blood relations."

The English guidebook, *Bharat Mata Mandir: A Candid Appraisal (BMM)* opens with a discussion of the reasons why Satyamitranand decided to build the temple. This decision is depicted as arising from a "vision," an "almost divine inspiration" which "dawned on Pujya Swami Satyamitranand Giri Maharaj in an auspicious tranquil moment" (*BMM*, i). After sharing his vision with some close disciples, he began to speak publicly about the need to build the Bharat Mata temple in Hardwar. The text draws readers into an intimate, inclusive relation with its logical arguments by using first-person-plural pronouns: "We may wonder about the basis for the iconic representation of Bharat Mata." It assures readers that worship of the Divine Mother is universal and normative; it is "as old as civilization" and exists in India as it has in "all ancient cultures." In India, the Divine Mother as the "Cause of Creation, as the symbol of Primal Energy and the source of Power—Shakti—is well within our comprehension." Tantric tradition worships the mother as goddess at "shakti-peeths" throughout India. There are "iconic manifestations" of the Divine Mother as Ganga, Yamuna, and Gita: "why not then Bharat Mata????" (i).

Indeed, such a manifestation of Bharat Mata is necessary because "to us all Mother-Land is sacred" (i). A temple would propagate the worship of Bharat Mata. It would also be a medium to enlighten visitors about the power and glory of the holy motherland:

> May this beautiful, yet powerful symbol of Mother India entice the hitherto uncommitted passerby, who happens to be a chance visitor, to the glory of Bharat Mata in her manifold facets, to the vastness of her resources and power, to get a glimpse of her history, culture, traditions, and hopefully, be rejuvenated. . . . It is hoped that a visit to the shrine will be a satisfying and lasting spiritual experience that will inspire devotion and dedication to Mother-Land. (i–ii)

The iconic representation of Bharat Mata in sculpture is described as both an artistic expression and a devotional act. The temple is a means to promote this devotional attitude to Bharat Mata, something which "historians and mythological story tellers may have missed" (1). Satyamitranand selected Hardwar as the site for the Bharat Mata temple because it is famous for the austerities of ancient sages; it is "the holiest of holy pilgrim centers." Every year "millions of Indians and others" retreat from "the din and bustle that engulfs our modern world" and come to Hardwar for an atmosphere "sublime, captivating, full of divine vibrations" that can "uplift the human heart." Thus, the temple in Hardwar gives visitors both aesthetic and spiritual satisfaction by presenting "a unique majestic appearance soothing to the eye and the mind" (ii).

The temple is said to synthesize the best of ancient and modern architecture. This notion of a synthesis of traditional and modern also informs ideas concerning Hinduism and Hindu society promoted by the VHP and its affiliated religious leaders, who claim to interpret ancient traditions and adapt them to the conditions of modern life. Not everyone, however, concurs with this estimation of the temple's architecture. Many Indians told me that the temple is imposing, but as ugly as an office or apartment block; it lacks the beauty and grandeur befitting a temple. An Indian architect working in Delhi, who visits Hardwar several times a year, asserted that the Bharat Mata temple "is not architecture but it is an important vision of India's unity." When I asked him what he thought the political implications of worshiping India as a Hindu deity might be, he replied, "Villagers like the temple, especially the views of Hardwar which can be seen from the top." The English guidebook, however, does not restrict to villagers the pleasure of this view from the top: "The view of the Himalayas: of the Sapta Dhara [seven streams, said to have been formed so that during its descent the Ganges would bypass the ashrams of the seven ancient sages]; of the scenic view of entire campus of the Sapta Sarowar area from the balconies of this floor, is breath-taking and tranquilizing to the eye" (18).

The Bharat Mata temple's embodiment of the vision of India's unity, of the nation's history and heritage, is a recurrent theme in the guidebook. Even though India "is saturated with temples" and its entire landscape is "an Abode of God," the Bharat Mata temple meets the urgent need to "keep our history and heritage alive." This knowledge "about our ancestry, about the founders of our faith, culture and tradition . . . is often sadly lacking." Muslim and Christian youths are said to be more knowledgeable about their heritage than Hindu youths: "Can we afford such gross nescience about our ancestry, about our heritage?" (iii).

More than many other Hindu pilgrimage centers, Hardwar is a place that encourages interest in ancestry. Through reference to ancestry persons define their individual and social identity in terms of past and present relationships and duties based on kinship and caste. Hardwar's origin is attributed to the desire of Raja Bhagirath to reverse the curse placed upon his ancestors. The popular Saptarishi Ashram near the Bharat Mata temple celebrates the past presence in Hardwar of the seven original rishis, whom brahmans claim as their ancestors. Many pilgrims perform mortuary rituals and rites honoring ancestors during their visit to Hardwar. As well as being pilgrimage guides and ritualists, Hardwar's brahman pandas are professional genealogists who keep registers which record births, marriages, and deaths in their patrons' families. These records also provide information on the patron's residence, caste, and sectarian status as well as on the kinds of rituals performed while in Hardwar and the size of the donation made to the panda and other ritualists (Goswamy 1966; Jameson 1976). Pandas' records can also be used as evidence in legal cases concerning property rights and inheritance. The pandas' genealogical services document important persons and events for particular patrilines. To have one's ancestry thus recorded by pandas in Hardwar and in other pilgrimage places is a source of pride and prestige for Hindus.

Like the patrons viewing the records of their lineage kept by pandas, visitors to the Bharat Mata temple are presented with a genealogical record. In addition to its purpose of fostering devotion to Bharat Mata, the temple is said to commemorate "the persons who have generated the alpha and gamma of our culture" and provide visitors "a glimpse of our nation's illustrious sons and daughters: saints and seers, philosophers and theologians, the originators of our unique thought; gallant men and women who have sacrificed their lives for the nation" (iii). By thus presenting the nation's lineage of illustrious forebears, the Bharat Mata temple is said to inspire in visitors "pride, faith and confidence in Bharat, and a resolve for dedication to the cause of our Motherland" (iii). Through its presentation of the motherland as an object of devotion and sacrifice, the temple, like the VHP, defines national identity in terms of Hindu piety and activism. Such an identity contributes to the VHP's ability to mobilize large numbers of people for specific Hindu nationalist causes—the Sacrifice for Unity, the demolition of the Babri Mosque and the construction of a Rama temple at Ayodhya.

The guidebook sets forth how the Bharat Mata temple explicitly aims to provide for its visitors an emotional experience of religious and national unity. The temple unifies sectarian diversity "under one umbrella" and strives to promote an appreciation of the diversity of religious teachers as "different interpreters of the Same Manifest." The temple's presentation of diversity as encompassed by unity is said to be the basis for instilling "the feeling that 'We are one,' 'Bharat Mata is our mother'" (iii). The ideology of Hindu nationalism as expounded by Savarkar and the VHP creates a composite religious and national identity. It figures loyalty to the nation in terms of devotion to and sacrifice for one's sacred motherland. The temple guidebook propagates the position that "religion and nationhood should be complementary to each other. Religion motivates culture while nationhood evokes sacrifice for one's religious identity. Nothing of lasting value can be achieved without this sense of self-sacrifice and dedication. The welfare of our nation demands sublimation of our individualistic drives and the creation of a true spirit of humanism and brotherhood" (iv).

The Bharat Mata temple is a means for teaching a particular conception of Indian history. So numerous have been the contributors to the "many millennia of our history" that it is impossible to include all of them in a single temple. Regarding the principles informing the selection of personages who have "created our unique, intransient civilization," the text offers an ambiguous explanation: "to apply criteria of selection would defeat the aim. Bharat Mata Mandir is just a humble effort at highlighting some important epochs in our social history that may encourage further research" (iv). Despite the guidebook's claim, further research suggests that the figures included in the Bharat Mata temple have been carefully selected according to specific criteria. These criteria primarily relate to the themes structuring the Hindu nationalism of the VHP, as prefigured in Savarkar's militant teachings. The criteria are not, however, exclusively Hindu nationalist; there is some overlap with other forms of Indian nationalism.

The deities represented in the temple are the VIPs of the Hindu pantheon. Some are worshiped throughout India, others are leading deities of particular regions who are worshiped in major pilgrimage centers. The Hindu nationalist tenet which asserts that Sanatanis, Jains, Buddhists, Arya Samajis, and Sikhs are all Hindus is enshrined in the level of the temple that is specifically dedicated to saints and religious teachers. But before examining in detail the contents of the temple, I shall turn the discussion to the next section of the guidebook, where Satyamitranand further explains the temple's purpose. This explanation is framed by a narrative which charts Satyamitranand's achievement—from the temple's conception to its construction and consecration. The narrative also provides an occasion for Satyamitranand to set forth and apply principles of Hindu nationalism.

BHARAT MAHATMYA: THE LAND OF DIVINE REVELATIONS AND SPIRITUAL GLORY

Satyamitranand praises the glory of Bharat Mata and the holy soil of the motherland. The incarnations in Bharat of Shiva, Krishna, Rama, and all the gods of heaven as well as saints and religious teachers have consecrated Bharat's soil. The ideals and values they embodied and taught have created the culture and nation of Bharat. Their presence has "divinised this land," and the most important feature of Bharat's "matchless and prodigious" soil is its capacity to nurture the spiritual:

> The unique, singular feature of this holy land of India is that it fosters and sustains spiritual life: it is the land leading in the world for yoga and ecstasy. The august tree of spiritualism grows and thrives on this land, through its branches and sub-branches and spreads far and wide and bestows gentle peace and sweet transcendence to us all who absorb it. (3)

Like Vivekananda, Aurobindo, Tagore, Mahatma Gandhi, and others, Satyamitranand contrasts Bharat's spirituality with the rampant materialism of Europe and America. Bharat's reputation is such that "for the quest of the saffron of spiritualism the entire universe is drawn to the sacred soil of Bharat. There is no equal to it" (3).

Bharat Mata may be the divine embodiment of Bharat's holy soil, but like the social identity of a Hindu woman, her identity is defined in reference to a male: "As I ponder over the format and facet of Bharat Mata I fancy that total aspect of her is symbolized in Lord Shankara" (Shiva). Satyamitranand envisions Shiva as the "Supreme Lord—the Lord of Lords" and as the "characterization of our nationhood" (1). He equates "our nationhood" with Shiva's status as supreme overlord, an equation which embeds within the concept of nation the ideals of Hindu militancy and ascetic discipline. The menacing trident and aum, more recently deployed by the VHP, have long been emblems of Shiva, the Supreme Lord whose asceticism increases his already awesome powers. Furthermore, the concept of Shiva as Lord of Lords also suggests the political ambitions of militant Hindu nationalists: to gain control of the Indian state. Hindu nationalists use symbol, ritual, and discourse to link culture, politics, religion, and nation-state. Satyamitranand does not use the term Hindu in his discussion of nation and culture. He uses either Bharat or India. However, he not only equates the nation with a Hindu god and goddess but also pronounces that "the culture flowing through her is portrayed in the life of

Lord Rama. It is difficult to conceive of a culture in the absence of nation-hood while the absence of culture cannot give entity to nationhood. Thus we need both: Lord Shankara as the manifestation of our nationhood and the modesty and adeptness as personified by Lord Rama" (1).

Rama is widely revered by Hindus as the divine embodiment of dharma—he is duty incarnate. For Satyamitranand, Rama is culture incar-nate and provides the model for proper social and religious conduct. Like the self-representations of the VHP and Satyamitranand, Rama is por-trayed as being concerned with social problems. Had he not been exiled from Ayodhya, "He would have forgone personal experience of the prob-lems of the multitude in India" (8). Even "without rolling in the Indian soil" Rama could have achieved "his goal of social uplift" (3–4). However, Rama chose to "flounder" in Bharat's soil as a child and to traverse it dur-ing his exile in order "to inspire the future generations in the piety of the soil of Mother India" and to "set standards and norms of socio-moral in-telligence" (9). The text implies that by emulating Rama's self-sacrificing adherence to dharma, that is, his deference to all figures of patriarchal authority—his father the king, brahman gurus and priests—Indian society will be able to achieve "social uplift" and solve its problems. Through his exemplary actions and his blessings, Rama "gives contentment to one and all" (9). While Shiva characterizes nationhood and Rama is the manifesta-tion of ideal culture, Satyamitranand names Krishna as the "persona-grata of such idealised personality" and proclaims that these three male Hindu deities represent the totality of Indian culture: "Thus, the total panorama of Indian culture would appear to be a synthesis of the personalities of Lord Rama, Lord Krishna, and Lord Shankara" (9).

According to Satyamitranand, Indian culture owes its idealism to Hindu gods and its continuity to saints and ascetics. Through their divinely inspired knowledge and their travels throughout Bharat and the world, Hindu saints interpret scriptures and propagate the principles of Indian culture. Satyamitranand extols sainthood as constituting the eternal roots of both culture and nation. Sainthood is defined as "piety coupled with strict self-discipline"; it has "penetrated the heart-centre of our nation and planted the imperishable Banyan tree (like the one on the River Ganges at Prayag) of our culture" (2). Shankaracharya and Vivekananda receive spe-cial attention in Satyamitranand's discussion of saints. They are revered for their teachings on and achievement of self-realization, and for founding monastic institutions. Satyamitranand belongs to an ascetic order founded by Shankaracharya, and his depiction of him suggests a venerable progeni-tor for the VHP's mission to unify Hindu society and codify Hindu rituals and beliefs. Shankaracharya's mission was to "synthesize and unite the strands of ethos and logos of our worship" (9). He traveled throughout In-dia and conducted religious discussions and disputations; this enabled him to "scrutinize, collate and authenticate our theology." In order to propagate his teachings, he established four ascetic orders, one each in the north, south, east and west of India.

Satyamitranand introduces other religious teachers, devotees, and saints, who are declared to be ubiquitous in the holy land of Bharat. Whenever society was weak, saints strengthened tradition and "thus rejuvenated and rescued our culture in times of peril" (10). When despair brought desolation to human hearts, the Krishna devotionalism taught by Chaitanya brought hope to the masses. On other occasions when "Indian life was dissipated" on account of "foreign invasions, laxity, indifference and internal quibbles," Gyaneshwara, Namdev, and Shahjobai "rescued our society and re-established its splendour and tradition" (10). Like Savarkar, Satyamitranand has a special place for Ramdas, guru of the Maratha warrior Shivaji. His passage concerning Ramdas echoes Savarkar's paean to the guru, who, like Krishna in the *Bhagavad Gita,* inspired his disciple to battle. It also encodes within it Savarkar's claim that the Hindu nation owes its continued existence to Maratha warriors and that Hindus should emulate Maratha militarism and heroism: "At another time in our history when physical exertion and inaction had demoralised our nationhood, our able Guru Ramdas preached chivalry, competence and confidence to his great disciple Shivaji Maharaj, who rose to the occasion, obtained the blessings of Mother Bhavani and became the saviour of our culture and inspired gallantry among his compatriots" (10).

From the many saints who have contributed to the continuity of Indian society and culture, Satyamitranand singles out Swami Vivekananda as most representative. He highlights the same qualities and achievements of Vivekananda that his own disciples attribute to him, particularly popularity in India and abroad for dynamic and persuasive speeches that express a modern approach and a pride in Indian heritage. Satyamitranand extols Vivekananda's message of fearlessness and strength: "India needed 'muscles of iron,' 'nerves of steel' and a 'gigantic will' " (11). This imagery connotes the political goals of Hindu nationalism: militarization, industrialization, and a centralized, authoritarian state.

Having detailed the reasons for building the Bharat Mata temple, Satyamitranand summarizes them in the final section, "A Moment of Volition." Readers once again hear Satyamitranand thinking aloud, as he wonders if all these wondrous aspects of Bharat Mata would remain buried in history books. Next, he asks how they could be "meaningfully projected in some monumental form that can inspire the ordinary man of India and enrich and uplift his life." And he concludes on a practical note: "if the total aspect of the excellence of Bharat Mata can be capitalised in one place to enable recapitulation of its glorious past, it could serve as an impartial motivation conducive to the future prosperity of the nation. Is this not obligatory?" (11). Satyamitranand recalls having speculated that Lord Brahma may have erred in giving him, a poor ascetic, the mission of building the Bharat Mata temple. However, he accepted the responsibility and attributes its fulfillment to divine will. Indeed, he proved himself skillful in raising money for building this monumental means to enshrine and popularize Hindu nationalism. It is also a means to solicit monetary donations that fund other organizations and campaigns led by Satyamitranand and his allies in the VHP.

A COVETED STATUS OF NATIONAL SIGNIFICANCE

The guidebook describes the Bharat Mata temple as unique, "a pioneer in its field"; this "marvel of engineering skill" has "acquired a coveted status of national significance" because it is a shrine designed to "spread a message of universal harmony and brotherhood" in a country with a variety of religions and languages (13). From its 180-foot summit visitors gaze down on Hardwar, and the temple's lofty golden dome can be seen from afar.

A statue of Bharat Mata greets visitors when they enter the temple: "the sons and daughters of Bharat Mata get a glimpse—Darshan—of the Mother whose love flows to her subjects in abundance" (14). The inspiration for the Bharat Mata statue is attributed to "Bande Mataram" in Bankim Chandra Chatterji's *Anandamath*. The guidebook associates Bharat Mata with the freedom struggle by explaining that Bankim Chandra visualized her during the movement for independence from British rule. Although the statue could not include all the aspects expressed in "Bande Mataram," it manifests them in an "abbreviated" form. Bharat Mata holds a milk urn in one hand and sheaves of grain in the other and is described as "signifying the white and green revolution that India needs for progress and prosperity" (13; see plate 15). The milk urn belongs to other chains of significations that the text does not discuss—cows, the cow protection movement, gifts to brahmans. The milk urn also suggests ritual vessels like the ones filled with Ganges water, worshiped and sold during the VHP's Sacrifice for Unity.

A sign in Hindi and English identifies the statue as Bharat Mata. Below that is another sign with black letters on a white background with a green and orange border, evocative of the Indian flag. Its devanagari script reads, "Vande Bharat Mataram" (Praise to Mother India). In the front point of the triangular pedestal is an orange aum. Large brass oil lamps burn on either side of the statue. The shrine also incorporates tantric elements of goddess worship by including a yantra, an abstract geometric icon of the goddess; on the wall behind the statue "the mighty Bharat Mata Yantra is installed to give her power and glory" (13).

Like another yantra, a large map of India is mounted on a raised platform in the center of this ground floor shrine. On it are marked mountains and rivers, major centers of Hindu pilgrimage, and "all important centres of culture" (13). Thus the map represents the political boundaries of the Indian state while inscribing its topographic features in terms of Hindu cosmography. Besides the statue of Bharat Mata and the map of India, upon entering the temple visitors also see large color photographs showing Satyamitranand, Indira Gandhi, the Shankaracharya of Dvaraka, and others who participated in the temple's consecration ceremonies. The next three floors above this entry level contain shrines dedicated to the nation's heroes, satis, and religious teachers:

> The stalwarts in any nation can be categorised as: the heroes on the battle front; the noble women of character at home; and the philosophers who have given ideas and set ideals. By the grace of the Lord, our culture is endowed with innumerable brave gallantry (Shoor), chaste womanhood (Satee) and pious Acharyas and pious Saints (Sant). This is true not only for our past history but also for the present generation. It is hoped that the visitors to the Shrine will be able to pay their respects to them under one roof, and get inspiration from them for their own life. (14)

The guidebook explains that although it may seem as if the temple includes too many manifestations of deities and heroes, holy men and women, each floor of the temple was consecrated by the Shankaracharya of Dvaraka and constitutes an autonomous shrine.

On this entry level is also a book display which sells publications such as *Divyalok*, the Hindi and English temple guidebooks, *Sadhana* and other collections of Satyamitranand's spiritual teachings. Postcards of the temple are also sold here, either individually or in a sixteen card set showing a selection of the temple's deities, heroes, satis, and saints as well as a photo of Satyamitranand flanked by sacred texts. A popular feature of the temple is its elevator, which—for a modest fee when it is not malfunctioning—whisks visitors up to the temple's penultimate level.

The Shrine of Heroes occupies the second level. Like the shrines on four other floors, it consists of a large room with statues in display cases lining three walls. The fourth side opens to a veranda and views of the Ganges. Signs in Hindi and English naming the figures are propped against the base of the statues. Bharat's forebears are worshiped in this shrine for their sacrifices to defend the sacred motherland and Hindu religion: "The first floor is dedicated to the sacred memory of our valiant ancestors, bold and gallant sons and daughters of Bharat Mata, who sacrificed their lives for the patriotic cause of protecting the Sanatan Dharma and the glory of the Motherland" (14). Satyamitranand and his associates have selected a dozen personages to include in this shrine: Madan Mohan Malaviya, Veer Savarkar, Subhash Chandra Bose, Mahatma Gandhi, Maharana Pratap, Chatrapati Shivaji, Guru Govind Singh, the Rani of Jhansi, Shaheed Bhagat Singh, Chandra Shekar Azad, Hemu Kalani, and Asphak Ulla.

The selection of these figures is consistent with the lineage of Hindu nationalists that Satyamitranand and the VHP construct for themselves. This lineage draws upon those whom Savarkar had celebrated as defenders of the Hindu nation—Maharana Pratap, Shivaji, Guru Govind Singh, and the Rani of Jhansi. Mounted upon her horse with baby swaddled on her back, the Rani of Jhansi raises her sword with one hand and holds reins and shield in her other hand. Her clothing and her horse's caparison are green and orange, the colors of the Indian flag. The lineage constructed by the Shrine of Heroes also incorporates revolutionary terrorists who were killed by the British: Chandra Shekar Azad and Bhagat Singh. The statue of Azad portrays the balance between traditional and modern that Satyamitranand and other contemporary religious teachers claim to offer. A white cloth tied at Azad's waist hangs down to shoeless feet; over his bare chest hangs a sacred thread. He wears a large watch on his left wrist, and a thick gold bracelet adorns his right wrist. His waist is encircled with a belt of bullets from which hangs a gun in a holster. In the gesture of a king or noble man, he twists the ends of a thick mustache (see plate 16). Next to Chandra Shek-har Azad in this shrine and on the set of post cards stands Bhagat Singh with both arms at his sides, like a soldier at attention. The image of Bhagat Singh shows a wholly modern militant matriot. He shares with Azad the bushy black mustache. Singh, however, is outfitted from head to toe in western style gear: fedora, long-sleeved white shirt, belted trousers, and black shoes.

During Satyamitranand's visit to Bardoli in Rajasthan, local notables described him as combining the qualities of two great men who had previously visited the city—Subhash Chandra Bose and Mahatma Gandhi. These two heroes of the independence movement are installed in the Bharat Mata temple as representatives of militarism and nonviolent noncooperation. Pandit Malaviya—founder of Benares Hindu University, Hindu political leader, and organizer of brahman priests in Hindu pilgrimage centers—is enshrined among these protectors of sanatan dharm, brahmanic Hinduism. Savarkar also stands with these national stalwarts, these "heroes on the battle front." Nehru is conspicuously absent in this configuration of Bharat's lineage of freedom fighters.

The floor above the Shrine of Heroes houses the Sati Shrine. The term sati has two connotations: it refers to a virtuous woman as well as to a woman who kills herself after her husband's death, usually by immolating herself on his furneral pyre. The guidebook describes it as being "dedicated to the glory of Indian Womanhood from Vedic times to the present era, symbolizing the chastity, loyalty and dedication of Indian wedlock" (15). A Sanskrit verse extolling the virtues of women is presented as evidence of the "sense of respect and reverence shown to our women." The guidebook maintains that such evidence refutes those who think women are oppressed in Indian society. This assertion belongs to the discourse concerning the high status of women in traditional Hindu society. Still pervasive today, this discourse perpetuates the apologetics of conservative upper-caste Hindu men who were responding to critiques by the British and by Hindu social reformers, critiques often directed against sati (Chakravarti 1990; Mani 1990). The critiques, like the practice and worship of sati, continue to this day. Hardwar is believed to be the site where the goddess Sati avenged her father's insult to her husband Shiva by jumping into the royal sacrificial fire. Two of the twelve "beautiful manifestations" in the Bharat Mata temple's Sati Shrine show a woman engulfed in flames. Sati Padmini, a Rajput queen, is celebrated for leading the women of Chitor to kill themselves after their husbands were defeated in battle by a Mughal army. With flames rising out of wood and up to her shoulders, Sati Padmini's half-open eyes and beatific smile make her look like she is in a blissful trance. Her hands are pressed together in a gesture that suggests she is respectfully fulfilling her duty and politely greeting those who come before her. Flames are etched upon her fair forearms, making her glass bangles glow (see plate 17).

Besides its two burning symbols of the "chastity, loyalty and dedication of Indian wedlock," the Sati Shrine includes wives of sages and other women who are exemplars of wifely virtue. Continuing the clockwise circuit of the statues, the visitor reaches the last sati. The final figure looks incongruous amidst the finery and glory of Indian womanhood. In a plain white dress, suggestive more of a widow rather than an auspicious Hindu wife, stands Annie Besant. She stares severely and clutches a book in one arm; her feet are shod with heavy, sensible shoes. Her inclusion in the Sati Shrine can be variously interpreted. She was a leading figure during the early days of the Congress and the independence movement; she supported the campaign for a Hindu University and extolled the spiritual riches of Hindu civilization. For visitors who might be less familiar with the specifics of Annie Besant's career in India, her presence might signify that even Western women aspire to the status of Hindu sati.

When I visited the temple in 1987 and 1988, there was an empty glass display case next to Annie Besant. In 1992 the case was no longer empty; Sister Nivedita, the Irish disciple of Vivekananda, had been enshrined and the Sati Shrine renamed the Matri (Mothers') Shrine.

Above the Shrines of Heroes and Satis is the Shrine of Saints, which consecrates a national lineage of religious teachers. The guidebook's discussion of this shrine reiterates the belief that sainthood is central to Indian culture:

> In a world of luxury, lust and power, Indian culture has upheld the ideals of Sainthood. This floor is dedicated to our great philosophers and Saints, who have infused unity in us, who have rejuvenated us; through love, devotion and knowledge they gave us inspiration, through captivating speeches they enriched our culture, through pious, austere life they set norms for our way of life. (*BMM*, 15)

Twenty-four statues crowd the shrine, so that the founders and teachers associated with major Hindu sects and ascetic orders can be included. Figures associated with other religious groups—Sikh, Jain, Buddhist—which are embraced by the VHP's conception of Hindu are also displayed here. The saints worshiped in this shrine are: Valmiki and Tulsidas, Rama's inspired devotees; the Buddha; Mahavira, the Jain saint; Nanak, the Sikh guru; Chaitanya, the Bengali devotee of Krishna; and Ramdas, the guru of Shivaji. The great religious philosophers of the South—the "miniature incarnations" of Indian culture—in the Shrine of Saints are: the Adi Shankaracharya, Ramanujacharya, Nimbarkacharya, Vallabhacharya, and Madhavacharya. Other saintly religious teachers depicted are Udasain Acharya Chandraji, Rang Avdoot, Garibdas, Raskhan, Hirjibapa, Narasingh Mehta, Gyaneshvara, and Shirdi Sai Baba (who perhaps doubles as a referent to the currently popular Sathya Sai Baba). Notably, all three members of the triad associated with the Ramakrishna Mission are also present: its founder Vivekananda and his guru Ramakrishna, together with Ramakrishna's wife and disciple, Sharada Ma, who is the only woman included in this assembly of spiritual teachers. Nearby stands the statue of Aurobindo, the anti-British revolutionary who retired from active politics to devote himself to spiritual pursuits at his ashram in Pondicherry. The alliance between the Arya Samaj and the VHP earns a place in the Shrine of Saints for Swami Dayananda Saraswati, the man who founded the Arya Samaj and propounded the supremacy of Vedic spiritual knowledge.

Although not formally a shrine, the Assembly Hall on the next floor portrays tenets of Indian and Hindu nationalism which celebrate the unity of all religions and the unified diversity of the peoples and cultures of Bharat. Painted on the walls are "important Dharma Sutras from all the religions of India: Hindu, Muslim, Christian, Parsee, Sikh, Jain, Buddha" (16). Just as the cooperation of Hindus, Christians, and Muslims in the Sacrifice for Unity is presented by the VHP as evidence of the unity underlying all religions, so the guidebook describes the quotations as "illustrating the brotherhood of man in a world of many beliefs and '-isms'" (16). In addition to the passages from scriptures, the Hall is also decorated with a series of paintings. Each one is labelled with the name of an Indian state and shows landscapes, temples, facial types, and clothing associated with that state. Modern technology is also recruited to the cause of national unity: the guidebook promises the imminent installation of a computer which will answer questions of cultural interest. Two years after the guidebook's publication, the computer had not yet arrived.

Above the Assembly Hall is the Shakti Shrine, dedicated to various forms of the goddess. Its thirteen statues of the "divine mother" are described as "the embodiment of spiritual and moral strength, the triumph of Truth over evil." The text refers to the *Markandeya Purana*'s enumeration of Durga's nine "invincible" manifestations, and each is represented in the Shakti Shrine as a form Durga took to slay a particular beastly foe. As noted earlier, the VHP also favors Durga: the cover of *Ekatmata Yajna,* the commemorative book celebrating the Sacrifice for Unity, shows Durga leaning on her lion with the orange Hindu flag in her hand. Bharat Mata embodies the divine mother's power to bestow prosperity; Durga's iconography emphasizes her power to vanquish enemies.

In addition to these nine forms of Durga, the Shakti shrine presents Saraswati, the goddess of knowledge and music. Visitors also have darshan of Ved Mata Gayatri, the goddess in her form as the Gayatri mantra. Although some religious teachers such as Krishnananda of the Divine Life Society continue to pronounce that this mantra should be the exclusive possession of upper-caste males, others popularize it among high and low castes, men and women. Just down the street from the Bharat Mata temple is the large ashram founded by Acharya Sharma and his Gayatri Parivar, another Hindu organization affiliated with the VHP. As mentioned in chapter 2, Sharma's teachings emphasize the powers which accrue to those who chant the Gayatri mantra and worship the divine mother in her various forms. Two further forms of shakti are figured in the shrine, and the guidebook associates them with specific regions of India: Jagadamba of Gujarat and Meenakshi of South India. Of the many popular regional forms of the goddess, Jagadamba may have been selected because Satyamitranand's Gujarati followers in India and abroad contributed money for the temple's construction. Meenakshi, the fish-eyed goddess worshiped at the wealthy Madurai temple in Tamil Nadu, may be included as a tribute to Hindus of South India.

Enshrined in the seventh and penultimate level of the Bharat Mata temple are nine forms of Vishnu. The guidebook describes these incarnations of Vishnu as symbolizing "Devotion (Bhakti) with Domination" and provides a Sanskrit quotation to emphasize Vishnu in his form as "Destruction to Wrongdoers" (17). By highlighting Vishnu's punitive powers, the guidebook affirms the duty and moral authority of righteous rulers to subjugate those whom it names as enemies of Hindu dharma. The shrine displays incarnations of Vishnu and his consort that are popular throughout India: Sita-Rama, Lakshmi-Narayana, Radha-Krishna. It also displays incarnations that have important but more regional and less ubiquitous followings: Dattatreya, Sri Nathji, Ranchod Raiji, Vyankatesh, Akshara Purushotta, and Vitthala-Rukmini.

Visitors must climb stairs to reach the summit of the Bharat Mata temple, which depicts Mount Kailash, the abode of Shiva. The guidebook describes this topmost level: "The massive Sanctum Sanctorum of this floor presents a wonderful view of Mount Kailas. In the center, under the huge dome, Lord Shiva is seated deep in meditation, a Maha Yogi" (17). With its glittering white plaster crags, the sanctum's mountainous scene resembles a stage set. Several statues of Shiva representing his different aspects populate the pinnacle. The central and dominant statue shows Shiva in solitary meditation, the form through which "he glorifies renunciation and asceticism: the qualities adored and adopted by seekers after Truth in India" (17). He wears and is seated upon animal skins. Cobras are entwined around his silver body. Another cobra rises out of the matted locks coiled on top of his head. The glistening cascade of the descending Ganges flows through his hair. Stuck in the ground next to Shiva is his trident, from which hangs the drum on which he beats his deathly rhythms.

Behind the solitary meditating Shiva, viewers see him in a family portrait. Here Shiva sits with Parvati and his elephant-headed son, Ganesha. In the wings of the shrine are two other forms of Shiva. One shows his androgynous form: "an idealization of Purusha and Prakriti of Shiva and Shakti in one moorti [image]" (18). Satyamitranand had earlier asserted his vision of Shiva, the Supreme Lord, symbolizing the total aspect of Bharat Mata. Shiva's representation as half-woman provides an iconic referent for Shiva's capacity to symbolize the totality of Bharat Mata. The fourth statue of Shiva shows him in his well-known form as Nataraja, Lord of Dance. Surrounded by a circle of fire, he dances destruction upon the body of Maya (illusion). The guidebook extols the statue maker's genius for making a "unique piece of art" that "concurs beautifully with the notion of perpetual motion as investigated by modern science" (18).

The guidebook repeatedly assures readers that the statues in the Bharat Mata temple have been consecrated and are worshiped with the proper rituals. Unlike visitors to other temples who bring food, cloth, and other goods as ritual prestations to the deity, visitors to the Bharat Mata temple arrive empty handed. There is no bell to ring to announce one's presence, and no priest awaits devotees to take their offerings and give them prasad. With its labeled statues in glass display cases, the temple seems more like a museum of Hindu nationalism than a Hindu temple where devotees come to worship. However, as is common in temples and ashrams, here too visitors are encouraged to donate money. A temple attendant ritualizes the act of donating money by marking donors' foreheads with red powder—an activity common in many temples and appropriate in other ritual settings—and by issuing receipts.

The guidebook's discussion of how donations to the temple are used echoes both Satyamitranand's and the VHP's pronouncements about their support for charitable projects that further national unity:

> It is our resolve to utilise all gifts and endowments received at the shrine towards the further service of our Vanavasi Brethren—the forest and hill dwellers, and the Harijans [Untouchables]. Along with this, a portion of this endowment will be utilised for the education of Brahmin youth in proper Vedic rites, rituals and research. We earnestly hope that in this way Bharat Mata Mandir can contribute to the socio-economic needs of our nation. (iv)

The training of brahmans as Vedic ritualists and scholars and the "service" to tribals and untouchables are heralded as ways in which the Bharat Mata temple uses its income to further the cause of strengthening the nation. Such activities are similarly undertaken and portrayed by the VHP and Satyamitranand. The Bharat Mata temple houses multiple elements of Hindu nationalism. It purveys to visitors a particular configuration of national identity in accordance with its definitions of Bharat's unified culture and religion. The temple encourages visitors to imagine their identities as devoted sons and daughters of Bharat Mata; to be edified and inspired by the ideals and deeds of their heroic and saintly forebears; and to prove their devotion by dedicating themselves as matriots to the defense of the holy motherland. Visitors to the Bharat Mata temple are enjoined to "depart with the noble concept that we all belong to One Family" (iv).

SEVEN

Sivananda and the Divine Life Society

THE VOICE OF SIVANANDA

The success of the Vishva Hindu Parishad derives in part from its ability to attract religious leaders who have followings among people from a range of class, caste, and regional backgrounds. This involvement of a variety of religious leaders in the VHP also facilitates the propagation of moderate and militant forms of Hindu nationalism. Whereas Satyamitranand and the Bharat Mata temple present a form of Hinduism which explicitly conforms with the VHP's tenets of Hindu nationalism, the Divine Life Society emphasizes the universality of Hindu religious thought and practice.

Swami Sivananda Saraswati founded the Divine Life Society in 1936. His lectures and prolific publications in English and their translations into Indian languages popularized the belief that advaita vedanta contains the spiritual truth underlying all religions, a belief also propagated by the Ramakrishna Mission, Radhakrishnan, and others. English speaking, well-educated, high-caste, upper- and middle-class Hindus have been and continue to be the principal supporters of the Divine Life Society.

Divyalok (Chaturvedi and Sharma 1986) recounts Satyamitranand's early association with Sivananda. Swami Chinmayananda, the founder of the VHP, is counted among Sivananda's early disciples. Sivananda's successor Chidananda, the current president of the Divine Life Society, has ties with both the VHP and the Bharat Mata temple. He is a member of the VHP's Central Advisory Council. In 1984 he lit the ritual lamp at the consecration of the Bharat Mata temple, and in 1987 he attended the celebrations marking the anniversary of the temple's consecration.

The events and participants in the celebration of Sivananda's birth centenary in 1986 and 1987 demonstrate the influential position which the Divine Life Society enjoys in contemporary India. This influence relates to its continued success in attracting support from politicians, bureaucrats, professionals, and business groups. Several of Sivananda's ascetic disciples have carried his message abroad and have established branches of the Divine Life Society or their own independent organizations to propagate the teachings of Sivananda in Mauritius, Malaysia, the United States, Canada, South Africa, Australia, South America, and Europe.

Foreigners are always present as residents and visitors at the Sivananda ashram, the headquarters of the Divine Life Society in Rishikesh. They come to study yoga, to ask for spiritual guidance from senior swamis in the ashram, to imbibe Sivananda's teachings on divine life. Their presence at the ashram and the reverence they show for senior swamis affirm claims that the Society is open to members of all religions and that Sivananda's teachings on "practical spirituality" can be adopted by Hindus and non-Hindus alike. When watching a promotional video made by the Divine Life Society, one Indian woman commented that this indeed is "export-quality religion and spirituality." Sivananda's teachings are not unique; there are numerous similarities between his universalist interpretations of advaita vedanta and those propagated by India's philosopher-statesman Sarvepalli Radhakrishnan, Sivananda's contemporary.

In order to protect its international reputation as a proponent of universal religion, the Divine Life Society does not publicize its links with Hindu nationalist leaders and organizations. For example, in official biographical accounts of Sivananda's leading disciples, it does not mention that Chinmayananda founded the Vishva Hindu Parishad.

When discussing my study of the Divine Life Society at a social gathering in the New Delhi home of a woman whose husband had been an Indian diplomat, one of the guests declared that the Divine Life Society was one of India's "worst communalist groups" and that it was closely associated with the RSS. During a visit with another well-educated Delhi woman, who also has lived overseas when her husband held a foreign posting, I heard an opposite position. This woman is a devotee of Chidananda and regular visitor to the Sivananda ashram in Rishikesh. When I asked her, she adamantly denied that the Divine Life Society had formal or informal connections with the VHP or the RSS. However, like the Hindu nationalist apologetics which were then increasingly fashionable in newspaper and magazine articles, she argued that the need to defend themselves against government favoritism of minorities was inducing "liberal, secular" Hindus like herself and her family to become increasingly militant. She related the growing influence of Hindu organizations like the RSS and VHP to their "promotion and protection of Hinduism within India and abroad." Assenting to this view, her very old grandfather reiterated her words with solemn conviction.

This same woman lamented that the Delhi branch of the Divine Life Society had been taken over by "unscrupulous businessmen." She criticized the Delhi branch for its lack of social service projects and noted that visiting swamis refuse to stay at its premises. When I asked for further details, she declined to explain what she regarded as their unscrupulous activities.

The centenary issue of the *Voice of Sivananda* (hereafter, *VS*), the journal published by the Delhi Branch of the Divine Life Society, suggests how Sivananda's teachings on spirituality are used to support Hindu nationalism. The issue opens with an article attributed to Sivananda. Extolling the spiritual preeminence of Hindu India throughout the ages and advocating the continued relevance of this heritage to both post-independence India and the whole world, this article reads like a VHP text or like the guidebook of Satyamitranand's Bharat Mata temple, discussed in the previous chapter. The article begins by asserting:

> India is the sacred land which has given birth to countless Sages, Rishis, Yogins, Saints and Prophets. India is the land that has produced many Acharyas or spiritual preceptors like Sri Shankara. . . . India is proud of Guru Govind Singh and Shivaji. . . . Krishna, Rama and all Avataras were born in India. How sacred India is! How sublime is India. The dust of Brindavan and Ayodhya, the land trodden by the sacred feet of Krishna and Rama, still purifies the heart of countless people. Even Jesus, during the missing period of his life, lived in Kashmir and learned Yoga from Indian Yogins. (*VS*, August 1987, 2)

The article expounds familiar tenets of Hindu nationalism. Indian culture and Hinduism, Indians and Hindus are used interchangeably as equivalent terms. India's sacred land, holy rivers, and "spiritual vibrations" make it "peculiarly suited for divine contemplation" (*VS*, 2). India is a spiritual country where religion governs all aspects of life. In exchange for "handfuls of rice" sannyasis travel door to door to distribute "priceless gems of Hindu religious thought and philosophy" (3). Hindu culture is older than any other culture, and Indian civilization has "influenced the history of the world at every stage." When ancestors of westerners "were completely uncivilized savages," India was full of self-realized saints and seers: "The Greeks and Romans imitated the Hindus and absorbed Hindu thoughts."

The *Ramayana* and *Mahabharata* are said to record the glorious past of ancient India and to be sources of inspiration "to make India great again." The "noble characters" of these epics provide models for "our domestic, social and national ideals" (3). No other country has produced so many great men—saints and philosophers, kings, heroes, and statesmen. To this day India "abounds in sages and great souls." Those who inherit this legacy should be proud and grateful to be Hindus: "The more you know of India and Hinduism, the more you will honor it and love it and the more thankful to the Lord you will be that you were born in India as a Hindu." After this introduction, "Spirituality the Bedrock of Indian Culture" provides the theme for the article's next section. England is famous for coal and iron, America for dollars, and Italy for sculpture; India is famous for religious devotion. India's history is the history of religion and its culture is "built around Dharma or righteousness." India would not be India without the *Gita* and the Upanishads. Political strife, alien invasions, and temporary political bondage have not "sullied the soul of India" (3).

Spirituality privileges ascetic values and practices as superior to all other human pursuits. Those who practice and espouse ascetic values uphold dharma and should be supported by householders with handfuls of rice, or as in the case of the precepts set forth by Sivananda, with donations of two to ten percent of a householder's income. Mastery over the senses and self-restraint are said to be the "key-note of India's culture." Self-realization through knowledge and service provide the basis of India's "national ideals." They are responsible for keeping "intact the virility of Bharatvarsha as a nation." These values constitute the "undying vitality" of Indian culture which its sages and saints "revitalize to suit the needs of changing times."

Its unique spirituality makes India "the most tolerant nation in the world." Like an indulgent mother, "she includes all nations in the embrace of her love"; even when oppressed by "greedy men" for over 800 years, she served them and made them happy and rich. High-caste, wealthy men who collaborated with Muslim and British rulers are thus portrayed as a bountiful maternal hostess with avaricious, ungrateful guests. With spirituality at her core, India is "ever rich, liberal, and catholic. She nourishes the whole world." Like a monopolist who is protecting his dominance of a particular market and commodity, Sivananda asserts that "the unity of mankind and universality of religion are the prerogatives of the Indian tradition."

India's superlative spirituality is commonly opposed to the West's rapacious materialism. Sivananda articulates this position with a series of oppositions: brahman is the only reality in India, matter is the only reality in the West; self-realization is the ultimate goal in India, power and domination are the ultimate goals in the West; Indians pursue happiness through self-restraint, Westerners pursue pleasure through self-indulgence; renunciation brings joy to Indians, possession brings joy to Westerners; nonviolence is the Indian ideal, killing and conquest is the Western ideal (5). Sivananda briefly replaces India with the East in his oppositional strategy: "The West is material. The East is spiritual." A couple of sentences later he resumes his use of India as the antithesis to the West. India may not be able to rival the West's dominance of physical sciences and modern technology. However, India commands the more important field of spirituality. Thus Sivananda asserts: "In the spiritual field, she will certainly be unparalleled. She will always guide the entire universe in spiritual matters, in Yoga, Vedanta, etc. She will ever be the world's preceptor, India will always lead the world in spirituality. She does not stand in any need of spiritual enlightenment" (3).

Embedded in Sivananda's assertions of India's spiritual preeminence are claims concerning his own authority to teach Indian spirituality and bestow its largesse upon India and the world. The West stands not only for foreign nations but also for groups within India—secularists, Muslims, Sikhs, Christians—who refuse to defer to the authority of Hindu leaders such as Sivananda. Through her saints and swamis, who knowingly teach the divine wisdom of the Upanishads, *Gita,* and advaita vedanta, India can "lead all to prosperity, peace and perpetual bliss. Let India lead countries which are spiritually bankrupt. She alone can undertake this gigantic task. India alone can lead the world towards better understanding, harmony, fraternity and peace" (6). Sivananda embroiders and reiterates these themes in the article's concluding section, "The Future of India." As elsewhere, he attributes to India the values and characteristics associated with Hindu asceticism. He asserts that because India's mission has always been spiritual greatness and not political eminence or military power, "India has never attached importance to wealth and power." India must not imitate the West; Indians who do so have lost their soul.

Sivananda addresses the government on behalf of his own occupational group by exhorting the rulers of India to honor and defer to the judgment of spiritual leaders:

> She cannot become glorious through building of more aeroplanes and warships. She should produce more Yogins, and victors over self. The governors of India should consult the saints on important matters of administration. They should accord them a high place of honour. Then and then alone will the Indian Government be righteous, divine and peaceful. (6)

Elsewhere Sivananda advises businessmen and industrialists to purify themselves of the "taint and corruption of business" and earn great merit through "abundant charity," giving generously to social and religious institutions, Sanskrit schools, and medical clinics (Divine Life Society 1987, 182; hereafter, *The Master, His Mission and His Works [MMW]).* Similarly, by supporting spirituality, i.e., organizations such as the Divine Life Society, India will purify public life and remove "ex-crescences which are poisoning the springs of national life in India at its very source. Let all live the Gita-life" (*VS,* 6).

India's future depends not on material wealth but on spiritual strength: "Atman or the spirit is the rock-foundation of wisdom, prosperity, strength and peace" (7). By building up one's own spiritual strength, one strengthens the country. Sivananda encourages Hindus to "be ever a beacon light of the spiritual essence of Bharatvarsha's culture. Live the exemplary personal and social life of the ideal Hindu." Sivananda closes his article with a patriotic crescendo: "India will rise. India must rise. It is a glorious land of Rishis and sages. It is a Punya-bhumi [holy land] with Ganga and Yamuna. It is the best of all lands" (7).

In this special centenary issue of the *Voice of Sivananda,* the editors include the article, "In Retrospection," by Sivananda's successor, Chidananda. He opens with paeans to Gurudev Sivananda and notes that in 1963 and 1964 the world mourned the passing of great leaders— Jawaharlal Nehru, John F. Kennedy, Pope John XXIII, and Sivananda. Through his revival of yoga and vedanta, "Swami Sivananda's name had become synonymous with the resurgence of India's ethical principles and spiritual ideals." Sivananda's "dynamic gospel of practical spirituality" saved India from the "rampages of agnostic materialism and hedonistic forces" (29).

Like Shiva himself, Sivananda roused himself from his austerities in "the northern apex of our Indian sub-continent." He preached his spiritual message with "the Voice of the Himalayas, the Voice of India" (29). Through "sweet persuasion," Sivananda captured the "hearts and thus saved the souls of India's children" at a time when "the strident voice of disbelief and skepticism was clamouring to claim the ear of a slowly awakening India." Chidananda presents Sivananda as a paternal, heroic leader who restored the preeminence of spirituality and the authority of Hindu ascetics. The reader might surmise that the official snubbing of Hindu ascetic leaders and their organizations, characteristic of the Congress government and Communists after Independence, was the menacing force threatening the souls of Mother India's children.

As successor to Sivananda and leader of the institution founded by him, Chidananda defines the identity and duty of the Divine Life Society. It must continue Sivananda's mission of unifying and coordinating the work of all spiritual institutions. He constructs a series of equivalences whereby the Divine Life Society today is the living presence of Sivananda and Sivananda is identical with India's spirituality. The Divine Life Society

> will not only identify itself with the great spiritual work and teachings of Gurudev Swami Sivananda but also will feel its oneness with all spiritual institutions in India and abroad. The Divine Life Society identifies itself with Indian spirituality. The great Sun Swami Sivananda might have gone beyond the horizon, but its light continues to shine and to illumine the path of man's life towards God realisation and ultimate Divine Experience. Swami Sivananda is Immortal in the same way as India's Spirituality is Eternal. (32)

Through such equivalences Chidananda argues for the authoritative role of the Divine Life Society in defining and protecting spirituality, the "foundation-rock" of Indian culture and society. Articles in the *Voice of*

India indicate how Sivananda participated in the nationalist discourse of his time and how his contributions are taken up by contemporary propagandists of Hindu nationalism. Just as Sivananda, Radhakrishnan, Gandhi, and Savarkar strategically interpreted the teachings of Shankaracharya, Ramakrishna, Vivekananda, and others, so too their own teachings are variously interpreted to authorize contemporary political and social projects.

Both outsiders and insiders speculate how success has affected or interferes with the Divine Life Society's spiritual mission. Venkatesananda, a close disciple of Sivananda, has perhaps been the harshest critic of the direction the Society has taken after Sivananda's death. During Sivananda's life, Venkatesananda lived in the ashram and worked closely with his guru. Some of Venkatesananda's disciples told me that he was so dismayed by the situation after Sivananda's death that he left the ashram to spread his guru's message abroad. In an article in the journal *Light,* published by the Divine Life Society in Mauritius, Venkatesananda critically comments on the commodification of spirituality. He argues that great spiritual teachers derive their power from their ability to attract followers. They are constrained from speaking the truth because it would cause "disaffection" among their followers. Given this dynamic, "corruption thus becomes pervasive. Non-corruption or the simple truth doesn't sell. That which sells is a consumer commodity which naturally promotes business organization, hierarchy, pyramidal power structure" (*Light,* July 1982).

An Indian acquaintance who had visited the Sivananda Ashram in 1987 while making a film on the Ganges described the Divine Life Society as a highly successful corporate enterprise. Indeed, Sivananda and his disciples have built an organization which purveys a variety of commodities, e.g., yoga of synthesis, ayurvedic medicines, Sivananda audio cassettes and wristwatches as well as a network of political and business contacts and hundreds of publications which promise to lead readers along the path to divine life and self-realization, success and prosperity.

The Divine Life Society is a prosperous, formidable, and complex institution which attracts support from members of India's ruling-class groups. Like other apparatuses of ideological powers, the potency of the Divine Life Society relates to the ability of its leaders, administrators, proselytizers, and followers to interpret its ideology and use its organization for a variety of personal and political purposes. These purposes do not necessarily conform to those officially pronounced by the Divine Life Society in its 1986 annual report:

> The Fundamental Aims and Objects of The Divine Life Society, as a whole, are spiritual, cultural and social, entirely non-sectarian, universally applicable and perfectly tolerant. The Society offers a peaceful haven wherein is

provided ample opportunity and actual help for the restoration of peace to the troubled, conflict-ridden and psychologically traumatised personality of modern man. (*Annual Report and Balance Sheet of the Divine Life Society* 1986, 22)

SIVANANDA—THE HEART OF LOVE

The story of Sivananda's life conforms to hagiographical conventions discussed in relation to Satyamitranand. He was born in 1887 in a village in Tamil Nadu into a pious and orthodox brahman family and named Kuppuswamy Iyer. From an early age his behavior revealed his saintly character: he was generous and loving, devout and intelligent. At school he always stood first in his class and won prizes every year. His athletic ability, and particularly his interest in gymnastics, prefigured his later mastery of yoga. In order to serve others he decided to study medicine. So great was his dedication to medicine that he spent his holidays working in the hospital. Even as a medical student "he possessed more knowledge than doctors with covetable degrees" (*MMW*, "Swami Sivananda," 10).

Sivananda's career as a writer and publisher began when he started a medical journal called *Ambrosia*. He wrote most of the articles and used a variety of pseudonyms to give the publication the appearance of being a conventional scientific journal. Sivananda's generosity extended to this publishing venture: "even then he used to distribute the journal freely: he was shy to ask people for contribution." Yet somehow Sivananda made it a profitable venture, for when his mother, who had given him money to start the journal, later required cash "for celebrating some festival," he had it ready for her (10).

The next phase of Sivananda's life began when "a call came to Dr. Kuppuswamy from Malaya (now Malaysia) soon after the death of his father." His 1913 sea voyage to Malaya provides an occasion to remind readers of Sivananda's high ritual status and his strict adherence to brahmanic dietary regulations. Belonging to an "orthodox Brahmin family," Sivananda was "afraid to take non-vegetarian food in the ship." His mother packed a large quantity of sweets for the journey, and when Sivananda arrived "he was almost half dead" (10).

Sivananda was hired to run a hospital on a rubber plantation in Malaya. His employer, Mr. Robins, was "a terrible man with a violent temper, a giant figure, tall and stout." Sivananda's hard work and extraordinary healing powers attracted people to him and brought him fame: "Hopeless cases came to him, but success was sure. Everywhere people declared that he had a special gift from God for miraculous cures effected in the patients and acclaimed him as a very kind and sympathetic doctor with a charming and majestic personality" (11). He treated poor patients for free and bought them food and medicine: "he gave money like water." Sivananda also gave generously to sannyasis, sadhus, and beggars.

"The dormant spirituality" in Sivananda was awakened when a sadhu gave him a book by Swami Satchidananda. This prompted him to study the works of great Hindu teachers such as Shankaracharya, Rama Tirtha, and Vivekananda as well as the Bible and literature of the Theosophical Society. Despite his busy work schedule, he was "very regular in his daily worship, prayer and Yoga Asanas." He also studied "sacred scriptures like the Gita, the Mahabharata, the Bhagavata and the Ramayana" and sang devotional hymns (11). During this period of his life, the young doctor was something of a dandy and enjoyed displaying the luxuries purchased with the profits of his successful medical practice: "high class dress and collection of curious and fancy articles of gold, silver and sandalwood always attracted the doctor. Sometimes he purchased various kinds of gold rings and necklaces and wore them all at the same time. He used to wear ten rings on ten fingers!" (11). However much Sivananda fancied luxuries and conspicuous consumption, readers are assured he was not a greedy materialist: "Nothing could tempt the doctor. His heart was as pure as the Himalayan snow." His philanthropy and renunciation endeared him to all and "people lovingly called him the 'Heart of Love'" (11).

Having "purified his heart through loving service," Sivananda was now ready to leave his "lucrative practice" and renounce the world (12). After nine years overseas, he returned to Madras in 1922 and from there began his pilgrimage. He traveled to Benares to visit gurus, yogis, and temples. By 1924 he arrived in Rishikesh and soon after met Swami Vishvananda Saraswati: "The doctor saw a Guru in the monk and the monk saw a Chela in the doctor" (12). After a "brief personal talk" Vishvananda initiated him as a sannyasi and named him Swami Sivananda Saraswati. Unlike Sivananda's own disciples, who continuously refer to their Gurudev, Vishvananda has a minimal presence in the Sivananda saga. He is invoked to authorize Sivananda's initiation into a specific ascetic order. After initiating Sivananda, he sent "the necessary instructions about Sannyasa Dharma from Benares" and accounts of Sivananda's life do not refer to him again (12).

During the next few years Sivananda lived in a dilapidated, "scorpion infested hut" at Swarg ashram in Rishikesh. He began a period of meditation and severe austerities during which he fasted, kept silence, studied scriptures, and "practiced all the various Yogas." He also attended to needy sadhus, begging food for them and carrying "sick persons on his back to the hospital." Despite his vows of renunciation Sivananda was not without personal financial resources: "With some money from his insurance policy that had matured, Swamiji started a charitable dispensary at Lakshmanjhula [Rishikesh] in 1927" (12).

His frugality was such that he collected used envelopes and scraps of old newspapers and stitched them into notebooks. In these notebooks he wrote out "self-instructions" which he later formulated as guidelines for spiritual seekers. He wrote of the need to give up salt, sugar, spices, and vegetables and to serve "bhangis [untouchables], serve rogues, serve inferiors, remove faecal matter, clean clothes of Sadhus." These self-instructions stress the virtues of kindness and compassion, forgiveness and love. They emphasize the need to "develop good manners, extreme politeness, courtesy, etiquette, good demeanour, nobility, gentleness, mildness. Never be rude, harsh or cruel" (13). These notebooks record behavior which Sivananda regarded as requiring careful cultivation, behavior helpful for assuming the duties of guru and saint, or in the words of Gayatri Parivar founder Acharya Sharma, behavior useful "to convince others of one's superiority."

Sivananda's years of "intense and unbroken Sadhana" bore the desired fruit: "he enjoyed the bliss of Nirvikalpa Samadhi. He had come to the end of his spiritual journey" (12). Thus, the text attributes to Sivananda the attainment of his spiritual goal—merger of self with God. Having come to the end of his spiritual journey, Sivananda next set out on a pilgrimage through "the length and breadth of India." During these travels he lectured and led groups in singing bhajans (devotional songs).

In 1933 Sivananda formed the Swarg ashram Sadhu Sangha, his first attempt at establishing a formal organization with himself as the head. The following year he and his disciples moved across the Ganges into a shack "which looked like an abandoned cowshed." The increasing number of disciples seeking Sivananda's "lotus feet" necessitated further expansion. They found more cowsheds and made them habitable. When the old cowherd who was living in one of them vacated, "the Divine Life army completed the occupation" (13). In Sivananda's own account of the founding of the Divine Life Society he expresses his gratitude for the grant of land from the Maharaja of Tehri:

> I should feel it a pleasure to bring to everyone's notice that the Tehri (Garhwal) State Durbar has been giving its full support from time to time, and that had it not been for the free grant of land sanctioned by the Durbar to house the Divine Life Trust Society and its feeder institutions, there would not have been any place for us all to cover our heads from sun and storm, and rain and ravage, and carry on our activities with added zeal and vigour. . . . I once again take this opportunity of conveying my deep indebtedness to the Durbar and to one and all for the help given to me and my cause and pray humbly that the Durbar would be pleased to extend its gracious and generous hand of support to the Trust Society from time to time. (*MMW*, "The Great Fulfillment," 205)

ESTABLISHING AND EXPANDING THE DIVINE
LIFE MOVEMENT

In an article entitled the "Divine Life Movement," Sivananda discusses why he established the Divine Life Society in 1936. He describes its moment of formation as a "critical juncture" when

> Students became irreligious,
> They lost faith in religion,
> Under the influence of Science,
> They neglected Dharma,
> They began to smoke and gamble,
> Girls became fashionable,
> Officers became materialists,
> Health of people deteriorated,
> People shunned the scriptures,
> Materialism had its sway.
> (*MMW*, "The Divine Life Movement," 22)

At this critical juncture, people needed to be awakened to their errors and were eagerly searching for guidance. In response to this need, he formed the Society and "now people consider it a blessing to the world." The Divine Life Society is based on the "quintessence of the teachings of all religions and of all saints and prophets of the world." As an "all-embracing and all inclusive Institution," it does not condemn any cult but rather includes the principles of all religions and cults. It is without "pet dogmas or sectarian tenets." Its teachings lead people to the spiritual path and enable them "to take easily to the Divine Life even while living in the world and following the teachings of some particular cult or religion" (23). In another statement, Sivananda maintains that the Divine Life Society has neither "secret doctrines nor esoteric sections or inner circles. It is a purely spiritual organisation having no leanings towards politics" (*MMW*, "The Great Fulfillment," 206).

The Society stresses the practicality and accessibility of a disciplined spiritual life and expounds "in a rational and scientific manner the Yoga of Synthesis." Divine knowledge is not "the sole property of Sannyasis." It can be acquired by any man "in his own station of life," "be he a Brahmachari, Grihastha, Vanaprastha or Sannyasi, be he a scavenger, Brahmin, Shudra or Kshatriya, be he a busy man of the world or a silent Sadhak" (*MMW*, "The Divine Life Movement," 23). Sivananda, thus acknowledges social distinctions but asserts that his teachings are relevant and accessible to everyone.

The formation of the Divine Life Society Trust is said to have taken place when Sivananda was touring in the Punjab and conducting week-long, nonstop sessions of chanting Hari Nam: "It was in this atmosphere of sacred ecstasy" that all of a sudden Sivananda remembered "his Postal Cash Certificates of Rs. 5000" (*MMW*, "The Great Fulfillment," 199). He had been using the interest on this capital to buy food and medicine for sadhus at Rishikesh, but now he resolved to "utilise the whole amount in the best possible way to serve the world on a wider scale." After consulting with a devotee who was a lawyer, he formed and registered the Divine Life Society Trust "as the legal body of the Divine Life Society" (199).

The production and distribution of publications containing Sivananda's teachings and reporting on the activities of the Divine Life Society contributed to the growth of the organization. Publication of the Society's journal *Divine Life* commenced in 1938. The following year saw the formation of the Sivananda Publication League, which attempted to control the publication of Sivananda's writings that were being produced by the Gita Press in Gorakhpur, Motilal Banarsidass in Delhi, and private presses in Amritsar and Lahore. Sivananda explains why the Publication League was formed: "With the object of reserving the rights of publication, reprint, sales, etc., and to preserve my writings forever to help the Divine Life Trust Society financially, through the proceeds of the sales of the books published, I started the 'Sivananda Publication League, Rishikesh'" (204). Through its own publications and the placement of articles by Sivananda in newspapers and magazines, the Divine Life Society publicized its activities and the teachings of Sivananda throughout India. Biographical sketches of his prominent disciples frequently note that they first learned of Sivananda through some chance encounter with his writings: an article in a women's magazine in the home of a relative; a booklet lying under a stack of office paperwork; a published piece recycled as a grocer's paper bag; a book in the library.

By 1940 Sivananda had initiated 200 sannyasis and brahmacharis as his disciples and had attracted numerous lay supporters. As the Society's financial resources and labor supply increased, its operations expanded. Sivananda put his disciples to work: printing Divine Life Society literature on its own presses; answering letters from people seeking advice; running the ashram's kitchen to feed not only residents and visitors but also local sadhus and beggars; staffing the charitable medical clinic; manufacturing and selling ayurvedic medicines.

Indian English was the lingua franca of the ashram. Sivananda's disciples and followers were generally educated in English, and many were university graduates from wealthy families. For example, the official biographical sketch of Chidananda describes him as the eldest son of a "prosperous zamindar owning several villages, extensive lands and palatial buildings." Sivananda called this disciple, who served him as personal secretary and succeeded him as president of the Divine Life Society, "a prince among sannyasis" (*MMW*, "Stones, Bricks, and Mortar," 220–21). When Krishnananda, the general secretary of the Society since 1961, first came to Sivananda as a young man in 1944, Sivananda encouraged him to remain in the ashram: " 'Stay here till death; I will make kings and ministers fall at your feet.' The young man who wondered within himself how this could ever happen at all, now realises the prophecy of the saint's statement" (223).

A prominent early disciple of Sivananda was Swami Paramananda, "the youngest son of a prosperous Brahmin couple" (211). He first learned of Sivananda by reading his *Practice of Yoga* when working for the railways in Madras. He began to correspond with Sivananda, asking for advice about his "innate urge for renunciation." Sivananda advised him against being hasty and suggested he offer his services to the local Ramakrishna Mission. However, Paramananda's "zeal could not be subdued" and he headed to Rishikesh to meet Sivananda (211). When Paramananda arrived, Sivananda was away on a long tour, and so he went to the Ramakrishna Mission ashram in Calcutta, where he became "an attache" to a prominent swami. When this swami died, Paramananda "felt impelled to reach the feet" of Sivananda, who initiated him as a sannyasi in 1932.

Paramananda is acclaimed for his "matchless guru bhakti." He served his guru with exemplary diligence and dedication:

> Even a mere catalogue of the services rendered by Paramananda to the divine cause espoused by the Master would fill the pages of a large volume. Suffice it to say that when a holy wish arose in the Cosmic love-lake of Swami Sivananda's heart, it flooded Paramananda's entire being; when a word issued from Swami Sivananda's lips, Paramananda was ready with the response, "It is done, Swamiji." (212)

Sivananda publicly praised his disciple: "He is a very hard worker. He works the whole night." The many services Paramananda rendered to his guru include organizing his sixtieth birthday celebrations and his tours, mounting an exhibition of "Sivananda Regalia," collecting money to build the bhajan hall, and arranging the translation and publication of Sivananda's books in French and German. His official biography notes:

> Paramananda was often called the "Bismarck of the Ashram," meaning thereby that he was virtually the foundation, the basic structure of the edifice of the Divine Life Society, which he managed to maintain with all its strength and stability, by his sternness, precision and unparalleled devotion to Sri Gurudev Swami Sivananda." (212)

Sivananda also attracted older men who had retired from successful careers in law, medicine, education, business, and government administration and wanted to live in the ashram. Swami Swaroopananda, like Paramananda, was among Sivananda's first disciples. At the time he met Sivananda he was an elderly man, "well-read in English, Hindi and Sanskrit." He is described as a "talented Swami, a good orator and Kirtanist" (211). He toured with Sivananda, translating his guru's lectures into Hindi; Sivananda conferred on him the titles of Vachaspati (Master of Oratory) and Vedanta Kesari (Lion of Vedanta). When forming the Divine Life Society, Sivananda appointed him as a trustee and first general secretary.

Sivananda thus had valuable resources in the form of dedicated personnel—eager, energetic young men and experienced, well-connected older men with financial security and leisure. Some of them might leave the ashram after a while and others might live elsewhere and make annual visits, but whoever came to the ashram was expected to perform as guru seva whatever tasks Sivananda might assign. "The marvellous expansion in the activities of the Society" is attributed to Sivananda's ability to encourage in each person "the expression of his talents and genius." However, as a "Great Master and Avatara," Sivananda did not require the help of his disciples. Rather, part of his "multifaceted and cosmic" mission was to provide a "favorable atmosphere for the ripening of evolved souls": "Thus did Swami Sivananda cause the gravitating of exceptionally talented, rare and evolved souls towards himself" (211).

Sivananda's growing reputation also attracted curious, skeptical young men. A journalist in Delhi writing for the *National Herald,* Balakrishnan Menon (later known as Swami Chinmayananda), was one such man. He went to Rishikesh intending to "expose the whole racket" but was favorably impressed by Sivananda and the work of the ashram (Patchen 1989, 34). He described Sivananda as continually busy, working seven days a week without holidays and yet exuding a "dynamic peace." Sivananda paid special attention to Menon and induced the journalist to extend his stay from a few days to one month.

According to Patchen, ashram residents became jealous and wondered why Sivananda was favoring Menon, a chain smoker and compulsive tea drinker. Yet even they could see in Menon's "big, bulging yogic eyes and extra long arms" the signs of "spiritual tendencies from previous lives" (34). Menon returned to Delhi and wrote articles about the marvelous personality and practical, yet sublime teachings of Sivananda and the important work of the Divine Life Society. Later in 1947 when the Divine Life Society was concurrently celebrating Sivananda's sixtieth birthday and India's independence, Menon was invited back to the ashram to edit the commemorative volume being published for the occasion. His second visit lasted three months, and during this time Sivananda began to train Menon to speak to audiences on religious topics. He returned to Delhi with Sivananda's books, which he reviewed in the *National Herald.*

In 1948 Menon returned to Rishikesh and decided to remain in the ashram. He was initiated by Sivananda and named Swami Chinmaya-nanda. He later studied Vedanta with another swami and then began to tour India in order, as he put it, "to convert Hindus to Hinduism." In conceiving his mission, Chinmayananda asked himself: "Can I face the educated class of India and bring to their faithless hearts at least a ray of understanding of what our wondrous culture stands for?" (ix). His biographer notes that Chinmayananda's social background equipped him for this mission: "He had been one of the educated elite. He knew their weaknesses; he knew their strengths" (4). His training as a journalist, his study of Sivananda's teachings, and his knowledge about the operations of the Divine Life Society prepared him for establishing and running his own organization, the Chinmaya Mission. He began with yajna tours throughout India which included singing, chanting, vedic fire sacrifices, and lectures on topics such as "Let us be Hindus." Indian president Rajendra Prasad presided over Chinmayananda's 1956 yajna in Delhi.

Like Sivananda, Chinmayananda's tours and publications attracted supporters and raised money. He published a journal that included his own writings as well as excerpts from the writings of Sivananda, Aurobindo, Vivekananda, and St. Francis. His growing success is said to have created tension with Sivananda's disciples, who accused him of egotism and the desire for fame and glory (197–98). When he increasingly became a source of discord within the Divine Life Society, Sivananda is said to have told Chinmayananda, "From this moment, let us worship each other in our hearts" (198).

Whatever may have been the reasons for the acrimony between Sivananda's disciples and Chinmayananda, it has eased sufficiently for the Divine Life Society to include his biographical sketch with those of other important disciples in its Sivananda centenary commemorative volume (*MMW*, 236–37). Indeed, Chinmayananda is perhaps Sivananda's most famous disciple: he was founder-president of the Vishva Hindu Parishad and heads the Chinmaya Mission, an organization with ninety-seven branches throughout India and abroad, which also has numerous affiliated schools, ashrams, study groups, and medical projects. In a speech to the 1987 graduating class at one of the Mission's training centers, Chinmayananda reminded the audience of the Mission's purpose: "We are creating an army of workers for the protection of Hinduism and for its further development—to rediscover the true heart of Mother India for the people" (Patchen 1989, 255).

This brief account of Chinmayananda's association with Sivananda and the Divine Life Society suggests how Sivananda attracted and trained ambitious, talented young men as his followers. Chinmayananda adapted Sivananda's teachings on practical spirituality and his techniques of propagation; he became a major ideologue and leader of the Hindu nationalist movement. Discussion in chapter 9 of Sivananda's disciples who returned to the ashram with their own disciples for the Centenary Celebrations will introduce some others who have followed career trajectories similar to Chinmayananda. Their association with Sivananda and their training in the ashram provided them with important skills and linked them with networks of potential patrons useful for building up their own organizations.

Sivananda's and other official accounts of the Divine Life Society record the events considered to be significant to its expansion and mission. Sivananda founded the All World Religions' Federation in 1945 and the All World Sadhus' Federation in 1947. Vivekananda had to travel to Chicago to address an assembly of representatives of the world's religions; Sivananda convened his own World Parliament of Religions in 1953 at his ashram in Rishikesh. The president of the Hindu Mahasabha was one of the speakers who addressed the parliament's 1,000 delegates. In 1948 Sivananda opened the Yoga Vedanta Forest Academy to promote the Society's status as a center of spiritual scholarship. Three years later he began the Yoga Vedanta Forest Academy Press to publish more literature. To expand the work of translating and distributing publications, the Sivananda Literature Dissemination Committee was formed in 1959.

Accompanied by an entourage of fifteen of his ascetic disciples, Sivananda went on a "lightning" two month All India and Ceylon Spiritual Awakening Tour in 1950. During this tour Sivananda and his assistants publicized the Divine Life Society through lectures, radio talks, and the distribution of literature. The tour was also a debut for Sivananda's protégé, Chidananda: "Together they attracted to the Divine Life Movement great political and social leaders in India, high ranking Government officials and rulers of Indian states" (*MMW,* "The Divine Life Movement," 22). The Society describes the effect of this tour as "tremendous." Sivananda "virtually awakened the moral and spiritual consciousness in the hearts of the people." This awakening aroused the desire for divine life and brought increasing numbers of people to the ashram. After the tour, "there was an incessant flow of seeking souls to the Ashram, as also a greater inflow of letters from aspirants from the entire country, which demanded more intense dissemination of knowledge" (*MMW,* "The Divine Life Society," 25).

Like other religious and political leaders, Sivananda had enemies. One particular incident is consistently recounted to illustrate Sivananda's saintly capacity to reform even the most vile of characters. During an evening assembly at the ashram in 1950, a man attacked Sivananda with an ax. Sivananda was unharmed but much to his disciples' dismay, he refused to turn his attacker over to the police. Instead, he showered love and forgiveness on his would-be assassin, gave him books on practical spirituality, and sent him home.

Throughout Sivananda's life, the Society's activities continued to expand. By the time of his death in 1963 his work was complete: "He came with a Mission and it was FULFILLED" (*MMW*, "The Great Fulfillment," 209). Although "such a Soul was neither anxious about his Mission nor did he nominate anyone as his successor (though he had the power to do so)," Sivananda's careful training of his talented disciples ensured that "they would carry forward his noble Mission." With its celebration of Sivananda's birth centenary, the Divine Life Society describes itself as entering "another era of dynamism." It continues to be "wholly guided by the Master's Divine Will" (209). The "Miracle-Man" and his Mission live on through his disciples, who "are small miracles in themselves": "It would be no exaggeration to say that Sivananda, on his attaining Mahasamadhi, has verily entered his disciples, in and through whom he carries on his noble Mission, in a more vigorous manner, even to this day" (209).

SERVING THE NATION

In a section entitled "After the Master's Passing," the Divine Life Society discusses how it furthers Sivananda's mission. After Sivananda's death, the Society's trustees elected Chidananda as president. Under his leadership the Society works "ever more vigorously" to disseminate throughout India and the world "the Divine Life Gospel, summed up by the Master in six succinct words: 'Serve, Love, Give, Purify, Meditate, Realise'" (*MMW*, "The Divine Life Society," 25). The Society represents its activities as pursuing national goals and complementing the work of the Indian government. Without offering any specific evidence, the Society asserts that its nonsectarian, fully tolerant teachings provide "a cementing factor amongst the people of this country. The Ashram has drawn its residents from all provinces in India. Its Branch Centres are to be found throughout the country and their spiritual work fosters tolerance and encourages national unity" (26). As part of the Society's annual national and state conferences, it sponsors "one or two sessions as All-Religious-Meet or Sarva-Dharma-Sammelana." These sessions are said to promote peace in Indian society. The Society claims that both its spiritual teachings and its activities "make it evident that it has been propagating practices and indirectly working for targets for which the government is now working" (26).

As a "pioneer" advocate and popularizer of yoga, the Society promotes "national health and physical fitness" (26; see Strauss 1995). It also contributes to national health through its free medical facilities: the ashram hospital, annual eye camps, first aid training courses, women's and children's medical camps, and educational exhibits on health and nutrition. Its branches similarly provide a variety of medical and other social services. The Society's work with the lepers of Rishikesh has "reclaimed from the streets a large number of leper beggars." It not only provides lepers with housing, medical care, and clothing but also "bears a major part of the financial burden" of running Kushtha Ashram, a colony for 120 lepers (27).

The Society presents its involvement in educational activities as another way it serves the nation. It financially supports over one hundred "deserving students" from "very poor and backward" areas as well as "poor and deserving" local schools (27). Through these and numerous other charitable activities, the Sivananda Ashram extends its influence throughout the region and upholds its authority by enacting the role of benevolent patron of the needy. As recipients of the Society's patronage, students and their families, lepers and local educational institutions become its clients. Continued assistance requires that they repay their debts in the terms explicitly or implicitly set by the creditor.

The Society involves itself in educational activities by supporting "normal schooling" and through classes conducted at the ashram on "Yoga, Vedanta and Indian Culture in general, including classes in Sanskrit language, music, physical culture, etc." Furthermore, the Society sends its "trained Instructors" to teach special courses at the National Academy of Administration in Mussoorie and the Officers Training School in Nanital. These formal links with institutions which train members of India's ruling classes provide the Society with further opportunities for recruiting highly placed and influential supporters. Similar training courses are also offered by the Society at "factories, industrial townships, universities like Pantnagar University, the Delhi University, the Jawaharlal Nehru University, New Delhi, etc." (28).

The Society's financial investments are presented as further evidence of its service to the nation. Since its founding the "Institution has been a regular and unfailing participator in a number of national schemes by contributing appreciably towards the Small Savings Fund, National Savings Certificates, Defence Bonds and collection drives undertaken by the Government" (27). Thus, even when the Society is making money through its investments, it serves the nation. Readers learn nothing about the sources and circulation of this investment capital. To what extent might it be black money which the Society purifies and transmutes into social and political capital for its donors, and uses to fund its own operations? Vanaik offers as a conservative estimate the value of India's illicit or black economy to be forty to fifty per cent of the recorded economy. He describes the black economy as "closely integrated with the 'white economy.' Black savings flow into the capital market and into bank deposits (with few questions asked), thus providing resources for investment" (1990, 36). Following the statement about its investments in "national schemes," the Divine Life Society assures readers that, like the government and other prominent religious or-

ganizations, the Society "also contributes its share in times of natural calamities like famines, epidemic, flood, etc." (*MMW,* "The Divine Life
Society," 27).

The Society's depiction of the succor provided by its "Headquarters-
Ashram" recalls the bountiful, wish-fulfilling cow which two rival sages
fought to possess. At the Sivananda ashram no hungry person is refused a
meal; no "shelterless person is turned away without a night's shelter here."
If this were the case, the ashram's resources would have dried up long ago.
The Society reports that it fed approximately 500 people daily and accommodated 10,987 visitors in 1986.

The text emphasizes the spiritual resources of the ashram. It is a "haven for persons in distress" that provides a place for them to "rest and recover . . . and return in a better condition to face their problems and
situations." Men and women of all ages and backgrounds come to the ashram "seeking to fulfill some inner want, some indefinable need." The Divine Life Society attempts to define and evaluate these inner wants and
needs. It also promises to provide the means to fulfill them—"Serve, Love,
Give, Purify, Meditate, Realise"—means that in turn fulfill needs of the organization. However, the text asserts that "the value and importance to
their lives of what they find here is only known to them and can be assessed
only by them" (28).

SPIRITUALITY: AN INVISIBLE YET A TANGIBLE ASSET

In the *Voice of Sivananda* article discussed at the beginning of this chapter,
Sivananda proclaims the universal and inestimable value of India's unique
spiritual heritage. This theme is also introduced in the discussion of the
Society's service to the nation. The translation of Sivananda's writings on
yoga into European languages is presented as an example of national service. His works have been translated "with the earnest objective of bringing about the widest possible spread of our country's most precious
spiritual heritage. The dignity and eagerness of the country's cultural heritage has obviously risen high in the eyes of the people's of other nations by
this institution's work" (*MMW,* "The Divine Life Society," 26). This "eagerness of the country's cultural heritage" takes the form of "spiritual
teachers" deputed by the Divine Life Society; they are "welcomed everywhere as the country's cultural and spiritual ambassadors of goodwill"
(26). Using the language of capitalist economics, the text hints that the Society's work expands the profitable markets for Hindu spirituality: "The
vast goodwill thus earned for India and its spiritual science (Adhyatma-
vidya) is an invisible and yet a tangible asset whose value cannot be
easily estimated. This good work is spreading progressively all over the
world" (26).

As a registered society, the Divine Life Society is required by law to report on its tangible assets and declare their value. The *Annual Report and Balance Sheet of the Divine Life Society (AR)* for 1986 includes eight fold-out pages showing its audited annual accounts. The following discussion of the 1986 *Annual Report* is based on this material concerning its formal structure and public disclosures of financial operations. The first half of the *Report* addresses the main activities of the Society's twenty-two departments, which are divided into five categories: Dissemination of Spiritual and Cultural Knowledge; Practical Training in Yoga and Vedanta; Humanitarian and Social Welfare Service; Branches; and Miscellaneous Activities. The *Report* asserts that through these activities "the Society aims to remove the unwarranted distinction between the spiritual and the secular, and endeavours to present an integrated view of life as a whole" (*AR*, 1). The Auditors' Report and balance sheet constitute the remaining sixteen pages of the *Report*.

Many of the activities referred to in the *Report* have been introduced above in the discussion of the growth of the Divine Life Society. Other activities will be addressed in later discussions of daily life in the ashram and the celebration of the Sivananda birth centenary. In 1988, when I asked a member of the board of management about the Society's financial situation, he replied that although its fiscal practices may appear unsound and idiosyncratic to an outsider, the Society not only keeps intact a sound financial base but also considerably expanded it through funds raised during the Centenary year.

Of the 226 branches affiliated to the Society's Headquarters, twenty-one are outside India. In 1986 the affiliation of fifty-one branches was pending for "non-fulfillment of conditions necessary for affiliation." The *Report* does not specify what constitutes these conditions. Official affiliation fees are minimal. Notes in the Auditor's report state that the branches are "only affiliated bodies functionally independent from Head Office." Each branch is a "separate financial unit," and hence branch accounts are not incorporated in the report of Head Office accounts. The branches, however, do provide important services for the Head Office: they sell Divine Life Society publications and ayurvedic medicines; they arrange public functions for swamis on tour; they recruit members and supporters whose donations may go directly to the Head Office.

A review of the Society's annual financial report is suggestive rather than conclusive. A chartered accountant in Hardwar whose clients include numerous ashrams told me that such official financial reports conform to legal requirements of charitable trust societies; their relevance for an inquiry into a trust society's actual financial condition and the scope of its operations is limited. Furthermore, evaluations of property and assets are not unequivocal. For example, the 1986 written down value of the Society's fixed assets, which include extensive landholdings and numerous buildings—temples, offices, residences, a library, hospital, and clinic—and their fixtures and equipment, as well as a farm, dairy, tractor, and motor vehicles, are valued at the seemingly low figure of 6,550,009 rupees (approximately U.S. $730,000). Whatever the fixed assets' current value may be, the Divine Life Society's occupation of the banks of the Ganges at Rishikesh which began in 1934 continues apace, transforming the riverfront and forested hillside into a concrete jungle.

EIGHT

Arenas of Ashram Life

AN OFFICIAL TOUR OF THE SIVANANDA ASHRAM

During my first days in Hardwar at the guesthouse of the Gurukul Kangri University, I was invited on a sight-seeing tour of the area by Bhaiji, the head of a music school in Delhi, who was also staying in the guesthouse. The tour included an excursion to Rishikesh and a visit to the Divine Life Society's Sivananda ashram. When we arrived at the ashram, Bhaiji introduced himself at the reception office, reminding them that he had brought his choir to the ashram six months earlier to sing at the opening ceremonies of the Sivananda Birth Centenary. When he asked if we might meet with Chidananda, we were brought to Guru Niwas, Chidananda's residence. As we passed through a room filled with video equipment, we were told that a film was being made about the ashram. We were seated on a balcony and asked to wait there until Chidananda was ready to see us. As we waited on the balcony enjoying the fresh breeze and commanding view of the Ganges, ashram personnel served tea and snacks and gave us some Divine Life Society books. It seemed as though we were receiving VIP treatment.

After nearly an hour we were told that Chidananda was outside in his car and we could meet him if we hurried downstairs. Several of Chidananda's attendants hovered around the car. Chidananda was alone in the back seat with a wet orange towel atop his shaven head. He looked a frail and elderly man. He graciously greeted Bhaiji, saying that he was unaware of his visit. Bhaiji replied that he had given his card to one of the attendants. Chidananda tactfully changed the subject to Bhaiji's choir, saying that people were still talking about its performance and that they must perform again at the ashram. His assistants told us we must not further delay Chidananda, since he was already two hours late for an appointment in nearby Dehra Dun. As the driver started the car, Chidananda directed his assistant to give us refreshments, books, and a thorough tour of the ashram.

Bhaiji seemed perturbed at this snub and blamed it on the assistant's 185 failure to give his card to Chidananda. Bhaiji reasoned that had Chidananda known we were waiting, he certainly would have given us a private audience. Instead we were given a private tour, which began with a visit to one of the ashram's senior swamis, Nadabrahmananda. At the age of twenty he began seventeen years of "arduous discipline and austerity" associated with his musical training under three "illustrious masters" (*MMW*, "Stones, Bricks, and Mortar," 246). He later became a professor of music at Benares Hindu University and court musician for the Maharaja of Mysore. At the age of fifty-seven he came to the ashram, and Sivananda initiated him as a sannyasi.

Rotund and looking twenty years younger than his ninety-two years, Nadabrahmananda's regal posture was buttressed by orange cushions. Photographs filled the walls of his reception room. They documented his travels through the world and pictured him with foreign admirers and music students. Like other fashionable and successful swamis, photographs show him with western celebrities—film stars, musicians, politicians, and the Pope. His official autobiographical sketch records his acclaim:

> His ability to present himself as a master musician was really superb and people got thrilled, and thousands of devotees and eager students especially in the United States of America were trained by him. . . . His departure from the United States due to age and fatigue and his coming back to the Ashram on that account brought a sense of bereavement, as it were, among the students in America who considered him as a father, a Guru and almost a Godman in the field of Music. (246)

Nadabrahmananda also had for ready display an album with photographs showing him wired up for all sorts of medical tests and surrounded by doctors and scientists. He explained that they were studying the extraordinary physical abilities which he developed through his training in yoga and music. He then gave us a brief demonstration: for several minutes he kept himself from blinking while flexing various muscles—calf, forearm, pectoral, stomach—pulsating them to count time like a metronome.

His official biography maintains that despite "numerous commercial offers" Nadabrahmananda kept the vow he made to his music guru and "steadfastly refused to compromise the spiritual purity of his music" (246). The "spiritual purity" of Nadabrahmananda's yogic and musical talents, however, have earned him both fame and fortune. Marble plaques outside the ashram's dining hall and Vishvanath temple announce donations of 250,000 rupees made by him in memory of his mother.

After our visit with Nadabrahmananda, our guide showed us the principal places of worship in the ashram: Sivananda's samadhi shrine and the Vishvanath temple. We also visited the bhajan hall where ashram residents continue without cessation the Sanskrit chanting which was begun by Sivananda in 1943. As our guide led us around, I asked him how he came to live in the ashram. He replied that he had been a businessman in Bombay and came to live in the ashram two years ago. Chidananda had initiated him as a brahmachari. If and when his guru deems him ready, he will be initiated as a sannyasi. The guide then showed us the printing press that produces much of the Divine Life Society literature. Next we visited the library, an attractive and airy octagonal building. It houses 10,705 books in English, Hindi, Sanskrit, and other Indian languages. An average of 450 people use the library every month (*Annual Report [AR]* 1986). On the walls of the library hang large photos of Sivananda, Ramakrishna and Sarada Devi, Vivekananda, Anandamayi Ma, and Indira Gandhi.

When we completed the tour, I told the guide about my research and asked if it might be possible to arrange a future stay in the ashram. He encouraged me to return in September for the finale of the Centenary Celebration but suggested that at that time the ashram would be very crowded and it would be better to arrange accommodation elsewhere. However, after September, the ashram would be quiet again and if I wrote in advance, a room could be reserved for me.

ASHRAM ROUTINES AND HOLIDAYS

In accordance with the advice given about future visits, I returned for the September finale of the Sivananda Centenary year. Before examining materials concerning the Divine Life Society's Centenary celebration, I shall discuss aspects of ashram life which I became familiar with during subsequent visits. Both in my letter asking permission to stay in the ashram and when introducing myself to people around the ashram, I explained that I was a Ph.D. student conducting research on religious organizations. I wanted to distinguish my purposes from those who stay in the ashram in order to serve a guru, practice yoga and meditation, study Hindu philosophy, and seek spiritual liberation. Yet, I was often reminded during my visits that staying in the Sivananda ashram could not but be spiritually beneficial.

To avoid unnecessary attention and supervision from male ashram officials during my visits, I minimized contact with them and sought out the women residents of the ashram. In an environment where misogynist ascetic attitudes arouse sexual suspicion concerning women, and particularly foreign women, it is also strategic for a woman to seek out and spend time with other women. Most of all, I enjoyed conversing with these women residents and listening to their stories about life in the ashram. Had I been less aloof from the male officials and senior swamis, I might have gathered more information about certain aspects of ashram business, but in order to guard my autonomy and reputation I considered it more prudent to keep my distance. As in other ashrams, officials and residents prefer to talk with outsiders about spirituality. After a while, however, a few residents spiced their discourses on spirituality with stories and gossip about curious characters as well as past and ongoing scandals in the ashram. One resident likened the function of an ashram to a sewer: through it flows human filth.

Visitors hoping to stay in the ashram first report to the reception office that is on the main road which divides the ashram into two sections. The lower section stretches along the riverside, and its buildings—hospital, residences, offices, shops selling books and ayurvedic medicines—are interspersed with other shops, tea stalls, and taxi and scooter stands which cater to ashram visitors and pilgrims. Across the street from the reception office is a steep stairway and a driveway leading to the main portion of the ashram that climbs up the hillside. This upper part with its residences, temple, bhajan hall, Sivananda samadhi shrine, and library, provides a quiet retreat from the bustle of the bazaar which characterizes the lower portion of the ashram.

Compared to other ashrams with guards at their gates and guides directing visitors' movements, the premises of the Sivananda ashram are more open. People can enter off the street and wander about without being questioned. Those visitors who want to stay in the ashram or want more information about its activities make their inquiries in the reception office. As elsewhere in Hardwar and Rishikesh, the busy season extends from late April until October, the months when roads to the Himalayan pilgrimage centers are passable. The ashram is particularly crowded during these months, and visitors who have not made prior arrangements for their stay are often turned away.

After earlier visits when the ashram had been packed with summer and Centenary visitors, I returned during the winter and early spring lull and stayed in the ashram for several visits extending from a few days to two weeks. Because there were relatively few visitors when I arrived in November, I was assigned a commodious room in the new guest house, complete with private bath and sunny balcony. On later visits I was given more modest rooms and usually paired with other foreign women.

Conversations with ashram personnel in the reception office and with visitors about their reception by these personnel indicate that room assignments in the ashram relate to a complicated calculus of social and official status. For instance, on one occasion, I was told that I would have to stay elsewhere for a few days. No rooms were presently available because forty government officials had come to Rishikesh for business, and they wanted to stay in the ashram. The man in the reception office apologetically explained that the ashram was obliged to accommodate these government officials. Later in the day I was informed that a room had been found for me.

During another visit I was assigned a dark and drafty room made icy by the winter wind howling down the narrow valley. A sunny room across the hall had been empty for several days, so I asked in the reception office about switching rooms. They informed me that it was reserved for a group of important devotees which included the wife of the Tamil Nadu minister of transport. Their arrival had been delayed by the death of the chief minister of Tamil Nadu, but they could arrive any moment. On another occasion, an official in the reception office sighed after appeasing a group of disgruntled visitors who had demanded that they be given rooms with private facilities. He explained to me that they "require their amenities" because they were members of the Nepalese royal family.

Besides accommodating itself to the requirements of its VIP visitors, reception office personnel size up foreign visitors according to nationality, appearance, age, gender, and social connections. They send some away immediately and send others to Krishnananda, who decides if and how long they will be permitted to stay in the ashram. Foreign travelers arriving without prior arrangements are often turned away. An English woman told me that when she arrived unannounced, the reception office had told her that nothing was available. As soon as she mentioned the name of the man in Bombay who had suggested that she come to the ashram after her visit with his (wealthy) family, they became more cordial and gave her a VIP room.

Individuals or groups from abroad are encouraged to make bookings for their visits. In 1986 the ashram sponsored special courses for six different groups of Japanese yoga teachers. A Japanese woman arranged to come by herself to the ashram after learning about it from the Indian tourist office in London. She felt her conversations with Krishnananda had been spiritually beneficial but she did not like the fact that the ashram refused to charge fixed fees. Visitors might make a donation in remuneration for their food and lodging, but she wanted to know exactly how much to pay. After a week she moved to a small ashram which not only has specified rates for room and board but also at that time had a dozen other Japanese people staying there.

Approximately 150 people live permanently on ashram premises and include sannyasis, lay devotees, and male students studying in local schools. In 1986 the ashram reported accommodating a total of 10,907 visitors, of which 403 were from abroad. Due to the Centenary celebrations and the publicity generated by them, the numbers visiting the ashram increased in 1987 and 1988.

After registering in the reception office, visitors are given a schedule of ashram activities and are urged to attend them. They also are given a pass for meals in the dining hall and are reminded to be punctual. A list of "Instructions to Visitors" is included with the schedule. The following are "strictly forbidden" by the ashram: smoking and the consumption of eggs, meat, fish, liquor, and intoxicating drugs. Violators are liable to expulsion.

Cooking and the "usage of electric gadgets" in rooms are prohibited. In accordance with the ashram's spiritual purpose, "an atmosphere of peace should be maintained at all times."

The ashram's daily regime has three foci: the temple with its morning, midday, and evening rituals; the samadhi shrine and bhajan hall where people gather at set times throughout the day for meditation, chanting, devotional singing, and lectures; and the dining hall which serves breakfast, lunch, afternoon tea, and supper. Yoga classes also meet twice a day but are suspended whenever the yoga teacher is away on tour. By talking to ashram residents I learned of other regular activities such as morning and afternoon lectures by a learned swami and an early morning session of devotional music.

The daily regime of the ashram is frequently embellished by rituals and other observances associated with numerous Hindu holidays, anniversaries related to Sivananda, and the birthdays of senior swamis, particularly Chidananda and Krishnananda. The ashram celebrates Hindu holidays such as Mahashivaratri, Ram Navmi, Devi Navaratri, the birthdays of Krishna, Hanuman, Adi Shankaracharya, and the *Bhagavad Gita*. The ashram also celebrates anniversaries associated with Sivananda—his sannyas initiation, his birthday, his death, and Guru Purnima (the full moon, usually in July, when disciples and devotees worship and make special gifts to their guru). It also has annual observances to mark the commencement in 1943 of non-stop Sanskrit chanting *(akhanda sankirtan yajna)* and the consecration of the Vishvanath temple. Special rituals are performed on particular dates in the lunar calendar, particularly full moon days. The purpose of these rituals is said to be "world peace and human welfare." The performance of pujas on dates requested by individual devotees is an important source of revenue for the ashram. The 1986 balance sheet shows an income of over four and a half million rupees from this source.

Although most ritual activity is conducted in the temple and Sivananda samadhi shrine, the library is used for ceremonies associated with Durga puja and Christmas. A temporary shrine is set up in the library for Durga puja during which ashram residents and visitors gather for rituals and readings of the *Devi Mahatmya*. During one session, several women were so overcome with emotion that they began to weep. The reading was led by the librarian, a sannyasini named Krishnapriya who knows the Sanskrit text by heart; she did not allow the others' displays of devotion to interfere with the rhythm of her chanting.

The ashram's elaborate Christmas observances form part of its annual festival cycle and provide an occasion for the Divine Life Society to enact its embrace and patronage of Christianity. Foreigners residing in and visiting the ashram are particularly prominent in the Christmas celebration. They gather a few days in advance to plan the proceedings and practice singing

Christmas carols. In 1987 the musical portion of the program was greatly enhanced by the talents of two professional musicians—a flautist and a trumpet player—whose yoga teacher in America had suggested that they visit the ashram during their trip to India. Several Japanese people staying at nearby ashrams also joined the chorus of carolers.

Christmas observances began in the library at dawn on Christmas eve. Accompanied by drums and cymbals, ashram swamis led the assembly in an hour of chanting various mantras, including "aum Jesus." Bookshelves were moved aside; tinsel garlands, a tree with flashing colored lights, and a nativity scene transformed the library into a Christmas chamber. The shrine with a garlanded picture of Jesus between two garlanded pictures of Sivananda suggests how the Divine Life Society encompasses Christianity within its cult of Sivananda.

The main Christmas eve observances began after dinner with swamis leading the audience in the chanting of "Jai Ganesh." This was followed by an hour of recorded carols during which people continued to crowd into the library, huddling together on a cold winter's night. An older Canadian man who has lived in the ashram for over a decade presided as master of ceremonies. With a detailed, almost scene-by-scene account, he introduced the film, Zefferelli's epic *The Life of Jesus*. It was an old print in English with Arabic and French subtitles.

After the film four westerners read passages attributed to Ramakrishna, Vivekananda, Mahatma Gandhi, and Ramdas concerning the life and teachings of Jesus. One reader particularly pleased the largely Indian audience by reading and making her remarks in Hindi. The next part of the program involved readings from the New Testament, which were punctuated by Christmas carols. The reader, a western woman and ashram resident for many years, became flustered because children sitting in front began to chatter and giggle. The master of ceremonies had to relieve her. When the readings were completed the foreigners circumambulated the library carrying candles and singing "Silent Night." After the candlelight procession of carolers, a Japanese man gave a modern dance performance. The dance involved puja-like movements with an oil lamp and flowers before the shrines of Jesus and Sivananda. Throughout the dance he chanted "I am the way, the truth, and the light." Finally, the proceedings were concluded with a swami leading rounds of chanting "Hare Rama." The moment which many in the audience had been awaiting at last arrived, distribution of prasad—slices of Christmas cake and Indian sweets.

Early on the morning of Christmas day, foreigners who were not already awake were roused by a knock at their door. The head of the reception office went to each room and personally invited all foreigners in the ashram to a special Christmas lunch. Like a solicitous host, he supervised the serving of the meal in the ashram dining hall. Women and men were seated on the floor in separate rows. Unlike the usual arrangement with women sitting with their backs to the men, for Christmas lunch they sat facing one another. Although diners are usually reprimanded for conversing during meals, an atmosphere of conviviality was allowed to prevail during Christmas lunch as people were permitted to talk amongst themselves. Ashram residents and visitors were also treated to special foods and delicacies—rich vegetable and rice dishes, salad, and sweets—a break from the simple daily fare. As always, the meal commenced with chanting of mantras. Pictures of Krishna and Arjuna in their chariot and of Sivananda as well as other Hindu devotional images decorate the walls of the dining hall.

As part of the ashram routine, visitors and residents are particularly encouraged to attend the two-hour evening gathering or satsang in the Sivananda samadhi shrine. Its program varies but generally includes chanting, singing, and a discourse on a topic related to spirituality. Sitting on cushions in front of the audience, Krishnananda and other swamis and senior brahmacharis resident in the ashram regularly lecture to the satsang audience. This evening assembly is particularly well attended if there are rumors that Chidananda is in the ashram and may come to the satsang. After the closing chant, residents and visitors swarm around the swamis to ask questions and seek their blessings.

Not listed on the schedule but another of the ashram's regular and more intimate activities is Vidyananda's early morning devotional music sessions, which meet for about two hours. On winter mornings willful effort is required to wrest oneself from a warm bed, have a cold bath, and face the icy darkness to reach Vidyananda's room by 4:45. However, discomfort dissipates when Vidyananda begins to play the vina, leading the few others gathered in his room—dimly lit and suffused with incense—in steady, sonorous chanting and singing. After working for twenty-five years as a musician in the film industry in Bombay and Madras, Vidyananda joined the ashram in 1956 and was initiated as a sannyasi by Sivananda. Now in his eighties, he teaches vina and conducts these sessions of devotional music. Another ashram resident commented that it is not unusual to see Vidyananda go into a trance while singing.

Like Vidyananda's music, Brahmananda's expositions of Sanskrit religious and philosophical texts also provide for ashram residents and visitors an experience of intimacy with a master of his medium. When his health permits, Brahmananda offers courses during which he explicates a specific Sanskrit text. The classes open and close with chanting of mantras. Eager brahmacharis, other ashram residents, and visitors gather on his veranda in the morning and afternoon to listen to him read passages in Sanskrit and explain them in English. Some of the participants study English translations of the texts on their own and prepare questions for Brahmananda.

Other questions arise during his expositions, e.g., to the question, "Why did Rama cry over Sita?" Brahmananda replied, "He did not care if he cried or did not cry." The classes enable people to participate in the dialogical tradition of religious teaching as well as to increase their knowledge of specific philosophical and religious concepts and texts and their fluency in discussing them.

AUTHORITY ENACTED: KRISHNANANDA'S DAILY DARSHANS

The veranda outside of Krishnananda's rooms is the setting for another master at work. Also not listed on the schedule but far more popular than Vidyananda's music or Brahmananda's classes is Krishnananda's morning darshan. As mentioned earlier, foreigners visiting the ashram are usually required to present themselves to him and ask for his permission to stay in the ashram. Indians arriving and departing from the ashram come for his darshan; some sit silently and others ask questions and seek his blessings. Ashram residents and visitors, who are particularly devoted to Krishnananda and want some edification or perhaps just a lively diversion, also attend Krishnananda's darshan. The door to Krishnananda's office is usually open and covered only by a curtain. People waiting outside can often hear him discussing with assistants matters related to the management of the Society and the ashram. Even when he does come out and seat himself in an armchair, his exchanges with the audience are frequently punctuated when his assistants bring him checks and letters to sign, bills to approve, and other business matters to manage. As general secretary of the Divine Life Society, Krishnananda upholds his predecessor Parmananda's style as the "Bismark of the ashram."

An Indian who characterized the ashram as a successful corporation attended Krishnananda's morning darshan. He described Krishnananda as a "fascist fraud," saying that the swami spoke in circles but had enormous power. People around the ashram often told me that behind Krishnananda's stern and forbidding exterior was a very soft heart. Many regarded him as the ashram's most learned swami. One resident encouraged me to discuss my research with Krishnananda during his darshan, telling me, "He could answer any questions you might have. He knows everything about India." Given his predilection for bullying foreigners and women, I chose to remain a silent observer rather than participate in the staging of his authority and superior knowledge. This discussion focuses on Krishnananda's commanding performances at his morning darshans. During my visits to the ashram, I attended about twenty of these sessions. The number of people attending the darshans ranged from about a dozen on a very quiet day to twenty or thirty on average days.

Some mornings Krishnananda emerges from behind the curtain promptly at 9:30 and remains the full hour and a half. Yet these timings vary, and those who have gathered to see him can never be certain if, when, and for how long they will be given darshan. Once he does appear, he might terminate the darshan at any time with a perfunctory Sanskrit chant before vanishing behind the curtain. While waiting for his appearance, people talk quietly among themselves, read, or sit meditatively with closed eyes. Except for a few whispered comments, the audience remains silent as long as Krishnananda sits before them.

A description of Krishnananda's darshan would be incomplete without mention of Narayani, his favorite devotee. This youngish Canadian woman publicly serves her guru in the capacity of a devoted personal attendant. If she is made to wait outside with the others, she peers behind the curtain for a quick darshan. When he comes out, she sits on the floor next to his chair, her eyes glued to him. Her fixation on Krishnananda conforms to ideals of guru bhakti and seva which encourage and applaud such displays of absorption in the guru. However adroitly Narayani enacts her role as the devoted disciple, she is not without critics, who will be discussed later.

Krishnananda is both the leading actor and director of darshan performances. Proceedings are structured by his roles, but they vary according to how he chooses to interact with those who present themselves to him. Deferred to as a learned swami, Krishnananda unhesitatingly and authoritatively makes pronouncements about all matters presented before him. He often changes the subject to proffer further evidence of his knowledge and erudition. In addition to his learning on spirituality, philosophy, and religious and social practices, he particularly likes to display his knowledge of world history and non-Hindu religious and literary traditions. He also likes to show off his linguistic abilities. Although he usually speaks in heavily accented Indian English frequently interspersed with Hindi or embellished with Sanskrit verses, depending on his interlocutor he may speak a few sentences in Telugu, Malayalam, Kannada, or Tamil. Krishnananda also gives copious advice on medical matters. Many people discuss their ailments and he instructs them on diet, exercise, yoga, and medication. Between hawking and while scratching at the eczema on his hairless head he often discusses his own state of health. Once he detailed his various allergies and concluded that since antibiotics have no effect on him, he must be "superhuman."

In his exchanges with his audience, certain items recur—his displays of authority and knowledge, his hostility towards Christianity and women, his penchant for playing to the audience by ridiculing certain of its members. On one occasion when a group of twenty Europeans, who were touring Rishikesh's ashrams with an Indian guide, conspicuously filled the audience, Krishnananda began to talk about Indian Christians. He maintained that Christians in India are only Indians in the political sense; they worship Jesus of Jerusalem and not Krishna of Mathura. The Indian Christian accompanying the Europeans began to tell Krishnananda how Indian Christians were increasingly adapting Indian cultural forms. Krishnananda interrupted him and asserted that unlike Hinduism, Christianity is an exclusive religion. It is part of western colonization and its imported culture. He reasoned that since most Indian Christians are Catholic [which is not true], "they take their orders from the Pope." Repressing Christian components within the teachings and structure of the Divine Life Society, components related to the influence of Christian missionary propaganda and educational institutions on many of its early members, a Hindu nationalist subtext can be read in Krishnananda's comments. This subtext reads: Indian culture is Hindu culture; a true Indian worships gods who are Hindu and who were born on Indian soil.

The Indian Christian had no opportunity to further pursue the issue as Krishnananda then turned his attention to a brahman priest who had just arrived. He discussed with the priest arrangements for a special ritual requested by a devotee in Bombay. Next, a European man, not in the group with the others, deferentially presented a book which Krishnananda had written and asked him to autograph it. Meanwhile two affluent-looking Indian women arrived late, pushed to the front, and touched Krishnananda's feet; later they asked for his blessings as they were departing from the ashram.

On another occasion a man looking seriously disturbed was brought before Krishnananda. The man accompanying him introduced himself saying they are cousins and he had written in advance seeking help. Krishnananda looked at the ill man and pronounced, "He is not like you. Look at his face, he is not at all well." Krishnananda then began to question him but he did not reply. The cousin explained the other's silence by saying that he is afraid. He had spent three years in mental hospitals, where he was often beaten up. Krishnananda then occupied himself with some paperwork. Later he addressed the pair again, "I have perceived the heart of the problem. I can look at a man and intuitively know the problem. This man must not be left alone, he must be looked after. Stay one week in the ashram and attend all the religious activities." After making this prescription, Krishnananda turned to a darshan regular, a doctor on an extended visit to the ashram. He ordered the doctor to prescribe some medicine for the sick man. The doctor replied that if he is not violent then there is no need to medicate him. Krishnananda, who does not brook even the slightest challenge to his authority, responded, "There are no ifs in this case, he is not all right in any way." The doctor then agreed to prescribe something for the man.

To start off another darshan, Krishnananda asked if there were any Tamil speakers in the audience. A man in the back stood up. Krishnananda recited a Tamil proverb and explained it in English. He then questioned the man about his visit to the ashram. The man replied that he had come on business to Hardwar and this was his sixth visit to the Sivananda ashram. He then told Krishnananda that he suffers from serious sinus trouble. Krishnananda inquired about the man's diet and past medical treatment and told him to do special breathing exercises. The man replied that he has tried breathing exercises but they aggravate the condition. Krishnananda advised that he take them up again and walk for an hour every evening after dinner. He then ordered his assistant to give the visitor a booklet on yoga.

A well-dressed young couple from Bombay approached Krishnananda, touched his feet, and requested his blessings. He instructed them to regularly read the *Bhagavad Gita* and called for his assistant to bring them a copy. When the assistant came out of the office empty-handed, Krishnananda commanded him to proceed immediately across the river to the Gita Press bookstore and replenish the supply. The couple assured Krishnananda that they already had a copy of the *Gita*. Upon their presenting a check to him, Krishnananda acknowledged the couple's donation, "You have now opened an account with us." Later a woman timidly came to the front and handed Krishnananda a check and a letter. When he frowned as she told him that the money is for the library, she quickly added that the letter says the ashram can do as it sees fit with the money. As she rose to leave, Krishnananda handed the check to his assistant saying, "Oh, this is nothing, it is not important."

Besides having a stock of books to give to members of his generally well-dressed and affluent audiences, Krishnananda also keeps a stock of cheap sweaters in his office for poorer clients of the ashram. One morning an old ashram servant in tattered clothes stood in the back. He asked one of the assistants for a sweater and was given one. Someone brought to Krishnananda's attention that the man had received a sweater the previous day. Krishnananda commanded the old man to return the sweater. With a bowed head he walked to the front and gave the sweater to Krishnananda, who led the audience in laughing at the servant for being found out. The assistants were then instructed to keep a list of recipients of free sweaters. The following day two lightly clad men came to darshan to ask for sweaters. Krishnananda recounted to the audience the episode of the previous day and asked the men if they had ever received sweaters from the ashram. When they replied that they had not, Krishnananda told his assistant to give each of them a sweater and to order some more.

One morning Krishnananda called an old woman sitting in the audience to the front. She told him that she wanted to remain in the ashram to practice sadhana and perform guru seva. He replied that the ashram is not the right place for her, she would not fit in. He reminded her that when she last visited the ashram she had not remained and likened her to a bird, "flitting here and there." He then corrected her earlier comment, asserting that there is no difference between sadhana and seva. As she began to plead that she was now retired and ready to remain in the ashram, Krishnananda turned his attention to two men who were approaching him. She moved aside to make way for them.

Krishnananda greeted these two men, calling them "Brigadier Sahibs" and complimenting them on their splendid attire. One wore an army uniform, laden with decorations, a maroon beret and sunglasses. The other's clothing was also impressive—white shirt and tie, blazer and checked trousers. Both men touched Krishnananda's feet and sat before him on the floor. The army officer explained that he was in the area on business and his companion was a retired officer now living in Dehra Dun. Krishnananda told the audience that in order to know how to behave with someone it is not necessary to know his name but one must know his position. He explained that this knowledge is important because the official position is the source of the person's authority.

The Brigadier Sahib began by discussing his companion's bad health which had just recently improved. Krishnananda replied that the man must have a good doctor. Then he reminisced with the Brigadier about their visit together in Rajasthan, where they had toured border posts, and how he had pitied the soldiers who suffered from the desert heat. He recalled that the Brigadier owned a Fiat and that he and his wife were very good drivers. When he remarked that he would like to visit Rajasthan again, the Brigadier eagerly replied that he could arrange another tour as his brother was now posted there. Krishnananda declined, saying it would not be the same since the Brigadier is no longer in command "with everything at his disposal."

The Brigadier's companion talked with Krishnananda about his sadhana and the relaxation and peace of mind he derives from it. When he asked, "How can one realize 'it is here?'" Krishnananda ordered his assistant to bring him a book of quotations. Then he read passages from Sufi and Zen masters and the New Testament. He commented that he has asked many Christians the meaning of the New Testament quotation about giving and taking, but none could adequately explain it. Krishnananda invited the men to stay for lunch but they politely refused. He then asked, "Any other seva?" While touching his feet, they again politely answered in the negative and marched out of the darshan.

Krishnananda follows his own advice and matches the solicitude he shows to people with his knowledge of their official position and authority. When the Brigadiers entered, he quickly dismissed the old woman who wanted to stay in the ashram. After they departed, he was no less brusque with an old man who asked if Krishnananda could help him arrange to have his cataracts treated. He lamented he could not clearly see Krishnananda because his cataracts made everything cloudy. Perhaps an assistant later referred the man to the ashram's eye clinic for treatment. Krishnananda, however, showed no interest in the matter.

Krishnananda's behavior with the Brigadier Sahibs disclosed a capacity for deference that he rarely reveals during these darshans. As with the forty government officials, the visitors from the Nepali royal family, or the wife of a Tamil Nadu cabinet minister, ashram personnel strive to please visiting VIPs who not only have the power and authority to bestow favors but also whose patronage earns prestige for the ashram. For example, friends of the ashram with the power to influence the Home Ministry are said to have assisted the Divine Life Society in the difficult process of procuring residential visas for foreigners in the ashram. Tributes to the Divine Life Society by government officials and politicians during the Centenary year also indicate the give and take between the ashram and powerful patrons; their specific forms will be discussed in the next chapter.

Sometimes as Krishnananda sat reviewing ashram bills and signing checks, he commented about the prices of various commodities. One morning he engaged the audience in a lively discussion about the price of ghee and gasoline. It was determined that compared to Bombay, commodities are less costly in Rishikesh. Apropos of this excursion into the world of buying and selling, a man came forward and offered his services to Krishnananda. He introduced himself as a painter who had been employed by other Rishikesh ashrams to paint signs and murals. Krishnananda told him that an assistant would inspect his work at the other ashrams. When he had the opportunity to consider the painter's merits, he would then decide if the ashram should employ him.

After this exchange, a young man approached Krishnananda and said he had been unwell and unable to work for the past two years. He reported that his condition had improved enough so that the previous day he was able to attend an interview for a position with police intelligence in nearby Tehri. Krishnananda replied, "How can a sick man join the police?" He told the young man to consult with the doctor, who was in the audience. After listening to the two discuss the young man's condition, Krishnananda chided the doctor for not asking about the medical history of the man's family. He told the doctor that the father had suffered from the same illness and decreed that it must be a hereditary condition. He then ordered the doctor to define a gene and concluded that one must never forget the importance of the "hereditary aspect." The young man might have both been asking for Krishnananda's blessings and tacitly appealing for Krishnananda to use the ashram's influence with district officials and recommend him for the police position.

On another occasion a middle-aged couple presented themselves to

Krishnananda. The husband asked if women are permitted to chant the Gayatri mantra. Krishnananda replied, "The mantra is forbidden by scriptures to women and shudras. Only after being initiated with the sacred thread does a male have the right to use it." The man further queried, "How can it be forbidden to women if the Gayatri mantra is a Devi?" With an exasperated sigh Krishnananda asserted, "The mantra is not a goddess; this idea came later. Gayatri refers to the meter of the mantra." He then asked the man, "Do you know what meter is? Do you know what poetry is?" Like a shamed schoolboy, the man responded with a nod. Krishnananda continued, "The mantra is for the sun god. Since menstruation and childbirth make women impure, it is better they do not say it because one must be pure to use the Gayatri mantra." Krishnananda reprimanded the man, "The mantra is your work, why are you making your wife do your work?" Before dismissing the couple he instructed them to perform daily puja in their home.

Besides being consulted and insulted by Krishnananda, the darshan doctor often asked questions related to philosophy and spirituality. One morning he inquired why it is said that unless the Gita Mahima is recited before reading the *Bhagavad Gita,* there is no benefit from reading the *Gita.* Krishnananda replied that the Mahima serves to remind people of the *Gita*'s importance. The *Gita* is great in itself and does not need the Mahima but people need it because they can forget the greatness of the *Gita.*

Many visitors to the ashram do not attend Krishnananda's darshan. When talking with a young man about his brother who had visited the ashram without coming to see him, Krishnananda commented, "It is strange." The man apologetically explained that his brother planned to come for darshan when he returned to the ashram on the following day. Krishnananda asked where his family lived in Delhi and the man replied that they own two houses there. He then took the envelope which had been sent from Delhi by the man's mother. He read aloud its contents: a check for 5,000 rupees, a request to perform a fire sacrifice for her son's birthday, and a check for 450 rupees as a donation for the ritual.

Another morning a sack of apples was set next to Krishnananda's chair. When he came out he asked who had brought them. An Italian man identified himself as the donor. He had visited the ashram on other occasions and was known to Krishnananda. He told Krishnananda he was now leaving the ashram and planned to cycle to Benares. The audience laughed when Krishnananda teasingly responded, "Why don't you take the train?" He then instructed the Italian to distribute the apples to the audience. Later, another foreigner, a tall German man, asked for permission to stay in the ashram. His request was approved and Krishnananda added, "God will take a big bite out of you." He then turned to an Indian man, an engineer with Hindustan Aeronautical, and teased him for being so reticent.

A Brazilian woman asked Krishnananda for advice about chanting mantras. When he commanded her to recite her Sanskrit mantra, she complied with a shaky voice. He criticized and corrected her faulty pronunciation and asked her, "Are you just a housewife?" She hesitated before answering, "Yes Swamiji." Krishnananda then rebuked her, "You should not consider yourself only a housewife, a person is more than what they do." He then went on to display his knowledge of Brazil: people in Brazil speak Portuguese; Latin America is called by that name because it is populated by people whose ancestors came from places with languages derived from Latin. When I related this exchange to a white South African woman, she recounted with disgust her own experience with Krishnananda. The first time she attended his darshan she had asked him a question about meditation. He replied by aggressively questioning her about her father. She decided not to stay in the ashram despite being given permission to do so. Describing her darshan of Krishnananda, she said it made her feel that "he's a bully who cannot help me at all." During another darshan an obsequious brahman priest presented himself to receive Krishnananda's instructions concerning the ashram's celebration of Shivaratri. Krishnananda also assigned him other rituals which had been requested by devotees. He advised the audience that the priest is also an astrologer; they should consult him if they want to know their future. Assistants then brought to Krishnananda's attention further ashram business. One handed him a book that had just come off the ashram press. Krishnananda immediately spotted an error on the title page. He shut the book and ordered the assistant to stop the press and correct the error before printing any more copies.

Another assistant reported that the night before some ashram buildings had been defaced with graffiti. The audience laughed at his reply, "We should paint a sign saying, 'Don't write here.'" He then added that he should be consulted before any signs are posted around the ashram and alluded to his displeasure at not being consulted about what was inscribed on the Sivananda Centenary Memorial Arch. Another morning as visitors awaited Krishnananda's appearance, they could hear him inside his office discussing income tax regulations related to the sale of old printing machinery and the purchase of new equipment. When he came out, an old couple touched his feet and asked for his blessings. They told him about their difficulties at home arising from an accident which had disabled their only son. Krishnananda blessed them and instructed them to continue praying.

That day, as on many others, Krishnananda recollected his experiences as a young disciple living with other brahmacharis in the presence of their beloved Gurudev Sivananda. He contrasted the "simple life" of those bygone days filled with reading and discussing scriptures with the present complexities of running the ashram. These memories of youthful golden days might be prompted by the young brahmacharis, who like Narayani, sit close to him in rapt devotion. Their prospects for moving up through the ashram hierarchy are improved if they can earn recognition and favor from senior swamis like Krishnananda.

Gurus who had previously lived with Krishnananda in the ashram as fellow disciples of Sivananda and now have their own establishments abroad often encourage their followers to visit the Sivananda Ashram when they travel to India. One morning Krishnananda asked how many in the audience were followers of Vishnudevananda, one such guru. About ten raised their hands; one said that they were all yoga teachers who had been trained in a course at Vishnudevananda's ashram. Perhaps an old sibling rivalry prompted Krishnananda to comment, "Vishnudevananda's people are taking over." He wittily embellished this comment with a Sanskrit verse about Vishnu pervading the earth.

Non-Hindu foreigners seem to be more welcome at the ashram than Indian Christians. Two Indian Christian nuns who had taken "ecumenical sannyas" and wore orange clothes told me about their experiences with Krishnananda. One woman now has her own Himalayan ashram but had previously been a regular visitor to the Sivananda ashram over a period of about ten years. She recollected that when she first visited in 1973, the ashram's grounds were spacious and quiet. Now, she observed, it had expanded into a sprawling, busy institution. During the first three years of visiting the ashram she had not taken to Krishnananda. Later, however, when he assisted her in preparing a book about meditation for publication by Bharatiya Vidya Bhavan, she "came to appreciate him." She described Rishikesh as a "Hindu Vatican" and asserted that "Christians are not accepted at Sivananda Ashram." Krishnananda had often insinuated that her real mission at the ashram was not to study religious philosophy but to convert Hindus.

The other Christian woman ascetic was less genial about Krishnananda. She recalled that when she arrived in Rishikesh from a Catholic ashram in South India she deliberately wore a bracelet with a cross. She wanted to find out if these Hindu ashrams practiced what they preached about tolerance and the "unity of all religions." She was refused a room at several ashrams. Someone in the reception office at the Sivananda ashram told her that no ashram would admit her as long as she wore that bracelet. Later she received permission from Krishnananda to stay in the ashram on the condition that she not proselytize. When she once asked him about sannyas, he told her to beg with the sadhus at the ashram gate. This bedraggled group of sadhus is not invited into the ashram's dining hall but rather line up on the street where they wait to be publicly fed by the ashram. Her stay in the ashram was terminated when Krishnananda told her to leave and go stay "among her own people." She concluded from her experiences that "in the ashrams of Rishikesh there is no correspondence between the ideal of Hindu tolerance and its practice."

A conversation with an intermittent ashram resident, a wealthy European woman, suggests still another perspective on the pursuit of divine life and its institutional forms. Krishnananda need not prohibit this woman from proselytizing: at the outset of our conversation she expressed her contempt for Christianity. At a young age she rejected Christianity, finding it to be evil, hypocritical, and the cause of great suffering; she began to search for a "higher truth." Later she started to practice yoga and study Indian religion and philosophy. She found that whereas the West separates religion from philosophy and from life, in India the three are integrated. Through her studies she also came to believe that unlike Christianity, in Hindu tradition there is no guilt, fear, or evil. After meeting Chidananda in Europe, she came to India in 1971 and stayed several months in the Sivananda ashram. As she had always worked—she had been a fashion designer in Paris—and did not want to sit and do nothing, she asked Chidananda what she might do while in the ashram. He arranged for her to supervise one of the three leprosy colonies which the ashram manages. Under her supervision a production unit was established to weave rugs. She explained that even lepers missing fingers could work on the unit's looms. According to her, work instilled self-respect in these lepers. She added, "it made a big difference for lepers to go to the bazaar in new clothes."

For six or seven years she came and stayed in the ashram through the winter, continuing to supervise the lepers and their weaving of rugs. Once she stayed in India for fifteen months. She said Chidananda had offered her a place in the ashram, saying that it would be her home in India. This "place" is a plot of land within the ashram on which she built for herself not merely a room or a suite of rooms within a residential building but a small villa. When I commented on the lovely view of the river that stretched before us from her veranda, she replied that the place was designed so that it would be private. She had selected a site where nothing could be built to obstruct the view. She noted with relief that trees obstructed the view of the recently built Sivananda footbridge: she was not subjected to seeing "that monstrosity and all the vulgar people."

Unlike when she first came to Rishikesh, it is now full of the horrors and ugliness of mass culture, just like Europe or America. She lamented that things had become so uniform and plastic: "You used to be able to tell where the pilgrims came from by their dress and its colors but now they all wear synthetics and look the same, rushing through Rishikesh up to the mountains." When I commented on the expansion of ashrams in Hardwar and Rishikesh and their role in attracting pilgrim crowds, she shifted into the panda's idiom, "Indians do not take holidays or honeymoons. They come to places like Rishikesh and have always come. If they are now more crowded it is only because the population has increased." About foreigners traveling in India and visiting Rishikesh, she grumbled that they used to be "horrible hippies," but now there are no hippies, only "drug addicts."

The elitism of her spiritual quest complements her disgust for the masses and mass culture. She spoke reverentially of Krishnamurti, praising him as a living Buddha. She came to realize this after repeatedly reading his works and listening to his tapes as well as through her studies with Tibetan lamas in Dharamsala from whom she had taken initiations. She particularly likes Krishnamurti because "he never came down to the level of others. He only raises people up." She contrasted the loftiness of Krishnamurti with the swamis of the Divine Life Society whom she derided for making a cult of the dead Sivananda. About the "frightening mass appeal" of the Sivananda Centenary celebrations she said, "to tell the truth, sometimes I feel ashamed to be here."

To learn more about her background and opinions, I asked if she had ever been interested in Communism, like many other Europeans of her generation. Her reply was direct, "No, I am a capitalist." She said that as a conservative she belongs to the right, not the left. Her scorn for democracy approximated her contempt for Christianity: "I am against democracy. I think democracy is a big joke. People are not ready for it, or maybe only in Switzerland and perhaps Sweden." In her opinion democracy is inextricable from the ugliness of mass culture. Europe, once a place with great cultural traditions, has been ruined by American mass culture. Everything that is beautiful has been built by "kings, the church, tyrants and dictators." She concluded her discussion of the topic by asserting that it is such a waste for "intelligent people" to have to cook, shop, and clean for themselves because servants are no longer a "part of culture."

Several times during the conversation she said that she felt the "circle" of her time in India was drawing to a close. Rishikesh had become too noisy and crowded. For Christmas she planned to visit friends in Kenya. She would then return to Rishikesh but probably would not stay very long. After her many visits over the past fifteen years she felt she had gotten from India what she needed—"to learn how to live alone." She likened being in India to going through psychoanalysis: both involve the search for the self. Their techniques are different but the principle and goal is the same: "so one can live with oneself."

During our visit she seemed to endure rather than enjoy my presence. When I had come earlier that day, introduced myself, and said that other ashram residents suggested I meet and talk with her, she readily invited me to return later in the afternoon. Throughout the two hours she kept herself occupied with needlework and punctuated the conversation with long, tense silences. When I thanked her and prepared to leave, however, she suddenly became almost friendly, or perhaps just polite. She thanked me for the visit and when I said I could see myself out, she asked if I knew how to close the gate. From a couple of people who had spoken to her later, I learned that she angrily described my visit as a presumptuous intrusion. By way of an explanation one of her acquaintances speculated that she was depressed and vented her hauteur on just about anyone.

Given her attitude to me during our visit and the subsequent reports, I did not attempt to make any further contact with this woman. One morning, however, she appeared towards the end of Krishnananda's darshan. He immediately acknowledged her presence, "What a rare event, what is the problem?" Then he jokingly said how jealous he was of her nice car which allowed her to go out for rides. She replied that if he wanted, she could take him for a ride. He then complained that her car made too much noise and asked, "Doesn't it have a silencer?" She countered, "What's the point? India is so noisy anyway." After this stand-off, she explained that she had come to darshan because she would like to speak with him when he had time. At the end of the darshan Krishnananda called her into his room for a private audience.

WOMEN IN THE ASHRAM

Unlike the resentment which the European woman seemed to have for my inquiries, other contacts with women in the ashram were generally congenial. Women are a minority in the ashram. Those who reside there have made and accommodated themselves to particular niches, often in the interstices of the ashram's hierarchical structure. Two women, Swami Hridayananda and Dr. Devaki Kutty, however, occupy important official positions within the Divine Life Society. Both are on the seven-member board of trustees, and Dr. Kutty served as general secretary of the committee which organized the Sivananda Centenary celebration.

Of the biographical sketches of fifty initiated disciples of Sivananda, the "Stones, Bricks and Mortar" of the Divine Life Society, only one concerns a woman, Swami Hridayananda. When she bought a second-hand book of Sivananda's and looked at his picture, "she instantaneously felt that she had known him intimately. That book possessed her and the same evening she had a vision of Swami Sivananda in her meditation, blessing her" (MMW, 250). She had been an opthamalic surgeon in a Madras hospital and later had a private medical practice. After coming across Sivananda's book, she left Madras for a short visit to Rishikesh. "Sivananda played the miracle" by putting her to work in the ashram hospital. Instead of returning to her husband in Madras, she received sannyas initiation from Sivananda. Later a "substantial contribution" from a devotee, Captain Srivatsava, enabled the ashram to build an Eye Hospital which Swami Hridayananda came to direct. Under her expert supervision the hospital's reputation spread, "reaching the ears of the officials of the Government in the State and the Centre, who were eager to assist our hospital by grants given by the Government" (250).

Hridayananda's guru seva was not limited to her duties in the hospital; "she was very personally associated with Sri Gurudev" and served him as both "personal assistant and personal physician" (250). In her capacity as a "spiritual seeker," she wrote books and essays on Sivananda and "became very famous as a spiritual guide to many people and seekers who came to the Ashram" (250). This fame brought invitations from seekers abroad, and after extensive touring she settled "in Europe (France, Belgium and Holland), which is a delight and great satisfaction to seekers in those parts" (250). When I asked one ashram resident why Hridayananda had left Rishikesh, I was told that like a few other senior swamis, she preferred to live elsewhere after Sivananda's death. No one explicitly stated that she had been squeezed out by those who took command of the ashram. However, a couple of people intimated that with Sivananda's death came controversial changes which induced those who had not moved into powerful positions to leave the ashram. One person told me that the caste background of Hridayananda had attracted considerable critical speculation; she may have been a shudra.

When Dr. Kutty came to the ashram, Sivananda also put her to work in the hospital. She told me that at the time of her first visit she was the Professor of Gynecology and Obstetrics at Lucknow University. She came with an old couple on pilgrimage to Badrinath. They had been advised to seek lodging in Sivananda's ashram because in those days "most ashrams had many rules about caste," but the Sivananda ashram was known to be run by "educated, progressive people." After arriving at the ashram, she went to visit the hospital where she was encouraged to seek Sivananda's darshan. Dr. Kutty recalled that although at that time she was "indifferent to swamis," she went along to meet Sivananda. His appearance and bearing impressed her: "he was a huge man, about six feet tall and fat, a very imposing figure." He asked her why she was going up to Badrinath. Dr. Kutty interpolated for me by way of commentary, "We Hindus don't always know why we do such things." To Sivananda she had replied that she wanted to have darshan of the deity. He insisted that she not go to Badrinath but rather stay behind in the ashram and have darshan of the deity by serving the poor. She resisted and the old couple were hesitant to leave her, but Sivananda was adamant. When the couple returned from Badrinath and she was to travel with them to Mussoorie, Sivananda again insisted that she not go along and that she continue her seva in the hospital.

During that first visit, Sivananda told her that she should consider the ashram as her home and Lucknow as the hostel. She should come home whenever she could. Except for only a few years, she returned every summer to work in the ashram hospital. After her retirement from her post in Lucknow, she moved permanently to the ashram. Her spacious and well-appointed apartment is near the hospital and has lovely views of the Ganges. Dr. Kutty portrayed herself as an efficient and busy woman. She works in the hospital from six in the morning until early afternoon. She said that she is a contented and happy woman; she planned her life carefully and it has worked out well. She seemed to enjoy talking about herself and said that she always kept excellent health: she was always busy and was never tired. She described herself as never having been ambitious for wealth but that she "always enjoyed comforts." One ashram resident speculated that Dr. Kutty was a very wealthy woman.

Her father had been a judge in Madras, and she had a "comfortable upbringing." She said that her paternal grandmother, who was very learned in Sanskrit, had advised her father, "Do not force this daughter into marriage. She is very intelligent. If she finds a man she wants to marry, fine. Do not coerce her into marriage." Her father followed her grandmother's counsel and her parents never forced her to marry. Dr. Kutty said that had she found a man she loved, she would have married but that there is great risk with arranged marriages and women can end up very unhappy if the match is unsuitable. Dr. Kutty also attributed her capacity for independence to the fact that her family is from Kerala, where women have customary rights to property not enjoyed elsewhere in India. She had aunts who had never married but managed their own property. In her opinion, the ownership of property by women provides them with the means to live independently of men and marriage.

In describing her active family life, she noted that family members often come and stay with her in Rishikesh. As the eldest of five siblings, she said that she is consulted for advice on family matters. She noted that her brothers and sisters were all married and "comfortably settled": one brother and his wife had just left Rishikesh after a two week visit; she was planning a visit with her other brother, a neurosurgeon in London; one sister is married to an army colonel and the other to an engineer.

Like swamis and other ashram residents, Dr. Kutty likes to discourse on Hindu culture and society. She told me that the Hindus had a "very scientific" model for society with its four classes and prescribed duties for the four stages of life (*varnashramadharma*). She noted it was the donations of householders which supported both the students and sannyasis. As if I knew nothing about India, she told me that India is a complex society with great linguistic and cultural diversity. She prided herself on her wide-ranging interests and her capacity to talk to anyone.

When I asked if she planned to take sannyas, she said that when she was young and troubled she would think about renouncing the world. Later, she was no longer interested in sannyas. As she matured she found that she fully enjoyed "life in the world." She further explained that she has no inclination to take sannyas because in her life happiness has "won out" over sorrow. Although some of the ashram's senior swamis have encouraged her to take sannyas, she will not because its rules would restrict her freedom, "and freedom is very important." Even without sannyas, Dr. Kutty enjoys a position of status and authority within the Divine Life Society. At public assemblies and evening satsang she sits on stage alongside the other swamis, albeit on a white rather than orange cushion. Indeed, should she take sannyas, her position within the ashram hierarchy would change, since one important measure of seniority is defined in terms of when initiation as a sannyasi took place. Furthermore, her autonomy vis à vis the senior swamis could be compromised if she took sannyas because it would bring her under the authority of whoever initiated her. As it stands, like the other senior swamis, she need be grateful only to Gurudev Sivananda, whose photographs were plentiful in the room where she received me.

Dr. Kutty may well have acquired her facility for operating in male-dominated hierarchies during her successful career as a medical specialist and university professor. Such expertise would enable her to mediate in the disputes among the ashram's senior swamis. From various people I learned that tension and rivalry characterize the relationship between the two senior most swamis—Chidananda and Krishnananda. One ashram resident explained that Chidananda was selected over Krishnananda as president because when Sivananda died and others were confounded by what the loss portended, Chidananda remained clear-headed: "Power is exercised by those who seize and hold onto it." Krishnananda had proven himself effective in the day-to-day management of the ashram, but then and during other times of crisis he lacked Chidananda's capacity for taking firm and decisive action.

It is difficult to know the details about the dynamics of the relationship between Chidananda and Krishnananda. As is common among disciples, they had been rivals for the favor of their guru and for positions of authority within the organization. Later the rivalry focused on their ability to attract and keep their own disciples as well as on power struggles related to their positions as officials and trustees of the Divine Life Society. To some extent the potential for conflict between them is reduced by the fact that Chidananda spends most of his time on tour and Krishnananda remains in the ashram. However, several incidents which were recounted to me suggest that this arrangement does not wholly resolve the conflicts between them.

As mentioned earlier, Krishnananda does not discourage his Canadian woman devotee, Narayani, from publicly doting on him. Her intimacy with Krishnananda not only irritates other devotees, one of whom was described as being "murderously jealous," but also irks Chidananda. Although I did not personally witness any controversies concerning Narayani, the following episodes were related to me by a woman with a long association with the ashram. On one occasion Narayani arrived with Krishnananda at a meeting of the board of trustees. She did not attend the meeting, but when Chidananda emerged from it and saw her waiting at the door, he lost his temper. He ordered Narayani out of his sight, saying that Krishnananda was going to walk with him and not with her. Krishnananda, however, refused to budge without Narayani, and Chidananda had to back down.

During a special training program at the ashram for officers from the Indian Administrative Service, Narayani arrived late and sat in front, near Krishnananda. The following day, she again arrived late and the swami in charge of public relations for the ashram stopped her from entering. Krishnananda refused to lecture to the audience of government administrators and returned to his room. The swami went to Chidananda to ask what he should do and was instructed to apologize to Krishnananda. This was insufficient and Krishnananda demanded that he apologize to Narayani. Again the swami returned to Chidananda for instructions. In the end, he was ordered by Chidananda to apologize to Narayani.

The way women figure in the rivalry between Chidananda and Krishnananda was illustrated in another story told to me. Chidananda's sister's daughter had come to stay in the ashram. Her uncle was officially her guru, but during his absence from the ashram, Krishnananda lavished attention upon her and she spent much time in his presence. Despite Krishnananda's attempts to encourage the woman to attach herself to him, she remained loyal to his rival, her uncle and guru. She was later sent to visit other relatives in Canada.

The guru's favor is coveted yet fickle. The following account, a synthesis from what I was told by two ashram residents, concerns a woman who had been supplanted as Krishnananda's favorite devotee. She is said to have begun her ashram career as a young woman after working for a few years as a doctor. She first lived in Anandamayi Ma's nearby ashram, but was "too independent-minded" for the way they treated women there: "Ma was very protective of her girls." She did not find the regulations agreeable, and after much trouble, "Ma sent her to live in the Sivananda ashram." For a while she worked in the ashram hospital and came to be the known favorite of Krishnananda. Unlike Narayani, she did not appear publicly with him. However, I was told that he "pampered her in private" and she enjoyed the privilege of dining with him. After about fifteen years she lost her position as his favorite and became "one of the herd, looking on Krishnananda from afar." She now keeps largely to herself. One observer described her as very beautiful and sad, capable of being both nice and short tempered; "she is not a happy person."

From an ashram resident I heard the tale of another unhappy woman. After several extended visits to the ashram, she requested permission to live there permanently. She comes from a wealthy family in Orissa. Her family are loyal supporters of the Divine Life Society and operate a branch out of their home. She had the misfortune of falling in love with a young sannyasi. When she told the sannyasi that she loved him and wanted to be his wife, he "was very kind" but refused to marry her. The woman who recounted this to me said that young women often fall in love with brahmacharis, sannyasis, gurus, and even deities. Usually they get over it and consent to the marriage arranged for them. However, there is another cultural ideal concerning women's loyalty and love: once a woman sets her mind and heart on a particular man, she will accept no one else as her husband. This dedication is often explained in terms of karma and rebirth. The woman had been the man's wife in a previous life but in her present birth he is unavailable to her. The young woman from Orissa is resolved to remain loyal to the ideal and to her beloved sannyasi and has refused to marry anyone else.

The duty assigned to her while in the ashram involved the care of an elderly Tamil woman, revered by some as a saint. Known as Amma, this woman had come to Rishikesh many years ago for Sivananda's darshan. Her husband had been Sivananda's classmate. She has become sickly and senile in her old age. The events of her life and the miraculous signs of her sainthood have been recorded in a book written by a widower living in the ashram, whose wife had been Amma's leading devotee. The librarian, Krishnapriya, once brought me to meet Amma. She visited her daily to chant Sanskrit and perform puja before a shrine of faded pictures of Hanuman, Shirdi Sai Baba, Ganesha, and Sivananda. Amma sat on the floor in front of the shrine—hunched and silent. After the puja she gave us pieces of banana as prasad. Krishnapriya touched Amma's feet and we departed. Later I learned that Amma's son had brought her to live with him in Madras.

Residents commented that the ashram does not provide adequate care for its aged inmates. In some cases, after many decades of service in the ashram, swamis and other residents "retire" elsewhere when age or ill health renders them inactive. To a fortunate few, the ashram assigns brahmacharis, students, or women residents to provide them with personal care. Most are left to "fend for themselves" or are put into the ashram hospital where they remain until they die.

When an especially helpful ashram resident brought me to meet an old sannyasini in the hospital, she reminded me, "You must put her in your book" (see plate 18). The ashram's hospital was dim and dingy. Of the dozen beds in the ward, most of them were occupied by men, and all the occupants were old and dying. The woman I met there, Devasharanananda, had not yet lost her spark of life. My companion told me that Devasharanananda was thought to be 113 years old. Originally from a wealthy family in Mysore, she was married young and had no children. On her insistence—"We Hindus think a son is necessary" commented my companion—her husband later married her sister. After her sister had children, she came to Rishikesh to live in the ashram.

Her guru seva involved working in the temple, keeping it clean and making garlands. She was well known for her fastidiousness about food and dress. She was also "playful and a little cunning": for visitors she would tell stories about the gods, sing hymns, and chant, "Rama, Rama." They in turn would give her small donations which she would save up and offer to Sivananda or Chidananda. Both swamis made sure that she was rewarded for her devoted service. Chidananda gave her sannyas initiation and later brought her presents from his travels abroad. Once she told him that she wanted a steel trunk and was given money and taken to the bazaar to buy one. When she became too old to go to the kitchen for her own food, a student living in the ashram was assigned to deliver it to her. Although listless when we first arrived at her hospital bedside, Devasharanananda quickly perked up. Wearing a shabby orange sweater, she lay on her back under a blanket. Within minutes she began clapping and chanting, "Rama, Rama." My companion said, "God is teasing her by keeping her here," and then asked her if she was afraid of dying. She answered, "Is a bride afraid to go to her parent's home?"

In the ashram as elsewhere, people gossip. Residents speculate about each other's diligence and progress in pursuing the divine life; about if and when they will receive partial or full sannyas initiation; about squabbles among inmates or visitors; about others' financial circumstances and patterns of consumption; about sexual or other scandals. I was told that besides the kitchen, the residence of one widow was the "gossip center of the ashram." Many years ago this woman had come with her husband to the ashram, where he worked as a doctor. After his early death, she was permitted to remain in the ashram. As a childless widow she did not want to leave and live with her in-laws, and her parents did not want her to return to them.

Another widow living in the ashram attracts considerable gossip. Her husband had been a generous devotee of Sivananda, and they regularly visited the ashram. The ashram's austere regime was not for them. They arrived in a chauffeured car with an entourage including servants and a cook. People in the ashram debated about the sources of their wealth, and most thought the man was involved in Bombay's underworld of gangster-businessmen. After her husband's death, the woman's fortunes declined. She lives modestly in the ashram part of the year and with family members in Bombay for the rest of the year.

Another story about a woman ashram resident concerns a well-educated Punjabi woman who came to Rishikesh in the late 1950s. Since she was from an affluent and cosmopolitan family, her background enabled her to serve the ashram as an official host for foreign visitors and important Indian devotees. She was described as having been as beautiful as she was forceful and efficient in performing her seva. She has always kept her own cook, who prepared rich, savory food for her and the VIP visitors entrusted by the ashram to her care. Over the years she suffered from many prolonged periods of depression, and the ashram arranged various treatments, including electric shock therapy. For the past three years she has been almost fully incapacitated by her illness and vacillates between raging abusively and sitting silently in her rooms, which she shares with her elderly father.

When she was younger and less debilitated by her illness, she was reputedly "obsessed with sex," an obsession that made her into the ashram's greatest "scandalmonger." Although she was never known to have had any affairs herself and she was eventually initiated as a sannyasini, she tirelessly spread "vile rumors about everyone else." When I asked why the ashram permitted her to stay, I was told that since she had given so many years of service and her illness has become acute only in recent years, the ashram would not expel her: "she is like a daughter of the ashram; she is tolerated and this is her home." Whatever the reasons are that enable her to remain in the ashram—her service, her wealth, a sense of parental obligation, potential lawsuits from her family members should she be expelled—she and others who have made the ashram their home make it a place replete with the comedies, banalities, and tragedies of divine and mundane life.

NINE

Celebrating the Birth Centenary of Gurudev Sivananda

THE PRELIMINARIES

With the energetic Dr. Kutty as the general secretary of the Sivananda Centenary Celebration committee, the Divine Life Society mounted a year-long program of festivities in September 1986. After the celebration was completed, she spoke with me about the enormous amount of work involved in its execution. She marveled at the eagerness which people— "even perfect strangers"—had shown to help the Society. In Dr. Kutty's opinion such widespread goodwill contributed to making the Sivananda Centenary year a wondrous success. It also affirmed her belief that "people are basically good." These many helpers, like the young couple giving their donation to Krishnananda, were adding to or "opening their accounts" with the Society.

The centenary campaign enabled the Society to demonstrate its status as a premier Hindu religious organization. The spiritual eminence attributed to its ascetic leaders authorizes their pronouncements concerning Indian culture and society, pronouncements in accord with tenets of Hindu nationalism espoused by other organizations supported by ruling-class groups. Patronage by these groups is demonstrated not only through their support as private individuals but also in their capacity as government officials and politicians to confer on the Society various benefits from the central and state governments. Furthermore, through the Centenary campaign, the Society attracted new supporters and raised funds, resources necessary for the organization's continued growth.

The campaign had several phases: the initial planning, which began in 1982, and pre-Centenary publicity; the first nine months of the Centenary year commencing in September 1986; the "Hundred Days' Programme," from June through August 1987; "The Grand Finale" during the first week of September in 1987; and post-Centenary activities. Besides materials collected both during and after Centenary events, the following analysis draws on materials published by the Society: the Centenary commemoration volume, *The Master, His Mission, and His Works (MMW);* the 1986 *Annual Report and Balance Sheet of the Divine Life Society (AR);* and a report on the Centenary written by Dr. Kutty and described by her as being published "to record the Centenary's events, especially for those who were not able to attend."

According to official accounts, devotees were anxious to celebrate the Centenary: "Loving enquiries and even exhortations were being received constantly in this connection as early as 1982" *(MMW, 225).* In 1984 the Society responded to devotees' "wish that the Centenary of the Master should be celebrated in a befitting way" by forming the Centenary Celebration Committee *(Sri Swami Sivananda Centenary Celebrations: A Report [CR], 2).* In a section entitled "Preparing the Ground for the Centenary Celebrations," this report discusses how the 1985 All-India Spiritual Prachar Yatra [Publicity Tour] for National Integration served as the "flying start" of the Centenary celebrations (3–4).

The purpose of this eight-month Yatra by a party of senior swamis, brahmacharis, and devotees was "mass propagation, not only of Gurudev's teachings, but also of the country's culture and its message of unity, brotherhood, tolerance, harmony and high ethical ideals" (4). Throughout the Yatra "government officials, media people and people from every strata of society" demonstrated their interest in and support for the Society, making the tour "a resounding success" (4). The Yatra's progress through India was "well covered by the Press, All India Radio and T.V." *(AR, 8).* Provincial as well as national television news programs carried stories about the Yatra and its varied public functions, e.g., discourses by members of the Yatra party and participation in ceremonies to inaugurate the Swami Sivananda school, the Tagore Children's School, and the Sivananda Government Dispensary in Rajasthan (7).

Like the VHP's report on the 1983 Sacrifice for Unity, the Society provides statistics on its 1985–86 National Integration Yatra. The Yatra party covered 45,000 kilometers in nineteen states and three union territories; it visited seventy-five cities, 115 towns, and 143 villages. The party conducted 1,551 meetings—"including huge public functions"—and contacted 1,500,000 people "from all walks of life" (8). While in New Delhi "doing spadework" for the Yatra, the party's headquarters was the Sivananda Bhavan of the Swami Sivananda Cultural Association in Lajpat Nagar. The birth centenary issue of *Voice of Sivananda,* discussed earlier, the issue with the blatantly Hindu nationalist propaganda, was published by this Lajpat Nagar group.

To complement the work of the Yatra party, the Divine Life Society's public relations specialist, Swami Adhyatmanananda, also toured India. He gave lecture-demonstrations on yoga and made "effective use of the

Press, Radio and T.V. to spread information about Gurudev and his teachings" (*CR*, 4). Two other yoga specialists were sent by the Divine Life Society "on extensive world tours propagating the Master's message" (4). Meanwhile, Chidananda spent the early months of 1986 on a "cultural tour" in the United States and Canada (*AR*, 3). The tour was organized by a Sivananda Centenary Committee formed by devotees in America, Canada, and the Bahamas. Some of the stops on Chidananda's two and a half month tour included: satsang in the home of "Sri Venkateswaram of the World Bank" in Arlington, Virginia; a stopover in Portland to "pay his respects" to a mahatma of the Ramakrishna Ashram; lectures at yoga schools; talks at an ashram in San Francisco named after Nadabrahmananda, the yogi-musician discussed in the previous chapter; a visit to an ashram of Satchidananda, a disciple of Sivananda who later came to Rishikesh with an entourage of devotees for the Centenary's grand finale; a five-day program in Los Angeles, including talks at the Sivananda Yoga Vedanta Center of Vishnudevananda, another swami who came to Rishikesh with a group of followers for the Centenary's closing festivities; satsang in Nashville at a new Ganesh temple; and lectures in Montreal, Vancouver, and Toronto (3–5).

On returning to India after this foreign tour, Chidananda based himself in Hardwar for the Kumbh Mela (*CR*, 4). Never before had the president of the Divine Life Society set up a "Spiritual Camp" for Kumbh Mela crowds in Hardwar. The Society reports having spent 275,000 rupees on this Spiritual Camp and attributes its "grand success" to Chidananda's continuous presence (*AR*, 28). In addition to daily yoga classes attended by hundreds of people, Camp activities included lectures by scholars and prominent ascetics. Chidananda organized a Harijan Puja and Bhog feast as the "grand finale" of the Kumbh Mela Spiritual Camp: "A highlight of the programme was the Harijan-seva in which Sri Swamiji personally performed the worship of the Harijan guests with clothes, money, sweets, etc." (6).

Through the rituals of worshiping and feeding untouchables the Divine Life Society publicized its conformity to the ideology and practices promoted by the government and Hindu nationalist groups alike: paternalistic concern for the spiritual and physical welfare of untouchables. As mentioned earlier, the ashram celebrates Mahatma Gandhi's birthday with similar ceremonies. One untouchable woman, who came daily to clean the toilets in the ashram guest house, said that she and her family members were summoned every year to attend these celebrations. She declined to elaborate on them. She preferred to tell me that the ashram had helped her husband find a good job in Dehra Dun and that her two sons were studying in local schools.

Issues related to caste status seldom arose in my discussions with ashram residents. When I purposely raised them, they were usually deflected with assertions that, from its inception, the Divine Life Society challenged caste regulations. The priest in the ashram's main temple, who performs the daily pujas in its inner sanctum crowded with a Shiv linga and statues of Radha, Krishna, Hanuman, Sita, and Rama, was rumored to be an untouchable. He was also said to have "stubbornly fought for the post of pujari." One resident noted that the ashram does not publicize the caste status of this priest. The matter could generate controversy: many residents, devotees, and visitors continue to believe that temple ritual should be performed by a ritually pure brahman priest.

Building on the publicity campaign of the Prachar Yatra, Chidananda's cultural tours, and Kumbh Mela spiritual camp, "a select number of candidates" were invited to the ashram in order to further coordinate the branches' involvement in the Centenary celebration. Instead of the Sadhana Week which usually follows the July celebration of Guru Purnima, the ashram organized a "Special Training Programme and Sadhana Shibir" (Spiritual Camp). Its purpose was to give representatives from the Society's branches "intensive training for doing selfless service and Prachara of spiritual ideals according to Gurudev's teachings" (CR, 5). To further publicize the Centenary, the ashram placed numerous large signs in Hindi and English on the road between Delhi and Rishikesh to inform travelers about the Divine Life Society's celebration of the Sivananda Centenary year. Buses in Rishikesh and Hardwar were also painted with such signs.

THE CENTENARY YEAR COMMENCES

The Birth Centenary year officially commenced with evening satsang on September 7, 1986. During the satsang invited mahatmas spoke on the life and teachings of Sivananda. Choral singing by the choir from the Gandharva Mahavidyalaya in Delhi "delighted the hearts of everyone" attending the satsang (CR, 5). The following day "the usual spiritual activities" marked Sivananda's birthday. The day's high point, however, was the release of the Sivananda Commemorative Postal Stamp. The main ceremony for the stamp's release—"a really wondrous function"—was held at the auditorium of the Federation of Indian Chambers of Commerce and Industry (FICCI) in New Delhi where, "in the presence of a large and distinguished gathering," it was released by then Vice President R. Venkataraman (AR, 8; CR, 6). On the same day the postmaster general of Uttar Pradesh released the stamp at the Sivananda ashram. It was also released in twenty-two other cities and towns, including Pattamadai, the village in Tamil Nadu "sanctified by Gurudev's birth." To emphasize the prestige of the event, the Centenary Report notes that the simultaneous release of a stamp in such a large number of places was "unique in the history of the Postal Department" (CR, 6).

On the following day "hundreds of devotees and the public of Rishikesh participated" in a procession through Rishikesh, "a grand Nagara Sankirtan" (6). The procession was followed with nine days of "soul-stirring Ramayan Katha" by the renowned Ramesh Bhai Ojha, who returned in August 1987 to conduct a "final and majestic" recitation (14). In April 1987 the head of the Kailash ashram in Rishikesh gave an eighteen-day series of discourses on the Bhagavad Gita that "proved to be an unprecedented spiritual feast, a Jnana [knowledge] Yajna for the elevation of the soul" (14). The following month the ashram brought Pandit Manhar Maharaj and his sixty child disciples, who "to the delight of all" recited the Gita and sang bhajans. Next came senior Mahatmas of the Ramakrishna Mission from Hyderabad, Chicago, and Chandigarh who lectured on Vedanta. Meanwhile, in Delhi the Society organized the "Divine Meet 1987." The Dalai Lama was the chief guest at this "grand function" attended by over 8,000 people. The program included a bhajan recital by a popular musician. The Divine Meet is described as having given "a new fillip both to the Centenary celebrations and to the propagation of Gurudev's teachings in the capital" (15).

Prior to and throughout the Centenary year the ashram arranged daily readings of the Bhagavatam, the Valmiki and Tulsi Ramayana as well as daily chanting of mantras. The readings and mantra chanting are described as a means "to keep the atmosphere in the Ashram surcharged with spiritual vibrations and also benefit the world at large" (16). The ashram also invited brahmans from Madras, Kanchipuram, and elsewhere to conduct a series of vedic recitations and rituals.

CENTENARY PUBLICATIONS

From its earliest days, the Divine Life Society has devoted much of its resources to print media. It has promoted Sivananda's teachings by publishing books, pamphlets, and periodicals as well as by placing articles in newspapers and magazines. Motilal Banarsidass, a leading publisher of indological books, endorses the scholarly status of Sivananda's writings by publishing five of his books on yoga and his commentary on the Brahma Sutra. The Centenary committee resolved to continue this tradition and quicken the pace of publication. Branches within India and abroad donated money to support publishing by the Society's own presses and to pay for publication by commercial presses of materials in English and regional languages.

As a Centenary activity, "headquarters took up for execution a grand project to print a hundred books of Gurudev" (7). Difficulties, including frequent power cuts, are cited as reasons why ninety-four rather than the full one hundred titles were finally published in Hindi and English. The *Centenary Report* notes that the Divine Life Society of South Africa in Durban "donated magnanimously to the printing of quite a few of the publications" (7). It also provides figures on publications of translations into regional languages that were funded by branches. The "challenge" was to publish as many as possible by the close of the Centenary year. Branches "took up the challenge to get Gurudev's books translated into their regional languages" and published 108 titles in Tamil, 108 in Telugu, eighty-seven in Gujarati, and hundreds of booklets in Kannada (7). Branches donated the publications to the ashram, which in turn sold some and distributed others for free. In the sessions during the final week of the Centenary year, Chidananda ceremonially released these publications and publicly honored the branches and persons who funded them.

The Divine Life Society branch of Perth, under the direction of an Australian woman who had been initiated as a sannyasini by Sivananda's disciple Venkatesananda, prepared and paid for the publication of a nine-volume collection, *The Life and Works of Swami Sivananda*. Published in Hong Kong "to meet the standard required for world-wide distribution," the venture is described as a "labour of love," whose "production values are excellent and the books are already on the world market" (8). For the domestic market, a comic book version of Sivananda's hagiography was published by Argus Central Enterprises of New Delhi. The ashram provided the materials and guidance for this publication. It was later published in Hindi, Telugu, and other regional languages, and copies were on sale at the ashram. Sivananda now takes his place in the pantheon of gods, saints, and national heroes whose stories circulate in comic book editions.

Three special commemorative volumes were also prepared for the Centenary. The ashram's Hindi department prepared the *Swami Sivananda Janma Shatabdi Smriti Granth*, "a bumper volume containing articles by eminent writers on a variety of cultural, philosophical, religious, spiritual and social subjects, besides the life and teachings of Swami Sivananda. It is a magnum opus likely to be of immense use to research scholars" (8). A smaller volume in English, *The Master, His Mission, and His Works* is described as a "standard textbook," "a mini-encyclopaedia of spiritual teaching" (*MMW*, iii). The Society produced this "Comprehensive Souvenir" to serve as "a permanent guidebook to spiritual seekers the world over" (iii). It is divided into seven sections of approximately forty pages each: the first section includes articles by Sivananda, Chidananda, Krishnananda, and Venkatesananda which extol the purpose and achievements of the Divine Life Society. The next section contains excerpts from

Sivananda's commentaries on Hindu scriptures. This is followed by "Sivananda on the Religions of the World" and then his expositions on eleven types of yoga, culminating with the "yoga of synthesis."

The final sections include: his "advice and messages" to various groups—children, students, householders, teachers, women, doctors, businessmen, lawyers, industrialists, nations, the West—and an "inspiring message for everyone"; a section with biographical sketches of his disciples; and a synopsis of Centenary activities. The volume closes with an epilogue, "Heart of Sivananda's Teachings." It contains his twenty spiritual instructions; the science of seven cultures "for quick evolution of the human soul"; and various mantras with descriptions of their benefits such as preventing death by lightning, snakebite, motor accidents, drowning, and fire (*MMW*, 275–81). Devotees are enjoined to recite the mantra 100,000 times on their birthday, or at least 50,000 times, as well as to perform a fire sacrifice and to feed sadhus and the poor. They will be rewarded with "long life, peace, wealth, prosperity, satisfaction and immortality" (281).

The epilogue also includes a form showing how to keep a spiritual diary. Such a diary is described as a "whip for goading the mind towards righteousness and God" (282). The form asks twenty-seven questions whereby the devotee monitors diligence and lapses: "When did you get up from bed?" "How many Gita Slokas did you read or get by heart?" "How long in the company of the wise (Satsanga)?" "How many hours you spent in useless company?" "How many lies did you tell and with what self-punishment?" "How long in disinterested selfless Service?" "How much did you give in charity?" By keeping this diary spiritual seekers are assured of "quick progress" and "marvellous results." Devotees are advised to send a copy of the diary to Guruji "for getting further lessons" (282).

This quantitative approach is also evident in the form, "My Resolves for the Year." It has eighteen points concerning how much virtuous behavior devotees intend to practice during the upcoming year—celibacy, fasting, chanting, keeping silence, *Gita* study. Like the spiritual diary, the resolve form "should be prepared in duplicate and one copy duly signed and sent to your Guru so that you may not be tempted to relax your efforts, or ignore the resolves or break any resolve under the slightest pretext or lame excuse" (283).

Through these instructions and forms of self-assessment, Sivananda rationalized the procedure for achieving the divine life. Devotees are enjoined to submit their diaries and annual resolutions to the guru, i.e., mail them to the Divine Life Society and receive a response from its correspondence department. Through this process the Society encourages devotees to mold for themselves identities that conform to criteria which can be enumerated and evaluated. Such identities complement those which earn positions of authority based on complex calculations of self-discipline, spiritual and secular achievement, and wealth. Sivananda's insistence that these guidelines provide spiritual seekers with the means for "quick progress" and ultimate liberation recalls his advice about the need to be forceful and completely confident when treating patients:

> Gurudev's service has always been of the aggressive type. Very recently he remarked humorously: "You should not be diffident when a patient approaches you; you should assure him that you are giving the best medicine and that he will surely get well soon. You must go to the patient and say: 'Come to me and I will heal you in a day!' Be aggressive in service; and the Lord will crown your efforts with success." (Venkatesananda 1980, 148)

CONSTRUCTION AND CHARITABLE PROJECTS DURING THE CENTENARY

The Centenary also provided the Divine Life Society with the occasion and funds for making improvements on existing ashram facilities and constructing monuments to Sivananda and new buildings. The Centenary Report summarizes the purpose of ten major construction projects: "the Ashram campus as a whole underwent a face-lift on the eve of the Centenary" and the administration executed various construction projects "designed to fulfill specific needs" (*CR*, 10). With fresh paint on old buildings and freshly constructed buildings, the ashram presented to Centenary visitors an appearance congruent with its present prosperity.

The ashram's forty-year-old Bhajan hall was renovated and enlarged. The Vishvanath temple was expanded, since it had been unable to accommodate the hundreds of devotees who gather on festival days. The temple also had a face lift: "an artistic facade in traditional South Indian style has been added on to the temple which now presents a grand appearance" (11). The ashram also constructed an outdoor auditorium; six guest rooms were cleverly built beneath its stage. As this new auditorium's capacity of eight hundred people is greater than that of the Samadhi hall, it "came in handy to conduct the various programmes connected with the Centenary" (11). To enhance the "majesty and grandeur" of the marble statue of Sivananda in the Guru Mandir, the ashram commissioned the construction of an "artistic marble pedestal in the shape of an open lotus" (11).

The old rooms where Sivananda had lived were converted into a museum and shrine, the Sri Gurudev Kutir. Some of his personal effects—notebooks, desk, clothes—were placed on display. The renovations are said to have preserved intact "the floor of the room sanctified by the dust of the lotus feet of Gurudev" (12). The ashram also rebuilt the riverside ghat below Sri Gurudev Kutir and nearby ghats where Sivananda used to bathe in the Ganges. Adjacent to these concrete stairs leading to the river are large concrete platforms where visitors can sit. They are labeled with signs in Hindi and English: "Pray Here"; "Cogitate Here"; "Meditate Here." At dawn and dusk when the valley resounds with temple bells and loud-speakers blaring bhajans, solitary figures can be seen sitting silently on these platforms (see plate 19).

Not unlike commemorative columns constructed by bygone rulers of India, the Society constructed the Sivananda Dharma Stambha on a trian-gular plot of land at the crossroads of the main and bypass roads between Hardwar and Rishikesh. This pillar of white marble is similar to the one outside the Vishvanath temple at the ashram, and their inscriptions are identical. Chidananda consecrated the Dharma Stambha with a ceremony attended by "a distinguished gathering" (10). Commenting on the conse-cration, one resident in a Hardwar ashram was particularly impressed by the Divine Life Society's punctual and well-organized performance of the ceremony.

As travelers on the national highway enter the area of Rishikesh in-cluding and surrounding the ashram known as Shivanandanagar, they meet an even more impressive monument, the Sivananda Centenary Me-morial Arch. The Society describes the arch as "a fitting monument to the great saint who, more than anyone else, had been responsible for putting Rishikesh on the world map" (10). The trustees of the wealthy Tirupati temple in South India donated 250,000 rupees to build this "Sivananda Dharma Dwara," the gateway to the realm of Sivananda Dharma. The week before the Centenary's grand finale, "the Swami Sivananda Centen-ary Memorial Arch was inaugurated by Hon. Sri Vir Bahadur Singh, Chief Minister of Uttar Pradesh, in a very solemn function" (20). The presence of the chief minister, other officials, and the press at this ceremony attracted local political activists: members of the Uttarkhand Kranti Dal "demanded on the occasion a separate hill state" (*Times of India,* 26 August 1987). During his speech the chief minister promised that the government would build a paved road to connect Lakshman Jhula and Sivananda Jhula, the nearby footbridges across the river. The Uttar Pradesh government had completed construction of the latter—a suspension footbridge to connect Shivanandanagar and Swarg ashram—the year before the Centenary. The Government of India through its Ministry of Shipping and Transport also used the occasion of the Centenary for "paying their tribute to the worship-ful Master" (*CR,* 12). The Ministry proclaimed that the four-kilometer stretch of national highway passing through Shivanandanagar be officially known as Swami Shivananda Marg. These official tributes to Sivananda in-dicate how the Society works "to remove the unwarranted distinction be-tween the spiritual and the secular" (*AR,* 1). Organizations such as the Divine Life Society exhort government officials to fulfill their duty as protectors of India's valuable spiritual heritage and profit by providing occasions for officials to publicly discharge this duty.

Dharma also requires those who enjoy prosperity to publicly donate to charitable causes. The *Centenary Report* records the special "social welfare and relief work" projects undertaken by the Society. Although "Sadhu Bhojan and poor feeding is an important feature of the Sivananda Ashram even on normal days," throughout the Centenary year on the eighth of every month (the birth date of Sivananda) sadhus and "hundreds of poor were fed in an organised manner" (*CR*, 13). "On the happy occasion of Gurudev's Centenary" the ashram also provided assistance to "poor people" in Rishikesh whose riverside huts had been damaged by floods. The ashram donated money and labor for rebuilding their homes (14). The Society also increased to 400 the number of poor students whom it supports.

Another Centenary project involved expansion of the ashram's "medical relief" services and included renovating and enlarging the hospital. Despite its limited thirty-bed capacity, the hospital is described as providing the means "to cater to the needs of all people, particularly the poor in the surrounding area" (13). The ashram also extends its charitable medical aid to people in the surrounding area by sending doctors to conduct clinics in mountain villages. The sides of the large medical van bears the Divine Life Society's name as well as the name of the devotee from New York who donated funds for its purchase. In addition to the services of visiting devotees who are doctors, the ashram employs a full-time doctor, who is paid a modest salary.

The doctor working for the ashram in 1987–88, a man dedicated to serving the poor, had been an active member of the RSS since boyhood. He said that he was no longer involved in the organization, but his relatives continue to be staunch RSS supporters. He told me that the Rishikesh RSS branch was very active. The meeting that he promised to arrange for me with local RSS members never took place.

THE HUNDRED DAYS' PROGRAMME

"The second and more intensive phase of the Centenary" began on June 1, 1987, the anniversary of Sivananda's sannyas initiation (16). The *Hindustan Times* announced the commencement of these celebrations in Rishikesh (3 June 1987). Posters around Hardwar invited ascetics to the ashram for a Sadhu's Assembly on Sivananda's sannyas initiation day. Like the first months of the Centenary year discussed above, the Hundred Days' Programme involved a steady stream of special events: lectures on the *Ramayana,* on Sivananda's life and teachings, and on other religious topics; performances of devotional music and dance; rituals for Guru Purnima and anniversaries associated with Sivananda's life; processions; and consecrations of renovated and newly constructed buildings.

This three-month "more intensive phase" of Centenary celebrations began at dawn with meditation and prayers in the Sivananda Samadhi hall. These were followed by an early morning parade through Shivanandanagar and across the Shivananda footbridge to the hut where Sivananda had lived during his early days in Rishikesh. The procession returned to the ashram, where Krishnananda addressed the assembly with a sermon on "Sannyasa and Its Import." This was followed by "reverential tributes to Gurudev" by sixteen Mahamandaleshwars from Hardwar and Rishikesh. After their testimonials, these Hindu ascetic leaders "were reverenced with traditional feast and farewell" (17). The farewell for important guests at a feast traditionally includes a cash gift. In the evening the Society's vice president ceremonially inaugurated the renovated Gurudev Kutir. The crowd then proceeded to the river, where "hundreds of devotees went up and down the Ganga in boats singing special Kirtans surcharging the atmosphere with spiritual vibrations" (17). The first day of the Hundred Days' Programme concluded with a performance of dance and devotional music by the Art Group from the Bharat Heavy Electricals factory in Hardwar.

Two days later a pandit began a series of discourses on the Valmiki *Ramayana;* on the ninth day a vedic fire sacrifice marked the completion of the pandit's lectures. On the same day another fire sacrifice was performed as part of the consecration of the Vishvanath temple's new facade. A few days later, Tamil devotees from Delhi conducted a "Padi Vizha function." They stopped and sang a hymn as the ascended each step of the stairway from the road to the Vishvanath temple: "It was indeed a grand and inspiring experience to witness the devotion with which the whole programme was gone through" (18). Throughout the month of June devotees gave special musical performances at evening satsang. On two evenings those attending satsang were treated to a performance by a Garhwali dance and music troupe who "gave a variety programme depicting the cultural lore of Garhwal" (18). At these evening satsangs during the second half of June prominent sannyasins and scholars from Hardwar and Rishikesh lectured to "hundreds of eager people" on "various spiritual topics" (18).

July began with a series of lecture-demonstrations by the ashram's yoga expert. This was followed by a series of discourses on the role of the guru by the Society's vice president that concluded on Guru Purnima, which was "celebrated in the traditional way" (18). Next came the annual "Sadhana Week," during which several hundred devotees attended yoga classes and received "special instructions and guidelines for leading a spiritual life" (18). Rituals and "solemnity marked the occasion" of the anniversary of Sivananda's death on July 19th. The month of July closed with a series of lectures by Chidananda, during which he "narrated some thrilling and inspiring incidents in Gurudev's life which he had personally witnessed" (19). Due to the audience's enthusiastic insistence, Chidananda lectured ten days longer than planned.

During the first week of August devotees enjoyed a "veritable spiritual feast" (19). In addition to Chidananda's discourses on Sivananda, they were treated to "scholarly and inspiring" lectures by Krishnananda on "The Vision of Life." This feast also included talks by a "great exponent" of the Tulsi *Ramayana*. The visiting pandit lectured for five days to "thousands in a packed audience" about the spiritual basis of events in the *Ramayana* (19). Later in August Swami Jivanmuktananda, president of the Divine Life Society in Malaysia, lectured for a week on "Gita and Gurudev Sivananda." Through his lectures the swami from Malaysia "ably brought out the similarity between the teachings of Sri Krishna and Gurudev" (19). When the lectures on the *Gita* and Sivananda were concluded, a swami from Andhra Pradesh discoursed on the Upanishads "in a very simple and lucid style." The ashram involved local schools in the Centenary celebrations by sponsoring an elocution competition for college and high school boys. The assigned topics concerned Sivananda and the Divine Life Society. The competitors "showed considerable enthusiasm": "It was gratifying to know that amongst the younger generation, interest in saints and Adhyatmic [spiritual] studies was still present" (20). The ashram awarded prizes and gifts to winners and participants. The students also presented the audience with a "cultural fete."

Forty-one pandits from Delhi were invited by the ashram to perform the "sacred Ati Rudram" rituals: "such a grand and solemn function had never been witnessed by anyone in the Ashram" (20). The rituals "culminated" with a vedic fire sacrifice, and the Delhi pandits "were seen off with traditional gifts and Dakshina" (cash donation) (20). Like the legendary courts of Hindu kings, through such events the Sivananda ashram enacted the role of patron—sponsoring competitions and distributing prizes to students and rewarding brahmans for their ritual services. Other events during August included bhajan singing by musicians from Madras and a Hari Katha recital conducted by Sant Keshav Dasji, who was accompanied by his western disciples. For lighter entertainment the ashram invited two professional magicians, who delighted audiences on three evenings with their "very interesting magic performance" (21).

THE GRAND FINALE

By the end of August a huge tent was raised on ashram grounds: the site for the Centenary's "Grand Finale." Dozens of ceiling fans and cut-glass chandeliers were suspended from the tent's frame. Loudspeakers and florescent lights were mounted on poles throughout the tent. The billowing pink and white canopy was dotted with the emblem of the Divine Life Society: a lotus with a rising sun and aum in the center framed by the motto, "Serve, Love, Meditate, Realize." Rows of silvery aums glittered from the side panels of the tent. Nearly large enough for a symphony orchestra, the high stage had a colorful backdrop showing a blow-up of Sivananda's smiling face set amidst the snowy peaks of the Himalayas. On the right-hand side of the stage was a Sivananda shrine. It consisted of a bust of Sivananda and a life-size cutout figure of Sivananda, identical to the picture on the Centenary postage stamp. Every day devotees garlanded the figure and bust and performed puja before them. The Centenary tent, with its "tastefully decorated stage," was inaugurated by Chidananda the same evening that a week-long recitation of the *Bhagavatam* (Bhagavat Saptaha) commenced. Throughout the week, the singer-storyteller "enthralled" the audience with his "soul-stirring" performance (20–21).

Like an orchestra pit in an opera house, in front of the stage was a section with chairs where VIP guests were seated. Behind this lower section was a raised expanse covered with cotton rugs. The bright orange of its occupants signaled that the front was reserved for sannyasis and sadhus. Whereas in the VIP section men and women were not segregated, in the rest of the audience men sat on the right and women on the left. The tent accommodated about 7,000 people. The audience passed through a miniature bazaar when entering at the rear of the tent. Devotees staffed stalls selling not only books but also an array of Centenary souvenirs—plastic briefcases, wristwatches, wall clocks, decals, cloth shoulder bags, and t-shirts emblazoned with Sivananda's face and the Society's Centenary logo. Representatives from branches had available Sivananda booklets and prayer cards printed in English, Hindi, and regional languages which devotees had donated for free distribution.

The Grand Finale in the first week of September "marked the culmination of the Centenary celebrations" (21). These eight days were packed "with one programme or the other, spiritual or cultural." The *Centenary Report* acknowledges the "cooperation and goodwill" shown by the people of Rishikesh and Hardwar and considered this evidence of the "love and reverence in which the great Master is held by them even today" (21). The Society expressed its gratitude to ashrams, dharmshalas, and hotels in Rishikesh and Hardwar for helping to accommodate "the honoured guests who poured in from all parts of the world" (21). It is likely that these accommodating hosts appreciated the extra business generated by Centenary guests. When I had inquired about staying in the ashram during this busy week, I was advised to stay at the nearby government tourist bungalow where rooms had been reserved for Centenary visitors.

The printed program of the week's events announced the schedule: daily sessions; a three-day Cultural and Spiritual Conference; a three-day

Seminar on Spiritual and Humanitarian Values; and the activities for the penultimate and final days, a procession through Rishikesh and birth anniversary worship. The daily sessions started at dawn with chanting, meditation, readings from Sivananda's books, and talks by senior swamis. Visitors were encouraged to attend sunset Ganga arti conducted by the ashram every evening at the riverside Shivananda ghat. The ashram had also arranged programs of devotional music and dance by professional performers for each night of the week.

During the three-day Cultural and Spiritual Conference, speakers uniformly extolled the importance of Sivananda's life and teachings. Chidananda's lecture, "The Personality of Sri Gurudev Swami Sivananda," opened the Conference's first session. Krishnananda spoke authoritatively on "Ethical Ideals in the Religions of the World." The relevance of Sivananda's teachings for contemporary life, and particularly his interpretations of the *Gita* and the life of Rama, figured prominently in the lectures of the other eight senior swamis. The schedule of the Conference and the Seminar, with lectures from nine until eleven in the morning and between four and six in the afternoon, provided ample time for the audience to line up for meals in the dining hall, rest through the heat of the day, shop in the bazaar, and visit other ashrams and temples.

Throughout the proceedings, Chidananda, as president of the Divine Life Society, was publicly deferred to as the ashram's highest ranking official and spiritual leader. Through his frequent comments expressing concern for the welfare of the guests and exhorting them to attend all the activities and to be punctual, Chidananda enacted the role of gracious host and paterfamilias. A wave of excitement passed through the audience whenever he entered the tent. When departing at the close of a session, he was usually thronged by devotees touching his feet and anxiously vying for a quick word with him. After one session a devotee wearing a VIP badge managed to gain Chidananda's attention. He asked about traveling with Chidananda's entourage to Badrinath after the Centenary; Chidananda agreed that he could join the group and instructed him to make arrangements with the office. Devotees also gathered around other senior swamis as they walked through the ashram grounds, but none seemed to generate as much excitement as Chidananda.

During the first day of the Cultural and Spiritual Conference I sat amongst the women towards the back of the tent. Posted throughout the tent were men and women with yellow kerchiefs around their necks and huge badges. They directed the crowd and sometimes commanded those talking to be silent. Many members of the audience were writing in Centenary exercise books which were distributed by the ashram. Devotees were instructed to fill the pages with mantras and then return the notebook to the office. Others in the audience occupied themselves reading through materials they had purchased or received. Most of the audience looked healthy and well dressed. Unlike crowds in the bazaar, at the bus stand, or at the railway station, few people looked rustic or poor.

When I took out my pen and notebook to record some of the comments of the speakers, an old woman sitting next to me looked alarmed. She grabbed the pen from my left hand and thrust it into my right. When I put the pen back in my left hand, she repeated her action. She thought I was writing mantras; the left hand is ritually impure. When I explained that I was not writing mantras she was slightly relieved but still disturbed to see the pen in my left hand. After this exchange she, like others in the audience, listened and dozed as the speakers rambled on and on.

Although there were microphones on stage and numerous loudspeakers, many of the speakers were barely audible from the back of the tent. Since I wanted to follow the proceedings more closely, I inquired in the reception office about sitting in the front. The staff referred me to Adhyatmanananda, the speedy swami in charge of public relations. He took me to the tent and seated me in the back of the VIP section and in front of a group of women ascetics. At that point I did not yet know any ashram residents, and he introduced me to Krishnapriya, the librarian who has lived in the ashram for over thirty years. He advised me to ask her any questions I might have. For the rest of the week I often sat near her and listened to her commentary on the proceedings.

The second day of the Cultural and Spiritual Conference involved more speeches about Sivananda and the important work of the Divine Life Society. Journalists working for national and regional newspapers and wire services spoke during the morning session. One opened his speech with a familiar refrain: "Rishikesh has always been a place for national integration." Senior swamis thanked these media men—no woman was among them—for their excellent coverage of the Centenary year and presented them with flower garlands, plaques, and Sivananda books. The afternoon session attracted a larger audience. Like the day before, the stage was ablaze with orange. Onstage upon their individual cushions senior swamis sat with their invited guests: the head of the Sri Swaminarayan Sampradaya and a group of his ascetic disciples. This huge and wealthy international organization celebrated the bicentenary of its founder in 1981. The scale of its celebration dwarfed that of the Divine Life Society and approximated that of a Kumbh Mela. This largely Gujarati organization raised not simply a large tent but rather an entire religious theme park in Ahmedabad. One particularly popular exhibition concerning the life of the founder attracted 1,500,000 visitors who paid a rupee each to enter (Williams 1984, 152).

Like Chidananda and Satyamitranand of the Bharat Mata temple, who also enjoys considerable support from Gujaratis, the head of the Sri

Swaminarayan Sampradaya is listed as a member of the Vishva Hindu Parishad's inner circle of ascetic leaders. The report on the VHP's Sacrifice for Unity includes numerous references to participation by representatives of the Swaminarayan Sampradaya (*Ekatmata Yajna*, 130—33). The Divine Life Society's own and its invited speakers' links with the VHP were never explicitly stated during the Centenary proceedings. However, the content of many of the speeches given during the six days as well as Centenary publications discussed elsewhere offer a toned-down version of militant Hindu nationalism.

The emotionality fostered by the Centenary, with its insistence on universal love, shares presuppositions concerning Hindu identity and spiritual superiority espoused by Hindu nationalist hatemongers: the important role of spiritual leadership in Indian society; devotion to Rama, the incarnation of righteousness; the sanctity of Bharat, the land of the gods and of the Ganges, the Vedas, and the *Gita*. The repetitiousness and shared content of the speeches fostered the ritual aura of certainty. Throughout the entire week, a procession of speakers repeatedly embroidered the themes of the need for a guru, Sivananda's divinity, and the spiritual basis of Indian/Hindu cultural and social values. Preserving the repetitiousness of the themes and content of these speeches in the following discussion suggests how repetition by speakers on the centenary stage operates ideologically to make specific ideas intensely familiar and gloss them with the patina of inevitable truth.

The Swaminarayan swamis set a pleasant and devotional tone for their speeches by first leading the audience in an hour of religious songs. Speaking in rapid-fire Hindi, H.H. Sri Pramukh Majaraj, the head of the Swaminarayan Sampradaya opened his speech by saying, "Bharat is Sivananda and the Divine Life Society." The crowd cheered. He continued to praise Sivananda and his mission while reminding the audience of the necessity of a guru: "there is no path without a guru." The next Swaminarayan swami addressed the audience in English. He began by referring to Sivananda and discussing the importance of the "saint's subtle work." He spoke of other famous leaders. Hitler was an evil genius. Churchill was a great leader: when London was on fire he led people to "V." But Churchill "was afraid of Gandhi." Gandhi too was a great leader, but he "only experimented with truth." "Sivananda, however, realized truth" and thus can "lead people to God." The swami then narrated a story about a guard in a lunatic asylum. The guard had no fear of the lunatics because "they cannot organize themselves." The moral is: "we must join together and unite in peace." The ideology of Hindu Sangathan espoused by Savarkar and more recently by the Vishva Hindu Parishad was embedded in this swami's speech with its concern for organization, potency, and unity. Catering to the sentiments of the crowd, the speakers concluded their talks by leading rousing rounds of "Jai Narayan, Jai Sivananda" with the audience raising their arms as they shouted "Jai Sivananda!"

Through its participation in the Grand Finale of the Sivananda Centenary, the Swaminarayan Sampradaya demonstrated its support for the Divine Life Society. Both the invitation to participate and its acceptance illustrate the concern of prominent Hindu leaders to publicly display their solidarity and promote each other's authority and organizations. The *Centenary Report,* for example, notes: "On the 2nd September, H.H. Sri Pramukh Maharaj and his disciples of the Swaminarayan Sampradaya graced the function. In fact, the entire afternoon was allotted to them and they gave us a memorable performance of music and discourses" (22). With this statement the Divine Life Society enhances its prestige by recording the participation of the Swaminarayan leader and disciples and also suggests the Society's deference for the powerful Swaminarayan organization by noting that an entire afternoon was devoted to its representatives.

Badges of various sizes and colors and more modest name tags distributed by the ashram allowed Centenary guests to display their relative rank. The ashram was selective about whom it accommodated on its premises and whom it fed. Only those with passes were admitted to the dining hall during the busy Centenary finale. There were several sittings for each meal, for which women and men lined up and dined separately. As I waited in line one afternoon for lunch, an obese woman pushed to the front and laid down across the doorway: no one was going to get ahead of her. As if reciting catechism, she said to me, "You may be Christian, but all religions are one." When the gate was opened, the women pushed upstairs into the dining hall and took their seats on the floor in rows. A swami marched up and down the rows like a drill sergeant. Before the meal he led diners in chanting, "Hare Krishna, Hare Rama." Later he supervised the servers, who hurried up and down the rows with buckets of rice, lentils, vegetables, and roti. He also ordered diners to leave no leftovers. The woman on one side of me smiled as we watched the big woman sitting on the other side of me devour a dozen rotis and numerous helpings of rice and vegetables. Diners ate quickly and in silence. Traffic was thick between the dining hall and the big tent. After morning and afternoon sessions people often rushed down the hill to get in line for meals. After meals they trudged slowly uphill in the humid heat, returning to watch the proceedings on the Centenary stage.

On the third day of the Cultural and Spiritual Conference, Dr. Kutty addressed the audience. She was introduced as a trustee of the Divine Life Society, the director of the hospital, and the general secretary of the Centenary committee. Speaking in English, she summarized Sivananda's mission and the purpose of celebrating his Centenary. Service, charity, dissemination and acquisition of knowledge, according to her—and the Divine Life Society's official statement—are the principal goals of the Society. She added that "transformation of the self" is also important but it is more difficult: "to have it done on the streets of New York is difficult." Dr. Kutty, like other speakers, used the West to signify forces such as materialism, technology, secularism, and modernism, forces portrayed as inimical to spirituality.

In her capacity as head of the Centenary committee, Dr. Kutty enumerated some of the religious activities sponsored by the Society during the past year. The continual bhajans, lectures, pujas, satsang, and lectures on the *Gita* and Shastras have "set up spiritual vibrations that have the potential to change the whole world." She embraced the audience as a collectivity by using the first-person plural: "We must purify ourselves so that Gurudev can be born everyday in our hearts." She likened the need for purification to the "proper preparations we make for special guests." Sivananda is the model and the goal is perfection: "Let us be the example of the perfect disciple. In every aspect of his life Gurudev was perfect."

SEMINAR ON CULTURAL AND HUMANITARIAN VALUES

The Seminar on Cultural and Humanitarian Values commenced the day after the Cultural and Spiritual Conference concluded. Despite being scheduled as two distinct events, the pious topics and tone of the speeches overlapped. The Seminar had a slightly more academic ambience. Speakers sat on chairs rather than on floor cushions as they did the during the Conference. Invited speakers included religious leaders, academics, and politicians: "The participation of great intellectuals . . . made the Seminar a veritable intellectual feast" (*CR*, 22–23). Krishnananda chaired the Seminar but Chidananda presided, sitting center stage on a raised dias. A large clock placed on the podium, as well as Krishnananda in the chair, reminded speakers to remain within the time allotted to them. Chidananda emphasized the need for punctuality by leading the audience in a round of "Punctuality ki Jai." At the beginning of a session after lunch he directed people to go out and round up "those gossiping in their rooms."

"Evaluation of Indian Culture in the Context of Modern Times" provided the topic for the initial day of the Seminar. The first speaker, Chandrashekhar Rath, the deputy director of education for the Government of Orissa, opened his speech by leading the audience in a long chant of aum. After this invocation he ponderously started speaking in English: "No words can express my experience." His lifelong dream of coming to the land of the rishis has been realized with this invitation to come to the "holy land." As the train passed through Jwalapur (the last town between Delhi and Rishikesh with a large Muslim population), he felt as though he was leaving the mundane world behind him. After these words, Krishnananda approvingly interjected, "very beautiful, very beautiful."

The speaker then introduced a philosophical tone by talking about the deceptiveness of appearances. He illustrated his point with the example of a beautiful woman who, by always looking in the mirror, turns her back on reality. As he spoke, a sweaty porter bent over by the huge metal trunk on his back walked down the side aisle toward the stage: a momentary reminder of the difference between the work in the ashram done by wage labor and the lighter tasks performed by devotees as guru seva. Taking no notice of the porter, Rath quoted the *Bhagavad Gita* and asserted that the roots of Indian culture are in the Himalayas, and that its branches stretch throughout the subcontinent. This image also evokes the image the Divine Life Society uses to describe its organizational structure, with its headquarters in Rishikesh and its branches in India and abroad.

The speaker's discussion of India's cultural identity and political history conformed to versions discussed elsewhere, e.g., those of Savarkar, Satyamitranand, and Sivananda. To edify the audience, the deputy director of education defined culture as "consciousness of life and values which formulates itself on three planes—transcendental, mental, and physical." During the nineteenth and twentieth centuries, Indian culture has suffered a "modern onslaught" associated with the "clash among cultures due to modern technology." In ancient times cultures grew independently, but even since vedic times India has been invaded. However, India has proven that it can "accommodate itself to everything new"; it has an "inherent resilience to everything new." Although at times India was politically submissive to its invaders, its culture was never defeated. Optimists feel that the "evils of modern times will pass and Indian culture will keep its head high." Others, however, "fear that modern influences lead to a decline in awareness of our culture."

Having distinguished these two views, Rath then expanded upon them. He lamented the fact that he meets children who do not know the *Ramayana* and the *Mahabharata,* who do not go to temples or study Sanskrit. He blamed parents and teachers for being remiss in their duty to educate children properly and instill pride in the glories of Indian culture. As an example of his own success at imparting cultural and spiritual values, he referred to a boy who had never heard of the Upanishads. Alarmed by his ignorance, Rath recited a passage in Sanskrit and gave him a commentary on it. Eager to know more, the boy began learning Sanskrit so he could study the Upanishads.

Rath equated the West with modernity and discussed how it lures and misguides Indian youth and intellectuals. For youth, the "West with its many temptations and physical comforts seems like a vital alternative to our culture." Modern education misguides people and produces hostility or indifference to spirituality: "To talk of the soul is an embarrassment for the educated man who protests that it is non-verifiable, that it is a non-issue, and that he is content without its knowledge." He described this situ-ation as leading to confusion about the proper role of India vis à vis the West, implicitly introducing the popular theme that India's spirituality earns for it the status as guru of the world: "Unfortunately we look up to the West for guidance, while they look up to us."

Whatever Indians may find in western culture and modern science, it has long existed in Indian culture. When faced with ancient Indian science, modern science bows in awe: "Modern astrophysicists crumble to their knees at what they cannot understand. All this is explained in the *Gita*." Rath then gave several examples of scientific theories which had been antic-ipated in Hindu scriptures. For Rath as for other speakers extolling Siva-nanda and the Divine Life Society's contribution to upholding India's national and cultural identity, Hindu and Indian are used interchangeably. He referred to Hindu scriptures not only in relation to modern science but also in relation to art and literature. Contemporary poets and painters look to the Upanishads and Puranas for inspiration.

Rath cloaked in culture and spirituality his support for the ideology of Hindu dominance espoused by others in explicitly economic and political terms. He prophesied, "The time will come when the weak are lost and only one culture based on love and truth will prevail." To achieve this goal, "India must solidify its cultural ground." Like Dr. Kutty, he figured himself and the audience as forming a single body with a shared goal: "We must meet modern times as equals and graft it onto our own soil." Just as mod-ern objects such as plastic briefcases and wall clocks are stamped with Siva-nanda's face and the events on stage could be seen on closed circuit television in the reception office, the grafting of modernity onto Indian soil requires that "everything must have the touch of this great culture." To il-lustrate his question, "Why look elsewhere for what is within our own cul-ture," Rath narrated the story of a senseless man who dug a well on the banks of the Ganges.

With his allotted hour coming to an end, Rath raised the issue of the need for a guru. He recounted a story about a young man, who after much searching and many doubts, at last found his guru. Rath reminded the au-dience that the guru is always present but one must prepare oneself and earn the grace necessary for meeting and recognizing a true guru. As he pronounced these words two policemen with rifles slung over their shoul-ders came down the aisle and seated themselves in the VIP section, momen-tarily distracting both the speaker and audience. Rath closed his speech as he had begun it, in an intimate and emotional tone: "I will not thank you because I love you. You love me to have invited me."

Unlike Rath's measured and careful English elocution, the next speaker, Sanskrit scholar Dr. Mahamahopadhyaya Brahmamitra Awasthi from Delhi, spoke breathlessly in highly Sanskritic Hindi. As might be expected from someone with the titles Dr. and Mahamahopadhyaya, Awasthi displayed his expertise by opening his speech with a long Sanskrit recitation. Not to be upstaged by a householder and scholar, the swamis on stage joined in with Awasthi. His lecture emphasized the importance of the Vedas for Indian society: "What the Vedas say is dharma—they teach faith in God." He recounted at length the story of Nachiketa, the brave seeker after truth who remained undaunted and triumphed over death. The audience's restlessness was relieved when he arrived at his conclusion: "Our vedic culture and traditions are alive."

Perhaps impatient for his opportunity to speak, Krishnananda fidgeted while Rath and Awasthi had the floor. When his turn came, he spoke in English and began by defining culture. According to Krishnananda culture is "appropriate behavior in the context of prevailing conditions." He warned the audience that culture was enigmatic, thus implying the need for religious leaders like himself to discourse on it: "We all know it is good to be cultured but what kind of behavior is cultured?" In Indian English as in other languages, culture and cultured are laden with ideological implications. "Culture" and "cultured" translate into the Hindi terms "sanskriti" and "sanskrit." These terms link lengthy chains of significations—Hindu gods whose language is Sanskrit, Hindu saints who preserve and interpret culture, Sanskrit pandits, vedic ritualists, dharmic rulers such as Rama, virtuous wives like Sita and Sati.

Krishnananda related culture to "norms of behavior accepted by our own species." In Indian English the term species connotes not simply human beings but also jati, the various socially constructed categories a person belongs to, particularly caste and gender. (Savarkar used "jati" to designate the categories of race and people who constitute a nation, e.g., Hindu jati.) Krishnananda posed the question, "Why behave according to norms and not according to impulses?" Correcting the "intelligentsia" for their mistaken belief that "social behavior is the highest standard," Krishnananda asserted, "There is a higher standard: spirituality." Like Rath, Krishnananda introduced the themes of unity and cooperation and added sacrifice, another theme favored by religious and political leaders. In his view the "cooperative spirit of society arises from common aspirations in the hearts of humanity." This spirit of cooperation and sacrifice is "engendered by our very nature." Krishnananda did not explain how people such as himself earn the authority to pronounce on culture and its higher standard of spirituality, on humanity's shared aspirations and on "our very nature." Instead he asserted that "no one can order anyone else; anyone can be equally disposed to this cooperation."

The unnamed agent in Krishnananda's speech is the spiritual leader, the guru with the divine capacity to awaken devotees: "The urge to cooperate lies dormant as an unconscious or subconscious longing and is submerged. It must be made conscious and supplant subconscious acceptance of rules and orders." Whatever the role of unconscious and subconscious processes, Krishnananda asserted that "all life is conscious behavior." He implicitly affirmed the authority of those with spiritual knowledge as being in the position to understand the "supernormal conditioning factor which is the transcendental aspect in material life." Reiterating the belief that spirituality—a seen and unseen force—is both the bedrock and pinnacle of culture, Krishnananda concluded: "There cannot be a culture unless it is rooted in divine content. God must come first. The invisible is the final value." Impressed by Krishnananda's lecture, Krishnapriya nudged me and noddingly commented, "You were able to get much from Swamiji's talk."

Chidananda followed Krishnananda, thanking the speakers and summarizing points from their talks on the Evaluation of Indian Culture in the Context of Modern Times. Speaking clearly and slowly in simple Hindi, he politely paused, asking if everyone could hear him. After these courtesies, he chanted some Sanskrit verses and translated them into English. He began his Hindi commentary on the verse by saying, "Egoism has brought man to the brink of destruction. What I have known is a grain of sand on the seashore. Our culture inculcates this humility. Indian culture (bharatiya sanskriti) is the strand of sanity which can save man from his vanity and egotism." Chidananda then related Sivananda's teachings to "the indispensable necessity of Indian cultural ideals." These ideals include humility in the presence of god, compassion, charity, and the belief that all are worthy of being served. Just as an earlier speaker asserted that Bharat is Sivananda, Chidananda concluded his speech by equating Bharatiya culture with the spiritual teachings of his master, "Sivananda, Guru Maharaj."

The topic for the second day of the Seminar, "Swami Sivananda's Concept of a Spiritual Life," generated more speeches in praise of Gurudev. The day's first speaker, a professor of Sanskrit, delivered his lecture in English with an excited and urgent tone, not unlike televangelists. He opened with the invocation, "Oh man, you are divine!" Next he reminded the audience about the need for "amalgamation and harmony of all cultures," describing this as the process of "cultural integration." Like an earlier speaker, he referred to Kipling's famous dictum, "East is East and West is West and never the twain shall meet," only to assert that Sivananda proved Kipling wrong. Sivananda's teachings and the mission of the Divine Life Society bridge the gap between East and West.

The Sanskrit professor pleased the audience by reciting a popular Sivananda epigram: "To the agnostic and atheist who say 'god is nowhere,' Sivananda says, 'god is now here.'" From Sivananda we learn that "by changing your angle of vision you can achieve divinity." According to the speaker, Sivananda was the "lion of Vedanta," who showed us how to "roar the truth like a lion and not bleat like a goat." Sivananda was Radha, a lover of Krishna. In his next statement, Sivananda becomes both Radha and Krishna: "There is no distinction between Radha and Krishna." He then expanded on the vedantin principle of identity: "There is no distinction between Har and Hari, between Hindu and Christian." The speaker concluded by exhorting the audience to follow the path to divine life as taught by Sivananda: "God first, world next, and self last. Improve self first and others will improve by following your example."

The theme of Sivananda's divinity was taken up by the next speaker, an ascetic disciple of Sivananda and head of a Divine Life Society ashram in the temple city of Madurai. He opened with a chant praising Sivananda as an avatar of Vishnu. Speaking clearly and slowly in Hindi, he occasionally paraphrased his comments in English. Like his own guru Sivananda and countless other gurus, he maintained that the three most important things in life are a human birth, the desire for moksha (spiritual liberation), and the loving care and protection of a saint. Just as Sivananda gave forcefully positive prognoses to his medical and spiritual patients, this swami asserted, "Whoever wishes for moksha will eventually get it just as people who want food get it." The speaker then turned to his personal experiences with Sivananda. He recounted a visit with Sivananda in 1962, when his guru instructed him to start an ashram in Madurai. He expressed his hesitation about this undertaking to Sivananda, claiming that he was too poor. However, Sivananda assured him, "Where my pictures and words are, there I am." The swami dutifully established an ashram and soon after "money and followers came." This theme of material success recurred in numerous speeches: the humble beginnings of the Divine Life Society or particular branches and the inevitable growth leading to present eminence and prosperity.

The next swami commenced his address with a long Sanskrit chant. He took up the topic of guru dharma, saying that one may have many teachers but only one true guru. He likened the relationship to the true guru to "stri pati dharma," the beliefs and practices concerning the wife's dutiful subordination to her husband and in-laws. Loyal disciples are rewarded, assured the speaker; he then intoned a Sanskrit verse and translated it: "True disciples distinguish themselves wherever they are." To illustrate this point, the swami referred to a disciple of Sivananda who served his guru "like a mother cares for her children." Often Sivananda gratefully acknowledged the services of this attentive disciple, saying that he could never repay his debt to him. The speaker contextualized the services of the disciple. Guru seva ennobles the disciple and contributes to the guru's higher task: "this disciple served Sivananda as selflessly as Sivananda served all people." The loyal disciple does not assume any authority which the guru does not confer on him, such as giving unauthorized initiations which diminish the guru's pool of potential followers, a common cause of schisms within Hindu religious groups. Whenever people came to this exemplary disciple and asked to be given sannyas by him, he always sent them to Sivananda or Chidananda: "This is guru parampara." Krishnananda interrupted the speaker, prompting him to conclude. The swami, however, took his time. The audience laughed when he continued talking after Krishnananda—with a scowl and an annoyed sigh— interrupted him for a third time. The swami finally finished by speaking of the growth of the Divine Life Society. He reminded the audience that Sivananda often said, "If God wills, he will send men and money."

The final speaker for the morning session was introduced as the oldest guest at the Centenary celebration, a 104-year-old swami from Madras. This hoary swami, author of many books, began by leading the audience in song. Like many others, he spoke thickly accented Indian English. He talked about the great saints he had met during his long life: Aurobindo, Shirdi Sai Baba, Sathya Sai Baba, Sivananda. The mission of Sivananda grows larger and larger "because of some great incarnate force. His body is gone but his soul lives on in the ashram." Implicitly introducing the theme of Hindu spirituality as an exportable good, he talked about his own trip to Russia: "They wanted me because no one talks of God in Russia." He claimed that he sat outside under a tree chanting and reading the *Gita*. This attracted people to gather around him and ask "questions about the soul." They told him that just by sitting near him "they felt happy." The swami concluded his speech with an imperative: "Read Sanskrit, the Vedas, the *Gita,* and Upanishads."

Throughout the six days of speeches, Chidananda punctuated the paeans to Sivananda by announcing new publications, honoring those associated with them, and presenting other honors. One group called on stage for honors offered an unusual sight—four sisters, all sannyasinis dressed in orange. Their father had been a disciple of Sivananda since 1934 and his devotion was such that he died on the same day as his guru. For the Centenary they had completed the work begun by their father before his death, a translation into Hindi of Sivananda's lengthy text, *Bliss Divine.* Krishnapriya informed me that two of the sisters live in the ashram and the others visit often but continue to maintain a large house in Delhi. On later visits to the ashram, I tried to speak with them and was directed by a younger sister to speak with the eldest. Unlike other more extroverted ashram women, these sisters avoided contact with outsiders.

A retired woman doctor, elderly and deaf, was escorted to the stage to be honored by Chidananda. He thanked her for funding the publication in Marathi of ten books by Sivananda. Acknowledging her donation of 25,000 rupees, he noted that "she even sold some of her gold jewelry" to raise the money. Devotees from Nagpur and Bombay were also thanked for assisting in the publication of these Marathi translations, which consisted of 1,000 copies of nine titles and 2,000 copies of the tenth title in the series.

Emotional drama surrounded Chidananda's unveiling of two paintings by a Delhi artist. The first painting was of Sivananda; the second showed Chidananda as a boy with his mother, who had died when he was still a child. Chidananda bowed before both paintings and circumambulated them. Noting that the artist had also painted portraits of Aurobindo and Anandamayi Ma, Chidananda jokingly said that the Divine Life Society did not have wealthy patrons of the arts like Aurobindo and Anandamayi Ma. However, he pledged 7,000 rupees for the painting of his mother and later announced that the Bombay and Delhi branches had donated money to buy portraits of Sivananda. During another interlude between speeches Chidananda presented prizes to winners of the Sivananda Centenary essay contest. School and college students received books wrapped in brightly colored paper, and Chidananda announced the percentage marks awarded for each winner's essay. A schoolteacher was also introduced; two of her students had won prizes.

The entry of the chief minister of Rajasthan with an entourage, which included two armed guards, signaled that the proceedings of the afternoon session during the second day of the Seminar on Spiritual and Humanitarian Values would commence shortly. No less flamboyant in his entry was Swami Vishnudevananda, the afternoon's other speaker. He too entered with an entourage. It consisted of his personal attendant, a western man in sannyasi's orange, and a group of about forty western devotees, most of whom were young and middle-aged women. After his devotees were seated in the VIP section, Vishnudevananda was introduced to the audience as one of Sivananda's most senior disciples. He had taken Gurudev's mission abroad and now has centers in the United States, Canada, Britain, and the Bahamas.

When Vishnudevananda began his speech with a Sanskrit verse, his followers loudly and enthusiastically joined in with their guru. He greeted the audience, "Maharajas, Guru Bhais [brothers], and Guru Bahins [sisters]." Reverentially, he said that Gurudev's greatness makes it "difficult to talk about him." However, he proceeded to acquit himself of this difficult task as well as talk about himself. Likening Sivananda to Lord Krishna, he described him as "cosmic love." To inform the audience of his own importance while keeping to the subject, Vishnudevananda referred to his recent meeting with the president of India. He reported that the president had characterized Sivananda as "the sort of person who makes everyone that meets him feel that he loves them more than anyone else." "This," Vishnudevananda proclaimed, "is divine power." The disciple spoke of the early poverty of the Divine Life Society, recalling how Sivananda had lived in a "damp room." Marveling at its success, Vishnudevananda said, "Now the ashram is like a big palace. Look at that power." Krishnapriya, who has lived in the ashram during this transition to prosperity, chuckled and commented, "the power of money." While his own devotees along with ashram and press photographers stalked the stage with their cameras and video equipment, Vishnudevananda recalled how, as far back as 1946, "movie cameras" were used in the ashram: "Since it was helpful for devotees, Sivananda never objected to photography."

Like other disciples, Vishnudevananda noted that he first learned of Sivananda through his publications, saying that his writings "appealed to my intellect." He took leave from the Army and traveled to Rishikesh for Sivananda's darshan. On his second visit to the ashram for Sivananda's sixtieth birthday in 1947, the guru told him to stay in the ashram and he did. Two years later Sivananda initiated the twenty-two-year-old Vishnudevananda as a sannyasi. He recalled that at first he was too proud to bow before Sivananda, but Sivananda, "who had realized that everything is brahman" taught him humility by bowing before him: "there was no difference between Gurudev's private and public behavior."

Before continuing his praises of Sivananda, Vishnudevananda asserted, "science is not absolute but relative." He then talked about receiving Sivananda's permission to take his message abroad and attributed all his achievements to Gurudev: "I am like a puppet in his hands." Vishnudevananda spoke of receiving his guru's assistance for his ventures as a high-flying swami. He recounted his flights for peace, when he dropped flowers as he piloted small planes over the Suez canal zone and the Berlin Wall. During the flight over the Berlin Wall, thick clouds had made it difficult to land, but he prayed to Sivananda and the clouds cleared. About these flights, Vishnudevananda speculated, "Maybe the flying was my big ego, for show business, I don't know." Like a gracious guest, Vishnudevananda concluded with compliments to his host, "Sivananda's successor, Chidananda, like Gurudev is all heart, from head to toe." Saying in unison, "Chidananda is all prem" (love), Krishnapriya and sannyasinis sitting with her affirmed Vishnudevananda's praise.

The Centenary celebration also provided Vishnudevananda an opportunity to publicize his international organization to an Indian audience. A half-page newspaper advertisement placed by his International Sivananda Yoga Vedanta Centers and Ashrams and the Swami Ramachandrananda Sivananda Yoga Vedanta Dhanwantari Ashram in Trivandrum presents a melange of spiritual themes and icons (*Times of India,* 26 August 1987). Under the ad's banner headline, "Sivananda Centennial Celebrations," the text asks, "Can we reach the 21st century? We must learn to live as global citizens and love each other." On the left of the Centenary banner is an outline map of India with an image of the Devi (possibly but not definitively Bharat Mata) inside it holding the Indian flag. Figures of men and women holding hands are drawn down the front as the folds in Devi's sari. Over her left shoulder and amidst the mountains is Sivananda. On the opposite side, under the Indian flag is a drawing of Vishnu spinning his discus. Under this image of Bharat is an invitation: "Join us on 8th September for the All India Peace Mala, at Har Ki Pauri (Hardwar), Sivananda Ashram (Rishikesh), Rajghat (Delhi) and Nagercoil (Kannyakumari) between 11 am and 12 noon chanting Om Namo Narayana and Havans."

To the left of the banner is a drawing of a light aircraft and under that Vishnudevananda's "True World Order Message":

1. Drop flowers not bombs.
2. Cross the borders with flowers and love, not with guns and bombs.
3. Radiate love not nuclear radiation.

Across the width of the page are printed twelve quotations concerning love. Each is attributed to a particular religious tradition and accompanied by a symbol, e.g., a cross for Christianity, aum for Hinduism. Under these scriptural injunctions regarding love, readers see in boldfaced print, "UFOs in science and myth!" The questions follow in fine print:

Are UFOs real?
Are they trying to communicate with us?
Are they trying to warn us of the imminent destruction of our planet by terrorism or nuclear holocaust?

Under these provocative questions are two pictures, one a blurry photo with a bright circular shape, "a telescopic photo taken in Dec., 1952 in California." Readers are instructed to "compare it with the 18th century painting (on the right) depicting a 'vimana' (aerial car) in the epic Ramayana." The lengthy text explains that for years Vishnudevananda "has spoken of the UFO phenomenon as the appearance of beings from both other planets and astral or celestial planes of existence. Swamiji feels that they are attempting to warn the inhabitants of our planets of the precarious global imbalance we have created."

The ad discusses how reports of UFOs, "more frequent in the past few years," are also to be found in "ancient scriptures of diverse cultures." The correlations between ancient "citings" and "hauntingly similar" modern ones provide "new perspectives to one of the most perplexing mysteries of 'our' time." Readers are told that India's great epic the *Ramayana* "contains many references to vehicles and weapons vastly more advanced technologically than those we know of today." This assertion is followed by a quote from the Valmiki *Ramayana*: "Beholding the car coming by force of will Rama attained to an excess of astonishment. And the king got in, and the excellent car, at the command of Raghira, rose up into the higher atmosphere. And in that car, coursing at will, Rama greatly delighted."

To buttress this evidence, the ad includes a quotation from Ezekiel. The apparition described there is "remarkably similar" to that reported by a Chinese pilot flying a jumbo jet across Mongolia. "New patterns for thought" emerge with the consideration of this evidence, particularly when examined "in light of theories of quantum physics and psychological research." The text's final paragraph relates this concern for UFOs to Vishnudevananda's True World Order message: "Should the general public accept the existence of populated worlds other than Earth, the current fragmented territorial and sectarian consciousness could possibly be superseded by a global identity. This increased awareness might help alleviate many national and religious tensions and also the ominous threat of nuclear war and imminent ecological disaster."

Having expounded the grounds and evidence for fearsome forces menacing the world and prescribing the means to face up to them, the ad's inset along the bottom with the emblem of Vishnudevananda's organization informs readers: "a 24-page profusely illustrated 'Planet Earth Passport' can be collected from any of the addresses given. Carry it with you and radiate the message of peace to your fellow-brethren." The organization's emblem incorporates some features of the Divine Life Society's: the aum in the center and the motto, "Serve Love Meditate Realize." Above this motto has been added, "True World Order," and "Unity in Diversity" embellishes its lower border. Next to its emblem the ad announces, "Donations for the cause are welcome and can be sent to any of the addresses given below."

After Vishnudevananda's oration, the audience was addressed by a Congress party politician. Before beginning his brief speech, Harideo Joshi, the chief minister of Rajasthan, respectfully touched the feet of Chidananda and Krishnananda. He opened by recounting the familiar story of Nachiketa. Then he posed the question, "What is the divine life?" Our saints, he maintained, provide the answer to this timeless question. Joshi spoke slowly, looking back and forth at the swamis sitting on stage and at the audience before him. Like others, he asserted that Sivananda lives on in his disciples: "When Vishnudevananda spoke, it was like having darshan of Sivananda." He closed his speech by thanking the Divine Life Society for the opportunity to participate in the Centenary celebration of this great spiritual teacher. As soon as Joshi finished speaking, his aide handed him some tablets. Perhaps the chief minister was unwell. An event had occurred just the previous day in Rajasthan, an event indicative of the political and social conflict within the state and the cause of further conflict—the sati or burning to death of the young widow Roop Kanwar in Deorala.

After Joshi had finished his talk, Chidananda took the microphone. He praised the previous speakers. Commenting on Vishnudevananda's discourse, he said that "superconsciousness leads to bliss." The knowledge leading to this superconsciousness is dormant in society. Hence the need for sages and saints "to awaken it, to keep it alive." Chidananda distinguished Chief Minister Joshi from other politicians. While leading a political life, Joshi manages to "keep his personality as a bharatiya integral." According to Chidananda, Joshi "seeks knowledge" and is "firmly grounded in an inner center."

After these words of praise for Vishnudevananda and Joshi, Chidananda broke into a song, a taped version of which was played frequently over the loudspeakers during lulls between sessions. Its English lyrics concerned the destruction wrought by two world wars and the need for spiritual knowledge. Chidananda then encouraged the audience to return later for the evening's dance drama based on the *Devi Mahatmya*. He also announced that the following night's performance would be a dance drama based on the *Ramayana*. Like a mantra, he pronounced "national integration" to be the theme of these dance dramas.

The government official from Orissa had spoken of feeling that he had left behind the mundane world as he approached Hardwar and Rishikesh. The Centenary celebrations—with their speeches on spirituality, ritual activities, catered meals, evening performances of religious dance dramas and music—created an environment in which worldly worries receded. Everyday angsts were allayed by the Centenary's carefully cultivated preoccupation with a reality focused on an emotional and edifying experience of Hindu spirituality. Drought was ravaging much of northern India and floods had recently devastated vast areas of eastern India. Only a couple of months earlier in the nearby city of Meerut, riots and the police and paramilitary forces sent to suppress them, had killed hundreds of people, mostly Muslims. In response to sustained violence and riots between Muslims and Hindus in north Indian cities during a hot season prolonged by failed monsoons, the government imposed shoot-on-sight curfews in Delhi and Meerut. During the Centenary year there were also retaliatory riots against Sikhs in Rishikesh after a busload of Hindu pilgrims on their way to Rishikesh had been murdered by militant Sikhs.

Roop Kanwar burned to death while swamis and scholars were discoursing about the Evaluation of Indian Culture in the Context of Modern Times. No one spoke about dowry extortion and bride burning, bonded and child labor, or the countless impoverished Indians who never get enough to eat. Although there was plenty of talk about Rama and the *Ramayana,* no one spoke about the controversy in Ayodhya or related it to the ambitions of political parties and militant Hindu nationalist organizations. These topics, like the death of Roop Kanwar, or the drought and floods, were prominently absent from the Centenary's agenda. Instead, the audience was given a reprieve from the issues of the day while being assured that their involvement with the Divine Life Society and their pursuit of divine life was the highest and most noble value that their heritage offered them: "Serve, Love, Give, Purify, Meditate, Realise; Be Good, Do Good."

Chief Minster Joshi did not cancel his engagement in Rishikesh on the day following Roop Kanwar's death. Instead of attending to the problems arising in its wake, he chose to attend the Sivananda Centenary celebration. Immediately following and for months after the death of the eighteen-year-old Roop Kanwar on the funeral pyre of her husband, Joshi's Congress government was under siege. Many felt that his government consistently compromised with militant pro-sati Rajputs who were backed by Hindu nationalist groups and political parties. Those who decry the Kanwar sati claim that the police could have but did not take the necessary actions to prevent it, that Roop Kanwar was forced by her in-laws to burn with her dead husband, that the police allowed a crowd of over 10,000 people to witness the event, and that those arrested on suspicion of having conspired in the sati were unlawfully released (Hawley 1994, 84). Court orders against ceremonies at the site of Kanwar's death were delivered but not enforced by the Rajasthan government. Several hundred thousand people were said to have gathered for the ceremonies held twelve days after the death. The Mahasati Roop Kanwar Samiti, hastily formed to organize the capitalization on the death, reported that after this ceremony, of the 2.5 million rupees it had collected, it set aside 500,000 to build a temple on the site and prospects for further funding were favorable: " 'Money is not a problem anyway,' explained members of the Mahasati Committee. Leading industrial houses of the country, they added, had offered 'to do the needful'" (*Sunday Mail,* 26 September 1987).

Joshi later refused to comment on the presence of members of his party at the ceremony or on the government's failure to enforce the court order prohibiting it (*Times of India,* 21 September 1987). Joshi maintained in his reports to the press that Kanwar's death occurred only because government officials did not have knowledge of the situation.

In India's upper house of Parliament, Shanti Pahadia, Congress member from Rajasthan (and also wife of a former Rajasthan chief minister), "did not go the whole hog in demanding the sacking of the Harideo Joshi ministry" (*Times of India,* 11 November 1987). However, she attacked Joshi for saying that "incidents of sati had taken place earlier and also elsewhere. 'He was trying to show that what happened in Deorala was nothing out of the ordinary. We should feel ashamed about this stand'" (*Times of India,* 11 November 1987). A letter to the editor commends a politician who spoke in the Rajasthan assembly against Joshi's handling of the aftermath of Roop Kanwar's death (*Times of India,* 18 November 1987). Its contents provide additional background concerning the Bharatiya personality that Chidananda lauded Joshi for keeping integral whilst leading a political life:

> Mr Narender Singh Bhati deserves the gratitude of all progressive forces for the scathing attack he mounted on Mr Harideo Joshi in the Rajasthan assembly for the latter's failure to prevent the glorification of the gruesome murder of Roop Kanwar. Mr Bhati's allegation that Mr Joshi is hand in glove with pro-sati element may have some substance if the Rajasthan chief minister's past record is taken into account. In fact, Mr Joshi has always sided with revivalist leaders. Again, in Nathdwara a mob of upper caste Hindus prevented Harijans from entering the Shree Nathji temple. Despite the alleged involvement of a Congress MLA in this shameful act, the chief minster took no action against him. By lashing out at such a chief minister, Mr Bhati has served the cause of humanity. (*Times of India*, 18 November 1987)

The complexities of the Roop Kanwar case, the ensuing court orders and legislation, and the varied responses by politicians and Hindu religious leaders are legion. What is clear is that Joshi chose to be on stage with the swamis at the Sivananda ashram at a time of political crisis. When Joshi returned to Rajasthan after paying his tribute to the Divine Life Society, he refused to meet representatives of women's groups who were protesting Kanwar's death and the subsequent ceremony (*Sunday Mail*, 26 September 1987). However, two months later, at a politically more opportune moment, Joshi "offered his full cooperation to women's organisations in creating awareness against sati." Inaugurating the All India Women's Writers' Conference in Jaipur, Chief Minister Joshi said "men and women should work together to remove social evils and build a new egalitarian society." About the Deorala incident, Joshi said the government was unable to prevent Roop Kanwar from committing sati because at that time, it did not have any advance information warning them about the event: "The chief minister also expressed the hope that the new legislation on sati would not leave any scope for recurrence of such incidents" (*Times of India*, 6 December 1987).

SPIRITUAL IDEALS AND SOCIAL VALUES

For the third and final day of the Seminar speakers were assigned the topic, "Spiritual Ideals and Social Values." The day's first speaker, M. P. Pandit, chairman of the World Union International, Sri Aurobindo Ashram, Pondicherry, covered familiar ground. He heralded the Centenary as "countrywide and worldwide celebrations." As head of the Aurobindo Ashram, he informed the audience that before coming to Rishikesh Sivananda had gone to Pondicherry for darshan of the Mother, Aurobindo's successor. Belying the upper- and middle-class character of the Divine Life Society, Pandit praised Sivananda for "bringing god to the door of the common man." He also noted that in South Africa the Divine Life Society enjoys a "distinguished name."

Pandit introduced the theme of cooperation and unity. He elaborated it in terms of the need for Hindu religious leaders and their organizations to strengthen themselves and minimize debilitating divisiveness: "There must be strong, cooperative relations among ashrams. There are no differences among realized teachers; it is disciples who create the differences." He affirmed that unity is grounded in the "spiritual ideals of Indian culture which have shaped collective and individual life in India." Pandit then assumed the panda's role and took the audience on a pilgrimage into world history. He discussed the types and achievements of great civilizations. "Until recent events," China provided the model for an ethical civilization. Roman civilization is renowned for its "legacy of jurisprudence and political ideals." The greatness of India's civilization lies in its "spiritual destiny": "The invasion by India has always been spiritual."

Like Savarkar and the guidebook for the Bharat Mata temple which identify the land of India with a deity, culture, people, and divine purpose, Pandit pronounced that "divine reality chooses a people for a particular manifestation. Truths are released in the atmosphere of a particular country; ideas form the daily life of a people." Indian culture recognizes that the technical, scientific side of life is subsidiary to the dominant force of spirituality, the "one reality." Spiritual knowledge is rooted in the Indian soil and expressed in particular beliefs: "The truth is embedded in the most average man of Indian soil in his belief in dharma and karma." Westerners are wrong to think of karma as a pessimistic world view. Karma bears with it the idea of the "importance of self-effort."

Pandit then introduced another familiar theme, reminding the audience that the guru is "the special institution of Indian spiritual idealism." The guru may take human form to communicate with people, but the guru is no mere human: "Never self-made, the guru is always god-appointed. The guru is god with a mission." The true guru cannot be found by searching. When the disciple is ready, the guru appears, but may or may not be in human form. Pandit emphasized the importance of the distinction between a disciple and a devotee. The disciple is bound to the guru by initiation; the devotee often "flits from guru to guru." The true guru has no personal will. The guru's actions are the expression of divine will. The true guru has the power to take on the karma of the disciple. Pandit, however, remained vague on this karmic dynamic of the guru-disciple relationship: the guru's "grace can cancel the disciple's karma."

The lecturer next related the role of the true guru to that of the teacher.

According to Pandit, "in India the institution of the guru is naturally translated into the institution of the teacher." Because the teacher "transmits to the student the capacity to study, to absorb and understand the shastras" the teacher occupies a place of honor in the student's family. He then discussed the terms of exchange between the student and the teacher and related it to the importance of oral transmission of knowledge: "Indian tradition has always undervalued the written text because emphasis is on oral instruction and learning from an adept. The student must first serve the teacher."

Having equated the guru with divine power and the guru with the teacher, Pandit asserted, "Never think of the teacher as a human figure." Just as the material is subordinate to the spiritual, oral tradition only approximates spiritual truth. Krishnananda had said that "the invisible is the final value," and Pandit reminded the audience that the "teacher communicates in silence." He illustrated this point with a story from the Upanishads and asserted that "words confirm and stabilize on the physical level what is communicated in silence."

The importance of silence according to Pandit also pertains to activities of daily life. For example, the injunction to eat in silence arises from the view that eating is a "sacred task," a sacrificial offering to Agni, who resides within one's own body as the digestive fire. The consecration of food to Agni through the act of eating is best done in silence. This "feeding of the self" forms part of "spiritual science." Pandit's description of rituals of eating presumes the central tenet of advaitin interpretations of spiritual knowledge, the identity of self with the divine. Gurus and teachers use silence to communicate this knowledge to disciples and students. Pandit added that silence while eating is preferable to "discussions of politics or finding fault with the housewife." During the Conference and Seminar sessions when the only female to sit on stage was Dr. Kutty, young women, like attentive, dutiful housewives, frequently came on and off the stage serving the seated swamis and other male dignitaries glasses of water and carrying messages.

Continuing his discourse, Pandit demonstrated a disdain for relativism: "Our social values and standards are based on universal truths." As if it were a defiling foreign import, he asserted that "it was only because of the influence of Buddhist thought that life became viewed as a snare and is consequently devalued. This idea is not in the Vedas or Upanishads." On the contrary, the Vedas and Upanishads teach that "the world is the habitation of god." Implicitly invoking the popular interpretation of the *Bhagavad Gita* concerning non-attachment to the outcome of one's efforts, Pandit said, "Life can be fully enjoyed only when you renounce proprietorship."

This point was elaborated in reference to the spiritual goal of Indian art and aesthetics. In India the "science of aesthetics" has a spiritual basis. It is informed by the concept: "God is delight." The aim of art is beauty; always fresh and never stale, this beauty is suffused by "divine breath." Thus Indian art seeks to "represent supraphysical realities and express delight in existence." Wearing householder's white and not sannyasin's orange, Pandit concluded his lecture with plaudits for rishis and their authority as spiritual teachers. Rishis represent a "spiritual tradition of life-affirming teachings." They were not "anchorites but householders and leaders of society." The teachings of rishis "form the cornerstone of Indian life."

The next speaker, Professor of Sanskrit S. P. Singh, respectfully referred to Pandit as a "cardinal of the country." Conferring equal rank on the president of the Divine Life Society, he acclaimed Chidananda as "the country's other cardinal." Both belong to a "broad ocean" and as mahatmas they are "qualified to speak on spiritual values." Further exhibiting his humility, Singh claimed to be "closer to social values." The academic then proceeded to discourse on the lives of spiritual teachers. Gautama Buddha and Adi Shankaracharya were both renouncers and teachers. At a young age Shankara "attained divine bliss." To share his spiritual knowledge he traveled and preached throughout India. Extending the catholic reach of the metaphor introduced at the outset with his reference to Pandit and Chidananda as cardinals not of Hinduism or Vedanta but of India, Singh likened Shankaracharya to Christ. Both were "traveling preachers."

Next Singh analyzed the "recurrent pattern" in the lives of religious teachers: "a period of separation and isolation followed by a return to society." Even Toynbee, despite incorrectly interpreting the Vedas because he used inaccurate translations, had asserted that retreat and transfiguration are the two stages in the lives of saints. From these observations Singh concluded that "there must be continuous give and take between society and spirituality." For Singh as for others employed in professions based on knowledge of Sanskrit texts and interpretations of their spiritual and social import, intellectual work such as science and its technological products cannot fulfill human's higher needs: "Science has its own ethics and values but still man is not feeling more comfortable than earlier. This catastrophe of nuclear weapons is thrust upon us; they are giving us a certain technology as well as a certain philosophy." Science and its products threaten human life and cannot provide society with the guidance it requires. According to Singh, "intellection and reason cannot give us anything of value in the realm of social life. History and geography clarify obscure points but they cannot make us happy." Was Singh suggesting that compared to the boons to be earned from associating with religious teachers, university professors like himself have less to offer? Sivananda's "Song of

Eighteen Ities," suggests the ascendancy of Hindu religious institutions like the Sivananda ashram with its Yoga Vedanta Forest University over secular, government-run universities:

> Serenity, regularity, absence of vanity,
> Sincerity, simplicity, veracity,
> Equanimity, fixity, non-irritability,
> Adaptability, humility, tenacity,
> Integrity, nobility, magnanimity,
> Charity, generosity, purity,
> Practice daily these eighteen ities.
> You will soon attain immortality.
> Brahman is the only real entity.
> Mr. So and so is a false non-entity.
> You will abide in Eternity and Infinity,
> You will behold unity in diversity.
> You cannot attain this in the university.
> You can attain this in the Forest University.
> (MMW, 278)

Singh next discoursed on psychological issues. In today's world "individuals are becoming more withdrawn rather than expanded, which is the goal of life." He then launched into a lengthy discussion of Jung's research concerning dream journals kept by his patients. From this research Jung concluded that "through dreams patients learn of the self's center." This finding, according to Singh, affirms that "spiritual experience is always concentric." Further displaying his erudition, Singh referred to Kant and how his ideas about "reality and its moral imperative were already present in the Vedas."

Turning his attention to the structure of Indian society, Singh asserted that it is based on "spiritual truth." The Purusha mantra "has had stupendous effect on Indian society." The mantra figures the cosmos as an organismic being, and this provides an organic model for society. By dividing the cosmic man into different parts—brahman, kshatriya, vaishya, shudra— "spiritual values gave structure to the society for millennia." The mantra prescribes a flawless structure for society. Defects in actual social structure are due to human error: "Today the effects may be felt as contrary to the original intention but along with this criticism is the fact that the development which took place is not what was really meant in the mantra."

Mindful of the swamis on stage and the audience before him, Singh next discussed the importance of visiting spiritual teachers at their ashrams and encouraging others to do the same. He asked, "Why do you come to the ashram?" Certainly, he presumed, it is not for the physical comforts; travel is difficult and ashram life austere. Nevertheless "one feels delighted here at the ashram." The enjoyment of this delight must be propagated: "You should also try to make sure your neighbor is delighted. This is the social effect of spiritual values."

To support his assertion, "intellect cannot generate moral values," Singh cited passages from Bertrand Russell and Einstein. Intellectuals grope for answers that "we already have in crystallized form. Spiritual values provide the answers but mismanagement, misperception, and misunderstanding are responsible for poverty and problems." To teach these spiritual values, "universal beings such as Ramakrishna, Vivekananda, Aurobindo, and Sivananda" are active in society. Sometimes universal beings retreat to caves "for protection." However, they return to society and through their ashrams they provide a place where others can seek protection and guidance: "The whole world needs to come to the feet of sages and learn the mystery of that spiritual being that can solve today's problems."

Sitting at the feet of a senior disciple of universal being and Gurudev Sivananda, the audience next heard the words of Krishnananda. When he commenced his speech, not with a Sanskrit mantra but by intoning in English a series of oppositions—spiritual/social, god/man, subject/object, transcendent/imminent—Krishnapriya chanted along with him. To banish these illusory intellectual oppositions with the truth of advaita vedanta, Krishnananda recited in Sanskrit a passage from the Upanishads. Krishnapriya and other sannyasinis again chanted along with him. He then equated this passage with the laws of thermodynamics and recited another passage equating it with the theory of evolution. After this exercise, Krishnananda pronounced: "It is not that the Upanishads were unaware of the findings of modern science. They knew them intuitively." Like the other speakers on the topic, the general secretary of the Divine Life Society concluded that "all values are spiritually oriented."

Quickly capping off the morning session, Chidananda instructed the audience that a "good self" is the best contribution a person can make to society. The positive effect on society of this contribution is certain because "each person is a nucleus in a particular environment." Putting Krishnananda's conclusion in slightly different words, Chidananda asserted, "God experience is the highest value." Other speakers preferred to use the referent spirituality, but Chidananda's words indicate its linkage with a specific ideology of Hindu spiritual universalism: "Hinduism is concerned with the other-worldly life. To understand poverty and other problems in India as a result of spiritual values indicates the wrong conception of Hindu philosophy." Just when Chidananda was equating Hinduism with spiritual values, placing it at the heart of social values while detaching from it any culpability for poverty and other problems in India, a skinny, raggedly dressed man entered the tent at the front near the stage. A guard quickly forced this destitute-looking man out of the tent. Chidananda took no notice and concluded his speech: there is a "scientific progression of philosophy and ethics" which culminates in spiritual values.

As the audience awaited the start of the afternoon session, they heard tapes of Sivananda chanting Sanskrit and Chidananda singing a song with the refrain, "It is difficult to get a human birth." After conferring with Dr. Kutty about money, bills, and other complications, Krishnapriya told me that because a political rally was scheduled to interfere with the Centenary procession planned for the following day, the route had to be changed.

During the afternoon session of the final day of lectures, the locally prominent Gurukul Kangri University run by the Arya Samaj was represented by Professor Rakesh. Despite frequent references to sex and violence, English terms in an otherwise Hindi speech, the audience seemed bored by the monotonous drone and repetitious content of the Professor's speech. The audience showed more interest when, midway through this dull discourse, Vishnudevananda entered with his foreign entourage and created a commotion in front of the stage as they settled into seats in the VIP section. After decrying the vile influence of sex and violence in contemporary culture, Rakesh, in his Sanskritic Hindi, exhorted the audience to uphold the values of purity. Finally Krisnananda spoke up again; he was to be the last speaker of the day. He posited the gulf between social and true man. Asserting that this "schism is in the structure of the psyche," Krishnananda surprised no one when he announced that "spiritual life bridges this divide."

TESTIMONIALS TO GURUDEV

On the seventh day of the Centenary Program, the participants gathered in the morning for another session in the big tent and after lunch for a procession from the ashram to Rishikesh. Unlike the previous days of lectures and sermons by swamis and academics, this morning's session consisted of testimonials to Gurudev Sivananda by disciples and devotees (see plate 20). It was also another occasion for branches and individuals to be publicly honored by Chidananda for donations which funded Centenary publications and activities.

The first speaker, the head of a branch of the Divine Life Society, recalled how Sivananda had tested him. When his son fell seriously ill, his trust in Sivananda wavered. However, his faith in Gurudev was restored when his son recovered. The father-guru-son theme was also taken up by the next speaker, a middle-aged man from the Bombay branch of the Divine Life Society. He started by speaking about his parents' numerous visits to the ashram; later they became ashram residents. After his father's retirement, he took up his father's "Divine Life Society work" as he had taken up "the other business of my father." Often he had wanted to visit Rishikesh but his father did not allow it. Finally he visited the ashram to perform funeral ceremonies after his father's death. His voice became choked with emotion as he recalled the events of the visit. Swamiji (Chidananda) called him for guru mantra. In his excitement he forgot to bring the materials necessary for the ceremony but when he arrived they were ready and waiting. In his talk it was unclear whether he was referring to Sivananda or Chidananda. He clarified the ambiguity by asserting that "there is no doubt that Sivananda and Swami Chidananda are one." Winding up his testimonial, he spoke of his recent Divine Life Society work, Centenary fund raising in Bombay. At first "all looked hopeless." However, eventually "money started pouring in" and he announced that the Bombay branch had raised 1,100,000 rupees for the Centenary.

The comments of the next speaker, a young doctor from Jodhpur, were brief. Like the others, he addressed the audience in English. Divine will, in his view, brought participants in the Centenary celebrations to Rishikesh: "We are gathered here by divine dispensation from god and Gurudev." Sivananda's teachings provide the solutions for the "chauvinistic nationalism plaguing society." The Centenary is an important occasion for "uplifting mankind."

Dressed in ascetic orange, the fifth speaker began by greeting the audience as "members of the Divine Life Society family." A woman sitting near me explained that Sivananda is the "grandfather of us all." Her own guru is Chidananda, the guru of others might be disciples of Sivananda who had gone abroad such as Vishnudevananda, Venkatesananda or Satchidananda, but all are linked to Sivananda, the grandfather guru. The swami on stage remembered first hearing about Sivananda in 1954 while a college student. From that time he "looked upon Sivananda as guru." Four years later he was initiated. After further reminiscences, he closed by returning to the present, "Now I find my guru in Chidananda."

The audience became more attentive when the next speaker came to the microphone. Wearing orange clothes and with a shaven head, a German woman with the Indian name of Jyoti began her testimonial to Sivananda and Chidananda by singing a bhajan in Hindi. Like others, intense emotion occasionally caused her voice to falter. During her first visit to India eleven years before, she became a devotee of Chidananda. During the past year and a half she has lived in Rishikesh to be near her guru. From others I later learned that she is no longer permitted to reside in the ashram. Her behavior is deemed too erratic, e.g., she likes to sleep outside on the banks of the Ganges during the summer, and the ashram does not want to be responsible for her safety. She rents rooms in other ashrams and sometimes travels around India following Chidananda.

Jyoti related how through Chidananda she has had darshan of Sivananda. Once Sivananda appeared to her in a dream and transformed into Chidananda. During the last Kumbh Mela she saw Sivananda sitting on stage during the ceremonies marking Krishnananda's birthday. Her most recent darshan of Sivananda occurred during these Centenary celebrations: she saw him on stage wearing "dark specs." Later he removed them. She explained that he wore sunglasses so that she would realize it was really him when he took them off, adding that he never wore "specs in life, there are no photos of him with specs." To assure the audience of her modesty on these matters, she said, "I don't usually speak of spiritual experiences." However, inspired by the other speakers, "I felt compelled to share them with you."

The morning's last speaker was Chidananda in his role as master of ceremonies. He announced that a charitable homeopathic dispensary run by a branch in the Punjab had recently begun rural clinics on Sundays. He also gave figures for the numbers of patients the dispensary has treated since opening in 1980. Then Chidananda introduced the Seth family. Originally from Amritsar, where much of Sivananda's early work had been based, this family has supported the Divine Life Society "since its earliest days." Now the Seths, with their cloth manufacturing business, are based near Bombay. As early as 1980 the Seth family began a "savings plan" to set aside money for a Centenary donation. Chidananda praised their foresightedness and thanked them for their 121,570 rupee donation. He also announced the name of a devotee who donated 100,000 rupees and thanked all devotees for their contributions to the Centenary fund.

Referring to Jyoti's speech, Chidananda said that she "filled in a glaring gap." There had been no woman and no foreigner among the scheduled speakers, but Jyoti's appearance on stage—through her own insistence rather than by invitation I later learned—proved that the ashram was really "not male chauvinist." Chidananda then released an export-quality book on yoga written by the ashram's head yoga teacher. The book was first offered to the Sivananda shrine with a box of sweets which the yoga teacher later distributed among people sitting on stage and in the front rows. Chidananda also presented to the audience notecards and bookmarks with sayings of Sivananda, thanking the various devotees and branches for donating them for free distribution. Before closing the morning session, Chidananda announced the afternoon's activity: a procession from the ashram to Rishikesh. He advised the audience to assemble in the order listed on signs posted throughout the ashram. There would be separate contingents for sadhus, foreign visitors, women, men, and the representatives of the various Divine Life Society branches. He told people to assemble in silence and again reminded them that there should be "no gossiping."

THE CENTENARY PROCESSION

Consistent with its hyperbolic tone, the *Centenary Report* describes the Shobha (auspicious) Yatra as "the grandest procession the town had ever witnessed" (*CR*, 23). After heavy rain throughout the morning, by the time "eight or nine thousand people" gathered for the afternoon procession, the sky had cleared. The *Report* implies that this break in the rains was by divine intervention: "Strangely enough, once the Shobha Yatra was over, the sky started pouring again." The procession included a "beautiful Rath in the shape of a peacock" made of flowers, which was placed on the back of a jeep. Riding in the Rath was a life-size portrait of Sivananda. During its progress, the Rath frequently stopped to give onlookers the opportunity of worshiping Sivananda. All along its route the "processionists were accorded great hospitality in important places like the Gurudwara, Bharat Mandir and important hotels and shopping complexes." The devotional atmosphere of the procession was such that "people lost themselves in singing and dancing." Yet, these emotional displays never became indecorous: "withal, the whole procession was orderly and disciplined."

While the groups were assembling at the ashram, I headed up the road to find a spot where I could view the procession and take photographs. About a quarter kilometer past the Centenary arch I found a suitable perch on a stone embankment beside the road. As I watched the stream of people going towards the ashram to join in the procession, a rotund sadhu called to me from across the road, asking if I wanted a chair. He too was preparing to watch the procession. Although I said no, he brought me one anyway. Just after I seated myself, a bird's dropping splattered on my bare arm. As I wiped it off, the friendly sadhu assured me that it was an auspicious sign. Nearby two western disciples of Vishnudevananda busied themselves setting up their video equipment. Paper banners with the Divine Life Society motto were strung along the parade route. Storm and sun had faded their colors and left them fluttering in tatters.

Heading the procession was a group of men carrying a banner for the Divine Life Society Headquarters and long bamboo poles with orange and yellow pennants. Policemen walked in front of the banner, clearing the road for the procession. Stretching behind this first group were dozens of other groups carrying Centenary banners that named the branch of the Divine Life Society which they represented. Some were in English and others in the language of the state where the branch was based. A group of boys from Orissa in white shirts and red shorts marched behind the banner of their Sivananda Centenary Boys High School in Bhubaneshwar. Local boy scouts dressed in khaki shirts and shorts with red neckerchiefs and blue berets and boys from Rishikesh's Bharat Mandir school formed other contingents. Other groups in the procession included ashram residents, Vishnudevananda with his bevy of foreign devotees, and orange-clad sadhus living on their own and in ashrams around Rishikesh. Narayani walked beside Krishnananda, devotedly fanning him to ease the heat of the sultry afternoon.

Behind the group of sadhus came the Rath carrying the image of Sivananda. It was surrounded by a cordon of hand-holding men and policemen carrying rifles. Behind the Rath were sannyasinis, including the four pious Sharma sisters and other women associated with the ashram. Not far behind came a tractor pulling a trailer of ashram swamis and brahmacharis who, aided by microphones and powerful amplification, were leading processionists in songs and chanting (see plate 21). A group of Punjabi women sang and danced, adding exuberance to the procession. Behind the chant-and-song leaders stretched more banner-bearing contingents from Society branches. Drawing up the rear of the procession were cars and buses bedecked with signs and full of devotees singing and chanting.

Slowly advancing to central Rishikesh, the procession terminated after about three hours at the Bharat temple. After the buses and cars in the rear of the procession had passed and I had listened to the friendly sadhu's enthusiastic commentary on the spectacle, I made my way to the Bharat temple, approximately four kilometers from the Sivananda ashram. Those who took part in the procession and others who gathered at the temple were rewarded with free tea. The Bharat temple is one of the leading pilgrimage sites in Rishikesh. With a half-page advertisement in the *Nav Bharat Times*'s Sivananda Centenary supplement, the Bharat temple displayed its support for the Divine Life Society (7 September 1987). Amidst the ad's numerous citations of Hindu scriptures that refer to the Bharat temple are pious references to the Divine Life Society, Sivananda, and Chidananda. The temple is said to have been built even before the time of Adi Shankaracharya (the late eighth century), and its history is synonymous with the history of Rishikesh. It commemorates the site where an ancient sage had darshan of Vishnu. The deity instructed the sage that during the kali yug, he would be known as Bharat. The name Bharat also refers to the brother of Rama, who performed elaborate sacrifices and severe austerities on the banks of the Ganges at Rishikesh and was rewarded with Vishnu's darshan and blessings.

Not unlike the boons promised in the Sanskrit texts quoted in the advertisement, the Government of India's brochure on Rishikesh concludes its account of the Bharat temple: "Any pilgrim who does 108 parikramas [circumambulations] of this temple on Akshaya Triteeya Day will enjoy the blessings of Bardrinarayan [Vishnu] without going to Badrinath," a pilgrimage site in the Himalayas. The Hardwar-Rishikesh guidebook sold in the bazaar relates the importance of the Bharat temple to its age and the deity it enshrines, "Shri Bharata Ji the loyal brother of Shri Ram." The guidebook's description of the temple provides an occasion to remind readers of the depravity of Muslim iconoclasts: "The light gray plaster on the main temple displays a grave aspect to the scene. It appears that the shabby plaster covering the walls was overlaid in haste to hide the gleams of the once brilliant temple during the raids of the Moslem invaders" (N. Singh n.d., 60–61). Since those grave times, however, the Bharat temple's fortunes have improved: "The Mahant of the temple owns large properties in the city as well as in the suburbs and is reported to be very respectable" (61).

THE SIVANANDA CENTENARY ADVERTISING SUPPLEMENT

The front page of the *Nav Bharat Times* Sivananda Centenary supplement's six pages shows a large photo of Sivananda. He stands in the clouds with arms raised. The text printed on the photo is in English and includes a quote attributed to Sivananda as well as the following message from Chidananda: "Swami Sivananda showed us the way of 'Divine Life.' The world over, millions have been guided to this way of life. Millions more will be benefited, if we follow his teachings of self upliftment and serve the under-privileged, the poor and the sick" (*Nav Bharat Times*, 8 September 1987). Many other photos illustrate the supplement: Sivananda bandaging a man's head; his room in the renovated cottage; a Mauritius postage stamp with a big aum floating above mountains and next to Sivananda's figure; Sivananda and a young Chidananda reading a book; a sketch of the Sivananda footbridge; the Sivananda samadhi shrine at the ashram; Sivananda strumming a vina; Sivananda standing with India's first president, Rajendra Prasad; Sivananda seated in an armchair beside India's second president, Sarvepalli Radhakrishnan.

Under a half page of articles in English by Chidananda and Krishnananda is a box running across the page listing the names of fifteen individuals or branches, mostly from Baroda. Presumably the names refer to the donors whose money bought the space for the articles. Befitting an advertising supplement for a Hindi newspaper, most of its articles are in Hindi. However, only about half of the advertisements are in Hindi; the other half are in English. The Society advertises itself with articles and boxed inserts of Sivananda's twenty spiritual guidelines and universal prayer. The goods and services of other advertisers are announced in boxed display ads. Many are filled with quotes from Sivananda to demonstrate the advertisers' embrace of Gurudev's precepts. Indeed, these advertisements suggest that patrons have taken up the challenge offered by Chidananda in the supplement's article, "Spiritualise All Activities."

A Hardwar hotel quotes Sivananda, "Speak a helpful word, give a cheering smile, do a kind act, serve the maximum" and adds, "this is the tradition at Hotel Arti." The Surprise Hotel, which pampers its guests with "five-star facilities," quotes Sivananda: "Divine grace is in proportion to the degree of self-surrender." The Hotel Mandakini International, "the only luxury hotel with moderate tariff on the bank of holy river Ganges," shows a photo of the hotel with a Centenary sign painted on its outer wall. Its Sivananda quote reads, "Give and you will get in abundance." A Rishikesh building contractor quotes Sivananda in its ad, "Ingratitude is not a crime but a sin." In addition to other contractors and building supply businesses, pharmacies and photographers, travel agents and hotels, other Hardwar and Rishikesh ashrams placed ads in the supplement. "Life is a valuable asset. Utilise it for attaining God realisation" is the Sivananda quotation selected by the Krishna Sewa Ashram of Rishikesh.

Various government bodies also advertised in the Centenary supplement. The Rishikesh Municipal Corporation placed a quarter-page ad announcing recent improvements carried out by the administration and asking visitors not to defecate and urinate on the banks of the Ganges. The manager of the regional office of the State Bank of India in Dehra Dun sent "heartiest felicitations on Swami Sivananda's Birth Centenary Celebrations." A factory in Hardwar placed an ad that honored Sivananda as belonging to the lineage of great saints that have made India famous in the "field of spirituality."

An advertisement for the Hotel Natraj in Rishikesh occupies the entire back page of the supplement. The top half shows an outline of India with a halo-like double circle around it. The text inside the shape of India is entitled "A Lover's Call" and reads:

> Our nation was enslaved when we had stopped loving our country. Independence was won when we woke up from centuries of slumber and rediscovered India. Let us launch a nationwide Programme *I love my India*. It is not a slogan but our hearts' cry, a lover's call. "*India first, religion next, myself last*" India means everything to us. Some do not know they love India, others do not express it. Anybody can say—I love India but only an *Indian* may acclaim "*I love my India*." Apply this test and redeem your birth-right of serving mother, father and friend that *India* is. Forgetfulness of our country has resulted in problems of poverty, untouchability, Integrity and regionalism. Sure solution is in "loving India." Love is life, it gives ability to see mistakes and wisdom to correct them. *Beloved Mother India* seeks your *Love*.

Next to the southern tip of India, which protrudes from the circle, a quote attributed to Sivananda is appended to the above text: "India includes all nations in the embrace of her love. India will rise, India must rise, it is the best of all lands." Below this the Hotel Natraj adds—perhaps a continuation of the Sivananda quotation—" 'Lands comprising of exciting forests, Holy rivers, best of flowers, the touch of dew.' Lands consisting of places like Nataj." Under these materials, the lower half of the page shows a photo of a model of the hotel and a list of forty services contributing to its five-star facilities: shopping arcade, central air conditioning, beauty salon and florist, banquet halls and board room, putting green, swimming pool, tennis court and jogging track, drivers' dormitory, nonstop electricity supply, modern hygienic food production unit, bank, and safety deposit lockers.

"A Lover's Call" was not singularly devised for the Hotel Nataj advertisement. It was part of the Sivananda Centenary publicity kit. The same image and text called out from the back cover of the *Voice of Sivananda* Centenary issue, which was full of other Hindu nationalist sentiments. Over the reception desk at the Basera Hotel in Rishikesh I saw this same "Lover's Call" hanging as a plaque of etched metal. The receptionist told me the plaque had been presented to the hotel by Satchidananda when he stayed there with his foreign followers during the Centenary.

THE BIG DAY

The *Centenary Report* describes the final day of the year-long Centenary celebrations as "the big day, the most sacred Hundred and First Birthday of Sri Gurudev" (*CR*, 23). The day began with morning meditation, prayers, and a procession around the ashram. The day's main event began later that morning in the big tent: "a grand Paduka Puja," the worship of Sivananda's sandals, cast in silver for posterity. Decorating the stage with flower garlands, ashram staff and devotees busily prepared for the ritual. Others circulated through the audience with baskets of flowers so people could touch the flowers that would be offered during the ritual. As people filled the tent an announcement was made telling them to remain in the back; the front being "only for VIPs."

Set up on either side of the stage in front of people who already had premium seats were two closed circuit television screens. They appeared more as reminders of the ashram's modernity and prosperity than as necessary means to enable viewers to see the ceremony. The televisions in the back of the tent, however, provided some with a better view of the proceedings than they had at that distance from the stage.

While waiting for the ceremonies to begin, the man sitting next to me introduced himself. He said he came from Sivananda's village in Tamil Nadu. He described it as a "very cultured village" which has had a branch of the Divine Life Society since 1946. He has been associated with the ashram ever since he first met Sivananda during his 1950 tour. Our conversation was cut short when this man along with a group of others from his village were called to the stage to participate in the puja. According to the *Centenary Report,* "only a select few could be allowed on stage": the ashram's senior swamis and their colleagues returning from abroad, Satchidananda and Vishnudevananda; the 104-year-old swami from Madras; Krishnapriya and Vasantananda, a mataji from Bangalore; a western woman devotee; and members of the Seth family and other prominent persons, who were being further honored for their generous support of the Divine Life Society.

A drum and an oboe-like shehnai signaled the entry procession of swamis bearing the materials for the puja. They arrived on stage, joining the thirty or so others gathered around Sivananda's silvered sandals. Throughout the hour-long puja two pandits accompanied by Krishnapriya and another sannyasini chanted Sanskrit into the microphone. The puja began with participants placing flowers on the sandals and then pouring Ganges water and milk over them. Throughout the ceremony numerous people with cameras jockeyed for positions in front of the stage; a video camera was set up directly in front of the sandals. After the libations of milk had been offered, the sandals were wiped clean and anointed with red powder and garlanded. Women in the audience made a high pitched trilling noise and then everyone joined in the repeated chanting of "Aum Namo Bhagavate Sivanandaya." Again the sandals were excavated from the floral and other offerings. Garlands, sweets, and fruits were then carefully arranged around the sandals and an enormous lotus garland placed on top.

The excitement in the audience intensified when Chidananda entered to conclude the rituals for worship of Sivananda's sandals. Meanwhile, a woman at the microphone led the audience in song, a song whose vogue at many ashrams and temples around Rishikesh and Hardwar was attested to by the numerous loudspeakers which broadcast it daily during morning and evening worship. Next, the senior swamis ceremonially displayed their solidarity and the mutual esteem they supposedly have for another as fellow disciples of Sivananda: they garlanded each other and touched each other's feet.

The tempo then slowed down. Everyone on stage sat down and Chidananda began to chant Sanskrit. In Hindi he praised and thanked everyone whose efforts had made the ceremony "so beautiful." He then announced the publication of another book, written by Vasantananda, a mataji from Bangalore who had received her sannyas initiation from Sivananda. Chidananda also introduced Satchidananda—an impressive figure, tall and slender with long flowing white hair and beard—as one of Gurudev's senior disciples who has successfully propagated his message abroad.

A biographical sketch of Satchidananda is included with those of other senior swamis in the Centenary Commemorative volume. Satchidananda, the second son of "a very devout couple," was born in Tamil Nadu in 1914 (MMW, 238). "After pursuing a highly successful business career," he left home to visit pilgrimage places and ashrams following the death of his wife. He met Aurobindo, Ramana Maharshi, and other saints and "finally arrived" in Rishikesh where he met Sivananda, who initiated him as a sannyasi in 1949. Sivananda sent him on an All India tour in 1951. During this tour Satchidananda lectured, taught yoga, and organized branches of the Divine Life Society. Later Sivananda sent him to Sri Lanka "in response to an ardent request" by a woman devotee. Satchidananda's assistance was required because this woman "had not the ability to maintain the Centre being a lady herself and not very much acquainted with the knowledge of the Shastras, much less of Yoga" (239).

After the Sri Lankan centers were in operation Satchidananda went to the United States. The text describes the obstacles he faced and overcame:

> This Swami has also veritably worked a miracle in the West, and in one of the movies that he has produced he has portrayed the difficulties which he had to face in doing any good at all to people there as also the achievements which were to his credit by the grace of Sri Gurudev; because materialism, atheism and total non-acquaintance with the higher values of life etc., etc., were some of the negative sides which he had to face in Western youth especially, all which he handled very dexterously with his calm, quiet and poised nature, speaking slowly, powerfully, cogently and touchingly whatever be the disciples, students and enquirers that came to him for guidance. (239)

The biographical account concludes by praising Satchidananda's success abroad and his loyalty to Sivananda: "Swami Satchidananda is also a staunch devotee of Sri Gurudev though he stands by himself, on his own legs, in reputation as well as material security. He is one of the stalwarts who succeeded to the point of perfection in carrying the message of Sri Gurudev in the West" (239–40). Chidananda recounted to the audience how he presided over the consecration of the Sivananda Centenary Hall at Satchidananda's Yogaville ashram in Virginia. Satchidananda's organization also operates thirty Integral Yoga Institutes in the United States as well as ashrams and Institutes in Europe, Australia, and Sri Lanka. With only two centers in India, Satchidananda has not as yet encroached on the Divine Life Society's Indian terrain.

Integral Yoga, the journal produced at Satchidananda's ashram in Virginia, published a special Sivananda Centenary issue in September 1987. Like other Centenary publications it included an account of Sivananda's life, excerpts from his writings, and tributes to him by Chidananda and Satchidananda. Like the Centenary supplement to the *Nav Bharat Times,* in this issue advertisers from Virginia and elsewhere in the United States quote Sivananda as well as Satchidananda while publicizing their goods and services: natural foods shops; health care products; professional cleaning; computer, satellite and communications systems; bicycles.

The issue also included an account of Centenary activities reprinted

from the pro-VHP American publication, *Hinduism Today.* Satchidananda's own links with the VHP are displayed in a photograph in this Centenary issue of *Integral Yoga.* It shows him on stage in front of a banner for
the New England Hindu Conference of the VHP of America. Sitting with
him on stage were other swamis active in India and America as well as
"prominent Hindu personalities such as Sri A. B. Bajpayee (Opposition
party leader of India)"—the leader of the Bharatiya Janata Party, the party
affiliated with the RSS and VHP (*Integral Yoga,* September 1987). The
photo also shows these Hindu leaders sitting behind a table that has draped
from it a banner with a big aum and in Sanskrit and English the pithy,
"Truth is one, sages call it by various names." The accompanying article
reports that approximately 700 people attended this VHP Conference in
Boston.

After praising Satchidananda, Chidananda gave equal time to Vishnudevananda, extolling his work toward establishing a "true world order." He also reminded the audience of Vishnudevananda's "peace
missions," recounting how he dropped peace literature while courageously
flying over the Suez Canal, Belfast, the Berlin Wall, and Pakistan just before
the end of the 1971 war. While Chidananda was making these comments
another of Vishnudevananda's peace missions was getting under way: the
All India Peace Mala.

A western devotee of Vishnudevananda explained to me that her guru
had wanted to organize a mala or chain of people holding hands from the
Sivananda Ashram to Kanyakumari at the southern tip of India. However,
when it was estimated that 650,000 people would be required for this
cross-country venture, Vishnudevananda decided to settle for a mala from
the Sivananda ashram to Har ki Pauri in Hardwar and separate gatherings
at Rajghat in Delhi and at Kanyakumari. Later after leaving the morning
session, I saw schoolchildren and sadhus milling along the road. The hand-
holding and chanting had finished, and they were enjoying boxed lunches
which the organizers distributed to participants. This event received the
following coverage in a newspaper report:

> Rishikesh: Amidst chanting of Vedic hymns, the year-long birth centenary
> celebrations of Swami Shivananda Saraswati concluded here on Tuesday.
> About 25,000 men, women and children lined the 30 km road from Shiva-
> nanda Ashram, Rishikesh, to Harkipauri, chanting "Om Namo Narayana"
> for one hour to bring about national integration and world peace. (*Times of
> India,* 10 September 1987)

After commending the activities of Vishnudevananda and Satchidananda, Chidananda then invited the audience to come forward to make
offerings and have darshan of the sandals. The crowd was immediately on
the move, eager to touch Gurudev's sandals and Chidananda's feet. He

commanded the audience to be orderly and disciplined, saying that it should form a moving queue like those in Tamil temples, where visitors are not allowed to stop and stand in front of the deity but must keep moving. Policemen at the front and volunteer guards throughout the tent regulated the flow of the surging crowd. At the microphone stood a professional singer wearing a tinsel garland that Chidananda had presented to him. His soothing strains complemented the commotion of the crowd while "Swami Chidananda sat for hours receiving homage and blessing people individually" (CR, 24).

DISCOURSES ON SRI GURUDEV AND HIS MESSAGE BY VENERABLE MAHATMAS AND DEVOTEES

After a morning of ritual pageantry, the audience gathered again in the late afternoon for a "Special Satsanga: Discourse on Sri Gurudev and his message by venerable Mahatmas and devotees." Like many of the previous speeches, testimonials delivered that afternoon sounded as if they had been lifted from passages in the *Centenary Commemorative Volume* or other Divine Life Society publications. However, this uniformity was punctuated by some speakers' personal references to encounters with Sivananda that had transformed their lives.

Opening with "we are here assembled on the sacred banks of the Ganga," Professor Sharma set the reverential tone for his speech. Like others who had spoken during the course of the Centenary week, he recollected his first encounter with Sivananda: he was a college student and read a book on yoga by Sivananda. Inspired by this book, in 1948 he wrote to Sivananda, whose reply was a promise to help the young man in his spiritual endeavors. On his first visit to the ashram he arrived unannounced, but Sivananda—presumably by his supranormal powers and not by information from his assistants—immediately recognized Sharma and called him by name. For many years Sharma spent his summer holidays at the ashram. He found that Sivananda "encouraged everybody's latent talent." In 1958 Sharma, the dutiful devotee, wrote a biography of Sivananda. Many young men who took Sivananda as their guru did not take sannyas and remain in the ashram. Sharma explained his situation: although he had "spiritual inclinations," his own "destiny was to become a householder." Family obligations had kept him away from the ashram for many years, and now many of the senior swamis he had known as a young man were gone. The ashram's senior swamis of today were the other young men who, like Sharma, served Sivananda during the 1940s and 1950s.

The importance for Indian society of Sivananda's message was the theme of the second half of Professor Sharma's talk. Sivananda's teachings "serve the timely need of today—emotional and national integration."

The Sivananda ashram stands as a "model for bringing together castes, re-ligions, and cultures." Indeed, "integration is the miracle of Sivanandaji's grace." Sharma represented conflicts over access to political and economic resources among social classes, castes, and religious groups in spiritual and moral terms: "We need to forget individual tendencies which are disin-tegrating the country." Sharma then related this "need to forget" with "true religion," which he described in terms synonymous with the Divine Life Society's self-image: "the religion of love and compassion."

Spiritual teachers are necessary because of the "glaring disparity of our dual life." They provide society with the model for the "unity of thought, word, and deed which is sadly lacking among our people." Sharma closed by speaking of Chidananda's efforts to spread Sivananda's teachings throughout India, emphasizing his important work in "remote areas and eastern India." These are the same areas where the VHP and its allied organizations—in the name of tribal uplift and protecting vulnerable Hindus from Christian and Muslim conversion—are also busy establish-ing bases from which to propagate Hindu nationalist sensibilities and culti-vate support for local and national campaigns.

The next speaker, Swami Vasantananda Mataji Maharaj of Bangalore, had been introduced in a previous session when Chidananda announced the publication of a book she had written. She was also among the select few invited on stage to perform the paduka puja. When Sivananda gave her sannyas in 1957, "there was hardly a sprinkling of ladies to whom he gave sannyas." At that time she had just graduated from medical college. Through this initiation she felt that Sivananda gave her the "courage to teach the Brahma Sutras, which was a male preserve." The Mataji reiter-ated the motto of the Divine Life Society, "serve, love, give, purify, medi-tate, realize"; again Krishnapriya joined in the recitation. Vasantananda reminded the audience that Sivananda had shown how the spiritual path must begin with service because humanity is the manifestation of the di-vine. The guru teaches through words and example, and "Sivananda's ex-ample was always impeccable: Gurudev was an ocean of love."

The theme of love dominated the next speaker's talk. This devotee, an older woman doctor practicing in nearby Dehra Dun, engaged the audi-ence more than most other speakers during the past week. Loving adora-tion suffused her testimonial. Krishnapriya and the other sannyasinis applauded her opening statement, "Gurudev was so great, very great, infi-nitely great." His "multi-dimensional" personality made "every day with him a new day, every night, Christmas night." This ardent devotee spoke of her own limitations and of Sivananda's acceptance of them: "I'm not spiri-tual and Gurudev recognized this." She boldly stated her feelings for Siva-nanda, "I have fallen in love with him." Sivananda's multi-dimensional personality made him all things to all people: "he is father, mother, sister, brother." His mission was to bring happiness into the lives of others, and "he lived to make us happy." She spoke of Sivananda's infinite capacity to alleviate suffering; she had seen "people coming here to commit suicide, people who are ill, many examples."

Sivananda was love incarnate with the power to lead others to liberation: "Wherever he appeared it was as if love was moving. He was father, mother, brother. He came to lead humanity across the ocean of samsara." With a strong yet sweetly melodious voice she started to sing, "Hail, Hail, we find all in him." She concluded with an emotional crescendo and a crowd-pleasing comparison of Sivananda to Rama: "Like Kaushalya said of [her son] Rama, I say of Gurudev: those days spent with the guru are the only days I have truly lived, all others are meaningless." Her intensity and sincerity prompted an enthusiastic round of applause from an audience which seldom expressed its appreciation or approval for speakers in this way.

The next speaker's austere appearance and sober style contrasted to the corpulent figure and exuberance of the previous devotee. In a controlled monotone he briefly spoke about his childhood friendship with Sivananda. The man was old but not old enough to have shared childhood with Sivananda. Yet he seemed to be intimating this as he said that "even then everyone felt Sivananda's love and divinity."

When the next speaker, Mr. Bhaguna, went to the lectern, Krishnapriya said solemnly, "He is a very great man." He was introduced as an ecologist, a leader of the Chipko movement fighting against deforestation, and a social activist with his own ashram in the Himalayas. Bhaguna was a courteous Centenary guest and advocated spiritual rather than political solutions to contemporary problems. Ordinarily an outspoken voice on environmental issues, he did not comment on an immediate and obvious case of environmental degradation, i.e., the expansion of the Sivananda ashram, which was steadily deforesting the hillside on which he stood. Nor did he address the issue of the controversial Tehri Dam project upriver from Rishikesh, which ecologists and scientists throughout India were decrying as a project with disastrous consequences for the Himalayan environment. Instead he offered the familiar lamentation: "The progress of science and technology has merely brought us poverty and war." Bhaguna's solution: "Exploitation of nature would be curtailed if people followed the precepts of bharatiya sanskriti which teach respect for all life."

Bhaguna detailed the "price of prosperity." By the year 2000 over 60,000 plant species will be extinct. He also gave figures for the increasingly insufficient supply of water: by 2010, the per capita water supply would be reduced by twenty-five percent. Whereas bharatiya sanskriti or "true culture" involves the subjugation of nature for improving the life of all beings, today "we are butchers of nature." He described war as the "collective expression of individual dissatisfaction" and prescribed that "the current pillars of society—authority, wealth, and weapons—should be replaced by service, austerity, and peace."

The final testimonial of the afternoon came from yet another doctor and disciple of Sivananda. Now an elderly man, Dr. Adwari had practiced as an eye specialist and later retired to the ashram. His words, like those of Professor Sharma, echoed the Divine Life Society's official pronouncements; yet, they were not without his own interpretative embellishments. He reminded the audience of Sivananda's divine mission: "While most people come to the planet, Sivananda was sent to the planet to assist humans." He too offered the common observation, "Our religion is popular in words but not in practice." Bhaguna and other speakers portrayed the values of science and spirituality as rigidly opposed to one another in the contemporary world and regarded bharatiya sanskriti as the means to transcendence. Adwari embedded this idea in a ritual idiom: "Sivananda was a priest presiding over the marriage of science and religion." Affirming Chidananda's rightful succession as president of the Divine Life Society, Adwari invoked an artisanal metaphor: "Call Gurudev a great sculptor who selected hard stone and carved images. He left the polishing to Chidananda." Keeping the balance of praise even, the speaker extolled Krishnananda as an "incarnation of Shankaracharya." He recalled how Sivananda used to say that Krishnananda's learning was so great that there would be no need to worry about the future of the Divine Life Society.

The audience's attention was momentarily distracted from Adwari's speech and some even applauded as Satchidananda strode down the aisle, followed by two foreign women devotees laden with cameras and video equipment. A little later, a sudden deluge brought a dog scampering down the aisle; the dog, like the man in rags who had strayed into the tent the day before, was promptly shooed away. Adwari, however, gave no pause for these off-stage events and talked of Sivananda's teachings concerning self-purification through selfless work. Although karma yoga was first introduced by Vivekananda, it was "elevated to the highest position by Sivananda, who taught that karma yoga is necessary for the purification of mind and heart." He speculated that Sivananda's special affinity for doctors related to the fact that he was a doctor. This speculation enabled Adwari to suggest that he, as a doctor, enjoyed an affinity to Sivananda. He did not suggest but stated that he had enjoyed a special intimacy with Sivananda: whenever he visited the ashram Sivananda gave him "a one hour private audience."

After Adwari completed his speech, Chidananda announced the publication of a few more books and introduced the program for the evening. Prayers for world peace would be followed by a yoga demonstration by 230 boys from the Sivananda Centenary School in Orissa and then by devotional music by the "famous" Anup Jalota. The *Centenary Report* records an audience of 10,000 people for this last evening of the Centenary Celebration. In his capacity as the gracious host, Chidananda acknowledged the cooperation of those who had assisted the ashram during the Centenary week. He thanked the Rishikesh municipality for fulfilling its promise to provide a continuous supply of electricity and water while "elsewhere loadshedding is usual." The Uttar Pradesh government was thanked for the Shivananda footbridge. He also expressed gratitude to the Jai Ram ashram in Hardwar for accommodating one hundred devotees from Malaysia and to the Swarg ashram across the river and other Rishikesh ashrams for providing rooms during this busy week. Smiling, Chidananda thanked the tent maker for fulfilling his promise to make the enormous canopy completely waterproof. Chidananda then asked the audience to leave notes with comments and suggestions in the donation boxes around the ashram, saying that these "will be useful even for daily life in the ashram." Perhaps Chidananda wanted to alert casual visitors to the donation boxes conveniently located throughout the ashram. Devotees usually make their tax-deductible donations to ashram officials who issue receipts.

DEPARTURE DARSHANS AND POST-CENTENARY PROJECTS

The Centenary celebrations at the Sivananda ashram concluded on September 8 with the evening session of prayer, yoga demonstrations, and devotional music. The *Centenary Report* notes that all musical and dance performances were presented "as love offerings unto the great Master." It closes by summing up the Society's successful celebration of the Centenary: "Every function connected with the Centenary, be it spiritual or cultural, had such a touch of excellence about it, absolutely matching the supreme spiritual grandeur of the Great Master, that everyone felt his invisible presence everywhere" (*CR*, 25). The following day departing devotees lined up outside the library for a final darshan of Chidananda who sat inside. As after the paduka puja the previous morning, ashram personnel kept the queue of devotees moving. After touching Chidananda's feet and receiving his blessings, devotees were given prasad of fruit and sweets and directed to the exit.

While Chidananda was thus attending to devotees, Krishnananda occupied the nearby Sivananda samadhi hall. He presided over another paduka puja, whose performance had been specially requested by a group of departing devotees. After the puja Krishnananda also made himself available for darshan. As Narayani sat at his side fanning him, another woman expressed her devotion by laying herself at his feet. Other devotees approached him and asked for his blessings. Like his daily darshan and in contrast to the queue of devotees filing past Chidananda in the library,

Krishnananda took more time with those who came for departure blessings.

Outside the samadhi shrine and library, groups were gathering with their luggage, taking photos of themselves in front of the Vishvanath temple or the Sivananda obelisk, and preparing to return home or continue their pilgrimages with visits to Himalayan shrines, Hardwar, Mathura, and Brindavan. One group of devotees from Orissa asked me to take a photo of them; they did not have a camera but wanted a photo of themselves in front of the Sivananda obelisk. A few men and about ten middle-aged and older women formed this group. One of the men told me that he was working for a "land settlement office" funded by the World Bank. He explained that the project aims to consolidate landholdings into more rational and productive units for efficient irrigation. He spoke of meeting a Swiss man who told him that he came to India to find peace and then asked me, "Isn't there peace in western countries?" The speeches which he had heard during the previous week supported the view that India is the fountainhead of spirituality and peace. He gave me his address for mailing the photo and explained that their group was off to Brindavan because "the ladies especially wanted to go there."

A young woman standing nearby was staring at me, and so I started a conversation with her. She told me that her family was Sindhi and they lived in Delhi where they owned a clothing export business. She was studying in a South Delhi college. In reply to my question about her family's association with the Divine Life Society, she said that they have been followers of Chidananda for many years. Her extended family has diversified investments in religious organizations: some family members are devotees of Satya Sai Baba and others are followers of a Sindhi saint who has a shrine in Lajpat Nagar, a wealthy New Delhi suburb. She then talked about the need for strong leaders to solve India's problems. In her view the country requires a strong leader like Indira Gandhi "to stop the poor from cutting down the forests" and to curtail corruption.

This young woman's blaming of the poor for problems such as deforestation baldly states a cynical attitude towards the poor embedded in the ideology of organizations such as the Divine Life Society and the Vishva Hindu Parishad. It is an attitude common among middle- and ruling-class groups in India and elsewhere. The unseemly behavior of the poor needs to be suppressed and corrected. Powerful authoritarian leadership supplemented by paternalistic concern for the poor—Indira Gandhi's photo hangs with Sivananda's in the library where this young woman just had darshan of Chidananda—and not structural changes in economic and political processes that would empower the poor are presented as the necessary moral and spiritual solution for problems of pervasive poverty and corruption.

The "be good, do good" precepts of the Divine Life Society bear with them a rationale for self-righteousness and self-satisfaction. This rationale allows do-gooders to feel good about themselves while making tax-deductible investments in powerful organizations such as the Divine Life Society. Such strategies of self-aggrandizement are favored by privileged classes everywhere. The ideology of spirituality and charity camouflages the political and economic activities of religious and charitable organizations, activities which serve to reproduce exploitative social relations of production and exchange.

The numerous Centenary commodities on sale at the ashram embody the Divine Life Society's spirit of free enterprise and entrepreneurial zeal. A yoga teacher from Delhi also used the occasion to publicize his goods and services. While people were waiting for darshan and preparing to depart, the "world renowned Yogi Prof. Shankar" distributed a promotional pamphlet printed for the Centenary. It advertises a video cassette of him teaching yoga: "For beauty, fitness, health and longer life, learn yoga—a new workout at home for body and mind." The pamphlet shows two photos, one of Professor Shankar in a difficult yoga posture and the other of Sivananda to whom the video is dedicated, "for the welfare of humanity." The product's exceptional quality is suggested by references to the international market. The video "was shown during the tenth International Film Festival." It is also said to be "highly appreciated in USA and other European Countries." The brochure gives the address of the Sewanand Yogashram in Delhi where one can purchase the video, "take free guidance book," and consult Yogi Professor Shankar on yoga as well as on "numero-palmistry-herbal-medicine-gem therapy."

The Centenary year seemingly ended on September 8th. However, "Post-Centenary projects" as well as the ceremonies associated with the completion of Centenary projects such as the Sivananda Centenary Charitable Hospital in "Holy Pattamadai" and the renovation of another former Sivananda residence ensured that the Divine Life Society could extend its "glorious" Centenary celebrations. Post-Centenary projects were planned "as a continuation of the Centenary Year Programme, to perpetuate the memory of the God-Man, Swami Sivananda" (MMW, 272). These projects include the establishment of a Corpus Fund for Social Welfare; the formation of special Chairs at the Yoga Vedanta Forest Academy to invite Indian and foreign scholars for "cultural and spiritual study exchange"; the establishment of a prize to be awarded to a scholar for writing a doctoral dissertation on Sivananda, "who brought about a spiritual renaissance and philosophical reformation in the Twentieth Century"; and the investment of 100,000 rupees in a Capital Fund with the Bharatiya Vidya Bhavan for instituting a Swami Sivananda Centenary Memorial Lecture (272).

Later in September I returned to the Sivananda ashram for Chidananda's birthday observances. The celebrations were muted because Chidananda was away. They included a morning puja in the Sivananda samadhi shrine followed by a brief talk by a senior swami to a gathering of about one hundred devotees. The highlight of the day was a luncheon feast. The ashram doctor and his wife casually invited me to attend with them. Only later did I learn that attendance was by official invitation. The guests numbered about 250 men and a handful of women. Among them were ashram residents and devotees as well as local sadhus, businessmen, and personnel from other ashrams and temples. All were being formally rewarded for their assistance during the Centenary year. Besides a lavish meal, guests were given a Sivananda plastic briefcase in which was a Centenary souvenir package of decals, booklets, a metal calendar, an exercise book for writing mantras, and fifty-one rupees.

To mark the completion of the hospital in Sivananda's birthplace of Pattamadai, the Divine Life Society scheduled two ceremonies: a consecration of the building in November which included four and a half hours of vedic fire sacrifices; and on December 25, when Headquarters was celebrating Christmas, Chidananda presided over the hospital's "dedication function." To prospective participants, the Society mailed a six-page brochure giving detailed information and instructions about travel and accommodation. The text suggests both the importance of the December dedication function and the Society's connections with government officials by assuring readers that transport authorities have been advised to provide supplementary services "to accommodate and clear the rush of passengers at this time."

The following February, in conjunction with the celebration of Shivaratri, a contingent from the Divine Life Society paraded across the Sivananda footbridge to the other side of the Ganges where Sivananda had lived during his early days in Rishikesh. The old one-room dwelling had been transformed into a small temple. Chidananda presided over the consecration ceremonies. Outside the temple a group of swamis sat with Chidananda under a colorful canopy; tinsel garlands glittered in the morning sun. To the rear of the enclosure a television showed a promotional video about the Divine Life Society. Powerful loudspeakers broadcast the suave voice of the video's narrator: "The Divine Life Society was founded by Swami Sivananda in 1936. He wrote the highest possible ideas in the simplest possible language so that everyone, everywhere could understand."

At the gate of the temple an ashram official distributed a Hindi booklet prepared for the occasion (Rao 1988). Its text, written by Chidananda during his early days as Sivananda's disciple, gives an account of the time Sivananda spent in this cottage on the grounds of the Swarg ashram. Photos of Sivananda, the cottage-turned-temple, and the Hindi and English plaques marking the site are included in the booklet. The plaque reads:

Sri Swami Sivananda Birth Centenary Year
1986–1987
OM
Here in this kutir Sri Swami Sivananda Ji Maharaj, founder
of the International Divine Life Society, P.O.
Shivanandanagar 249192 Rishikesh, performed austere
spiritual sadhana during the period 1924–1934. This holy
abode is a place of pilgrimage for his numerous devotees.

Swargashram Trust

Milling around the edges of the crowd were stocky men in plaid sports jackets who looked like gangsters in Hindi films. These Marwari business-men were the official representatives of the Swargashram Trust, which is the major property owner on this side of the river as the Divine Life Society is on the other side. The audience of about three hundred was a mixture of ashram residents and visitors as well as sadhus, pilgrims, and others from the vicinity, who were attracted by the loudspeaker's promise of a spec-tacle. One sadhu appeared as if he had just emerged from a Himalayan cave. The audience watched him as he strutted around naked, wearing only long matted locks and carrying a large stick. He spoke to no one and stared up at the sun as he passed through the crowd.

After Chidananda cut the ribbon across the doorway, a group of men and Dr. Kutty crowded in behind him, filling the small temple. The pro-ceedings within the temple were brief, and Chidananda returned to the stage outside to lead the crowd in singing and chanting before beginning his discourse on Sivananda. Inside the temple stood a life-sized cutout fig-ure of Sivananda, the same image as on the postage stamp and which had been worshipped on the Centenary stage and on the float in the Centenary procession. A string of flashing colored lights and flower garlands hung around this icon of Sivananda. Also within the shrine, on both sides of the image, were tables laden with books by Sivananda. After the VIPs ad-journed to the stage outside and darshan seekers departed with their prasad of sweets, only three sannyasinis remained inside the temple sitting in meditative silence. Like other Centenary events, the ashram's public re-lations staff arranged for the consecration of the renovated cottage to be duly announced in the *Times of India* (21 February 1988).

BHARAT IS SIVANANDA AND THE DIVINE LIFE SOCIETY

The teachings of Sivananda, their current interpretations, and the activities of the Divine Life Society are neither unprecedented nor unique. The belief that spirituality is the essential and definitive feature of Indian national identity is a common thread in different strands of Indian and Hindu nationalist ideology. "Bharat is Sivananda and the Divine Life Society" announced a speaker in his testimonial during the Centenary celebrations.

When placing spirituality at the center of individual and social life, Krishnananda asserted that "the invisible is the final value." M. P. Pandit, the head of the Aurobindo ashram who also spoke at the Centenary celebrations, claimed silence to be the voice of spiritual truth but that "words confirm and stabilize on the physical level what is communicated in silence." A persistent and strategic silence permeates the garrulous repetitiveness of speakers discoursing on spirituality. This silence contributes to both the persuasiveness and power of this component of nationalist ideology. By addressing the political and economic aspects of organizations claiming to be custodians of spirituality, this study attempts to interrupt a pervasive silence on these issues. Towards this end I problematize how spirituality, with its privileging of transcendental values, is used by specific groups to simultaneously advance and mask their own interests. This orientation involves treating spirituality as a historical discourse with political practices and implications.

The discussion and analysis of materials concerning the Divine Life Society is underpinned by consideration of its linkages with other ideological and institutional formations, both historical and contemporary. Because a central theme of this study concerns contemporary forms of militant Hindu nationalism, I have selected Savarkar for an extended treatment of the relation between spirituality and national identity. Following this trajectory, I have emphasized the ideological and institutional connections between the Divine Life Society and Hindu nationalism by analyzing texts such as the Centenary issue of the *Voice of Sivananda* as well as by providing information on the Divine Life Society's links with Satyamitranand of the Bharat Mata temple, Chinmayananda, and the Vishva Hindu Parishad. In the final chapter, I examine pronouncements by Vivekananda and Nehru concerning spirituality and national identity to further demonstrate how the teachings and activities of religious organizations such as the Divine Life Society and Satyamitranand's Samanvaya Parivar are embedded in complex discourses on spirituality, culture, and the Indian nation.

In order to situate the activities of religious organizations within a larger context of public political activity and the staging of state patronage of India's spiritual culture, it is helpful to keep in mind the rituals performed by public officials such as the prime minister, president, and vice president on behalf of the nation-state. Such rituals include observances of birth and death anniversaries honoring Mahatma Gandhi and members of the Nehru family as well as the joint celebration in 1987 by the Indian government under Rajiv Gandhi of Nehru's birth centenary and the legacy of freedom fighters on the fortieth anniversary of Indian independence.

Political leaders use Hindu religious arenas, e.g., official visits to temples and participation in anniversary functions of religious organizations, for making pronouncements on spirituality and national unity. Such pronouncements echo the comments made by Professor Sharma in his Centenary address: "Sivananda's teachings serve the timely need of today—emotional and national integration." Press attention to these activities of important political figures not only publicizes and enhances the prestige of the religious organizations which stage such events but also contributes to representing politicians as dutiful patrons of India's spiritual culture. Chidananda's praise for Chief Minister Joshi as a politician who keeps his bharatiya personality integral to his public life is an instance of how this image as patron of spirituality is publicly staged. Joshi is not alone in receiving an ascetic's approbation. Swamis throughout India continuously bestow similar accolades on selected politicians to represent them as exceptions in a profession that is widely considered to be as corrupt as it is lucrative and powerful.

Professor Singh suggested this dynamic of mutual admiration between political and religious leaders in his Centenary speech when he asserted that "there must be continuous give and take between society and spirituality." The give and take between society and spirituality operates as publicized and covert dealings between representatives of ruling-class groups and religious leaders, between political parties and religious organizations. Spirituality and society are signifiers for complex and heterogeneous agents intertwined with each other and with the political economy of India. Chidananda expressed the ambitions of many religious leaders and their organizations to extend the reach of their power and authority when he wrote of the "supreme necessity" to "spiritualise all activities." Similarly the *Annual Report of the Divine Life Society* described its activities as aiming "to remove the unwarranted distinction between spiritual and the secular." Chidananda and other Centenary speakers, however, censured unbridled ambition on the part of any one organization by emphasizing the need for cooperation among religious organizations.

The Vishva Hindu Parishad institutionalizes this "cooperation" among religious organizations with its regional, national, and international infrastructure of trustees, committees, offices, and projects. It also attracts the support of religious leaders and their followers by interpreting political conflict in terms of the need to protect spirituality, a signifier of political and cultural dominance by upper- and middle-class, high-caste Hindus. With its yajnas and conferences, processions, rallies, and campaigns, the VHP provides numerous public stages for religious leaders to enact the role they reserve for themselves as the premier custodians and interpreters of spirituality. These are also means whereby it attracts and mobilizes religious leaders along with their own followers, as well as other political and social groups.

The dynamic of the relation between political and religious authority is also demonstrated by the close public association between President Venkataraman and Jayendra Saraswati, the Shankaracharya of Kanchi. Venkataraman is a devotee of this prominent and highly publicized Hindu leader. The Kanchi Shankaracharya, looked to as a religious and social authority by many high-status groups and particularly south Indian brahmans, sent brahman representatives to New Delhi to perform rituals on the morning of Venkataraman's inauguration as president of India. As the prevailing definition of secularism became more consonant with the ideology of Hindu nationalism, i.e., state support for all religions with the greatest share going to Hinduism, the "religion of the majority," the Kanchi Shankaracharya, whose photograph hung in Ashok Singhal's VHP office, changed his view on secularism.

In a press interview in 1987 Jayendra Saraswati condemned secularism as meaningless and harmful to the country (*Illustrated Weekly of India,* 13 September 1987). Two years later when speaking about his new political party with its platform of national unity and controlling prices, he asserted that "true secularism is our objective" (*Illustrated Weekly of India,* 1 October 1989). He had previously demanded, like Savarkar before him, that India be renamed Hindustan; he also claimed to be the protector of Hindu religion and society. As Hindu nationalist ideologues had become increasingly successful in conflating the terms Indian and Hindu, he later claimed: "In our lexicon we don't have the word Hindu at all. Our party will be called Bharat Jan Kalyan. It is a party of Indians. It is not my intention to mix religion with politics. That has always been my view'" (*Illustrated Weekly of India,* 1 October 1989).

The contributions of the Divine Life Society to the formation of official or national culture in India as outlined in the discussion of its ideology, activities, and Centenary celebration can be further understood by relating it to the representations of pilgrimage and spirituality promoted by government tourist departments. I have introduced some such representations in the discussion of Hardwar. Through its infrastructural support for Hindu pilgrimage—advertisements, tourist literature, facilities for transport, and accommodation—the Indian government contributes to ideological constructions not only of Hindu pilgrimage as a component of Indian national culture but also to the belief that Hindu deities populate and sanctify the landscape of India.[1] The Divine Life Society enacted its role as custodian of

---

1. "Faith is the force of life—Leo Tolstoy" headlines one in a series of advertisements placed by the Himachal Pradesh Tourism Development Corporation (*India Today,* 30 September 1987). Divinity is heralded as Himachal's timeless essence: "There is an aura of sublime divinity mingled with true peace of mind and soul in this sacred home of the gods—Himachal." As in another Himachal advertisement, a sketch of a Hindu temple fills the upper

culture by sponsoring Hindu devotional music and dance performances during the Centenary. On a much larger scale the central and state governments, through their departments of culture and tourism, act as patrons of religious culture by organizing festivals of religious music and dance in Hindu pilgrimage centers.[2]

---

half of the page. The text lists just some of Himachal's famed temples: "One can go on and on . . . endlessly." When readers turn the magazine's page on the reverse side of the advertisement, they meet a special report about "how Uttar Pradesh's Chief Minister Bir Bahadur Singh"—who recently had been the chief guest at the inauguration of the Sivananda Centenary Arch—"and his family are at the centre of a growing scandal revolving around the wealth they have amassed from real estate deals."

The logo of the Tamil Nadu Tourism Department, "Tradition and Tranquility," accompanies its quarter-page invitation to "Come, share the divine presence" (*Indian Express,* 14 August 1987). The text explains that this "divine presence is felt everywhere in Tamil Nadu," including at Madurai's "towering" Meenakshi temple, a photo of which dominates the advertisement. "The infinite presence of the omnipresent," however, does not confine itself to temples. In Tamil Nadu "divinity is close to everyone in every walk of life." The government tourist department heralds Tamil Nadu's thousands of temples not only as abodes of divinity but also as places which "depict the saga, the triumphs, the dedication of an era and above all Tamil Nadu's rich cultural heritage." Culture in Tamil Nadu is suffused with "divine delights."

2. Discharging their duty as official patrons of culture, central and state government's departments of cultural affairs advertise for the festivals and events organized by them. The following are a few examples from a large collection of such magazine and newspaper advertisements which I gathered during 1987–88. Illustrated with a line drawing of Radha and Krishna, the Uttar Pradesh Department of Cultural Affairs announces in Sanskritic Hindi, printed in bold devanagari typeface, "Vrindavan Sharad Utsav" (*Times of India* 28 September 1987). Under this calligraphic lead and in much smaller print is the translation, "Autumn Festival of Temple Dances." The remainder of the text is in English. The festival is to be held in Brindavan's Radha Madhav temple, and the public is apprised of "an unheard opportunity to witness the wide spectrum of Indian dancing in its variegated, many splendoured hues, spanning thousands of years of Indian performing arts and rituals, in the exotic setting of a magnificent temple in the holy town made sacred by the childhood 'lila' of Lord Krishna" (*Times of India,* 28 September 1987).

Two months later another advertisement announced the upcoming Ramayan Mela—"a tribute to our heritage at Ayodhya"—organized by the Uttar Pradesh Department of Cultural Affairs (*Times of India,* 24 November 1987). Just as Brindavan connotes the domain of Krishna and New Delhi the seat of the national government, Ayodhya connotes Ram and the campaign of the VHP to build a Ram temple there. The advertisement's illustration provides an iconographic referent for the nationalist tenet of religious tolerance. It shows the head and tail of a "Ram Siya coin issued by emperor Akbar in the year 1603." Nine Ram Lila troupes from Manipur to Bharatpur are scheduled to perform during the four-day festival. This reference to Akbar, a common signifier of India's tradition of religious tolerance, does not efface the other message of the advertisement: like rajas past and present, the government honors Ram by sponsoring Ram Lila performances.

An illustration of a fierce-looking Shaivite ascetic with a menacing trident dominates another advertisement's drawing. The illustration also shows two big bosomed women—a dancer and a worshiper—and a turbaned drummer arrayed around a scene of temples,

There are parallels between the drive of both the Indian government and Hindu organizations such as the Divine Life Society, the Vishva Hindu Parishad, and the Bharat Mata temple to act as custodians, patrons, and interpreters of Indian national culture. There are also parallels between their self-representations as being protectors of the weak and needy through supporting educational and medical facilities and providing disaster relief. Furthermore, the Sivananda ashram presents itself as a "peaceful haven wherein is provided ample opportunity and actual help for the restoration of peace to the conflict-ridden and psychologically traumatised personality of modern man," in other words, an asylum for troubled members of the dominant social classes who constitute the Society's leadership and supporters.

The Divine Life Society provides money and assistance to lepers and impoverished persons living beyond the ashram walls, but it is highly selective about whom it permits to reside within them. The gates of the Sivananda ashram may seem welcomingly open, yet many do not presume to walk through them. Beggars wait to be fed at the gates. Even middle-class Hardwar residents expressed deference when they learned of my visits to the Sivananda ashram, as if the superior social status of its swamis and followers rendered it a venerable and awe-inspiring institution.

Through their role as custodians of culture and uplifters of the downtrodden, representatives of the ruling classes—swamis, politicians, bureaucrats, industrialists, pandits, professors—claim to act on behalf of the interests of all Indians. Their policies and projects are said to promote the unity of the nation and provide the means of cultural integration. This claim, whether it be called upliftment, spiritual education, sanskritization, or the adaptation of traditional values to modern life, deflects attention from processes of political, economic, and often violent domination by ruling-class groups. Spiritual and moral arguments about self-purification through charitable concern for society's weaker members is an idiom and

---

bathing ghats, and boats. The Uttar Pradesh Department of Cultural Affairs thus publicizes its upcoming festival in Benares, the Ganga Mahotsav, "A tribute to Ganga, Shiva and Kashi" (*Times of India,* 15 March 1988). The program consists of three evenings of music and dance. Like a cautious investor, the Uttar Pradesh government through its cultural events shrewdly allocates its patronage to major Hindu centers and cults: Krishna in Brindavan, Ram in Ayodhya, Shiva and Ganga Ma in Benares.

The Magh Mela in Allahabad provides an occasion for Hindu ascetic orders, religious organizations, and politicians to gather and display themselves to the crowds that attend the festival. In its role as patron of national culture, the Government of India competes with these other groups for a share of the Mela audience. Its Department of Cultural Affairs advertises that it has organized an Inter-Zonal Cultural Programme for the Allahabad festival (*Times of India,* 16 January 1988). For twenty-one evenings each of the seven zones have arranged three performances by "prominent artistes" that represent music and dance forms associated with the particular zone.

means whereby hierarchical structures of power and authority are represented as just, respectable, legitimate.[3]

3. The materials concerning the Vishva Hindu Parishad, Satyamitranand, and the Divine
Life Society can be further contextualized by situating them in a field of public statements by
prominent and fashionable religious leaders, statements which receive frequent press coverage. Like politicians, presidents, and vice-presidents of India, they often make pronouncements on the unity of India, the heritage of religious tolerance, and the need to end communal
violence. Under its headline "New Crusade," *India Today* shows a photo of Baba Amte in
front of his bus and surrounded by followers. It describes him as a "lawyer, messiah, and
founder of Anandwan, a home for leprosy patients." His new crusade, Bharat Jodo Abhiyan
(Knit India March) plans to cover the 5,042 kilometers from Kanyakumari to Kashmir with
the aim "to re-infuse the spirit of national integration at a time of growing cynicism and communal strife." The crusade particularly targets youth to mobilize them "in the service of eradicating social evils" and involve them in "relief work at the grassroots level" (*India Today*, 15
April 1986).
    For the fortieth assembly of the Sant Nirankari Mission, a principally Sikh "movement of
universal brotherhood," the government temporarily allotted without charge a sixty-five
acre tract of land in North Delhi (*Times of India*, 30 October 1987). In order to prepare for a
crowd of over 300,000, approximately one thousand volunteers spent a month constructing
"a well-laid, full-fledged, glittering township" with electricity, water, roads, public utilities,
and residential camps. Visitors would be well looked after with facilities for first-aid, railway
reservations, telephones, post, and telegraph. A kitchen staff of one hundred volunteers
working around the clock will provide "free meals satisfying regional taste." Countless slums
lack daily water supplies, but the Municipal Corporation of Delhi has laid a water connection
for this three-day assembly. Within the camp 5,000 volunteers will "handle the security,"
while the police will take care of security outside the camp. According to Nirankari officials
the budget for this "miracle in the wilderness" is a minimum of two million rupees "besides
contributions made by the participants."
    At the opening ceremonies, Baba Hardev Singh, "supreme head" of the Sant Nirankari
Mission, "gave a call to end communal violence and bring about religious tolerance, so that
peace and unity were restored within the country and elsewhere." While he advocated the
need for continued scientific and technological progress, he stressed that the "need for spiritual advancement should not be lost sight of" (*Hindustan Times*, 1 November 1987). Baba
Hardev commended Nirankaris for their dedication to their mission and exhorted them to
maintain their "unflinching trust in almighty Nirankar" and increase their zeal and devotion
for their mission of "true spiritual regeneration and moral upliftment of mankind" (*Hindustan Times*, 1 November 1987).
    On the eve of a convention against communalism and separatism, Sadhu Mohan, "a wan-
dering renunciate from Kerala," advised convention organizers that they need to distinguish
between pure religion and pseudo-religion in order to restore pure religion "in the social consciousness" (*Times of India*, 12 October 1987). The present nexus of corruption in politics
and religion requires the intervention of "pure religionists" whose involvement in national
life "could be more effective than the tardy operations of the police and the administration."
The implicit assumption of Sadhu Mohan is that pure religionists like himself, who are the
guardians of "social consciousness," have the moral authority and duty to intervene in the
"affairs of the country."
    With the headline, "Rich, poor told to sink differences," a Delhi newspaper reports the
speech by Pandurang Shastri Athawale, the founder of the Shrimad Bhagavad Gita Pathshala
(*Times of India*, 5 January 1988). He spoke about the crisis facing the nation and the "intense
need to evolve new man" and a "society based on friendship of devotion." In Ahmedabad the

Publicity for Hindu religious organizations emphasizes both the universal need and desire for the commodities they produce and purvey. With the trademark of spirituality, such commodities include publications, ayurvedic medications, instruction in yoga and meditation, guidance by the guru, rituals of worship, and the opportunity to purify oneself through service and donations to the organization. Advertisements for its pilgrimage package tours and cultural events in Hindu pilgrimage places indicate that the government too is a vendor in the marketplace of spiritual commodities. The benefits to be gained by consuming these commodities are variously described: self-improvement and self-realization through spiritual disciplines; grace of the guru and boons of the deity leading to resolution of problems, to prosperity and success. Consumers of these commodities also accrue cultural capital. With the assistance of government tourist facilities, guidebooks, and panda's services, Hindu pilgrims extend their knowledge of myth and history, cosmography and geography. Visitors to ashrams expand and refine their understanding of various forms of culture as defined by Krishnananda as "appropriate behavior," e.g., by attending darshan with Krishnananda and observing how he sizes up and treats members of the audience.

As mentioned earlier, the "be good, do good" sensibility associated with consumption of spiritual commodities also bears with it a "feel good component"—the promise of security. Through support of religious organizations, not unlike employment by the government or involvement in political parties, people can earn access to potential sources of patronage and prestige which supplement family and caste networks. Participation in the activities of religious organizations as well as attendance at government-sponsored cultural spectacles also provide moments of pleasure and enjoyment. The propagation of ideas and beliefs concerning spirituality, culture, and nationality relies on both rational argumentation and the fashioning of

---

Pathshala celebrated its diamond jubilee in conjunction with the Vaghri Sanchalan. When welcoming Athawale, Vaghri leaders reminded the 250,000 attending this "mammoth" gathering, most of whom were Vaghri, that their group was "always ignored with a sense of degradation. . . . Whenever politicians wanted to serve their purpose, they distributed liquor and money among Vaghris. Once the purpose was served, they never showed their face" (*Times of India,* 5 January 1988).

At this assembly politicians were eagerly showing their faces. "Prominent among those who attended the meeting" were the chief minister, a judge, the city police commissioner, the mayor, and "several leading personalities of the city." Ten days later a press photo showed "thousands of fisher folk" with their decorated boats at Chowpatty Beach for the Bombay celebration of the Shrimad Bhagavad Gita Pathshala. The caption described the Pathshala as an organization that "works for the uplift of the downtrodden using Bhakti as a social force" (*Times of India,* 15 January 1988).

emotional and aesthetic experiences. Such experiences include the aural and visual delight of ritual, music, and dance; the soothing sound of Sanskrit chanting; the excitement of marching together in processions; the novelty of a boat procession on the Ganges; the wonder and amazement prompted by watching magic tricks on the Sivananda Centenary stage.

TEN

Shakti ex Machina

Previous chapters have examined how spirituality permeates political discourse and practice and have explored its relationship with nationalism and capitalism. The opening chapter presented theoretical and ethnographic materials to introduce these issues and linkages among them. Later chapters develop and elaborate these concerns. I have analyzed Savarkar's nationalist polemics and his leadership in the Hindu Sangathan movement as a prelude to a critical reading of not only contemporary forms of Hindu nationalist discourse, but also the organizational form and activities of the Vishva Hindu Parishad (VHP). I then turned to specific Hindu religious organizations and examined regimes of institutionalized spirituality as processes which produce ideological subjects and political activism.

This final chapter explores further some of the multitude of names and forms associated with these processes. The Gayatri Parivar portrays the endeavor of its founder, Acharya Sharma, as "brain-washing" and as a "man-making mission." The VHP variously calls its projects the awakening and revitalization of Hindu society, Hindu homecoming, and upliftment of the downtrodden. Satyamitranand's Bharat Mata temple describes its goal as imparting to visitors a "satisfying and lasting spiritual experience that will inspire devotion and dedication to the Motherland." A speaker at the Sivananda Centenary celebration characterized the Divine Life Society's mission of spreading Sivananda's teachings as a force for "emotional and national integration."

Institutionalized spirituality celebrates subordination to leaders whose authority is said to derive from their possession of knowledge and power. Another speaker at the Sivananda Centenary assured the audience that the "guru is always god-appointed, the guru is god with a mission." Submission to the authority of divinely inspired leaders is represented as the solution to all problems facing individuals, social groups, nations, and the world. However, the politics of spirituality does not demand passive subordination. It is an arena in which identities are formed through active engagement in the projects articulated by leaders.

The Hindu nationalist movement is by no means a monolithic entity. It is supported by a spectrum of leaders, groups, and individuals whose ideological positions range from moderate to militant and whose projects vary from charitable work and religious education to political power, hate-mongering, and communal violence. The Divine Life Society is genteel in the demands it makes of followers: "serve, love, give, purify, meditate, realise." Satyamitranand describes the Shrine of Heroes in the Bharat Mata temple as being dedicated to the sacred memory of "heroes on the battle-front," who have "sacrificed their lives for the patriotic cause of protecting the Sanatan Dharma and the glory of the Motherland." Savarkar stands with these enshrined heroes. Militant Hindu nationalist leaders today—like Savarkar in the past—exhort followers to be prepared to die for the movement. Like Savarkar, who maintained that "nothing can weld peoples into a nation and nations into a state as the presence of a common foe," there still are Hindu nationalists who espouse hatred for and violence against individuals and groups deemed to thwart their drive for political and economic power.

Savarkar insisted that the history of Hindu-Muslim relations in India is one of perpetual war, and that to counter the "Islamite peril" Hindus must "mobilize everything on a war scale." Militant Hindu leaders continue to figure Muslims as the foe to be vanquished. On numerous occasions Savarkar criticized the RSS for shirking from effective political activity. One more recent critic of the RSS is Ishwar Dutt. He explains his response to directives against taking "an aggressive posture'" issued by his superiors in the "RSS front organization," the Hindu Manch: he formed another organization because "We are tired of pleading and requesting. The government does not understand the language of memoranda. Fine, we will take up the gun to achieve our cherished goal of Hindu Rashtra" (*Sunday*, 23 August 1987).

GIRDLED WITH HUMAN SKULLS

Like Hindu goddesses, generically known as the Devi, whose different iconic forms and mythic elaborations portray particular aspects of her many powers (shakti)—one of which is Bharat Mata—nationalism in India as elsewhere has numerous forms and purposes (see plates 22 and 23). In its avidly violent forms Hindu nationalism fosters fear and hatred of a shared enemy to define a militant and activist group identity. Other forms have the potential to variously mask political commitments and the violence entailed in their pursuit with the language of charity, universalism, and religious idealism. At the Bharat Mata temple the goddess appears on the ground floor as a bounteous and stately matron bearing ritual pot and sheaves of grain. The Shakti Shrine on the fifth floor is "dedicated to the Mother Goddess: the embodiment of spiritual and moral strength, the triumph of Truth over evil." Of the thirteen forms shown, nine are of the goddess in her "invincible form" as Durga, the goddess which figures so prominently in the pantheon of the VHP. However celebratory of violence the image of Durga with her sword raised to vanquish demonic forces may be, the goddess in her manifestation as Kali celebrates the lust for blood even more explicitly. Linked with Kali as the manifestation of the mother's dark face and terrible ferocity is that of Bhavani, the mother's more luminous form. Savarkar reverenced Guru Ramdas for inspiring Maratha warrior Shivaji with the words, "Die for your Dharma, kill the enemies of your Dharma while you are dying, in this way fight and kill and take back your kingdom." Satyamitranand in the Bharat Mata temple guidebook writes of the heroic deeds of Shivaji, the "saviour of our culture" whose success was secured through the guidance of Guru Ramdas and the blessings of goddess Bhavani.

Before Aurobindo retreated to Pondicherry and established himself as guru, he briefly but intensely involved himself with the most radical and militant factions of the early nationalist movement. Fox argues that during Aurobindo's period of political activism he "adopted passive resistance expediently . . . soon after he urged passive resistance in print, he seems to have started planning violent revolution in private" (1989, 118). The imagery in the following passages translated from Aurobindo's Sanskrit poem, "Bhavani Bharati" (BB) bears the influence not only of Ramakrishna, Vivekananda, and Bankim Chandra Chatterji, but also of his study of Sanskrit texts and European revolutionaries such as Mazzini. In 1908 the Calcutta police confiscated the notebook in which it was written. I purchased a copy of the poem at the Aurobindo ashram in Hardwar.

The editors of *Sri Aurobindo: Archives and Research* note that the poem was left untitled by Aurobindo, but for several reasons they have named it "Bhavani Bharati, Mother of India." Arguing that the poem has "evident connections" with Aurobindo's 1905 text *Bhavani Mandir*, they cite a passage from it where Bhavani declares: "I am the Mother of the Universe, the Mother of the Worlds, and for you who are children of the Sacred Land, Aryabhumi, made of her clay and reared by her sun and winds, I am Bhawani Bharati, Mother of India." The editors further justify their selection of the title on the grounds that in the poem, Bhavani is the "name most often used for the supreme Goddess in her luminous form," and because in one verse she is called Bharati "to denote her special aspect as the Shakti of India." The editors of "Bhavani Bharati" conclude their introduction to the poem: "The translation attempts to convey some impression of the literary qualities of the original, the language of which is characterised by energy, directness and rhythmic vitality" (BB, 30). The following excerpts indicate that like Savarkar, Aurobindo displays a formidable and powerful command of passion-provoking language.

The ninety-nine stanza poem opens with the narrator "sunk in the comfort" of his couch, composing lyrics of "sensuous passion." Absorbed in self-interest and pleasure, and paying "homage to the feet of the evil one stained with the blood of my brothers," suddenly Kali appeared before him:

> Garlanded with the bones of men and girdled with human skulls, with belly and eyes like a wolf's, hungry and poor, scarred on her back by the Titan's lashes, roaring like a lioness who lusts for kill, with her fierce, hungry, blazing eyes irradiating all the worlds, rending the hearts of the gods with the piercing ring of her war-cry, filling the world with bestial sounds and licking her terrible jaws, fierce and naked, like the eyes of a savage beast in the dark—thus did I see the Mother. (BB, 134)

Chastising the narrator for neglecting dharma and serving the "foreign exploiter" who oppresses her and her people, Kali commands him to action:

> "Offer sacrifice to me; give, for I am thirsty. Seeing me, know and adore the original Power, ranging here as Kali who roars aloud and hungers to enjoy the heads of bodies of mighty rulers. . . .
>
> "Wheresoever are great heroes and leaders engaged in continual self-sacrifice for the good of their race, towards those nations does Kali grow gracious, nourished with blood, and they crush their enemies." (BB, 137)

Obeying Kali's command and "shaking off my pleasures," the narrator beholds "this land of India, the Aryan country, wrapped thickly in darkness, suffering, blinded." His heart fills with "undying wrath" for the unrighteous oppressor, the lordly Titan who boasts of righteousness, brandishes a harsh sword, and feeds "the hordes of his offspring with the tears of the Mother mixed with a hundred streams of her blood" (BB, 139). Amidst this terrible scene, the narrator sees armies of the Mother's sons turn against the Titan, "dire with rage." In the distance he views "a white light in the form of a Woman delightful in beauty." She is coming to annihilate all enemies and dispel anguish; he names her Chandi, Rudrani, Bhavani.

After a vision of victorious battle against the Titan, the narrator records the praises of the omnipotent goddess chanted by "the great Yogis." Being "steadfast in meditation," these Yogis of the Himalayan summits "through numberless ages have guarded India's destiny" (BB, 143). They salute the "Goddess omnipotent" and describe the return to the reign of dharma:

> "Thou indeed art Kali and utterly ruthless thou art; thou art Annapurna the merciful and gracious. I bow to thee as the Violent One, O ender of the worlds; I bow to thee, O Radha, in thy ecstasy of love.
>
> "The mighty Mother of creatures has vanquished the Age of Strife. Once again the movements of freedom are abroad; I observe them following the paths of the ancient scriptures.
>
> "Once again I hear in the forests the chanting of the Veda which is a fountain of immortalising nectar to the heart. An overflowing river of humanity streams to the hermitages of the sages perfected in self-knowledge.
>
> "Once again the eternal ways of the Dharma are guarded by one nobly born in the Solar Race. And once again resplendent Lakshmi, a smile on her lips, reigns steadfast among the Bharatas.
>
> "In East and West I hear the cry and stir of the whole world hastening with praise on its tongue to this country, the ancient Mother of the Vedas.
>
> "Praising the gracious and awe-inspiring Mother as the source of the true Law, the fulfiller of mighty vows, they revere as a place of pilgrimage this land dear to the Goddess beginningless in her power.
>
> "As those who dwell in Shiva's sacred city of Kashi are liberated by the auspicious touch of the Lord, so all this Aryan country where the Goddess has set her purifying feet shall be the Kashi of the world.
>
> "O infinite in thy forms, thou art contentment, compassion, patience and indomitable heroism, faith and endurance and knowledge of every kind. Be gracious, noble goddess; dwell long in the hearts of the Indian people!
>
> "Illumining these rivers and snowy mountains with a most gentle lustre, be firmly established in the Aryan country. Abide forever gracious in this land, O Mighty One, for the good of the world." (BB, 149–51)

SWAMI VIVEKANANDA: UP, INDIA CONQUER THE WORLD WITH YOUR SPIRITUALITY

Vivekananda is enshrined with Aurobindo in the Bharat Mata temple. In the temple guidebook Satyamitranand writes of Vivekananda's pride in India's heritage and his "modern approach." He reminds readers that Vivekananda "beseeched his audiences to shed fear and be strong: India needed 'muscles of iron,' 'nerves of steel,' and a 'gigantic will.'" Satyamitranand also emphasizes that Vivekananda's tours in Europe and America "created a yearning for oriental scholarship and wisdom." Like Aurobindo's vision of Bhavani Bharati, Mother of India, leading her devotees to victory, Vivekananda's formulations of the mission of Indian spirituality are sedimented in contemporary Hindu nationalism.

Opponents of British rule in India confronted an enormous project: to formulate a national identity capable of setting in motion a movement for Indian national sovereignty. This required that Indians articulate through strategic redefinitions and refutations a sustained challenge to the hegemonic ideology of British imperial sovereignty. Nationalist ideologues also had to provide a language and logic to mobilize against the formidable martial and administrative infrastructure of the British Raj, Indians who themselves were variously resisting, abetting, serving, and profiting by Imperial rule. Attacks on British imperialism, in oratory and in print as well as through assassinations, rebellions, strikes, riots, and everyday resistance, were variously articulated and executed throughout the subcontinent.

Swami Vivekananda was a leading exponent and organizer of a religiously infused national identity and an astute commentator on capitalism in the late-nineteenth century. His Irish disciple, Sister Nivedita, was also a leading propagandist of both Indian political independence and an "affirmative Orientalism" (Fox 1989, 113–17). Sister Nivedita, not included in the Bharat Mata temple's pantheon of satis in 1988, had by 1992 been installed next to Annie Besant in what was formerly the Sati Shrine which had been renamed the Matri (Mothers') Shrine. The valorization of spirituality in Vivekananda's nationalist formulations and the need for aggressive propagation of advaita vedanta to combat the menacing forces of western materialism resound in the pronouncements of Savarkar, the VHP, Satyamitranand, and the Divine Life Society, which have been examined in the preceding chapters. Along with Hindu religious leaders and militant nationalists, politicians continue to invoke Vivekananda to authorize their assertions concerning the unity and integrity of India and to add emotional force to them.[1]

Swami Vivekananda denounced the materialism of western nations and asserted that "religion and spirituality form the foundation and national backbone of India" (1985, 27). He warned Indians of the seductive powers of western materialism and reminded them that "extreme self-sacrifice" formed the basis of Aryan society. He juxtaposed the "unfelt desires" aroused by the "luxuries and intense sense pursuits" of "rank materialism" with a "stern presence, Sita, Savitri, austere religious vows, fastings, the forest retreat, the matted locks and orange garb of the semi-naked Sannyasin, Samadhi, and the search after the Self" (1958, 104). He maintained that in the West the goal of life is individual independence, the lan-

---

1. For a discussion of the VHP's appropriation of Vivekananda during its 1993 Global Vision 2000 conference in Washington, D.C. and in its publicity for the 1993 Parliament of the World's Religions in Chicago, see McKean (1994).

guage is "money-making education," and the means is politics. However, in India "the goal is—Mukti, the language—the Vedas, the means—renunciation" (1958, 104).

Empowered by experiences with his guru Ramakrishna and later by the hero's welcome he received on return in 1897 from the World Parliament of Religions, which was convened in conjunction with the 1893 World's Fair in Chicago, and a four-year lecture tour abroad, Vivekananda arrived in India to discover that " 'the nation had already accepted him as its Guru' and he eagerly embraced the role" (Dalton 1986, 277). Vivekananda relentlessly argued that spirituality is the mainspring of Hindu revitalization. Through it Hindus could recover and assert their virility and simultaneously free their motherland and themselves. Like Sivananda and Chinmayananda after him, Vivekananda directed his attention toward urban, educated, upper-caste Hindu audiences and instructed them in "practical Vedanta," which propagated belief in the divinity and essential unity of all persons and the spiritual benefits of serving others.

Vivekananda condemned western nations for their materialism and godlessness. He also calculated ways of gaining access to their wealth. In an idiom akin to the protestant work ethic, Vivekananda equated money with "social virtue" and disclosed his keen appreciation of the profits to be earned by spirituality's exchange value: "As our country is poor in social virtues, so this country (U.S.A.) is lacking in Spirituality. I give them spirituality, and they give me money" (quoted in Singer 1967, 150). Vivekananda depicted the world's desire, need, and hunger for great spiritual ideals to be dependent on India's unique resources, for in "God's economy everything, good and evil has its place" (1985, 30). He anticipated more vigorous entry of India into this divine economy: "I am anxiously awaiting for the day when mighty minds will arise and go forth from India to the ends of the world to teach spirituality and renunciation—those ideas which come from the forests of India and belong to Indian soil alone" (30).

Vivekananda exhorted young Hindu men to go forth with the "wonderful treasures of our forefathers" and to use them to procure material profits: "You must go out and exchange our spirituality for anything they have to give us; for the marvels of the region of the Spirit we will exchange the marvels of the region of matter" (73). Although glossed differently, Vivekananda's prescriptive calculations are recognizable in the Divine Life Society's evaluation of its own work abroad: "The vast goodwill thus earned for India and its spiritual science (Adhyatma-vidya) is an invisible and yet a tangible asset whose value cannot be easily estimated. This good work is spreading progressively all over the world."

Vivekananda often described the worldwide propagation of spirituality in militant terms—propagation as a form of conquest: "Up, India, and conquer the world with your spirituality. Aye, as has been declared on this soil first, love must conquer hatred, hatred cannot conquer itself" (1958, 100). Armed with the spirituality of advaita vedanta, young Hindu men are given the mission of conquering the world and thereby reestablishing the power of their own nation. Because of their materialism western nations also require "spirituality to preserve them as nations" (100). Like a general recruiting troops, Vivekananda announced:

> Heroic workers are wanted to go abroad and help to disseminate the great truths of Vedanta. The world wants it; without it the world is destroyed. . . . We must go out; we must conquer the world with our spirituality and philosophy. There is no alternative, we must do it or die. The only condition of national life, of awakened and vigorous national life, is the conquest of the world by Indian thought. (100)

Vivekananda regarded spiritual conquest as an imperative for himself and for all Hindus. Using the language of nineteenth-century natural scientists, social theorists, and monopoly capitalists, Vivekananda related the necessity of spiritual conquest to the law of survival based on the principle of expansion. Extinction is the penalty for breaking this natural law: "India must conquer the world and nothing less is my ideal. You have to expand or perish. This is the law of life" (1985, 73). In a similar vein Savarkar reasoned that Hindus have emerged as the majority in India "because they proved themselves fit to struggle for national existence."

Vivekananda implicitly invoked a metaphysics of asymmetrical exchange in his discussion of spirituality as India's gift to the world, and in his definition of the brahman's role in the process of uplift of low-caste groups. His travels through the world have convinced Vivekananda that India is a uniquely sacred place, a holy land:

> If there is any land to which all souls on the earth must come to account for their Karma and attain that last birth before salvation—the land where humanity has attained its highest towards gentleness, generosity, purity and calmness, and above all, the land of introspection and spirituality—it is India. (1985, 2)

The malaise of materialistic western civilization will receive its cure from India. The incomparable value of India's gift of spirituality makes the world indebted to Hindus, who have given it freely throughout history: "Comparing country with country, there is no other race on this earth to which the world owes so much as to the mild Hindu" (2).

Vivekananda refuted the claims of "the Western Pandit" that Aryans came from outside India and conquered and enslaved the original inhabitants. This is the procedure of western, not Indian civilization which instead places the sword at the "feet of Dharma and the weak" (144). He cited the *Ramayana* as evidence of the processes of Aryan expansion in southern India. Unlike Europeans whose expansion relies on the sword, Rama "only allies himself with the powers of the south. He never annihilates any people" (145). According to Vivekananda, the swordless division of society into varnas, a hierarchy of social classes, constituted the method of Aryan expansion through the subcontinent.

Whereas European civilization destroys in order to live more comfortably, "the aim of the Aryans is to raise all up to their own level or even to a higher one" (145). Just as Aryan dharma encompasses the southerner and Indian spirituality the foreigner, in Vivekananda's formulations, the brahman commands righteous authority over spiritual, cultural, social, and moral inferiors. Vivekananda defined the qualities of the true brahman: "no secular employment"; "treasury of virtue"; "trustee of the culture" (63). His views on culture, caste mobility, the importance and prestige of Sanskrit learning are later elaborated in the theories of social scientists, particularly G. S. Ghurye and M. N. Srinivas, who formalize these ideas into the concepts of Hinduization and sanskritization.

Vivekananda argued that Sanskrit must be popularized because although knowledge can be communicated in any language, "what is called culture can be imparted in India only through Sanskrit" (62). Like Shankara and Ramanuja in the past, religious teachers continue to be instrumental in raising lower castes closer to "Brahmanahood" (62). Repeatedly Vivekananda warned against solutions to the caste problem which "degrade" the highest caste: the "Brahmana, the man of God, the one who has the knowledge of the Veda, must remain" (62). Vivekananda decried claims to exclusive privileges by caste groups, but he unequivocally placed at the pinnacle of society those who possess and command spiritual knowledge and Sanskritic learning:

> To the underprivileged I say, "Why do you fret and fume because somebody else has more brains, more energy, more pluck to go ahead than you?" Instead of wasting their energies in quarrels, let them absorb the culture of the Brahmanas, and this will take place if all people take to Sanskrit education, because Sanskrit and prestige go together in India. (63)

Vivekananda spoke and wrote with passion about potential foreign conquests by Hindus bearing spirituality. Foreign conquerors, however, require a fortified home base. He related the success of spirituality abroad to vigorous promulgation throughout India of his teachings on practical vedanta. The activities of Savarkar the Sangathanacharya—the organizer of militant Hindus and head of the Hindu Mahasabha—like those of Mahatma Gandhi and his civil disobedience movement, had precedents in the ideas and work of Vivekananda concerning organization and mobilization of followers within India:

> To his disciples he repeatedly urged, "You must have a hold on the masses," "We must reach the masses." If only the people could unite, that would mean "infinite power. . . . Therefore, to make a great future India, the whole secret lies in the organization, accumulation of powers, co-ordination of wills. . . . That is the secret power of India." (Dalton 1986, 279–80)

The Hindu Sangathan movement also took up this task of mass organization. One of its successors, the Vishva Hindu Parishad, describes itself as "a dedicated organization for serving the masses. This is its strength and inspiration. The VHP bows to the masses."

Vivekananda's writings and activities disclose his project of building a mass movement. Through his teachings on advaita vedanta he created an idiom for speaking about a unified identity and purpose for Indian leaders and masses. He prophesied the enormous power that could be generated if leaders mobilized the masses to work toward one goal:

> The future of India depends entirely upon all its people working together with one will. Power is gained only through the concentrated will of a group of people. This is how small nations with united will have been able to dominate over vast masses of men, all divided among themselves. (1985, 63–64)

Through an interpretation of advaita vedanta as the timeless spiritual essence of India's superior culture and society, Vivekananda propagated both a theory and practice for engendering consciousness of national unity and for mobilizing diverse audiences. In militantly charged spiritual and moral terms, Vivekananda espoused practical vedanta as the ideology and discipline for Indians to individually achieve their latent divinity, and to collectively realize the heroic spiritual and political destiny of the Indian nation. Vivekananda infused this spiritualized nationalism with potent emotional appeal. He presented it as that ever popular patriarchal and martial mission: the challenge and quest for valorous virility and fraternity that face sons of the Mother:

> Wouldst thou attain, by means of thy disgraceful cowardice, that freedom deserved only by the brave and heroic? . . . Thou brave one, be bold, take courage, be proud that thou art an Indian, and proudly proclaim: "I am an Indian, every Indian is my brother." . . . Say brother: "This soil of India is my highest heaven, the good of India is my good," and repeat and pray day and night, "O Thou Lord of Gauri, O Thou Mother of the Universe, vouchsafe manliness unto me, O Thou Mother of strength, take away my weakness, take away my unmanliness and make me a Man!" (118–19)

NEHRU: WE MARCH TO THE ONE WORLD OF TOMORROW

Values and practices associated with spirituality set forth in Vivekananda's practical vedanta—self-sacrifice and austerity, service, discipline, and the liberating realization of unity—were adopted by political leaders during the Indian independence movement to establish their own moral and political authority. Gurus as well as politicians continue to epouse these values and practices, which in turn support their claims to be leaders and guardians of the nation and its culture. The following examination of Nehru's treatment of spirituality, national unity, and Mother India indicates further variations on these themes.

This book emphasizes Hindu nationalist interpretations of spirituality, yet the discourse of spirituality and the image of Mother India are so pervasive and potent that political leaders who staunchly opposed Hindu nationalism resorted to using it. The use of referents to spirituality and Mother India by nationalists who advocate secularism and oppose militant Hindu nationalism suggests that they are innocuous cultural and political pieties. However, such use also has the potential to foster among Hindus, who consider themselves heirs of Nehruvian secularism, identities imbued with devotion to Mother India and pride in India's superior spiritual heritage. The Hindu nationalist movement's successes arise not solely from its appeal to angry, militant Hindus, but also from the support of moderate Hindus who believe themselves noncommunal and yet have come to feel sympathy for the argument which contends that traces of Muslim rule— both Indian Muslims and mosques—diminish the glory of Hinduism in post-independence India, and are an affront to Mother India.

Indian nationalism, Nehru observed in *Discovery of India (DI)*, was "dominated by Hindus and had a Hinduised look" ([1946] 1989, 351). As rival political ideologues and leaders, Nehru and Savarkar accused each other of similar crimes—harming the nation and spreading lies. (Savarkar's denunciations of Nehru and the Congress have been discussed in chapter 3.) Nehru described the Hindu Mahasabha as the "chief Hindu organization" and characterized it as being as "aggressively communal" as the Moslem League (*DI, 386*). He deplored the Hindu Mahasabha, maintaining that

> it tries to cover up its extreme narrowness of outlook by using some kind of vague national terminology, though its outlook is more revivalist than progressive. It is peculiarly unfortunate in some of its leaders who indulge in irresponsible and violent diatribes, as indeed do some of the Moslem League leaders also. This verbal warfare, indulged in on both sides, is a constant irritant. It takes the place of action. (*DI, 387*)

Violent diatribes, however, are not a form of political inaction, but are rather a potent means for inciting rage and rationalizing political mobilization. Propagating the desire to conquer hated enemies is as integral to political discourse as propagating love and loyalty for the reference group which constitutes one's own identity, groups defined in terms of religion, culture, land, race, nation, or humanity. In his "manual for underground revolutionary activity," the *Indian War of Independence, 1857,* Savarkar instructed readers on how the discontent and dislike of foreign rule felt by diverse social groups should be "intensified into active hatred by Revolutionary Preachers."

Nehru's discussion of the spirit of the age *(yugadharma)* accommodates the ideas of practical spirituality espoused by Vivekananda, and later institutionalized by Hindu organizations such as the Ramakrishna Mission, the Divine Life Society, and the VHP, to name but a few. He described this yugadharma as being "governed by a practical idealism for social betterment": "Humanity is its god and social service its religion" *(DI, 557)*. Nehru assumed that "the better type of modern mind" which forms the yugadharma "has discarded to a large extent the philosophic approach of the ancients, their search for ultimate reality, as well as the devotionalism and mysticism of the medieval period" *(DI, 557)*. However, Hindu gurus and proponents of Hindu nationalism have incorporated the ideal of social service into the same institutional apparatus which promotes devotional worship and pursuit of spiritual liberation. Nehru, of course, could not forsee that militant Hindu nationalism would later draw on the capacity and authority of religious leaders to transform and appropriate the meanings of secularism and scientific rationalism, which for him constituted the spirit of the age.

Heir not only to the legacy of nationalist ideologues such as Vivekananda, Tagore, and Gandhi but also to the political legacy of British imperialism in the office of independent India's first prime minister, Nehru's views and policies regarding Indian culture were informed by nationalist, internationalist, and imperialist concerns. Like Vivekananda and later Sivananda, Radhakrishnan and the VHP, Nehru related Indian national culture to a global context. Others asserted the supremacy of India's spiritual culture, but he believed that internationalism must be rooted in an equality among autonomous national cultures. Grafted to his narrative of Indian history, which is structured by the concepts of assimilation, tolerance, and unity, is an assessment that Indian culture was particularly well-suited to the requirements of internationalism:

> It was India's way in the past to welcome and absorb other cultures. That is much more necessary today, for we march to the one world of tomorrow

where national cultures will be intermingled with the international culture of the human race. We shall therefore seek wisdom and knowledge and friendship and comradeship wherever we can find them, and cooperate with others in common tasks, but we are no suppliants for others' favours and patronage. Thus we shall remain true Indians and Asiatics, and become at the same time good internationalists and world citizens. (*DI, 566*)

As did other nationalists, Nehru claimed emotional and intuitive experiences as the basis for the authority of his views on the fundamental unity of India:

Though outwardly there was diversity and infinite variety among our people, everywhere there was that tremendous impress of oneness, which had held all of us together for ages past, whatever political fate or misfortune had befallen us. The unity of India was no longer merely an intellectual conception for me: it was an emotional experience which overpowered me. That essential unity had been so powerful that no political division, no disaster or catastrophe, had been able to overcome it. (*DI, 59*)

If nationalist leaders disputed among themselves about the strategies and ethics for involving individuals and groups who constituted the "essential unity" of India in the independence movement, imprisonment gave them a common idiom for asserting their moral authority. Letters, diaries, biographies, and press reports publicized the hardship and deprivation endured by imprisoned freedom fighters. Musing on the effects of political imprisonment, Nehru wrote: "Prison affects people in various ways; some breakdown or weaken, others grow harder and more confirmed in their convictions, and it is usually the latter whose influence is felt more by the mass of people" (*DI*, 442).

Accounts of imprisoned freedom fighters' experiences use terms associated with the potency and moral authority of particular figures—the disciplined householder-patriarch, the yogi, the sannyasin. Through ritual, sacrifice, and charity, the high-caste householder earns merit to counter the ill-effects of misdeeds and earn the favor of divine powers. Hindu ascetics make a sacrifice of themselves and strive to merge self with the all-pervading Self. Through austerities and physical and mental disciplines, they steadfastly pursue the ultimate goal of life: liberation from the bondage of rebirth. Austerities and disciplines facilitate mastery over mind and body, and earn powers *(siddhi)*, which can be used to effect desired results in the world.

In their fight for freedom from British rule, nationalist leaders voluntarily sacrificed wealth, comfort, and years of their lives. Just as "meeting Gandhiji changed Bhai's [Nehru's] outlook on life, both politically and socially" leading him to "shed his immaculate suits to don rough hand-spun and hand-woven cloth called 'khadi,' " so Nehru, Savarkar, and other nationalist leaders converted many to their styles of thinking and living (Hutheesing 1963, 10). The determination of many freedom-fighting leaders was contagious. Writing from prison to his sister about a reverie of "Rajas and Ranis and their satellites and parasites" dancing upon a "seething mass of hungry and famine-stricken humanity," Nehru reflected on his commitment to the fight for freedom: "I am myself so consumed by my own aim and objective that I find it extraordinarily difficult to appreciate the want of aim of anybody" (Hutheesing 1963, 30).

Nationalists yoked themselves to an ideal other. They yearned to liberate Mother India. Like the renouncer's cave, forest, and ashram, the jail cell provided a site for nationalist leaders to enhance the moral authority and potency of their actions with powers earned through austerities, disciplined reflection, and self-realization. An imprisoned Nehru wrote, "Meanwhile there is much to do and I want to do it with every ounce of energy. And if, as at present, I cannot indulge in activity I prepare myself for it, physically and mentally and store up energy" (Hutheesing 1963, 84). Mahatma Gandhi's efforts at transcending his sexual appetites are widely known. Figured as fundamental ascetic disciplines, celibacy and continence—especially for males—are regarded as sources of potency and power. Imprisoned nationalists had limited if any access to women. Nehru commented on this feminine absence: "It struck me as an odd and arresting fact that for nearly twenty-six months—for 785 days to be exact—I had not seen a woman even from a distance. Previously it was not so for even in prison we had interviews occasionally. And I began to wonder—what are women like? How do they look—how do they talk and sit and walk?" (Hutheesing 1963, 67).

With India already prefigured as a mother goddess by Bankim Chandra, Vivekananda, Aurobindo, and others, imprisonment gave nationalists further emotional impetus to imagine India as a feminine object. Struggling with their loneliness, nationalists in their prison cells conjured images of Mother India. Such images of Mother India create an emotional utopia based on patriarchal social relations, which make men not only foci for the doting and devotion of female kin, but also wary of their own and other men's desires and pleasures associated with intimacy with women.

Writing in prison, Nehru recollected the thoughts he had when officials released him so he could visit his wife Kamala, who was dying of tuberculosis in Switzerland. He reflected on his marriage, his wife, and himself:

> My past life rolled itself before me and there was always Kamala standing by. She became a symbol of Indian woman, or of woman herself. Sometimes she

grew curiously mixed up with my ideas of India, that land of ours so dear to us, with all her faults and weaknesses, so elusive and so full of mystery. What was Kamala? Did I know her? understand her real self? (*DI*, 43)

At the end of his *Discovery of India* Nehru elaborated his feminine characterization of India. Without the conventional piety for her expressed by other nationalists, Nehru imagined India as a beguiling, irascible, and elusive woman, whose pride, loyalty, and harmless foibles attract and endear those who approach her. India is at once a defiant moll and a reliable maternal presence in realms of threatening darkness. This portrayal of India follows Nehru's speculation on the difficulty of grasping the present as embodied in the private universes of four-hundred million individual Indians and in the "multitudinous past of innumerable successions of human beings":

> Something has bound them together and binds them still. India is a geographic and economic entity, a cultural unity amidst diversity, a bundle of contradictions held together by strong but invisible threads. Overwhelmed again and again, her spirit was never conquered, and to-day when she appears to be the plaything of a proud conqueror, she remains unsubdued and unconquered. About her there is the elusive quality of a legend of long ago; some enchantment seems to have held her mind. She is a myth and an idea, a dream and a vision, and yet very real and present and pervasive. There are terrifying glimpses of dark corridors which seem to lead back to primeval night, but also there is the fullness and warmth of the day about her. Shameful and repellent she is occasionally, perverse and obstinate, sometimes even a little hysteric, this lady with a past. But she is very lovable, and none of her children can forget her wherever they go or whatever strange fate befalls them. For she is part of them in her greatness as well as her failings, and they are mirrored in those deep eyes of hers that have seen so much of life's passion and joy and folly, and looked down into wisdom's well. Each one of them is drawn to her, though perhaps each has a different reason for that attraction or can point to no reason at all, and each sees some different aspect of her many-sided personality. (*DI*, 563)

Nurtured in a family milieu characterized by the tensions between a devout brahman mother and a secularist, liberal brahman father, Nehru regarded the essence of Indian civilization as an ongoing interaction between tradition and change. Imbibed through his father, and through his English public school and Cambridge education, Nehru regarded himself as "too much influenced by the humanist liberal traditions to get out of it completely" (quoted in Pillai 1986, 269). Later he turned to socialism as a "vital creed which I hold with all my head and heart." He considered it his duty to try "to convert the Congress and the country to it" (Nehru 1958,

349–50). The traditional culture of India "is fighting silently and desperately against a new and all-powerful opponent—the bania civilization of the capitalist West" (1958, 364). Offsetting the "evils of this cut-throat civilization," however are its science which "brings food for the hungry millions," and "the principles of socialism, of cooperation, and service to the community for the common good. This is not so unlike the old brahman ideal of service, but it means the brahmanization (not in the religious sense, of course) of all classes and groups and the abolition of class distinctions" (1958, 364–65).

Contradictions within Nehru's own political ideology, as well as the political and economic power of opposing groups, consistently compromised commitment to and the efficacy of secularist socialist policy and institutions. Like the bania businessmen whose patronage secures their livelihood or whom they themselves may be, brahmans too calculate profits, risks, and losses. These calculations concern brahmans' work as ideologues and publicists, who serve not an abstract community for the public interest, but rather participate in advancing the interests of particular regimes of power and authority.

M. N. Srinivas (1967), like many other scholars writing on Indian society, acknowledges the political import of the religious and social dominance of brahmans. He asserts that "brahmins were predisposed to reverence power," and through their performance of "essential vedic rites" which proclaim the "kingly status of the actual wielder of power," brahmans "helped to legitimize power into authority" (1967, 74). Those who are brahmans by birth may be more likely than members of other caste groups to be vedic ritualists and prominent ascetic leaders, and they may fight to retain dominance in these professions. They do not, however, monopolize them. Moreover, the use of "essential vedic rites" for political purposes does not belong exclusively to bygone eras as Srinivas's usage of "kingly status" suggests.

Soon after independence President Rajendra Prasad attended Chinmayananda's vedic sacrifices. The Gayatri Parivar makes vedic sacrifice the focus of devotees' domestic ritual and encourages its public performance in India and abroad as a means to publicize the organization and raise funds. The VHP described its major propaganda campaign, the Sacrifice for Unity, as a "sacrifice in the vedic sense." Brahmans, like other members of ideological professions, do not merely reverence power and legitimate it; they participate in the very act of its construction and deployment. They formulate the terms and forms that constitute the ideological apparatus of Indian society, the apparatus which socializes people to fear and "reverence power" as embodied in individuals—the guru, the tantrik, the corporate karmayogi, the party boss—in social institutions and in the state.

Nehru's characterization of the brahman ideal of social service stresses its voluntary aspect. This conforms with his celebration of the creative spirit and energy of the individual. His views about political and personal freedom echo Tagore's, and place creative, free individuals at the pinnacle of socio-moral value. Nehru differs from Vivekananda, who advocates bartering India's spiritual wealth for necessary material goods, and Gandhi, who chastises "the Poet" and other aristocratic aesthetes for the arrogated wealth that provides the resources and leisure for their artistic pursuits. Writing about the necessity to engender freedom through democratic processes which complement socialist economic institutions, Nehru decided what is non-negotiable: "It is not enough for us merely to produce the material goods of the world. We do want a high standard of living, but not at the cost of man's creative spirit, his creative energy, his spirit of adventure, not at the cost of all fine things which have ennobled man throughout the ages" (quoted in Pillai 1986, 287).

The Nehruvian "we" belies certain singular facts. Unlike hundreds of millions of Indians, he already enjoyed a high standard of living which could sustain a healthy body and educated mind, as well as foster a "spirit of adventure" which led to his *Discovery of India*. Inheriting high social status from his wealthy brahman parents and adopted by Gandhi as political disciple and heir, Nehru treated Indian civilization as if it were his undisputed patrimony. He claimed that his realization of India's unity arose from intense and repeated experience and contemplation of its people, history, and culture. He envisioned an India whose essential unity embraces all its diversity, and he returned the embrace. Nehru expressed his identification with India—past and present—in proprietorial terms: "I felt also that the whole of the past belonged to me in the present" (quoted in Singer 1981, 94).

JUSTLY, EQUITABLY, AND NATIONALLY THEIRS

The issue of proprietorship also concerned Nehru's nemesis, Savarkar. The "nation's barrister" argued to prove the patrimonial claims of the Hindu nation: "What the Hindu Mahasabha can never tolerate is to despoil the Hindus of anything which is justly and equitably and nationally theirs. Simply because they constitute the overwhelming majority in Hindustan their own Fatherland and Holyland" (n.d., 192). If Vivekananda, Mahatma Gandhi, and Nehru have been abundantly treated in the history of the nationalist movement, their writings prolific, their activities open for scrutiny, Savarkar is a far more shadowy figure. He advocated clandestine political activity. As Hindu Sangathanacharya he articulated and promoted a national identity based on hatred and desire for vengeance. I do not suggest a simple opposition between Savarkar as a force of darkness and evil versus the Mahatma and Nehru, as forces of light and goodness.

Like other arenas—religious, cultural, intellectual, economic—where power, wealth, and prestige are produced and fought for, politics has numerous dimensions, many of which are purposely hidden and disguised, others of which are studiously ignored or widely publicized.

Successful religious organizations, political parties, and movements require popular leaders to attract followers, skilled strategists to raise money, and disciplinarians to keep the organization intact. Sivananda, the "heart of love," had Parmananda, the "Bismark of the ashram." Besides familiar leaders such as Mahatma Gandhi, Nehru, Indira Gandhi, and Rajiv Gandhi, included in the survey, "Fifty Politicians Who Made all the Difference in the Four Decades since Independence," are those like S. K. Patil, "the Boss of Bombay." Patil is characterized as being "essentially a back-stage technician" whose expertise and "talents were vital for the Congress to put its act together on the federal proscenium" (*Illustrated Weekly of India*, 27 December 1987).

Patil's skill as a fund-raiser is likened to that of another party boss, Atulya Ghosh. This politician, "the Congress version of Cardinal Richelieu," is described as "having always operated from the shadows." He ran the Congress party in Bengal "with an iron hand." Ghosh never stood for election but rather "preferred to manoeuvre events and personalities like a puppeteer at a Punch and Judy show. Unseen, yet omnipresent." Ghosh is said to have been "feared and respected for his catholic temperament and unwavering devotion to his assignment" (*Illustrated Weekly of India*, 27 December 1987). The reader might wonder what is fearsome about a "catholic temperament," and sense the menace of violence lurking in Ghosh's shadow.

Acharya Sharma claims to be a puppet of God, Congress party boss Ghosh is figured as a puppeteer pulling political strings, and disciples and devotees of gurus claim to be but puppets of their masters. Metaphors such as these are as suggestive as they are misleading. They suggest that people are willing to be manipulated and misled by representing the manipulators as mechanically wielding power and authority over the manipulated. Such reductive metaphors, however, belie the complexity of the social relationships that constitute power and authority.

The book opened with materials selected to highlight the relationship between politics, capitalism, and institutionalized spirituality. Throughout I have analyzed the pronouncements and practices of Hindu religious organizations and the implications of contradictions between them. The organizations that have been examined embody these contradictions to a greater extent than many of the less socially and politically powerful organizations that I studied in Hardwar. Like the various forms of power (shakti) figured through different manifestations of the goddess, the power of spirituality relates to its widespread presence in Indian society and to its broad range of discourses and practices. The discussion now turns to a few further modes which deploy signifiers of spirituality in contemporary India.

SPIRITUALITY IN ADVERTISING

Government agencies and the press contribute to the construction and marketing of spiritual commodities, e.g., Hindu pilgrimage. Spiritual referents are used by advertisers to signify the desirability of consumer goods and services and the boons of ownership. An advertisement placed by the Central Cottage Industries Emporium and the Development Commissioner for Handicrafts uses a large image of the meditating Buddha to promote a special exhibition and sale that features daily demonstrations by craftspeople (*Hindustan Times,* 23 November 1987). Aesthetics is united with spirituality in the text of the advertisement to sanctify the objects sold at the Emporium:

> The Man Who Taught the Art of Living.
> Transformed into Living Art.
> The Buddha, immortalised in everything from small figurines to immense and awesome statues, by the hands of master craftsmen. In Stone. Wood. Brass. Bronze. Ivory. Alabaster. And depicted in paper and silk paintings, batiks and tankhas. Masterpieces that pay homage to the master who taught the art of living, with living art.

As befits sanctified commodities, in New Delhi's Central Cottage Industries Emporium prices are prominently marked and non-negotiable. Buyers need not squabble over the cost of hallowed objects, trinkets, or treasures, and they can pay with cash, traveller's checks, or credit cards. As promised in its seductive, glossy tourist brochures, the Government of India stages here a purchasers' paradise. An in-house packing and shipping service ensures buyers are not burdened by their purchases.

The text of an advertisement for Handloom House celebrates the spiritual fabric of Indian national culture, "In its warp, in its weft, in its weave . . . India lives." It also announces that the entire National Design Collection is sold in twenty-one Handloom House shops throughout India and is available for discriminating consumers "at specially subsidized prices right through the year." The advertiser eloquently extols the sublimity of the goods it purveys and stages their purchase as a spiritual and aesthetic encounter with "India. Primordial, deep, faceted. The wellspring of countless creative impulses. Palpably alive, to this very day. Strikingly and most colourfully manifest in the handspun magic of its fabrics. The handlooms of India. Resplendent, intricate, patterned, rustic, sophisticated, earthy, ethereal. In Indian handlooms rests India's very soul."

Poompuhar, the Tamil Nadu Handicrafts Development Corporation, advertises a special exhibition of Chola Bronzes at the Azad Bhavan Art Gallery in New Delhi and announces that Pupul Jayakar, "Adviser to Prime Minister on Heritage and Cultural Resources," will open the exhibition (*Times of India*, 12 March 1988). The advertisement's text, like that for the Handloom House, extols the importance of arts and crafts to the glory of Indian civilization. Here too aesthetics is represented as infused with spirituality:

> Equally with the philosopher and the king, Indian civilisation was advanced by the potter, the weaver, the carpenter, the mason, the ironsmith and the goldsmith.
>
> Indian sculpture, stone and bronze, like Indian painting, took for its material the symmetry of the human body, male and female, and the asymmetry of human emotions. Both these were then transposed on to gods and goddesses, just as the human body itself was transfigured in the architecture of the temples and in the seven basic notes of Indian music.
>
> The Chola bronzes express, more than the preceding Pallava rock-cut sculpture did, the fullness of the human body and emotions. The virility and strength of the male figure, and the sensuousness and grace of the female acquired in them very nearly a life-like quality.

The "bronze icons" displayed in the exhibition are "mostly replicas of 10th-12th century Chola bronzes." However, lest prospective viewers be discouraged because they are not going to see originals, the advertisement assures them that the bronzes have been "sculptured strictly on the lines prescribed in the Shilpa-sastra texts" in the workshops of the Tamil Nadu Handicrafts Development Corporation. The bottom line reads: "Buy Tamil Nadu Handicrafts. Preserve an Indian Heritage."

Spiritual referents are used to sell more than arts and crafts. The Cement Corporation of Gujarat—a joint sector (private and public) company—names its product Siddhi Cement. The corporation advertises its product with an illustration of a meditating yogi sitting atop a mountain (*Times of India*, 27 November 1987; *India Today*, 31 December 1987). Turn the page that heralds the "Perfect Strength Perfect Consistency" of Siddhi Cement and read about the "public outcry" over the dowry death of Shashikala in Karnataka (*India Today*, 31 December 1987). Her diary records her being tormented by her physician husband and rich, landowning in-laws for her insufficient dowry—25,000 rupees and 430 grams of gold. The report assures that her death will be avenged by society: her husband has been expelled from the local Rotary Club and may lose his membership in the Indian Medical Association; local lawyers refuse to defend the husband and his parents.

In the Siddhi Cement ascetic mode, a two-page color spread for Raymond's textiles shows a photograph of a chic young man and woman sitting on the ground, each wrapped in a blanket (*India Today*, 31 November 1987). Behind them are trunks of coconut palms and a wooden cart. In the darkness blazes an open fire. They look at a barefoot, bearded man in homespun clothing. At his side are a lantern and ascetic's pot. The text reads: "'To reach true love, you have first to climb a ladder of thorns,' he replied, his eyes glowing like embers." The advertisement entices viewers to eavesdrop on an imaginary intimate moment when this attractive young couple learns lessons of love from an ascetic guru.

Like the physical flexibility learned through training in yoga, the suppleness of the yogic image suits the requirements of commodity production. Indrajal Comics announces with a newspaper advertisement its latest "Super Hero," Aditya, "the Man from Nowhere" (*Times of India*, 21 October 1987). This barefoot young man with halo around his head "tackles terrorists without firing a single gunshot." If you want to know how "his yogic powers help him," buy the latest Indrajal Comic.

Religious and cultural icons such as cows, peasants, and the Buddha are used to advertise commodities to monied urban consumers. An advertisement for Garcoat supergloss synthetic enamel paint shows a group of turbaned peasants painting the horns of their sacred cows with blood-red paint (*India Today*, 30 November 1987). In its "Better Life-Style" series of advertisements, Shalimar Chemical Works, manufacturer of Shalimar coconut oil, celebrates the "lifestyle of ancient India" in the time of the Buddha as "simple yet beautiful" (*Hindustan Times*, 1 November 1987). The advertisement recites a familiar litany that glorifies Indian culture:

> Religious inspiration apart, Buddha Period is golden in India's history for excellence in Architecture, Fine Arts, Education and Culture. The stamp of absolute, class of artistry in Architecture and Inscriptions, replate [sic] in many a Temple, Cave, Pillar, Bronze and Wood of that period, reflect, their delicate sense of beauty and amazing heights of excellence in various Arts and Crafts.

Through the "aid of science" and ceaseless work, "hundreds of new commodities are born, old items are improvised," and Shalimar's coconut oil with its "modern pressunizing [sic] equipment and scientific falter system" contributes to "this time-honoured work" of making a better life-style. The advertisement's illustration shows a squatting man milking a cow, a Raja atop an elephant, temple buildings, and a busty, bejeweled young woman.

Like images showing a smiling woman feeding chocolates to a plump, overfed son or serving morning tea to a supine husband, emotive images associated with spirituality are regularly used to advertise consumer goods. Advertisements for the activities of religious organizations indicate another mode of marketing spirituality. Their frequent references to businesses which have funded the advertising disclose further circuits in the give and take between society and spirituality.

PAID ANNOUNCEMENTS: HOLY MISSION
OF INDIAN CULTURE

In addition to publicizing their events through listings in newspapers' calendars, religious organizations also announce their activities through advertisements. Most of these advertisements tend to be more modest and less costly than the six-page Centenary supplement placed by the Divine Life Society to publicize itself and its supporters. With the bottom line reading "space donated by," commercial concerns are often indicated as having paid for advertisements of religious events.

One advertisement attracts readers with the headline, "Holy Mission of Indian Culture." In this ad, Dada Ishwar Balani "cordially invites" readers to "exciting dramas" and "religious dances"; entry is free (*Times of India*, 4 July 1987). In advertisements for lectures at the Nehru Memorial Library sponsored by the Sadhu Vaswani Mission, Jay Pee Exports Pvt. Ltd. is prominently indicated as having paid for the ad. Elsewhere this same company advertised itself and the Mission with a large ad which pays obeisance to Sadhu Vaswani and attributes to him the success of Prakash Dudani, Jay Pee Export's managing director: "Even today when I have been honoured with this Udyog Patra Award, the award given to the Self made Entrepreneurs, I bow myself in front of Dada J. P. Vaswani because I owe my career to him. Even in my difficult days, I could feel the presence of the inner power of Dada Shyam Ji" (*Hindustan Times*, 18 May 1987).

The logo and motto of another company, Texla TV, "the right choice"—perhaps for watching the immensely popular television serialization of the *Ramayana*—appears in the bottom corner of an ad announcing the inauguration by Delhi's lieutenant governor of the Guru Ramdas naturopathy department and eye-care center (*Times of India*, 27 December 1987).[2] The Arsha Vidya temple advertises a discourse by Swami Dayananda to be held in Nehru auditorium at the All-India Institute of Medical Sciences (*Hindustan Times*, 22 May 1987). The Bharat Vikas Parishad (India Development Council) announces with an ad its series of three lectures by Swami Bhoomanand Tirth on the Yoga Vasistha, "dialogue between Young Rama and Sage Vaisitha (When Rama got disillusioned)" (*Times of*

---

2. The *Ramayana* serial was broadcast on Sunday mornings throughout India on government-run television in 78 weekly episodes during 1987–88 and it was also sold on videocassettes. For discussions of the political effects and debates surrounding the televised *Ramayana*, see Basu et al. (1993, 92–93) and van der Veer (1994, 8–9, 161, 178–79).

India, 12 October 1987). Those with the leisure, means, and inclination can find within the nation's capital countless occasions to improve their command of spiritual knowledge and to extend their familiarity and ties with the diverse organizations that promote it.

With space donated by Jay Cylinders Limited, makers of Suvidha Jay Energy Systems, the Sri Aurobindo Society announces an upcoming talk. The Chairman of the Aurobindo Society, M. P. Pandit is slated to speak on "Message of the Bhagavad Gita and Modern India" (*Times of India,* 13 September 1987). The Union Minister for Information and Broadcasting "will grace the occasion and preside over the function." This ad particularly caught my attention because a few days prior to seeing it, I had heard M. P. Pandit speak in Rishikesh. Acclaimed by another speaker as a "cardinal of the country," Pandit sat on stage with religious leaders and politicians, glorified the memory of Swami Sivananda, and basked in the limelight generated by the Divine Light Society's lavish celebration of Sivananda's birth centenary.

HINDU GROUNDBREAKING CEREMONIES IN THE CAPITAL

The ubiquity of linkages between spirituality and commerce perhaps inures the public to its implications. In addition to businesses paying to advertise the activities of religious organizations and the use of religious imagery in advertisements, businesses publicize their enterprises, their VIP connections, and their patronage of Hindu ritualists through advertisements announcing groundbreaking ceremonies *(bhoomi poojan).* Typically, these ads are decorated with the ceremonial water pot that is used in this ritual. Often decorated with the swastika, this pot is a distinctively Hindu emblem and is associated with a wide range of ritual activities. In an eighth of a page ad for its bhoomi poojan, Lawrence Food Industries "cordially invites friends and well-wishers" to attend ceremonies inaugurating the construction of a plant to manufacture fruit juices in "tetrapak" (*Times of India,* 17 January 1988). By stating in the ad that the Union Minister of State Industries will lay the foundation stone, Lawrence Food Industries signals its connections with high-ranking government officials.

Developers of commercial and residential complexes also advertise their bhoomi poojans. Contractors, builders, and architects associated with the specific construction project are often named in these announcements. The advertisement for the bhoomi poojan of Savitri Market in NOIDA, an industrial and residential development outside Delhi, announces that there are still some shops left, and guests may inquire during the ceremony about this "golden opportunity to become pride [sic] owner of shop in Ultra Modern unique Market with two lifts" (*Times of India,* 11 September 1988). With a quarter-page advertisement, the Army Welfare

Housing Organisation announces the bhoomi poojan inaugurating construction of "177 Super Deluxe Flats of NOIDA Authority" (*Times of India*, 21 November 1987). The Chairman of NOIDA and an Indian Administrative Service (IAS) officer will preside over the ceremonies. Similarly, members of the managing committee of the Bharat Co-operative Group Housing Society, Ltd., invite "you with family" to attend its bhoomi poojan function (*Hindustan Times*, 3 July 1987). The registrar of Cooperative Societies, Delhi, "has kindly agreed to lay the foundation stone of 308 flats." The morning's program begins with a vedic fire sacrifice and concludes with a luncheon feast.

These bhoomi poojan ceremonies provide an occasion for members of business, government, and religious groups to publicly demonstrate the relationships that bind them as allies and competitors, patrons and clients. Like temple consecrations, weddings, and other important socio-religious rituals, bhoomi poojans vary in size, expense, and spectacle. Through the organization and execution of these rituals, their sponsors redistribute resources in prestigious and efficacious ways which enlarge connections conducive for the potential profits of favor-trading and patronage.

DEAD BUT NOT FORGOTTEN: REVERENCING SUCCESSFUL CAPITALISTS

The press publicizes commemorations of death and birth anniversaries of past national leaders sponsored by the government and by political parties. Sponsors and participants use such occasions to publicly refigure alliances and update the terms of political discourse. Businesses and families use newspaper advertisements to announce deaths and commemorate birth and death anniversaries of prominent businessmen. Often the ads include long lists of family members giving names, professions, and relationships. Such lists suggest the dense interconnections among family, social, and business networks. The tone of these advertisements, like that of the testimonials to Sivananda discussed in chapter 9, is predominantly reverential and celebratory. They extol the exemplary leadership and the spiritual and philanthropic virtues of industrialists and businessmen. Moreover, as reiterated by speakers during the Sivananda Centenary, the ads celebrate the financial success of the deceased's endeavors and present this success as the just reward for selfless service by superior beings.

With one such advertisement, the family and staff of the Parle Soft Drinks Group commemorate the fourteenth death anniversary of the company's founder, Jayantilal Chauhan (*Times of India*, 22 March 1987). The ad includes the founder's photograph, which shows a dignified looking, gray haired man in a suit and tie. With imagery familiar in tributes to gurus and politicians, the text reads:

You smoothed the path for us to follow
You gave us the courage to pursue the right
You shared all that you learned and experienced
Today we still see your guiding light.

Another advertisement announces "with profound grief the sad demise of our respected Shri Gopal Chandrajee." The advertisement includes a photograph of Chandrajee wearing a business suit. It also announces the time and place for the ceremonies honoring him (*Times of India*, 18 March 1987). The deceased is celebrated as "a great philanthropist and industrialist," who founded the Shri Madan Mohan Damma Mal Trust Society, Dau Dayal Girls Inter College, and Dau Dayal Women's University, Firozabad. By using profits he accumulated as an industrialist to found educational institutions, Chandrajee earned for himself and his heirs social and economic profits of prestige, influence, and patronage generated by such institutions. The ad's lower third is filled with the names of family members. It lists Chandrajee's descendants, careful to delineate the patriline. In one column are listed the names of the son and daughter-in-law, granddaughters, grandsons, and two companies, Kumar Aerosols and Dhiraj Agencies, giving the addresses and office and residential phone numbers. In the other column are listed the names of one daughter and son-in-law ("Kunti-R.M. Agrawal, I.A.S.") and another married daughter.

Enclosed in a black border and with "Obituary" in bold type, six brothers, a sister, and mother announce the death of G. Parameswaran, "Auditor of U.R.G. and Company, Erode" (*The Hindu*, 17 March 1987). The advertisers note that they are "grateful to all the eminent doctors who attended on him." They also pay the following tribute to Parameswaran as the family's patriarch: "Since the day of our father's demise for the last 33 years, you shouldered responsibility, guided, educated, gave position, taught importance of love, unity and affection. Your untiring services will be ever remembered. With tears." Appended to the list of the six brothers are their various professions and affiliations: Lion; Assistant Director of Industries, Tamil Nadu; Dental Surgeon; Pioneer Group, Madras; Medical Technologist; Union Motors, Madras. The photograph of the acclaimed leader of this formidable group of well-placed brothers shows an austere man with heavy glasses and bare shoulders. A white string over one shoulder indicates the sacred thread and his status as an initiated high-caste Hindu male.

A larger ad commemorates the first death anniversary of Seth Shri Sadajiwatlal Chandulal Bahl (*Indian Express*, 27 December 1987). At the top of the ad are two lines in Sanskrit from the *Bhagavad Gita* with the following English translation: "Whatsoever a great man does, the same is done by others as well. Whatever standard he sets, the World follows." Below this quotation is a circular photograph bordered with stars and flowers. Seth Bahl is acclaimed as one "who all his life followed the path of Devotion and Love. A *Philanthropist* for the cause of *Hinduism.*" This commemorative ad is "A tribute from members of Bahl and Khanna Families, Relatives, Friends and Staff." In bold capital letters at the bottom of the advertisement is the name of the company and its Bombay address. The Seth's philanthropic activities are not detailed; instead they are generalized as having benefited "the cause of Hinduism."

"His virtues will plead like angels, trumpet-tongued" opens the text of a birth anniversary advertisement which covers about one-sixth of a newspaper's front page (*Times of India,* 18 March 1987). It shows a fleshy faced middle-aged man in a business suit. The photograph is set upon a bed of roses. The management and workers of Shree Acids and Chemicals, Ltd., and Delhi Cold Storage Pvt., Ltd., say of the departed Shri Suresh Kumar Mittal:

> He's not with us anymore. But he leaves behind for us the fame of his good works; his inspiring genius; his infinite capacity for work; his deeds; his virtues. He shall always adorn our dwellings.
>
> We all pay homage to this great soul today, on his birth anniversary. And remember him with a heavy heart and great respect.

This man is extolled not as one who made money with his chemical, acid, and cold storage businesses but as a great soul, who left for his heirs a legacy of famous good works. As is the case in many commercial establishments, residences, palaces, temples, and ashrams, where photographs of forebears and founders hang prominently, perhaps Mittal's portrait will indeed "always adorn" the offices and homes of the heirs to his businesses.

The linkage between the Arya Samaj and Punjabi Hindu business families is suggested in an advertisement for the funeral ceremonies of "our beloved Shri Wazir Chand Kawatra" (*Times of India,* 18 March 1987). The photograph shows a corpulent man in a business suit who was "past district governor Rotary International" and for whom a memorial service will be held at the Arya Samaj DAV College for Boys in Batala. Under the heading "Grief Stricken" are listed the names and relationships of twenty family members. The bottom of the ad shows the name and address of the deceased man's business.

No family members are mentioned in a quarter-page advertisement commemorating the seventeenth death anniversary of L. Ramlal Chandhok (*Hindustan Times,* 5 June 1987). With another invocation that could be of a disciple to a guru, the ad's text begins: "Be near us when we climb or fall: Ye watch, like God, the rolling hours. . . . " The qualities attributed to this successful businessman recall those attributed to Sivananda, the dynamo of divine life. The ad celebrates Chandhok's "immortal ideals" that continue to "inspire us," his "gentle soul," "strong work-ethic, indomitable will and cheerful optimism." While other advertisements close with a list of the deceased's relatives, this ad shows the names of twenty business firms from Kashmir to Madras, Delhi, Bombay, Bangalore, and Calcutta as the fruit of Chandhok's "indomitable will" and "humane nature." Like Sivananda through his Divine Life Society, Chandhok "still serves humanity" through the Shri Ramlal Kaushalya Devi Chandhok Charitable Trust.

The investment in charitable trusts by businessmen is noted by van der Veer in his study of religious institutions in Ayodhya (1988, 42). He observes that Marwari merchants have replaced landowning elites as leading religious patrons; their religious trusts are run according to bureaucratic methods. The business meetings of religious trusts "function as occasions for business contacts and community solidarity in a similar way to such organizations as the Lions clubs in western society" (van der Veer 1988, 42). Indian business groups involved with religious trusts may also have members who are active in organizations such as the Lions and Rotary Clubs and Chambers of Commerce, just as businessmen in western society may be active in such organizations as well as in the affairs of churches, synagogues, mosques, and temples.

Whereas capitalist businessmen with their charitable trusts are currently leading patrons of Hindu religious institutions, righteous rulers acting as patrons of religion are an enduring ideal. The government demonstrates its fulfillment of this duty of the ruler through a variety of activities—infrastructural support of Hindu pilgrimage, visits by government officials and politicians to temples, and their participation in the public celebrations staged by religious organizations. The association of such aristocrats as the Maharaja Bhagwat Singh Mewar and the Maharaja of Nepal with the VHP and their presence at the VHP's ritual functions has been noted in chapter 4.

This image of regal patronage is juxtaposed with that of the businessman in the following memorial announcement. Readers see two images of Raja Rattan Amol Singh: a photograph showing him in a business suit and portrait of him in traditional royal attire with jewels (*Times of India*, 10 September 1987). Above this diptych is a leonine crest and motto "Droit et Loyal," and below it the announcement of a "bhog ceremony and a convention of intercommunal national integration function." This ceremony at Fort Buria in Harayana commemorates the third death anniversary of "our dearest papa . . . who struggled the whole of his life for secularism, national integration and communal harmony." Three daughters, Rajkumaris of Buria, and his sister, Rajkumari Rattan Amol Kaur, are named in capital bold letters at the bottom of the advertisement. Heiresses no less than heirs can be invested in preserving the memory of prestigious, powerful forbears.

GIFTS AND THEFTS, BRICKBATTING AND POLICE PICKETS

The wealth and resources that Hindu institutions—temples, ascetic orders, religious schools, charitable trust societies—command through the support both of wealthy and of less powerful, more ordinary patrons receive regular press attention. The press regularly reports on the amount of income major temples earn through donations, and on thefts of statuary and valuables from temple sanctuaries and treasuries. Newspapers also bemuse and consternate their readers by reporting unusual gifts given to deities.

"Lord Venkateshwara, the presiding deity at Tirumala, received a strange gift yesterday" reported temple officials at Tirupati. A devotee placed a "modern mini grinding machine" in the temple collection box (*Times of India,* 14 December 1987). Perhaps the donor was a dealer or manufacturer of this new consumer gadget and hoped a donation would help the business to flourish. A more explicit example of the government-business-temple connection is suggested by a report on the donation to the temple of Venkateshwara of a forty-kilogram bag of fertilizer made by the state-owned Godavari Fertilisers, Ltd., on the day the factory started production (*Times of India,* 7 February 1988). Bemusing reports of offerings such as these—a grinding machine and sack of fertilizer—gloss with congenial levity the social relations that are mediated by Hindu institutions and rituals.

Other reports, however, more baldly indicate the violence that may structure these relations. At a Rajarajeshwari Mata temple near Ujjain and in the presence of other devotees, a police constable "cut out his tongue with a razor and offered it before his deity" (*Times of India,* 27 March 1988). The report explains that "the constable offered his tongue to propitiate the goddess." The report, however, does not include information on whom or what induced the constable to mutilate and silence himself.

The institutional and symbolic power of persons and groups associated with the operation of religious institutions attracts support from patrons who want to ally themselves with these sources of power. The economic power of temples in the form of their moveable assets attracts professional thieves. On two successive days reports of thefts from Ujjain temples reached Delhi newspapers via two different wire services. Silver statues of Rama, Sita, Lakshman, and Hanuman weighing a total of eighteen kilograms were stolen from Ujjain's Gopal temple (*Times of India,* 14 December 1987). The crown, umbrella, and silver and gold ornaments of

Goddess Harsiddhi, "who was believed to be worshipped by King Vikramaditya in ancient Ujjain," were stolen from another Ujjain temple the following day (*Hindustan Times,* 15 December 1987). In Madhya Pradesh police arrested eleven members of an interstate gang of idol thieves and recovered statues of Radha and Krishna valued at thirty million rupees (*Times of India,* 26 October 1987). The thieves were not successful in extracting the estimated seventy-seven kilograms of gold from the statues, but they managed to remove approximately ten million rupees worth of semiprecious gems adorning them. The newspaper reports that the police had not yet apprehended the gang's leader.

The police assist proprietors of religious institutions to recover stolen property and control agitated crowds. There are situations, however, when police are called upon to curb the powers and abuses of priests. From an article with the headline "15 Cops Hurt in Riot Over Temple Takeover," readers learn that police personnel were injured in "the brickbatting by some associates of the Chintpurni temple pujaris" (*Hindustan Times,* 3 June 1987). New legislation in Himachal Pradesh required that the administration of the Chintpurni temple change hands. To protest the government's involvement and resist the occupation of the temple by the police, the priests locked themselves in the temple sanctuary, preventing "pilgrims from having the darshan of goddess" Chintpurni. In addition to repelling the police by force, the priests' associates successfully obtained a court order requiring the police to vacate temple premises. In concluding its report on events, the article asserts: "the situation is presently under control." Under whose control? Temple priests and pilgrimage pandas employ their own brickbatting associates who use violence and intimidation to prosecute and protect their professional interests. The use of violence by brahman pandas in Ayodhya to defend and expand their share of the pilgrimage market is discussed in detail in van der Veer's study (1988). He describes how a single panda came to virtually monopolize Ayodhya's traffic in pilgrims and notes that this ruthless and powerful panda is regularly visited by important politicians.

Government tourist literature and travel journalism picture great Hindu temples as centers of timeless tradition, as places of sanctity and spiritual inspiration. A leading women's organization in Orissa has "demanded the posting of women's police pickets" within the grounds of the Jagannath temple in Puri (*Times of India,* 16 January 1988). The policewomen are necessary to "ensure the 'safety' of women visitors and pilgrims" and to counter their harassment by "a section of temple priests and antisocial elements." The demand relates to the criminal charges that two women—a noted Oriya writer and a college lecturer from Pune—have brought against Puri temple priests. During their visit to the temple, the women "were surrounded by about 25 priests who allegedly abused them and assaulted them and pushed them out of the temple." The temple administration defends itself by claiming that they too have requested increased policing of temple premises.

PLUMBING THE MURKY DEPTHS

In addition to reports on gifts, thefts, and violence at temples as well as advertisements and calendars of daily events, newspapers keep their readers abreast of the activities of Hindu religious organizations through regular reporting on their affairs in their snippets columns, news stories, and feature articles. Religious organizations attract considerable media coverage when politicians and public officials attend their gatherings. Religious figures and organizations have an almost numbingly commonplace presence in newspapers through news items placed in columns with other news-in-brief or scattered throughout the paper. These usually give two or three sentence reports relating to recent and planned events of organizations, criminal offenses and court cases, and accidents and deaths of religious leaders.

Besides reporting on the good deeds and pious pronouncements of religious leaders and organizations, newspapers and magazines regularly carry stories about their scandals, feuds, and court cases. Sex and financial scandals involving gurus and devotees are frequent and prevalent. The coverage they receive suggests the ambivalence that people feel for gurus, for the powers some are capable of wielding through their wealthy patrons and their connections with politicians, bureaucrats, and military and police officers, and for the influence they can exert over credulous devotees. Details of such stories also suggest the byzantine business and interpersonal intrigues that surround gurus.

In recent years the activities of gurus with transnational spiritual empires such as Bhagwan Rajneesh and Mahesh Maharishi as well as Chandra Swami, implicated in the Iran Contra scandal through his dealings with his devotee, the international arms broker Adnan Khashoggi, provide examples of gurus' skills and successes in exchanging spirituality for money. Details concerning these jet-setting gurus, whose business interests and ambitions are reported from time to time by investigative journalists and in press reports of property and account books seized during periodic raids on their establishments by income tax officials, are beyond the scope of the present discussion. Instead, I shall introduce a series of less complex cases of shady and often illegal activities of gurus that have been reported in the press.

The headline "Swami Abducts Teenager" begins a report on allegations concerning the abduction of an eighteen-year-old woman by her guru (*Hindustan Times*, 23 November 1987). A month later a full-page story in

India Today follows up this case, which involved an Ahmedabad industrialist who accused Swami Amarjyot Shyam—whose passport address reads "Amarnath caves in the Himalayas"—of kidnapping his daughter, Tamanna (*India Today*, 31 December 1987). The daughter and her mother had been followers of the thirty-year-old Swami for the past year. They were just two "among the many others in Ahmedabad who had succumbed to the mysterious spiritual powers of the Swami." The Swami and his supporters deny the daughter's official statement that he had promised her "moksha" (salvation) if she eloped with him. The Swami claims that he had received a message from his guru telling him "to settle for a worldly life" and that an Arya Samaji priest married him and Tamanna in Jaipur. Two weeks after her disappearance Tamanna was located by relatives in Jaipur and returned to her parents. She did not give a police statement because her father produced a medical certificate stating that she "was not in a proper mental condition." Her father filed charges against the Swami and six of his disciples for kidnapping his daughter. Among the accused is the dean of the College of Performing Arts at Baroda, the husband of a popular film actress.

Adding to the "sensationalism" of the story is the fact that the Swami has many "powerful followers" with whom he stays during his tours: the brother of the Union Minister for Steel and Mines, a major-general, a brigadier, a retired rear-admiral, and "a host of top government officials." The report also names "businessman" Sakalchand Patal as his main disciple in Gujarat. It does not indicate what the relationships among these devotees and Tamanna's industrialist father may be. Instead it closes the article by saying that all sides agree the relationship between the Swami and Tamanna "was strictly spiritual." However spiritual the Swami's intentions may be, "rumours that are circulating in Ahmedabad hint" that the Swami's interest in the industrialist's only daughter was pecuniary, i.e., procuring a lucrative dowry and a wealthy father-in-law.

A couple of months later, *India Today* devoted a full-page report to another "Godman's Gaffe" (15 February 1988). It details allegations of how a leader of a religious sect in Ahmedabad "lured women devotees into illicit relationships" by assuring them that he had been their husband in previous lives. The case arose when a video was released that showed a guru named Kalanidhi Goswami "in compromising positions" with his devotee Videhi, the "dusky wife" of an Ahmedabad "electronics engineer-cum-industrialist." The husband claims to have made the video with the cooperation of his wife in order to warn other women about the lecherous proclivities of the guru.

Goswami argues that he had been in bed "under duress" and that the couple used the video to try to blackmail him. He had helped Videhi's brother become a business partner of another disciple. When the partnership dissolved and the brother owed the partner 140,000 rupees, they hoped the threat of publicizing the video would induce the guru to pay them 170,000 rupees as well as order his disciple to "forget" the brother's debt. The article is illustrated with a photo of a few policemen standing amidst a crowd of plump well-dressed women who are protesting outside of Goswami's house. It concludes by noting that the scandal has not diminished Goswami's popularity: "As the sun sets, a steady stream of visitors can be seen going to the guru's house, ready to fall at his feet."

More frequent are the short scandal reports such as one from Aurangabad concerning the suicide of a "baba." The baba had been arrested on charges of "flirting with his disciple, a young eighteen-year-old married woman at her residence." Two days later he killed himself (*Times of India,* 27 March 1988). News reports suggest that boys, like women, are preyed upon by gurus and sadhus. The All-India Hijra Kalyan Sabha (Eunuchs' Welfare Society) sent a memorandum to Prime Minister Rajiv Gandhi concerning the "forcible emasculation" and initiation of "hundreds of boys" by the naga sect of sadhus (*Times of India,* 4 April 1988). Such boys came "from the lower strata of society" or had been kidnapped. The public has reason for being wary of nagas, who are notorious for public nudity and for displaying their often disfigured genitalia. They constitute trained fighting cadres used to defend and avenge the interests of their ascetic orders through intimidation and violence. When police force is insufficient or inadvisable, politicians and businessmen use goondas or toughs, and ascetic orders rely on nagas.

"Homosexuality and embezzlement" are the accusations that two swamis have been trading in "an internecine feud" that began in 1985 (*Statesman,* 6 April 1988). The feud involves the succession to the highest office of the Siddhanganga Virashaiva Math. The dispute has "plunged" the math "into murky depths." Besides the religious prestige this math enjoys among Virashaiva followers throughout Karnataka, it also commands considerable social and economic resources. It feeds five hundred people every day, operates over seventy educational institutions, and owns tens of millions of rupees of property in Karnataka. Trouble began when the "pontiff ousted Swami Gaurishankar and appointed Swami Siddhalinga as heir-apparent." The senior swami ordered Gaurishankar, "an engineering graduate" to go to Varanasi to study Sanskrit, but he refused and continued to live at the math. Supporters of the ousted Gaurishankar organized a protest. It quickly spread throughout the district and became violent. In response, the government posted four platoons of the Karnataka State Reserve Police at the math and special guards at the residence of the senior swami. The protesters plan to fight their battle in court.

The activities of swamis and "spiritual heads" of organizations and the feuding among factions of devotees frequently lead to civil and criminal court cases. With the headline, "Hardwar 'swami' granted bail," a newspaper reports a case in which one swami allegedly kidnapped a rival swami (*Hindustan Times,* 28 May 1987). The defendant pleaded that the other swami was hiding to make it seem as if he had been kidnapped. The two swamis are embroiled in a dispute over the ownership of the Ramayan Satsang Bhavan in Hardwar. In another case, the High Court in Madras ruled that the passport of the "spiritual head" of the Madurai Adheenam be returned to him (*Times of India,* 13 November 1987). Government officials had confiscated his passport "on the grounds that two criminal cases were pending against him." It was returned so that he could attend the sixth annual World Tamil Conference in Kuala Lumpur.

The Gurudev Siddha Peeth, an international organization with Chidvilasananda, the woman successor to Muktananda, as the current leader, bought a quarter-page newspaper ad to discuss its ongoing court case and the media coverage it has attracted (*Times of India,* 18 December 1987). The Peeth advertisement refers to its earlier ads that publicized their case against Subhash Shetty. Those ads stated that the *Illustrated Weekly of India* had published "slanderous" articles but had "apologized" for them. The present ad claims that the *Illustrated Weekly* has "taken exception" to their language. Peeth officials have discussed the matter with the editor and journalist responsible for the article. The *Illustrated Weekly* has since published a clarification of its article, and the Gurudev Siddha Peeth regrets "this unfortunate misunderstanding between the magazine and us" (*Times of India,* 18 December 1987). The ad suggests that both the *Illustrated Weekly* and the Siddha Pith want to publicly disavow their disaffection.

In a letter to the editor, one writer decries the defective legislation which permits the Mahabodhi Vihar in Bihar to be controlled by a committee dominated by Hindus (*Times of India,* 2 October 1987). He argues that Buddhists throughout the world are offended that "their sacred place of worship is being controlled, managed and administered by an orthodox Hindu Mahant [head of a math] whose practice has no connection with the Buddhist precepts of compassion and brotherhood. The Mahant maintains a private army to show naked and brutal force and controls vast landed estates illegally." The letter further alleges that this orthodox Hindu mahant appropriates a substantial portion of the funds donated to the Buddhist Vihar for his personal use. Disturbed by this situation the letter writer suggests: "Let the Hindus do some self-searching before they raise the issue of Ram-Janma Bhoomi" (*Times of India,* 2 October 1987).

A WORLD MORE MACABRE THAN A STEPHEN KING HORROR STORY

Public suspicion of gurus relates to the fear that false gurus can dupe devotees into thinking that malicious manipulation is in fact the assistance that a true guru—beloved, benevolent, omniscient, and omnipotent—is capable of providing. This opposition between authentic and phony, benevolent and malevolent gurus structures thinking about gurus and their organizations as expressed in written and oral discussions. People often asked me if I could tell them which gurus in Hardwar and Rishikesh were frauds and which were truly spiritual. The opposition upholds the belief that however few and far between, true gurus deserving of worship, obedience, and service do in fact exist and that their presence is a boon to both individuals and society. Such a view often marginalizes sustained critical thinking in sociological and political terms about the operations of gurus and their organizations. Furthermore, this view that regards false gurus as the norm and true gurus a rarity encourages devotees to inflate the value of their own true guru while regarding most other gurus with suspicion if not contempt.

Whereas the true guru is celebrated for possessing the power to raise devotees to the zenith of divine life, the fraudulent guru is feared for possessing powers that lead devotees to a deathly nadir, plunging them into "a world more macabre than a Stephen King horror story." For its sophisticated readers, *India Today* offers the glib Stephen King comparison after opening its story: "From the outside, the palatial, pink-washed house in Chandigargh's Sector 8 looked no different from its neighbours" (*India Today*, 31 May 1987). In this grisly case a guru and devotees behaved for twenty-two months as if the corpse of another devotee was alive but in a "spiritual coma." The media covered the story of guru Amir Chand Kaushal and the death of S. R. Dutta in considerable detail and illustrated it with ghoulish photographs of the dead Dutta's skull and skeleton (*Hindustan Times*, 5, 8, 10, 16 May 1987; *India Today*, 31 May 1987). Mrs. Dutta and her five children lived in a room with the corpse while staying in the home of her husband's "former colleague and close friend," Baldev Singh and his wife Daljit Kaur, who were devotees of the same guru. In fact, Daljit had been "miraculously 'pregnant' now for 64 months." The guru promised that Daljit's baby would be born the same day that Dutta would be cured.

The guru had treated other family members and was called in when Dutta, Assistant Conservator of Forests in Himachal Pradesh, fell ill. His condition rapidly deteriorated under his guru's care, but the guru prohibited the family from seeking other medical attention. For nearly two years Dutta's wife dutifully sponged her husband's blackened body and sent forms to his employer stating that he was in a "spiritual coma" and requesting his leave be extended. She and the children spent hours each day in the room talking to the dead man. Dutta's employer became increasingly suspicious and came to Chandigargh to investigate. After the case became public, Dutta's brother brought the police in and has filed charges of murder against the guru and a few of his disciples.

The guru denies being a tantrik and claims that his cult "centres around the belief that one should not believe in any religion" (*India Today*, 31 May 1987). He performs "moonlit" ceremonies during which his disciples chant prayers and "obey his every word, as if they were under some form of hypnosis." According to Baldev Singh, in whose house the dead Dutta lay for so long, his guru has about fifty people in his "inner circle." The guru has thousands of other followers, "mainly the rich and powerful." Guru Amir Chand Kaushal insists that his disciple Dutta is not dead and it is within his power not only to cure Dutta but also to cure AIDS victims. By profession Kaushal is a headmaster and teacher of English and social sciences in a middle school in the Punjab. Kaushal displays to reporters letters addressed to the director-general of the World Health Organization and to the chairman of Union Carbide which detail his miraculous spiritual healing of victims of the Bhopal disaster.

After news of the Dutta case broke, newspapers carried stories of two similar cases. One involved Sudesh Kumari, whose "mummified" body was kept in her mother's house for forty months (*Hindustan Times*, 15 May 1987). After falling ill with a stomach ache and being taken to the hospital, family members claimed she went to Agra. Soon after this her brother went to live in Chandigarh, but he denied any connection with the dead Dutta's guru. The brother did admit, however, that he had his sister treated by Hindu ascetics from Brindavan and Agra. The ascetic from Brindavan diagnosed her as being in a coma and visited every year to give her a special preparation.

As Sudesh Kumari did not improve, i.e., she remained dead, her family brought her to several other ascetics including one at a Kali temple in Pathankot who refused to treat her. When police discovered her body, it was blackened beyond recognition. The article reports that the family consisted of Sudesh's mother, four sisters, and three brothers. It also reports that the family "had little social contact with neighbors." Such isolation would increase the vulnerability of the mother and sisters as widow and unmarried daughters. Structurally, a widow and four unmarried daughters would be extremely vulnerable to abuses by adult males within and outside the family. All would be well aware of the expense and liabilities involved in arranging marriages for the girls. Perhaps the family was hoping Sudesh's death would obviate the expense of her marriage, and her miraculous remains would be a source of income—as the following case shows is possible.

In the wake of the Dutta case, the Uttar Pradesh government ordered an inquiry into "the sensational case of a saint preserving the body of his wife, Ganga, for the last eight years in the historic town of Bithoor in Kanpur" (*Hindustan Times*, 20 May 1988). The husband claimed that he was only fulfilling his wife's wish that her body be preserved. He relied solely upon his "spiritual powers" for preserving her body since her death. The government sent doctors with a police escort on an earlier occasion, but "stiff opposition from local residents prevented them to take any step." Like devotees crowding in for darshan of the dark and terrible Kali, "even today a large number of people thronged the Baba's residence to have a glimpse of Ganga."

The Hindu goddess manifests shakti in a myriad of social forms: Lakshmi embodies the power of wealth; Saraswati embodies the power of knowledge; Durga and Kali embody the power of violence—they vanquish enemies and bestow the boon of fearlessness upon devotees. Worship of Kali and Durga is particularly associated with those groups who wield weapons: rulers and revolutionaries, soldiers, police, and bandits. When Bharati Ma, the Mataji with whom I resided and traveled during 1987 and 1988, was preparing to consecrate the Kali temple at her Hardwar ashram, she clothed the naked Kali in red brocade sari. However, Kali's garland of skulls, bloody hands, and lolling tongue remained fully visible as did the body of Shiva upon which she stood (see plate 24).

Occasionally when people learned I lived in an ashram with a Kali temple, they lowered their voices and asked what kind of rituals were performed there. One sannyasini warned me that although in public pure rituals (no offerings of blood or alcohol; no sexual practices) were performed, one could never be certain what shaktas (worshippers of Kali) do during the dead of night. When I asked Bharati Ma about blood sacrifices, she acknowledged that some people do make them to Kali, but that she neither performs them nor permits their performance at her temple. She added that she refuses to comply with people's requests for assistance in harming their enemies. She believes that her power to help people would be lost if she used it for malevolent purposes.

Frequent press reports concerning human sacrifices to Kali and other Hindu goddesses heighten suspicion and unease concerning the pursuit of power through ritual violence. A newspaper editorial, "Shame for Hindus," enumerates six cases of child sacrifice that occurred between January and August 1987 and suggests further ones—"all this and more" (*Times of India*, 3 December 1987). "On the advice of a sorcerer from Meerut" a father sacrificed his six-year-old son before "Goddess Kali's idol" at a village near Ghaziabad (*Times of India*, 2 December 1987). The father was advised that through such a sacrifice to Kali he would "be blessed with lots of land and money and a big car" (*Times of India*, 3 December 1987). In his "greed for getting rich" the man beheaded his son, anointed his wife's forehead with their son's blood, and placed the severed head at the feet of Kali.

A case in Thane, Maharashtra, involved the arrest of five people, including a "temple servant," for their alleged involvement in the "ritual sacrifice" of a seven-year-old girl at the Adi Mata Shakti temple (*Times of India*, 24 March 1988). The case is the subject of an editorial entitled "Barbaric Practice" (*Times of India*, 28 March 1988). The editorial opens by referring to the response generated by the editorial on child sacrifice published three months previously:

> When we recently commented in these columns that the continuance of child sacrifice represented an aspect of their religion which brought shame on the Hindus, we received a spate of self-righteous indignant letters from those who profess and practice that faith. The more sensible among them argued that not all Hindus approved of child sacrifice. That it was not sanctioned by all Hindu sects and that, in any case, it was a disappearing phenomenon.

The Thane case is described as a "macabre murder which was carried out in line with tantrik rituals." The editorial asserts that performance of the sacrifice on "the auspicious Gudi Padva day" and the condition of the corpse "leaves little doubt about the religious content of the gory sacrifice, though the police are trying to make it out to be a rape case." It reports that according to "local people" this was not the first case of "macabre ritualism" occurring in either the temple or the adjoining Guru Nityanand Adi Mata ashram. However, allegations made on previous occasions were never investigated. Furthermore, the editorial suggests that the temple and ashram have powerful allies: a local politician, after being elected deputy mayor of Thane, "chose the temple as the place to express his gratitude to providence" (*Times of India*, 28 March 1988).

Institutionalized spirituality—the pursuit and deployment of powers associated with asceticism and ritual, knowledge and righteousness, wealth and violence—interprets and capitalizes on vicissitudes of life and fear of death. Sivananda and his followers built up the Divine Life Society into a formidable and wealthy institution by aggressively selling and astutely marketing spirituality. The Divine Life Society represents itself as having no murky depths: it claims to have no "secret doctrines nor esoteric sections or inner circles. It is a purely spiritual organisation having no leanings towards politics." Thus far its operations have not attracted disreputable publicity. The respectability of the Divine Life Society, no less than the sensationalization of guru scandals and human sacrifice, however, tends to obfuscate the problem which this book addresses: the relation of gurus, religious organizations, and rituals to circuits of power and domination in India.

The political economy related to belief in and worship of shakti or divine power, not only in the form of goddesses such as Bharat Mata, Ganga Mata, Kali, Durga, and other bejeweled golden deities in great temples but also in human form as gurus and tantriks, is complicated business. The myths and rituals, pilgrim and tourist literature, press coverage, and Hindu nationalist propaganda that promote awe for the omnipotence of Hindu deities and their embodiments in gurus and saints are similarly prolific and complex. This book grapples with these complexities and their implications. It explores how spiritual commodities are produced and advertised, circulated and consumed, as well as how spirituality contributes to the evaluation and circulation of cultural and religious, political and financial capital within Indian society. The prevailing polarization between true and spurious spirituality is presented as a problematic. The transnational operations of Hindu organizations are reminders that nationalist ideologies are served by those who identify Hindu India as the origin of spirituality, an identification used for authenticating the commodities they aggressively compete to exchange for money and symbolic capital in markets throughout the world.

EPILOGUE

"Hindu Rashtra Harbinger of Secular Nationalism and New World Order" is the headline on the first page of the 1992 annual brochure for the Chicago branch of the VHP of America. After the headline "Hindu Rashtra—Triumphant March" are several pages full of quotations from high-ranking officials of the Hindu nationalist movement's allied organizations: the VHP, RSS, and BJP. Ashok Singhal declares: "Arrangements for the construction of the disputed Ram Temple in Ayodhya in the state of Uttar Pradesh are on in full swing: no power on earth can stop the reconstruction of the temple." On the same topic and immediately following Singhal's words is a quote attributed to the then BJP chief minister of Uttar Pradesh, Kalyan Singh (whose government was dismissed after the destruction of the Babri mosque):

> For Hindus it is a matter of faith. Constructing a temple at the birthplace of Ram does not mean just construction of a place of worship. It is a symbol of our national self-respect: it is a symbol of our Independence. . . . The temple will be constructed. . . . It is a question of the Hindu faith.

The 1993 annual brochure celebrates the "successful culmination of the Ram Janmabhoomi Mukti Yogna," and BJP leader M. M. Joshi asserts: "A battle of ideology has started. The question is what constitutes the identity of the nation's mainstream; can this country remain united without Hindutva? A decisive moment has come." The 1994 brochure is even more exuberant in its references to the Ram Janmabhoomi campaign. Singhal describes the destruction of the Babri mosque as "a catalyst for the ideological polarization which is nearly complete" and again declares that the Ram temple will be built in Ayodhya. Following Singhal's words is a quotation from an RSS official acknowledging that the VHP was the prime mover of the Ram Janmabhoomi movement. The mainstreaming of Hindutva, 315 largely facilitated by Hindu organizations affiliated with the VHP such as the Gayatri Parivar, the Divine Life Society, and Satyamitranand's Family of Harmony and Bharat Mata temple—as well as militant activism—contributed to the events leading up to and following the destruction of the Babri mosque on 6 December 1992 in Ayodhya.

A young woman ascetic, Sadavi Rithambra, who is a member of the VHP's committee of religious leaders, invokes Bharat Mata when she speaks at rallies (Kakar 1992). Her speeches explode with rage and hatred directed primarily against Muslims (Basu et al. 1993, 99–102). They are so inflammatory that the government bans the sale of her cassettes. She tells her audience that Muslim atrocities against Hindus, which began when they invaded India, desecrated Hindu temples, and raped Hindu women, have neither ceased nor been avenged. Muslim separatists in Kashmir, she claims, are using "red hot irons to burn the slogan 'Long Live Pakistan' on the thighs of our Hindu daughters" (Kakar 1992). She exhorts the crowd to remember the blood of Hindu martyrs who died in 1990 during an attempt to build the Ram temple. She insists that the fight to build this temple is the fight to preserve their civilization, national consciousness, honor, and self-esteem.

References to the need for Hindus to protect themselves from brutal enemies intensify the emotive power of her speeches. It is a strategy used by nationalists and other groups to forge and consolidate a collective identity. The audience simultaneously experiences and affirms its collective identity, its imagined community, when it joins this young woman in a chant that begins and ends with invocations of Bharat Mata. The chant links the audience with gods of the past and Hindu martyrs of the present: all are children of Bharat Mata.

In 1987, when I first met VHP general secretary Ashok Singhal in his office and heard him and his associates talk about building a Ram temple in Ayodhya, journalists and academics generally regarded the VHP as a fringe group of right-wing Hindus. While meeting Singhal and his associates alerted me to the formidable determination of the VHP's leadership, later events disclosed the ruthlessness of its political will. The sustained activism of the VHP and its allies made Ayodhya into a prominent and volatile political issue. Support for the VHP steadily increased throughout the 1980s and early 1990s (Basu et al. 1993; Jaffrelot 1993; van der Veer 1994).

Following its 1983 All India Sacrifice for Unity, the VHP organized a procession in 1984 to demand the opening of the locked Babri mosque, where Hindus had placed an image of Ram in 1949. The VHP's persistence and growing political influence led to the 1986 court ruling which opened the mosque. Rajiv Gandhi's public support for this ruling in a 1989 campaign speech indicates the political ground the VHP gained in the 1980s (van der Veer 1994, 3). In 1989 the VHP organized people from throughout India and overseas to consecrate bricks for the Ram temple and bring them in procession to Ayodhya. Some of the processions provoked violent confrontations between Hindus and Muslims, particularly in Bihar. The following year a procession to Ayodhya—led by the VHP's ally, BJP politician L. K. Advani outfitted as Ram—incited even more violence. The police arrested Advani and opened fire on the procession because it defied an order banning its entry into Ayodhya. The VHP retaliated with video and audio cassettes as well as rituals throughout India that glorified those killed in the police firing as martyrs and condemned the government. These events were also bound up in electoral politics which brought the BJP to power in Uttar Pradesh in 1991. The following year the VHP and its allies again mobilized supporters to assemble in Ayodhya. This time they destroyed the Babri mosque.

In the widespread violence that followed the mosque's destruction, over 1,700 people were killed in fighting between Muslims and Hindus as well as by the police and army. Reports on the number and identities of those killed indicate that the majority were Muslims and that the police and military killed many more Muslims than Hindus. The Indian government is said to have ignored warnings from its own intelligence agencies that Hindu groups had specific plans to tear down the mosque. After a Supreme Court ruling supported the government's prohibition on the construction of the Ram temple at the disputed site, Hindu leaders assured the prime minister that the ceremonies they planned in Ayodhya would only involve a symbolic construction of the Ram temple. When the temple's symbolic construction turned into the mosque's actual destruction, the police fled and paramilitary forces were still in their camps. The government did not attempt to remove the Hindu activists from the site until the following day. And when troops did move in and clear out the activists, a Hindu priest was permitted to continue performing rituals at the newly erected Ram shrine.

The Government of India responded by imposing president's rule in Uttar Pradesh and banning the VHP, RSS, and the Bajrang Dal for their involvement in organizing the mosque's destruction. Ashok Singhal was among the Hindu leaders arrested on charges of inciting the crowd to demolish the mosque. Responding to the government's announcement that it would rectify the situation and restore rule of law by rebuilding the mosque, Singhal reportedly challenged the government to try and stop the temple's construction. The Ram Janmabhoomi Trust plans to spend 250 million rupees to build the largest temple in the world in Ayodhya; trustees include not only Singhal and two heads of ascetic orders but also G. P. Birla, G. H. Singhania, K. N. Modi, and R. N. Goenka, who number among India's leading capitalists (Jaffrelot 1993, 442).

The 1995 annual brochure for the Chicago branch of the VHP opens with a section called "Hindu Dharma and Hindu Politics," which begins with the following assertion: "Hindu Dharma and Hindu Politics are mutually interrelated, intertwined, and interchangeable; these are enunciated and elaborated by our Rishis, Saints and Seers, enshrined in our ancient scriptures as Four Vedas, Manusmriti, Purana, Upanishads . . . Ramayana, Mahabharat, Gita, Brahmanas, Arthashastra by Kautilya." The brochure's second section, "Hindu Rashtra Defined," is composed of quotations from VHP, RSS, and BJP leaders, including Ashok Singhal who writes:

> After all the Hindu Rashtra can only be a state where there must be Hindu churches and Hindu mosques, for Hinduism is not a religion. It is the collective experience of thousands of individuals unlike Christianity and Islam which are experiences of single individuals. In Hindu India, every one has to call himself a Hindu.
>
> The core issues in Ramjanmabhoomi are two, namely the site of the garbh-griha [sanctuary] and the proprietory rights of the land. On the first there is no room for compromise. The Hindu society will not accept the location of the garbh-griha at any other site than at the birthplace of Shri Rama, that is, the site of the make-shift temple. The entire acquired land, including the 2.7 acres of disputed land be vested in the deity Ram Lala. VHP sponsored nyas [trust] will be abolished after the completion of the temple; the Parishad was not interested in managing the temple, its mission was to rebuild the temple. (VHP 1995)

The campaign to destroy the Babri mosque and build the Ram temple in Ayodhya, like the Bharat Mata temple in Hardwar built by VHP leader Satyamitranand and the All India Sacrifice for Unity, are both ends and means. They are sites for the production and dissemination of national identity and cultural forms. They are means for raising money and attracting official and popular support for the Hindu nationalist movement. Movements to establish a Hindu nation-state in India have waxed and waned for nearly a century. Events surrounding the destruction of the Babri mosque suggest that the Hindu nationalist movement's political power, financial backing, and respectability among upper- and middle-class Hindus in India and abroad has never been greater. Its successes relate to complex dynamics associated with the domestic and transnational political economy and with the religio-cultural politics of nationalism.

After the demolition of the Babri mosque, Muslims in Pakistan and Bangladesh retaliated by attacking Indian consulates, businesses, and Hindu temples. Governments of Arab countries condemned the mosque's destruction. In Britain news about Ayodhya prompted fire-bombings of Hindu temples and cultural centers, a mosque, and a Sikh gurdwara. South Asian leaders feared that white racists would use this as an opportunity for further attacks. In New York, Black Muslims protested outside the United Nations. In Dacca 20,000 people gathered to march to Ayodhya and re-build the mosque. The Bangladeshi government, however, announced that it would stop the march at the border. The international responses to the mosque's destruction indicate that the politics of Hindu nationalism is not bounded by India's territorial borders. The Bangladeshi government may be able to prohibit protesters from crossing the border and entering India, but no single government can halt transnational circulation of money and support to Hindu nationalist groups and their opponents.

Although regional, ethnic, caste, and professional identities are strong among many diasporic Indians, groups such as the VHP in America invoke Hindutva to subordinate these identities to an encompassing Hindu reli-gious and cultural identity. As in India, the Hindu nationalist movement in the United States is composed of numerous groups, some of which operate as front organizations with nothing in their name to indicate their political commitments. For example, a group calling themselves Concerned NRIs [nonresident Indians] of Southern California bought a full-page ad in the *Indian Express* six weeks after the demolition of the Babri mosque (16 Jan-uary 1993; reprinted in *India-West,* 12 February 1993). They appealed to their "brothers and sisters in India" to protest the government's ban of "na-tionalistic organizations," i.e., the VHP, RSS, and Bajrang Dal, and to work toward "restoration of common sets of values and laws based on the 6,000 year heritage." They claim that they are concerned because "of the one million NRIs living in the USA, over 900,000 call Bharat as their Mother. Hindus have only one place (other than Nepal) to call home. Their roots are in Bharat." The appeal closes with a call for "fellow citizens of Mother Bharat to Awake, for without your action Bharat and Hindus are doomed." An ad replying to this was placed by "Indian Citizens in India" which challenged the NRIs' ad and asked, "Is it not presumptuous of the Indians who left 'mother Bharat' and caused a severe brain drain to dictate how we Indians, who remained behind should run our country?" (*Indian Express,* 26 January 1993; reprinted in *India-West,* 12 February 1993).

Strategies in struggles for power involve the use of cultural media to impart specific subjectivities and sensibilities; they also involve organiza-tional secrecy and dissimulation. Strategic deception makes it difficult for researchers and the public, and perhaps even government officials, to ob-tain and accurately interpret information about the Hindu nationalist movement's covert activities and sources of support. However, the move-ment's ability to organize networks of leaders and followers at local, na-tional, and international levels is apparent. Related to this ability is the movement's use of diverse media—television and radio, audio and video cassettes, mass rallies and festivals, pilgrimage and rituals—to propagate its ideology as well as raise money and attract supporters.

The most militant members of the Hindu nationalist movement consider their ultimate goal to be the transformation of India into a Hindu nation-state. Less militant Hindu nationalists emphasize the "protection" of the interests of a dominant Hindu majority within the framework of a secular state. It is difficult to know how many Hindu nationalists fit the former description and how many the latter, since to maintain its international respectability, the movement's publicists often mask or even deny the desire for a Hindu state. They may define Hindu nationalism in cultural terms and distance it from politics. Yet the range of identities and emotions that the Hindu nationalist movement constructs and imparts remains inextricable from the ideology propagated by the militants who destroyed the Babri mosque and call for similar campaigns in Mathura and Benares. For example, the 1995 annual brochure of the VHP's Chicago branch publicizes the campaign of Hindu militants to replace mosques in Mathura and Benares (Varanasi) with Hindu temples: "National progress is directly proportionate to the people's commitment to society oriented to a superior culture. Ramjanmabhoomi—Ayodhya, Krishnajanamsthan [Krishna's birthplace]—Mathura, Kashivishwanath—Varanasi are three essential perquisites for our mutural tolerance, coexistence, patriotism and progress, symbolize our aggrandizement and definable limits in the not too distant future." Some reports maintain that two thousand mosques throughout India have been targeted for destruction. Militant Hindu nationalists use the cult of Bharat Mata and belief in the supremacy of Hindu spirituality to mobilize support and to posit a dire dilemma. They propose that Hindus must either fight for the cause of Hindu unity, which should culminate with the establishment of a Hindu nation-state, or suffer the demise, defeat, and extinction of the Hindu people.

APPENDIX 1

The Manav Utthan Seva Samiti

After several visits to the Premnagar Ashram in Hardwar, I was advised that if I had any questions about the Manav Utthan Seva Samiti (Humanity Uplift Service Society), I should submit them in writing to the office. The Samiti's head, Satpal (Guruji Maharaj), as well as his mother and his wife would answer them. The following is the text of my questions and the answers which I received in writing from ashram officials in January 1988. (So that the reader can follow its distinctive flow, I have not edited the text.)

A. QUESTIONS ASKED OF SATPAL AND ANSWERS RECEIVED

What is the form of initiation offered to disciples?

Guru Diksha is a living sacred ceremony performed when the disciple is ready to receive the Knowledge. It is not a mechanical ritual but a sacrosanct divine ceremony in which the Guru bestows the divine vision to the disciple by which he can perceive the light divine within and connect his mind stuff with the cosmic vibration called Shabad Brahm or the Word. Guru Diksha is technically called initiation and imparting the Knowledge of the universal and internal techniques of self realisation. This initiation is primarily to unite the individual self with the cosmic self. It has a great spiritual significance because it is the rebirth in spirit. This is why the initiated one is called born for the second time. There is a clear cut distinction between those who have received initiation (Guru Diksha) and others who have not received Guru Diksha. It is like the one who is born in spirit and the other without initiation who still lives in flesh and mind.

Who is authorized to initiate disciples?

Some of the sannyasis can impart the technique of initiation by the grace of Guru Maharaj Ji. Guru Maharaj is a cosmic being who lives within and without the disciple and the experience of Knowledge by the disciple is always the grace of the Guru who manifests himself in the being of the disciple. And it is only in the pure heart that this manifestation becomes possible. Transmission of energy is a very inherent part of the initiation which only the Living Perfect does. Once initiated the process of evolution in spirit and revealing of the spirit starts naturally. The sannyasis who give initiation are not the Gurus but only the dedicated disciples of the Guru and his living mediums.

Do you give ascetic (sannyas) initiation to disciples?

Naturally Guru Maharaj Ji gives sannyas to those who want to dedicate their life totally to spiritual pursuits in their life.

What is your guru parampara (spiritual lineage)?

The living current of the Knowledge is eternal and same. Every perfect being called Guru manifests it in the heart of the disciple in his own lifetime. Therefore, our Knowledge is in total accordance with Adi Shankaracharya and Shri Hans Ji Maharaj [Satpal's father]. We are only keeping alive the torch of light ablazed by them. Basis is the same, expressions may be different.

How many disciples do you have?

In India our membership runs in millions and being a growing organisation its membership is swelling everyday. We have a few thousand members in Nepal and U.S.A. also.

Do you teach any specific form of yoga?

We don't believe in Hathyoga, we believe in Sahaj Yoga which is the blending of Knowledge, Karma, and Devotion. In fact there can be no action without Knowledge and there can be no service without devotion. Action saturated with love becomes service. So our object is to train the mind and the body and to bring them in unison with Knowledge and then manifest it in act of devotion for the service of the Society.

What is the importance of sadhana and what type do you recommend?

There is no question of personally preferred form of Sadhana. Sadhana (meditation) is universal phenomena. Sadhana in fact is to transcend likes and dislikes. It is as natural as the light of the Sun and is one for all. It is the natural process which the God created for the man as he created other things to unite with Himself. Sadhana (meditation) is linking up with the original source. All modes of sadhana created by or invented by some gurus by their ingenuity are not only against the revealed scriptures of the Great Masters but also artificial and imperfect.

What is the guru's role in contemporary society?

What to talk of contemporary society? The need of the Guru, the enlightened one, is always there for every society. But for the teacher we will be groping in darkness. If in this contemporary society we require all other types of teachers then why not a spiritual master? The spiritual master is the scientist of the spirit. It is only he who can kindle and awaken the spirit in man. And what is a man without a spirit? A breathing machine. Why not to replace the contemporary man with the Robot which can perform all mechanical actions like human beings. Man without the knowledge of the spirit is more or less like a Robot. The decline in the contemporary society, the tensions and the split in the personality of modern man, the increasing rate of suicides, the general sense of unfulfillment and restlessness among the people is simply because of the lack of spiritual growth. But for the knowledge of the spirit the vacuum that is created in man's life cannot be filled by statesman howsoever shrewd, by scientists howsoever inventive, and by political philosophies howsoever progressive in its contents. Therefore, the need of the Guru in the present society is evident. Guru symbolises Knowledge, enlightenment, peace, harmony. Moreover, the present upsurge in the Western Countries for spiritual search itself shows that nothing in the world can give peace to the man but the spiritual Knowledge. Therefore, if individuals and nations want peace the spiritual Knowledge is the only way and spiritual master is the only perfect being who can reveal the Knowledge within the heart of the people. Neither the books can do it nor institutionalised religion can do it.

Please comment on the involvement of religious leaders in political affairs.

Institutionalised religions should not dabble in politics because such religions become set of dogmas and rituals which divide society more instead of uniting it. In fact these develop vested interest and have become more hungry of authority than service. We know the role of Churches in Europe in politics and also in some of the Muslim states and here also in India. But I am in favour of that the politics and the administration of the countries should be based on ethical and spiritual principles. Otherwise, we will never create a just and unexploitative society. I would say in Plato's words that either the kings should have the wisdom of a philosopher, i.e., a seer of truth, or philosophers should be made kings, if real republic based on justice and morality are to be set up. War in nations living under constant fear and tensions is not the destiny of man. Therefore, the higher values must guide our rulers. Otherwise human societies will never get rid of afflictions.

Do you have any special teachings concerning women?

As far as the status of the women is concerned in India I am against all taboos social or religious which hinder their all round development. We should have the women of Vedic time participating in all activities with man equally. But at the same time I would like that the Indian women to maintain their grace and a glow which primarily they enjoy because of their grounding in spiritual traditions and culture of India.

How are your family members involved in your work as guru?

All the members of the family are as dedicated in the propagation of the spiritual Knowledge as I am and they help me a lot in multifarious types of duties that I perform. As far as my mother is concerned she is my Guru Mata and revered, loved, and obeyed by me as Shri Hans Ji Maharaj. In fact she is an ideal picture of Indian womanhood who not only performs her household duties but also looks after the Ashrams and widely travels for addressing the congregations. She is in fact ideal living model for us who is dedicating herself to the propagation of Shri Hans Ji Maharaj's teachings.

Are you training your eldest son to carry on with your work?

Naturally I would like my son to follow in my footsteps and lead a life of service and dedication and dedicate himself to spread this Knowledge, and carry on the torch of light ablazed by my father. I am also giving them that spiritual atmosphere and inspiration too like a good father but it is not a hereditary work which falls to son automatically. The son can inherit no doubt the external (material) property of the father but he cannot inherit the spiritual grace and wisdom till he deserves it and earns it through his own living. The inspiration for spiritual propagation must come from within. It cannot be inherited or imposed on any person. Ultimately it is the flowing of one's spirit which comes to the right person. We cannot deceive or break the laws of the spirit. Finally I believe in "Thy will be done on Earth as it is in Heaven."

Would it be possible to see a copy of your annual report?

You can see our minutes of the meetings and annual reports also. Ours is a registered charitable organisation and its accounts are audited and filed with the Government. [After receiving this permission to view their records, I asked several times to see them but they were never made available.]

B. QUESTIONS ASKED OF SATPAL'S MOTHER AND ANSWERS RECEIVED

What is your relation to the disciples of Hans Ji and Satpal?

I am their Guru Mata. They call me their Holy Mother. I treat the devotees as my children. In fact I have motherly love for all.

What type of sadhana do you practice and recommend?

No question of having a personally preferred form of Sadhana. I practice and preach the same Universal Sadhana as preached by all Divine Masters like Adi Shankaracharya, Guru Nanak, and even Christ. We are all one in spirit.

Please comment on the involvement of religious leaders in political affairs.

I have no interest in politics neither is it my field but I know that through the spiritual knowledge we can create good people and only good people can become good citizen. Dharma must permeate all our activities and norms of life. I appreciate Gandhi's idea of spiritualising politics.

Do you have any special teachings concerning women?

The Indian women should not lose its true identity in the mad craze for materialism and western style of life. They should be rather model of inspiration, purity, and service within the home and outside the home.

C. THE QUESTIONS DIRECTED TO SATPAL'S WIFE, AMITRA WERE ANSWERED WITH THE FOLLOWING RESPONSE

Like a devoted wife of Shri Satpalji Maharaj and daughter-in-law of Shri Mata Ji I readily perform the duties allotted to me by them because their service is my pleasure.

A Brief Account of Hardwar

by Pandit Rajkumar Sharma

Hardwar panda, journalist, and politician Rajkumar Sharma sent this unsolicited written account to me in 1989, about one year after I had left Hardwar. I have translated the text from Hindi.

ASHRAMS OF HARDWAR

In Hardwar there are about one hundred large and small ashrams built by sadhus and their organizations. Some ashrams are run by a single individual, others by groups. Pilgrims may stay in these ashrams; there are no fixed fees. Ashrams and sadhus are very important in Hindu culture. They are regarded with faith and reverence. The atmosphere in ashrams is pure and religious. Discourses, readings, and recitations of the Vedas, Puranas, *Gita, Ramayana,* and other religious books take place in ashrams. Each ashram generally has a temple of god, a Sanskrit school, and a stable for cows. Daily worship of bhagwan and arti take place in the ashram. Religion (dharma), morality, spiritualism (adhyatmvad), fulfillment of duty, and character are propagated in ashrams. Hardwar's sadhus propagate dharma in other regions of the country and abroad.

THE GURU

From ancient times the guru has been believed to have a superior place in Hindu society. A "guru" is one who is a benefactor and who bestows well being. Pilgrims come from various parts of the country and stay without charge with purohits (brahman priests). The purohit provides for pilgrims the conveniences of bathing, water, and electricity and sees to the performance of religious rituals and pujas on their behalf. The purohit takes pilgrims around Hardwar's various places. In times of difficulty, the purohit assists with money. He gives teachings *(updesh)* about ritual acts *(karm)*. The purohit helps the pilgrim should he fall sick or have difficulties with officials. The purohit treats you as if you were his own close kin. The purohit keeps registers of the pilgrim's ancestors. The names of ancestors are written in these registers. They are called registers or tomes. When the pilgrim is ready to leave Hardwar and return home, he gives the purohit a monetary donation *(dan)*. The purohit takes it and blesses the pilgrim.

HISTORY

Hardwar is an ancient pilgrimage center *(tirtha)*. It is mentioned in the Skanda Purana, which was written about five thousand years ago. For human welfare, Raja Bhagirath brought the Ganga from the Himalayan mountains across three thousand kilometers to Ganga Sagar. Hardwar is counted among Bharat's seven main pilgrimage centers. Its ancient name is Gangadwar, or Gateway of the Ganges. The name Haridwar arises from it being the gateway for going to Hari, namely Badrinath. The population of Hardwar is about fifty thousand. It is in the Shivalik mountains. In Hardwar there are more than one hundred dharmshalas, which are guest houses for pilgrims. Some dharmshalas are run by individuals, others by groups. They have been built by wealthy people. Now Hardwar has been made a separate administrative district.

THE FREEDOM MOVEMENT

The citizens of Hardwar took a leading part in the Cow Protection Movement of 1918 and the freedom movements of 1930, 1940, and 1942. In the 1918 Cow Protection Movement nine people were imprisoned in the Andaman Islands. Two hundred people were sentenced to two to seven years. Four were hanged. Most of these were purohits. People were arrested for opposing the British in 1930, 1940, and 1942 and were sent to jail. Hardwar's citizens had a strong drive to make the country free.

CHANGES

In 1947 the country became independent. Pakistan was made and Bharat was partitioned. Thousands of Hindu refugees came to Hardwar from Pakistan. In the changed economic circumstances, improvements occurred. Cultural changes also occurred. The population increased. The Bharat Heavy Electrical factory was built with Russian assistance in 1964; it manufactures turbine engines. Fourteen thousand workers and their families came from various parts of the country to live there, and it became a separate township. About twenty-five to thirty thousand people now live there. There has been development of trade in Hardwar, and economic conditions are greatly improved. New methods are used to construct stores and buildings. Buying and selling in the bazaar has expanded. The price of property has also increased. There has been advancement in education. In Hardwar there is one gurukul university, two degree colleges, six inter colleges, and two ayurvedic colleges. There are rail, bus, and other good conveniences. In Hardwar liquor and other intoxicants are prohibited. In Hardwar and Kankhal eating meat and catching fish are prohibited by law.

BIBLIOGRAPHY

BOOKS, ARTICLES, AND PAMPHLETS

Allen, M. R. 1990. The Hindu View of Women. In *Women in India and Nepal,* ed. M. R. Allen and S. N. Mukherjee, 1–20. New Delhi: Sterling Publishers.

Alper, Harvey, ed. 1989. *Mantra.* Albany: State University of New York Press.

Amin, Shahid. 1988. Gandhi as Mahatma. In *Selected Subaltern Studies,* ed. Ranajit Guha and Gayatri Chakravorty Spivak, 288–350. New York: Oxford University Press.

Anand, Vidya Sagar. 1967. *Savarkar: A Study in the Evolution of Indian Nationalism.* London: Woolf.

Andersen, Walter. 1972. The Rashtriya Swayamsevak Sangh. *Economic and Political Weekly,* March 11, 589–97; March 18, 633–40; March 25, 673–82; April 1, 724–27.

Andersen, Walter, and Shridhar Dalme. 1987. *The Brotherhood in Saffron: The Rashtriya Swayamsevak Sangh and Hindu Revivalism.* New Delhi: Vistaar Publications.

Anderson, Benedict. 1983. *Imagined Communities: Reflections on the Origin and Spread of Nationalism.* London: Verso.

Appadurai, Arjun. 1981. *Worship and Conflict under Colonial Rule.* Cambridge: Cambridge University Press.

———. 1988. Introduction: Commodities and the Politics of Value. In *The Social Life of Things: Commodities in Cultural Perspective,* ed. Arjun Appadurai, 3–63. New York: Cambridge University Press.

Appadurai, Arjun, and Carol Breckenridge. 1976. The South Indian Temple: Authority, Honor, and Redistribution. *Contributions to Indian Sociology,* n.s. 10:187–209.

———. 1988. Why Public Culture? *Public Culture* 1:5–11.

Arendt, Hannah. 1967. *The Origins of Totalitarianism.* London: George Allen and Unwin.

Asad, Talal. 1979. Anthropology and the Analysis of Ideology. *Man,* n.s. 14:607–27.

Aurobindo (Aurobindo Ghose). 1985. Bhavani Bharati: Mother of India. *Sri Aurobindo: Archives and Research* 9:130–51.

Babb, Lawrence. 1981. Glancing: Visual Interaction in Hinduism. *Journal of Anthropological Research* 37:387–401.

———. 1987. *Redemptive Encounters: Three Modern Styles in the Hindu Tradition.* Delhi: Oxford University Press.

Bagchi, A. K. 1970. European and Indian Entrepreneurship in India 1900–1930. In *Elites in South Asia,* ed. Edmund Leach and S. N. Mukherjee. Cambridge: Cambridge University Press.

Bagchi, Jasodhara. 1985. Positivism and Nationalism: Womanhood and Crisis in Nationalist Fiction—Bankimchandra's *Anandamath. Economic and Political Weekly,* October 26, WS58–62.

Bailey, G. M. 1988. An Essay on the *Bhagavadgita* as an Impediment to Understanding Hinduism. In *Religions and Comparative Thought,* ed. Purusottama Bilimoria and Peter Fenner. Delhi: Sri Satguru Publications.

———. 1989. On the De-construction of Culture in Indian Literature: A Tentative Response to Vijay Mishra's Article. *South Asia,* n.s. 12:87–101.

Baird, Robert. 1981a. "Secular State" and the Indian Constitution. In *Religion in Modern India,* ed. Robert Baird, 389–416. New Delhi: Manohar.

———, ed. 1981b. *Religion in Modern India.* New Delhi: Manohar.

Balse, Mayah. 1976. *Mystics and Men of Miracles in India.* New Delhi: Heritage Publishers.

Barthes, Roland. 1973. *Mythologies.* Trans. Annette Lavers. London: Paladin.

Basu, Tapan, Pradip Datta, Sumit Sarkar, Tanika Sarkar, and Sambuddha Sen. 1993. *Khaki Shorts and Saffron Flags: A Critique of the Hindu Right.* New Delhi: Orient Longman.

Baxter, Craig. 1969. *The Jana Sangh: A Biography of an Indian Political Party.* Philadelphia: University of Pennsylvania Press.

Bayly, C. A. 1973. Patrons and Politics in Northern India. In *Locality, Province, Nation: Essays on Indian Politics,* ed. John Gallagher, Gordon Johnson, and Anil Seal, 20–68. Cambridge: Cambridge University Press.

———. 1985. The Pre-history of "Communalism": Religious Conflict in India, 1700–1860. *Modern Asian Studies* 19:177–203.

———. 1988. The Origins of Swadeshi (Home Industry): Cloth and Indian Society, 1700–1930. In *The Social Life of Things,* ed. Arjun Appadurai, 285–322. New York: Cambridge University Press.

Beane, Wendell Charles. 1977. *Myth, Cult, and Symbols in Sakta Hinduism.* Leiden: E. J. Brill.

Bharati, Agehananda. 1963. Pilgrimage in the Indian Tradition. *History of Religions* 3:135–67.

———. 1970. The Hindu Renaissance and its Apologetic Patterns. *Journal of Asian Studies* 2:267–88.

Bhardwaj, Surinder Mohan. 1973. *Hindu Places of Pilgrimage in India.* Berkeley: University of California Press.

Bourdieu, Pierre. 1984. *Distinction: A Social Critique of the Judgment of Taste.* Trans. Richard Nice. Cambridge: Harvard University Press.

Bradford, N. J. 1985. The Indian Renouncer: Structure and Transformation in the

Lingayat Community. In *Indian Religion,* ed. Richard Burghart and Audrey Cantlie, 79–104. London: Curzon Press.

Brass, Paul. 1974. *Language, Religion, and Politics in North India.* Cambridge: Cambridge University Press.

———. 1990. *The Politics of India since Independence.* Cambridge: Cambridge University Press.

Breckenridge, Carol, and Arjun Appadurai. 1988. Editors' Comments. *Public Culture* 1:1–4.

Brent, Peter. 1973. *Godmen of India.* Harmondsworth: Penguin Books.

Brooks, Charles. 1989. *The Hare Krishnas in India.* Princeton: Princeton University Press.

Burghart, Richard. 1978a. The Disappearance and Reappearance of Janakpur. *Kailash* 6:257–84.

———. 1987b. Hierarchical Models of the Hindu Social System. *Man,* n.s. 13:519–36.

———. 1983a. For a Sociology of Indias: An Intracultural Approach to the Study of "Hindu Society." *Contributions to Indian Sociology,* n.s. 17:275–99.

———. 1983b. Renunciation in the Religious Traditions of South Asia. *Man,* n.s. 18:635–53.

———. 1983c. Wandering Ascetics of the Ramanandi Sect. *History of Religions* 22:361–80.

———. 1985. Introduction: Theoretical Approaches in the Anthropology of South Asia. In *Indian Religion,* ed. Richard Burghart and Audrey Cantlie, 1–14. London: Curzon Press.

Cameron, Charles. 1973. *Who is Guru Maharaj Ji?* New York: Bantam Books.

Cantlie, Audrey. 1985. Vaisnava Reform Sects in Assam. In *Indian Religion,* ed. Richard Burghart and Audrey Cantlie, 135–59. London: Curzon Press.

Caplan, Patricia. 1973. Ascetics in Western Nepal. *Eastern Anthropologist* 26:173–82.

Carrithers, Michael. 1979. The Modern Ascetics of Lanka and the Pattern of Change in Buddhism. *Man,* n.s. 14:294–310.

———. 1989. Naked Ascetics in Southern Digambar Jainism. *Man,* n.s. 24:219–35.

Carroll, Lucy. 1976. The Temperance Movement in India: Politics and Social Reform. *Modern Asian Studies* 10:417–47.

Caycedo, Alfonso. 1966. *India of Yogis.* Delhi: National Publishing House.

Cendrars, Blaise. 1979. *Moravagine.* Trans. Alan Brown. Harmondsworth: Penguin.

Cenkner, William. 1983. *A Tradition of Teachers: Sankara and the Jagadgurus Today.* Delhi: Motilal Banarsidass.

Chakrabarty, Dipesh. 1988. Conditions for Knowledge of Working Class Conditions. In *Selected Subaltern Studies,* ed. Ranajit Guha and Gayatri Chakravorty Spivak, 179–232. Delhi: Oxford University Press.

———. 1989. *Rethinking Working-class History: Bengal, 1890–1940.* Princeton: Princeton University Press.

Chakravarti, Uma. 1990. Whatever Happened to the Vedic *Dasi?* Orientalism, Nationalism and a Script for the Past. In *Recasting Women: Essays in Indian Colo-*

nial History, ed. Kumkum Sangari and Sudesh Vaid, 27–88. New Brunswick: Rutgers University Press.

Chandra, Bipin. 1981. *Nationalism and Colonialism in Modern India.* New Delhi: Orient Longman.

Chatterjee, Partha. 1986. *Nationalist Thought and the Colonial World: A Derivative Discourse.* London: Zed Press.

———. 1990. The Nationalist Resolution of the Women's Question. In *Recasting Women: Essays in Indian Colonial History,* ed. Kumkum Sangari and Sudesh Vaid, 233–53. New Brunswick: Rutgers University Press.

Chatterji, Bankim Chandra. 1992 [1882; 1941]. *Anandamath.* Trans. Basanta Koomar Roy. New Delhi: Vision Books.

Chaturvedi, Krishnakant, and Brahmajeet Sharma. 1986. *Divyalok: Parivrajak Ki Divya Yatra* [Heaven: The Divine Piligrimage of an Ascetic]. Hardwar: Samanvaya Prakashan.

Chaubey, B. B. 1976. The Nature of Guruship According to Hindu Scriptures. In *The Nature of Guruship,* ed. Clarence McMullen. Delhi: Christian Institute for Sikh Studies.

Chaudhuri, Buddhadeb. 1981. *The Bakreshwar Temple.* Delhi: Inter-India Publications.

Chidananda. 1987. In Retrospection. *Voice of Sivananda* 16:27–31.

Coburn, Thomas. 1986. Consort of None, *Śaktī* of All: The Vision of the *Devi Māhātmyā.* In *The Divine Consort: Radha and the Goddesses of India,* ed. John Hawley and Donna Wulff, 153–65. Boston: Beacon Press.

Cohn, B. S. 1974. The Role of Gosains in the Economy of Eighteenth and Nineteenth Century Upper India. *Journal of Social Research* 17:88–95.

Corbridge, Stuart. 1988. The Ideology of Tribal Economy and Society: Politics in the Jharkhand, 1950–1980. *Modern Asian Studies* 22:1–42.

Courtright, Paul. 1988. The Ganesh Festival in Maharashtra. In *The Experience of Hinduism: Essays on Religion in Maharashtra,* ed. Eleanor Zelliot and Maxine Berntsen, 76–94. Albany: State University of New York Press.

Coward, Harold. ed. 1987. *Modern Indian Responses to Religious Pluralism.* Albany: State University of New York Press.

Curran, J. A. 1951. *Militant Hinduism in Indian Politics: A Study of the R.S.S.* New York: Institute of Pacific Relations.

Dalton, Dennis. 1986. The Ideology of Sarvodaya: Concepts of Politics and Power in Indian Political Thought. In *Modern Indian Political Thought,* ed. Thomas Pantham and Kenneth Deutsch, 275–96. New Delhi: Sage Publications.

Darian, Steven. 1978. *The Ganges in Myth and History.* Honolulu: University of Hawaii Press.

Das, Veena. 1976. The Uses of Liminality: Society and Cosmos in Hinduism. *Contributions to Indian Sociology,* n.s. 10:245–63.

———. 1988. Shakti versus Sati: A Reading of the Santoshi Ma Cult. *Manushi* 49:26–30.

Derrett, J. Duncan. 1976. Rajadharma. *Journal of Asian Studies* 35:597–609.

Divine Life Society. 1986. *Annual Report and Balance Sheet of the Divine Life Society, 1986.* Shivanandanagar: Divine Life Society.

———. 1987. *The Master, His Mission, and His Works: Swami Sivananda Birth Centenary Volume.* Shivanandanagar: Divine Life Society.

———. N.d. *Sri Swami Sivananda Centenary Celebrations: A Report.* Shivanandanagar: Divine Life Society.

Dixit, Prabha. 1986. The Ideology of Hindu Nationalism. In *Political Thought in Modern India,* ed. Thomas Pantham and Kenneth Deutsch, 122–41. New Delhi: Sage Publications.

Dube, S. C, and V. N. Basilov, eds. 1983. *Secularization in Multi-religious Societies.* New Delhi: Concept Publishing Company.

Dumont, Louis. 1960. World Renunciation in Indian Religions. *Contributions to Indian Sociology* 4:33–62.

———. 1964. Nationalism and Communalism. *Contributions to Indian Sociology* 7:30–70.

———. 1970. *Homo Hierarchicus.* Trans. Mark Sainsbury. London: Paladin.

Eck, Diana. 1981. India's Tirthas: Crossings in Sacred Geography. *History of Religions* 22:323–44.

———. 1982. *Banaras, City of Light.* New York: Alfred A. Knopf.

Ekatm Saptahik. 1983. Bharat Mata Mandir Special Issue. *Ekatm Saptahik* 14 (April 28).

Elias, Norbert. 1978. *The Civilizing Process.* Trans. Edmund Jephcott. New York: Urizen Books.

Erdman, Howard. 1967. *The Swatantra Party and Indian Conservatism.* Cambridge: Cambridge University Press.

Eschmann, A., H. Kulke, and G. C. Tripathi, eds. 1978. *The Cult of Jagannatha and the Regional Tradition of Orissa.* New Delhi: Manohar.

Farquhar, J. N. 1967 [1915]. *Modern Religious Movements in India.* Delhi: Munshiram Manoharlal.

Fornaro, Robert. 1969. Sivananda and the Divine Life Society: A Paradigm of the "Secularism," "Puritanism," and "Cultural Dissimulation" of a Neo-Hindu Religious Society. Ph.D. diss., Syracuse University.

Foster, Robert J. 1991. Making National Culture in the Global Ecumene. *Annual Review of Anthropology* 20:235–60.

Fox, Richard G. 1987. Gandhian Socialism and Hindu Nationalism: Cultural Domination in the World System. *Journal of Commonwealth and Comparative Politics* 25:233–47.

———. 1989. *Gandhian Utopia: Experiments with Culture.* Boston: Beacon Press.

———. 1990a. Introduction. In *Nationalist Ideologies and the Production of National Cultures,* ed. Richard G. Fox, 1–14. Washington, D.C.: American Ethnological Society.

———. 1990b. Hindu Nationalism in the Making, or the Rise of the Hindian. In *Nationalist Ideologies and the Production of National Cultures,* ed. Richard G. Fox, 63–80. Washington, D.C.: American Ethnological Society.

Freitag, Sandra. 1980. Sacred Symbol as Mobilization Ideology: The North Indian Search for a "Hindu Community." *Comparative Studies of Society and History* 22:597–625.

Frykenberg, Robert. 1987. The Concept of "Majority" as a Devilish Force in the

Politics of Modern India. *Journal of Commonwealth and Comparative Politics* 25:267–74.

Fuller, C. J. 1984. *Servants of the Goddess: The priests of a South Indian Temple.* Cambridge: Cambridge University Press.

Gell, Alfred. 1988. Newcomers to the World of Goods: Consumption among the Muria Gonds. In *The Social Life of Things,* ed. Arjun Appadurai, 110–40. New York: Cambridge University Press.

Ghosh, Suniti Kumar. 1988. Indian Bourgeoisie and Imperialism. *Economic and Political Weekly,* November, 2445–57.

Ghurye, G. S. 1961. *Caste, Class, and Occupation.* Bombay: Popular Book Depot.

———. 1964. *Indian Sadhus.* Bombay: Popular Book Prakashan.

———. 1973. *I and Other Explorations.* Bombay: Popular Prakashan.

———. 1974. *Whither India?* Bombay: Popular Prakashan.

Gold, Daniel. 1987. *The Lord as Guru: Hindi Sants in the Northern Indian Tradition.* New York: Oxford University Press.

Gold, Ann Grodzins. 1988. *Fruitful Journeys: The Ways of Rajasthani Pilgrims.* Berkeley: University of California Press.

Gold, Daniel, and Ann Grodzins Gold. 1984. The Fate of the Householder Nath. *History of Religions* 24:113–32.

Gopal, Sarvepalli. 1989. *Radhakrishnan: A Biography.* London: Unwin Hyman.

Gordon, Richard. 1975. The Hindu Mahasabha and the Indian National Congress, 1915 to 1926. *Modern Asian Studies* 9:145–203.

Gordon, Stewart. 1971. Comment. *Indian Economic and Social History Review* 8:219–20.

Goswamy, B. N. 1966. The Records Kept by Priests at Centres of Pilgrimage as a Source of Social and Economic History. *Economic and Social History Review* 3:174–85.

Government of India, Department of Tourism. 1987. *Haridwar, Rishikesh, Mussoorie, Dehra Dun.* New Delhi: Government of India, Department of Tourism.

Graham, B. D. 1987. The Jana Sangh and Bloc Politics, 1967–1980. *Journal of Commonwealth and Comparative Politics* 25:248–66.

Guha, Ranajit. 1988a. Preface. In *Selected Subaltern Studies,* ed. Ranajit Guha and Gayatri Chakravorty Spivak, 35–36. New York: Oxford University Press.

———. 1988b. On Some Aspects of the Historiography of Colonial India. In *Selected Subaltern Studies,* ed. Ranajit Guha and Gayatri Chakravorty Spivak, 37–45. New York: Oxford University Press.

———. 1988c. The Prose of Counter-insurgency. In *Selected Subaltern Studies,* ed. Ranajit Guha and Gayatri Chakravorty Spivak, 45–86. New York: Oxford University Press.

Gupta, Chitra. 1939. Revised and brought up to date by Indra Prakash. *Life of Barrister Savarkar.* New Delhi: The Hindu Pushtak Bhandar.

Hall, Stuart. 1974. Deviance, Politics, and the Media. In *Deviance and Social Control,* ed. Paul Rock and Mary McIntosh. London: Tavistock Publications.

———. 1977. Culture, the Media, and the Ideological Effect. In *Mass Communication and Society,* ed. James Curran, Michael Gurevitch, and Janet Wollacott. London: Edward Arnold.

Hara, Minoru. 1967. Transfer of Merit. *Adyar Library Bulletin* 31/32:382–411.

———.1970. Tapo-dhana. *Acta Asiatica* 19:58–76.

Harpham, Geoffrey. 1987. *The Ascetic Imperative in Culture and Criticism*. Chicago: University of Chicago Press.

Haug, W. F. 1986. *Critique of Commodity Aesthetics*. Trans. Robert Bock. Minneapolis: University of Minnesota Press.

———. 1987. *Commodity Aesthetics, Ideology, and Culture*. New York: International General.

Hawley, John Stratton. 1994. Hinduism: Sati and Its Defenders. In *Fundamentalism and Gender*, ed. John Stratton Hawley, 79–110. New York: Oxford University Press.

Hawley, John Stratton, ed. 1994. *Sati, the Blessing and the Curse: The Burning of Wives in India*. New York: Oxford University Press.

Heesterman, J. C. 1959. Reflections on the Significance of the Daksina. *Indo-Iranian Journal* 4:241–58.

———. 1962. Vratya and Sacrifice. *Indo-Iranian Journal* 6:1–37.

———. 1985. *The Inner Conflict of Tradition: Essays in Indian Ritual, Kingship, and Society*. Chicago: University of Chicago Press.

Hoens, D. J. 1979. The Movements of Hams Ji Maharaj and of Chinmayananda as Processes of Change in Hinduism. *Religion and Society* 19:462–86.

Hubert, Henri, and Marcel Mauss. 1964 [1898]. *Sacrifice: Its Nature and Function*. Trans. W. D. Halls. Chicago: University of Chicago Press.

Hutheesing, Krishna Nehru, ed. 1963. *Nehru's Letters to his Sister*. London: Faber and Faber.

Inden, Ronald. 1985. Lordship and Caste in Hindu Discourse. In *Indian Religion*, ed. Richard Burghart and Audrey Cantlie, 159–79. London: Curzon Press.

———. 1986. Orientalist Constructions of India. *Modern Asian Studies* 20:401–46.

———. 1990. *Imagining India*. Oxford: Basil Blackwell.

Ivy, Marilyn. 1988. Critical Texts, Mass Artifacts: The Consumption of Knowledge in Postmodern Japan. *South Atlantic Quarterly* 87:419–44.

Jaffrelot. Christophe. 1993. *Les Nationalistes Hindous: Idéologie, implantation et mobilisation des années 1920 aux années 1990*. Paris: Presses de la Fondation Nationale des Sciences Politiques.

Jameson, A. S. 1976. Gangaguru: The Public and Private Life of a Brahman Community of North India. Ph.D. diss., Oxford University.

Jha, Akhileshwar. 1980. *The Imprisoned Mind*. New Delhi: Ambika Publishers.

Jha, Makhan. 1971. *The Sacred Complex in Janakpur*. Allahabad: United Publishers.

———, ed. 1985. *Dimensions of Pilgrimage*. New Delhi: Inter-India Publications.

Jhangiani, Motilal. 1967. *Jana Sangh and Swatantra: A Profile of the Rightist Parties in India*. Bombay: Manaktalas.

Jindel, Rajendra. 1976. *Culture of a Sacred Town: A Sociological Study of Nathdwara*. Bombay: Popular Prakashan.

Johnson, David. 1981. Religious Change, National Goals, and the Janata Party. In *Religion in Modern India*, ed. Robert Baird, 481–97. New Delhi: Manohar.

Jones, Kenneth. 1976. *Arya Dharm: Hindu Consciousness in Nineteenth Century Punjab.* Berkeley: University of California Press.

———. 1981a. The Arya Samaj in British India, 1875–1947. In *Religion in Modern India,* ed. Robert Baird, 27–54. New Delhi: Manohar.

———. 1981b. Politicized Hinduism: The Ideology and Program of the Hindu Mahasabha. In *Religion in Modern India,* ed. Robert Baird, 447–80. New Delhi: Manohar.

Jordens, J. F. 1978. *Dayananda Saraswati: His Life and Times.* Delhi: Oxford University Press.

Kaelber, Walter. 1989. *Tapta Marga: Asceticism and Initiation in Vedic India.* Albany: State University of New York Press.

Kakar, Sudhir. 1978. *The Inner World: A Psycho-analytic Study of Childhood and Society in India.* Delhi: Oxford University Press.

———. 1982. *Shamans, Mystics, and Doctors.* Boston: Beacon Press.

———. 1985. Psychoanalysis and Religious Healing: Siblings or Strangers? *Journal of the American Academy of Religion* 53:841–53.

———. 1992. "When Saffron Speaks." *The Sunday Times of India,* 19 July.

Kane, P. V. 1953. *History of the Dharmashastra.* Poona: Bhandarkar Oriental Research Institute.

Kapferer, Bruce. 1988. *Legends of People, Myths of State: Violence, Intolerance, and Political Culture in Sri Lanka and Australia.* Washington, D.C.: Smithsonian Institution Press.

Kaviraj, Sudipta. 1988. A Critique of the Passive Revolution. *Economic and Political Weekly,* November, 2429–44.

Keer, Dhananjay. 1966. *Veer Savarkar.* Bombay: Popular Prakashan.

Kelly, John. 1991. *A Politics of Virtue: Hinduism, Sexuality, and Countercolonial Discourse in Fiji.* Chicago: University of Chicago Press.

Khanna. Sushil. 1987. The New Business Class, Ideology and State: The Making of a New Consensus. *South Asia* 10:47–60.

Khare, R. S. 1970. *The Changing Brahmans: Associations and Elites Among the Kanya Kubjas of North India.* Chicago: University of Chicago Press.

King, Ursula. 1984. The Effect of Social Change on Religious Self-understanding: Women Ascetics in Modern Hinduism. In *Changing South Asia: Religion and Society,* ed. K. Ballhatchet and D. Taylor, 69–83. London: School of Oriental and African Studies.

Kolff, D. H. A. 1971. Sannyasi Trader-Soldiers. *Indian Economic and Social History Review* 8:213–20.

Kopf, David. 1974. The Missionary Challenge and Brahmo Response: Rajnarain Bose and the Emerging Ideology of Cultural Nationalism. *Contributions to Indian Sociology,* n.s., 8:12–23.

Kothari, Rajni. 1988. Class and Communalism in India. *Economic and Political Weekly,* December 3, 2589–92.

Kovoor, Abraham. 1976. *Begone Godmen! Encounters with Spiritual Frauds.* Bombay: Jaico.

Lal, Ratan. 1975. Sri Sathya Sai Baba. In *Gurus, Godmen, and Good People,* ed. Khushwant Singh, 1–6. New Delhi: Orient Longman.

Lipski, A. 1969. Some Aspects of the Life and Teachings of the East Bengal Saint Anandamayi Ma. *History of Religions* 9:59–77.

Lochtefeld, James G. 1992. Haridwara, Haradwara, Gangadwara: The Construction of Identity and Meaning in a Hindu Pilgrimage Place. Ph.D. diss., Columbia University.

Lorenzen, D. N. 1978. Warrior Ascetics in Indian History. *Journal of the American Oriental Society* 98:61–75.

Madan, T. N., ed. 1982. *Way of Life: King, Householder, Renouncer*. Delhi: Vikas Press.

———. 1983. The Historical Significance of Secularism in India. In *Secularization in Multi-religious Societies*, ed. S. C. Dube and V. N. Basilov, 11–20. New Delhi: Concept Publishing Company.

———. 1987a. Secularism in its Place. *Journal of Asian Studies* 46:747–59.

———. 1987b. *Non-renunciation: Themes and Interpretations of Hindu Culture*. Delhi: Oxford University Press.

Malik, Yogendra, and Dhirendra Vajpeyi. 1989. The Rise of Hindu Militancy: India's Secular Democracy at Risk. *Asia Survey* 29:308–25.

Mangalwadi, Vishal. 1977. *The World of Gurus*. Delhi: Vikas Press.

Mani, Lata. 1986. Production of an Official Discourse on Sati in Early Nineteenth Century Bengal. *Economic and Political Weekly*, April 25, WS:32–40.

———. 1990. Contentious Traditions: The Debate on *Sati* in Colonial India. In *Recasting Women: Essays in Indian Colonial History*, ed. Kumkum Sangari and Sudesh Vaid, 88–127. New Brunswick: Rutgers University Press.

Marcus, George, and Michael Fischer. 1986. *Anthropology as Cultural Critique*. Chicago: University of Chicago Press.

Marx, Karl. 1987 [1867]. *Capital*, vol. 1. Trans. Samuel Moore and Edward Aveling. New York: International Publishers.

Matthew, George. 1982. Politicisation of Religion: Conversions to Islam in Tamil Nadu. *Economic and Political Weekly*, June 19, 1027–33; June 26, 1068–72.

Mauss, Marcel. 1954 [1925]. *The Gift: Forms and Functions of Exchange in Archaic Societies*. Trans. I. Cunnison. London: Cohen and West.

McKean, Lise. 1994. The Transnational Context of Communalism: The 1993 Chicago Parliament of the World's Religions and Hindu Nationalism. Presented at the South Asia Regional Studies Seminar, University of Pennsylvania, January 1994.

Miller, David. 1981. The Divine Life Society Movement. In *Religion in Modern India*, ed. Robert Baird, 81–112. New Delhi: Manohar.

———. 1986. Swami Sivananda and the *Bhagavad Gita*. In *Modern Interpreters of the Bhagavad Gita*, ed. Robert Minor, 173–99. Albany: State University of New York Press.

Miller, David, and Dorothy Wertz. 1976. *Hindu Monastic Life: Monks and Monasteries of Bhubaneswar*. Montreal: McGill-Queen's University Press.

Mines, Mattison, and Vijaylakshmi Gaurishankar. 1990. Leadership and Individuality in South Asia: The Case of the South Indian Big-man. *Journal of Asian Studies* 49:761–86.

Minor, Robert. 1981a. Sri Aurobindo and his Experience: Yogic and Otherwise. In

Religion in Modern India, ed. Robert Baird, 277–304. New Delhi: Manohar.
————. 1981b. Sarvepalli Radhakrishnan and "Hinduism": Defined and Defended. In *Religion in Modern India*, ed. Robert Baird, 305–38. New Delhi: Manohar.
————, ed. 1986. *Modern Interpreters of the Bhagavad Gita*. Albany: State University of New York Press.
Morinis, E. A. 1984. *Pilgrimage in Hindu Tradition: A Case Study of West Bengal*. Delhi: Oxford University Press.
Murray, M. 1980. *Seeking the Master: A Guide to the Ashrams of India*. Jersey, U.K.: Neville Spearman.
Mujahid, Abdul Malik. 1989. *Conversion to Islam: Untouchables' Strategy for Protest in India*. Chambersburg, Penn.: Anima Publications.
Nandy, Ashis. 1980. *At the Edge of Psychology: Essays in Politics and Culture*. Delhi: Oxford University Press.
————. 1983. *The Intimate Enemy: Loss and Recovery of Self under Colonialism*. Delhi: Oxford University Press.
————. 1985. An Anti-secular Manifesto. *Seminar* 314:14–24.
Narayan, Kirin. 1989. *Storytellers, Saints, and Scoundrels: Folk Narrative in Hindu Religious Teaching*. Philadelphia: University of Pennsylvania Press.
Narayananda, trans. 1972. *Sri Guru Gita*. Shivanandanagar: Divine Life Society.
Negi, J. S. 1976. The Nature of Guruship: A Psychological Perspective. In *The Nature of Guruship*, ed. Clarence McMullen. Delhi: Christain Instutute for Sikh Studies.
Nehru, Jawaharlal. 1989 [1946]. *The Discovery of India*. Delhi: Oxford University Press.
————. 1958. Jahwaharlal Nehru: Democratic Socialist. In *Sources of Indian Tradition*, vol. 2, comp. Stephen Hay and I. H. Qureshi, 341–53. New York: Columbia University Press.
Obeyesekere, Gananath. 1970. Religious Symbolism and Political Change in Ceylon. *Modern Ceylon Studies* 1:46–47.
————. 1981. *Medusa's Hair*. Berkeley: University of California Press.
O'Hanlon, Rosalind. 1988. Recovering the Subject: Subaltern Studies and Histories of Resistance in Colonial South Asia. *Modern Asian Studies* 22:189–224.
Ojha, Catherine. 1981. Feminine Asceticism in Hinduism: Its Tradition and Present Condition. *Man in India* 61:254–86.
Oman, John Campbell. 1903. *The Mystics, Ascetics, and Saints of India*. London: T. Fisher Unwin.
Packard, Vance. 1975 [1957]. *The Hidden Persuaders*. Harmondsworth: Penguin.
Panandiker, V. A. Pai. 1987. India's Middle Class Power. *Hindustan Times*, July 25.
Pandey, Gyanendra. 1975. Mobilization in a Mass Movement: Congress "Propaganda" in the United Provinces (India), 1930–1934. *Modern Asian Studies* 9:205–26.
————. 1983. Rallying Round the Cow: Sectarian Strife in the Bhojpuri Region c. 1888–1917. In *Subaltern Studies 2*, ed. Ranajit Guha. Delhi: Oxford University Press.

————. 1988. Peasant Revolt and Indian Nationalism. In *Selected Subaltern Studies,* ed. Ranajit Guha and Gayatri Chakravorty Spivak, 233–88. New York: Oxford University Press.

Pandya, Pranav. N.d. *A Unique Heritage of Himalayan Hermits of Shantikunj.* Gayatri Parivar booklet. Hardwar: Yugantar Chetna Press.

Pantham, Thomas, and Kenneth Deutsch, eds. 1986. *Political Thought in Modern India.* New Delhi: Sage Publications.

Parekh, Bhikhu. 1989. *Colonialism, Tradition, and Reform: An Analysis of Gandhi's Political Discourse.* New Delhi: Sage Publications.

Parihar, Balram Singh. N.d. *Shantikunj and its Man-making Odyssey.* Gayatri Parivar booklet. Hardwar: Yugantar Chetna Press.

Parry, Jonathan. 1980. Ghosts, Greed, and Sin: The Occupational Identity of the Benares Funeral Priests. *Man,* n.s. 15:88–111.

————. 1982. Sacrificial Death and the Necrophagous Ascetic. In *Death and the Regeneration of Life,* ed. Maurice Bloch and Jonathan Parry, 74–110. Cambridge: Cambridge University Press.

————. 1986. The Gift, the Indian Gift, and the "Indian gift." *Man,* n.s. 21:453–73.

————. 1989. On the Moral Perils of Exchange. In *Money and the Morality of Exchange,* ed. Jonathan Parry and Maurice Bloch, 64–93. Cambridge: Cambridge University Press.

Patchen, Nancy. 1989. *The Journey of a Master: Swami Chinmayananda.* Berkeley: Asian Humanities Press.

Pillai, R. C. 1986. The Political Thought of Jawaharlal Nehru. In *Political Thought in Modern India,* ed. Thomas Pantham and Kenneth Deutsch, 260–74. New Delhi: Sage Publications.

Pollock, Sheldon. 1990. From Discourse of Ritual to Discourse of Power in Sanskrit Culture. *Journal of Ritual Studies* 4:315–45.

Prakash, Gyan. 1986. Reproducing Inequality: Spirit Cults and Labor Relations in Colonial Eastern India. *Modern Asian Studies* 20:209–30.

Price, Pamela. 1989. Ideology and Ethnicity under British Imperial Rule: "Brahmans," Lawyers, and Kin-caste Rules in Madras Presidency. *Modern Asian Studies* 23:151–77.

Radhakrishnan, Sarvepalli. 1970 [1937]. Introduction. In *The Cultural Heritage of India,* vol. 1. Calcutta: The Ramakrishna Mission Institute of Culture.

————. 1944. *Education, Politics, and War.* Poona: The International Book Service.

Ramanujan, A. K. 1986. On Women Saints. In *The Divine Consort: Radha and the Goddesses of India,* ed. John Hawley and Donna Wulff, 316–24. Boston: Beacon Press.

Rao, Shridhar (Chidananda). 1988. *Tapasvi Swami Sivananda.* Shivanandanagar: Divine Life Society.

Ratte, Lou. 1985. Goddesses, Mothers, and Heroines: Hindu Women and the Feminine in the Early Nationalist Movement. In *Women, Religion, and Social Change,* ed. Yvonne Haddad, 351–76. Albany: State University of New York Press.

Rawal, Ashok. 1981. *New Age Force: Gayatri*. Bombay: Bharatiya Vidya Bhavan.

Raychaudhuri, Tapan. 1988. *Europe Reconsidered: Perceptions of the West in Nineteenth Century Bengal*. New York: Oxford University Press.

Robb, Peter. 1986. The Challenge of Gau Mata: British Policy and Religious Change in India, 1880–1916. *Modern Asian Studies* 20:285–319.

Roy, Basanta Koomar. 1992 [1941]. Translator's Introduction. In *Anandamath*, by Bankim Chandra Chatterji, trans. Basanta Koomar Roy, 13–20. New Delhi: Vision Books.

Roy, Dilip Kumar, and Indira Devi. 1955. *Kumbh: India's Ageless Festival*. Bombay: Bharatiya Vidya Bhavan.

Rudolph, Lloyd I., and Susanne Hoeber Rudolph. 1983. Oligopolistic Competition Among State Elites in Princely India. In *Elites: Ethnographic Issues,* ed. George Marcus, 193–220. Albuquerque: University of New Mexico Press.

———. 1987. *In Pursuit of Lakshmi: The Political Economy of the Indian State*. Chicago: University of Chicago Press.

Saha, Suranjit. 1986. Historical Premises of India's Tribal Problem. *Journal of Contemporary Asia* 16:274–319.

Said, Edward. 1978. *Orientalism*. New York: Vintage.

———. 1985. Orientalism Reconsidered. *Cultural Critique* 1:89–107.

Samanvaya Sewa Trust. 1986. *Bharat Mata Mandir: A Candid Appraisal*. Hardwar: Samanvaya Publications.

Sangari, Kumkum, and Sudesh Vaid. 1990. Recasting Women: An Introduction. In *Recasting Women: Essays in Indian Colonial History,* ed. Kumkum Sangari and Sudesh Vaid, 1–26. New Brunswick: Rutgers University Press.

Sangren, P. Steven. 1988. Rhetoric and the Authority of Ethnography. *Current Anthropology* 29:405–35.

Sanskaran, Triteya. 1981. *An English-Hindi Dictionary*. New Delhi: S. Chand.

Saraswati, Baidyanath. 1972. Sacred Complexes in Indian Cultural Traditions. *Eastern Anthropologist* 31:81–92.

———. 1975. *Kashi: Myth and Reality of a Classical Tradition*. Simla: Institute of Advanced Study.

Saraswati, Satyananda. 1984. *Light on the Guru and Disciple Relationship*. Munger, Bihar: Bihar School of Yoga.

Satchidananda Ashram-Yogaville. 1987. *Integral Yoga* 18: Special Sri Swami Sivananda Centenary Issue.

Satyamitranand. 1986. *Bharat Mata Mandir: Ek Satvik Abhivyakti*. Hardwar: Samanvaya Prakashan.

———. 1987. *Sadhana*. Hardwar: Samanvaya Publications.

Savarkar, Vinayak Damodar. 1925. *Hindu Pad-padashahi* [Hindudom and Hindu Kingship]. Madras: B. G. Paul.

———. 1949. *Hindu Rashtra Darshan: A Collection of Presidential Speeches Delivered from the Hindu Mahasabha Platform, 1938–1941*. Bombay: Khare.

———. 1964. *Samagra Savarkar Wangmaya: Writings of Swatantrya Veer V. D. Savarkar,* vol. 6. Poona: Maharashtra Prantik Hindusabha.

———. 1967. *Historic Statements*. Ed. S. S. Savarkar and G. M. Joshi. Bombay: Popular Prakashan.

———. 1970 [1908]. *The Indian War of Independence, 1857*. New Delhi: Rajdhani Granthnagar.

———. 1985. *Six Glorious Epochs of Indian History*. Trans. and ed. S. T. Godbole. Bombay: Veer Savarkar Prakashan.

———. 1984 [1949]. *My Transportation for Life*. Trans. V. N. Naik. Bombay: Veer Savarkar Prakashan.

———. 1984. *Echoes from Andaman*. Bombay: Veer Savarkar Praksahan.

———. N.d. *Hindudhwaj: Public Statements of the President of the Hindu Mahasabha, 1938–1941*. N.p.

Saxena, Poonam. 1988. Women's Participation in the Nationalist Movement in the United Provinces, 1937–1947. *Manushi* 46:2–10.

Scholte, Bob. 1987. The Literary Turn in Contemporary Anthropology. *Critique of Anthropology* 7:33–47.

Schomer, Karine, and W. H. McLeod. eds. *The Sants: Studies in a Devotional Tradition of India*. Delhi: Motilal Banarsidass.

Seal, Anil. 1968. *The Emergence of Indian Nationalism: Competition and Collaboration in the Later Nineteenth Century*. Cambridge, Cambridge University Press.

Sharma, Jagdish Saran, ed. 1964. *India's Struggle for Freedom*. New Delhi: S. Chand.

Sharma, Bhagwati Devi. N.d. *Divine Culture Shall Expand, Not Remain Confined*. Trans. J. C. Pant. Gayatri Parivar booklet. Hardwar: Yugantar Chetna Press.

———. N.d. *Tested Experiments of Fruitful Gayatri Sadhana*. Trans. J. C. Pant. Gayatri Parivar booklet. Hardwar: Yugantar Chetna Press.

Sharma, N. K. 1976. *Linguistic and Educational Aspirations under a Colonial System: A Study of Sanskrit Education during British Rule in India*. New Delhi: Concept Publishing Company.

Sharma, Ram. N.d. *Basic Concepts of Material Achievements*. Trans. S. N. Pandya. Gayatri Parivar booklet. Hardwar: Yugantar Chetna Press.

———. N.d. *Deeds of Someone, Credit to Someone Else*. Trans. S. N. Pandya. Gayatri Parivar booklet. Hardwar: Yugantar Chetna Press.

———. N.d. *Let Spiritual Science Also Flourish*. Trans. S. N. Pandya. Gayatri Parivar booklet. Hardwar: Yugantar Chetna Press.

———. N.d. *Make God Your Partner in Daily Life*. Trans. S. N. Pandya. Gayatri Parivar booklet. Hardwar: Yugantar Chetna Press.

———. N.d. *Spiritual Training of Life Deity*. Trans. S. N. Pandya. Gayatri Parivar booklet. Hardwar: Yugantar Chetna Press.

Sharma, Shankar Dayal. 1989. Secularism in the Indian Ethos. *India Perspectives*, August, 4–9.

Shraddhananda, Swami. 1924. *Hindu Sangathan: Saviour of the Dying Race*. N.p.

Siegel, Lee. 1991. *Net of Magic: Wonders and Deceptions in India*. Chicago: University of Chicago Press.

Singer, Milton. 1967. Passage to More than India: A Sketch of Changing European and American Images of India. In *Languages and Areas: Studies Presented to George V. Bobrinskoy*, 131–60. Division of the Humanities, University of Chicago.

———. 1981. On the Semiotics of Indian Identity. *American Journal of Semiotics* 1:85–126.

Singh, Khushwant. 1975a. Balyogeshwar. In *Gurus, Godmen, and Good People,* ed. Khushwant Singh, 66–72. New Delhi: Orient Longman.

———, ed. 1975b. *Gurus, Godmen, and Good People.* New Delhi: Orient Longman.

———. 1988. Worship of the Ganga. *Sunday,* January 10.

Singh, N. N.d. *Hardwar, Kankhal, and Rishikesh.* Hardwar: Randhir Book Sales.

Singh, Tavleen. 1985. The Secular Myth. *Seminar* 307:25–28.

Sinha, Surajit, and Baidyanath Saraswati. 1978. *Ascetics of Kashi: An Anthropological Exploration.* Varanasi: N. B. Bose Memorial Fund.

Sinha, V. K. 1968. *Secularism in India.* Bombay: Lalvani Publishing House.

Sivananda. 1981. *Guru Tattwa.* Shivanandanagar: Divine Life Society.

———. 1987. India. *Voice of Sivananda* 16:2–11.

Smith, D. E. 1963. *India as a Secular State.* Princeton: Princeton University Press.

Spivak, Gayatri Chakravorty. 1988a. Subaltern Studies: Deconstructing Historiography. In *Selected Subaltern Studies,* ed. Ranajit Guha and Gayatri Chakravorty Spivak, 3–34. New York: Oxford University Press.

———. 1988b. *In Other Worlds: Essays in Cultural Politics.* New York: Routledge.

Srinivas, M. N. 1967. The Cohesive Role of Sanskritization. In *India and Ceylon: Unity and Diversity,* ed. Philip Mason, 67–82. London: Oxford University Press.

Staal, Frits. 1975. *Exploring Mysticism.* Harmondsworth: Penguin.

———. 1988. *Universals: Studies in Indian Logic and Linguistics.* Chicago: University of Chicago Press.

Strauss, Sarah. 1995. Reorienting Yoga: Transnational Flows from an Indian Center. Department of Anthropology, University of Pennsylvania. Manuscript.

Svoboda, Robert. 1986. *Aghora: At the Left Hand of God.* Albuquerque: Brotherhood of Life.

Tambiah, Stanley. 1976. *World Conqueror, World Renouncer.* New York: Cambridge University Press.

———. 1984. *The Buddhist Saints of the Forest and the Cult of Amulets.* Cambridge: Cambridge University Press.

———. 1990. Presidential Address: Reflections on Communal Violence in South Asia. *Journal of Asian Studies* 49:741–60.

Taussig, Michael. 1980. *The Devil and Commodity Fetishism in South America.* Chapel Hill: University of North Carolina Press.

Thapar, Romila. 1985. Syndicated Moksha. *Seminar* 313:14–22.

———. 1989. Imagined Religious Communities? Ancient History and the Modern Search for a Hindu Identity. *Modern Asian Studies* 23:209–31.

Thomas, George M. 1989. *Revivalism and Cultural Change: Christianity, Nation-building, and the Market in the Nineteenth-Century United States.* Chicago: University of Chicago Press.

Thompson, E. P. 1977. Folklore, Anthropology, and Social History. *Indian Historical Review* 3:247–66.

Thompson, John B. 1984. *Studies in the Theory of Ideology.* Cambridge: Polity Press.

Timpanaro, Sebastiano. 1975. *On Materialism.* Trans. Lawrence Garner. London: Verso.

Trautmann, Thomas. 1971. *Kautilya and the Arthasastra.* Leiden: E. J. Brill.

Trehan, Jyoti. 1991. *Veer Savarkar: Thought and Action of Vinayak Damodar Savarkar.* New Delhi: Deep and Deep Publications.

Tripathi, B. D. 1978. *Sadhus of India.* Bombay: Popular Prakashan.

Turner, Victor. 1972. The Center Out There: Pilgrim's Goal. *History of Religions* 12:191–230.

Uttar Pradesh Tourism. 1986. *Haridwar, Rishikesh.* Lucknow: U.P. Tourism.

Vaid, Sudesh, and Kumkum Sangari. 1991. Institutions, Beliefs, Ideologies: Widow Immolation in Contemporary Rajasthan. *Economic and Political Weekly* 26 (17): WS–2–18.

Vanaik, Achin. 1988. Ideology and Economics: The Case of India. *Times of India,* March 28.

———. 1990. *The Painful Transition: Bourgeois Democracy in India.* London: Verso.

van der Veer, Peter. 1987. The Gods Must Be Liberated: A Hindu Liberation Movement in Ayodhya. *Modern Asian Studies* 21:283–303.

———. 1988. *Gods on Earth: The Management of Religious Experience and Identity in a North Indian Pilgrimage Centre.* London: Athlone Press.

———. 1994. *Religious Nationalism: Hindus and Muslims in India.* Berkeley: University of California Press.

Venkataraman. R. 1989. Dr. Sarvepalli Radhakrishnan. In *Radhakrishnan Centenary Volume,* ed. G. Parthasarathi and D. P. Chattopadhyaya, 3–5. Delhi: Oxford University Press.

Venkatesananda. 1980. *Gurudev Sivananda.* Shivanandanagar: Divine Life Society.

———. 1982. Comment. *Light,* July (Journal of the Divine Life Society of Mauritius).

Venugopal, C. N. 1986. G. S. Ghurye's Ideology of Normative Hinduism: An Appraisal. *Contributions to Indian Sociology,* n.s. 20:305–13.

Vidyarthi, L. P. 1960. Thinking about a Sacred City. *Eastern Anthropologist* 13:203–14.

———. 1961. *The Sacred Complex in Gaya.* London: Asia Publishing House.

Vidyarthi, L. P., B. N. Saraswati and Makhan Jha. 1979. *The Sacred Complex of Kashi.* New Delhi: Concept Publishing Company.

Vigne, Jacques. N.d.a. Initiation et Réalisation Spirituelle. Manuscript.

———. N.d.b. Relation Guru-disciple et Relation Psychoanalytique. Manuscript.

Vishva Hindu Parishad. 1987. *Hindu Contribution to the World of Science.* New Delhi: Vishva Hindu Parishad.

———. 1988. Are the Hindus Communal? (advertisement) *Times of India,* February 13.

———. N.d. *Ekatmata Yajna.* Ed. Ramashankar Agnihotri and Dattatreya Tiwari. New Delhi: Vishva Hindu Parishad.

———. N.d. *The Hindu Awakening: Retrospect and Promise.* New Delhi: Vishva Hindu Parishad.

———. N.d. *Vishva Hindu Parishad: Messages and Activities.* New Delhi: Vishva Hindu Parishad.

Vishva Hindu Parishad of Chicago. 1992. *Fourteenth Annual Calendar.*

———. 1993. *Fifteenth Annual Calendar.*

———. 1994. *Sixteenth Annual Calendar.*

———. 1995. *Seventeenth Annual Calendar.*

Vivekananda. 1958. Swami Vivekananda: Hindu Missionary to the West. In *Sources of Indian Tradition,* vol. 2, comp. Stephen Hay and I. H. Qureshi, 94-107. New York: Columbia University Press.

———. 1985. *The Nationalistic and Religious Lectures of Swami Vivekananda.* Ed. Swami Tapasyananda. Madras: Sri Ramakrishna Math.

Wadley, Susan. 1977. Power in Hindu Ideology and Practice. In *The New Wind: Changing Identities in South Asia,* ed. Kenneth David, 133–58. The Hague: Mouton.

White, Charles, S.J. 1972. The Sai Baba Movement: Approaches to the Study of Indian Saints. *Journal of Asian Studies* 31:863–78.

———. 1974. Swami Muktananda and the Enlightenment through Sakti Pat. *History of Religions* 13:306–22.

———. 1980. Mother Guru: Jnanananda of Madras, India. In *Unspoken Worlds: Women's Religious Lives in Non-western Cultures,* ed. Nancy Falk and Rita Gross, 22–38. San Francisco: Harper and Row.

Williams, Raymond. 1984. *A New Face of Hinduism: The Swaminarayan Religion.* Cambridge: Cambridge University Press.

NEWSPAPER AND MAGAZINE ARTICLES

Day After
November 1987.   Chidananda Condemns.

Hindustan Times
5 May 1987.   Lest Last Thread of Life Snaps.
8 May 1987.   Dutta's Body Taken to Mortuary Amid Protest.
19 May 1987.   Tantrik Held for Dutta Murder.
15 May 1987.   Another Mummified Body Found.
16 May 1987.   We Are Crazy People. (Khushwant Singh).
18 May 1987.   Remand in Mummy Case.
20 May 1987.   Another Body Preserved in Bithoor.
28 May 1987.   Hardwar "Swami" Granted Bail.
3 June 1987.   Sivananda Centenary.
3 June 1987.   15 Cops Hurt in Riot over Temple Takeover.
7 June 1987.   How Can India Cope with Success?
25 July 1987.   India's Middle Class Power. (V. A. Pai Panandiker).
1 Nov. 1987.   Sant Nirankari Mission.
23 Nov. 1987.   Swami Abducts Teenager.

15 Dec. 1987.   Jewels Stolen from Temple.

Illustrated Weekly of India

13 Sept. 1987.   The Curious Case of the Missing Monk.

20 Sept. 1987.   Selling VP.

27 Dec. 1987.   Fifty Politicians Who Have Made All the Difference since Independence.

1 Oct. 1989.   Divine Intervention.

India Today

15 April 1986.   New Crusade.

15 May 1986.   Kumbh Mela Nectar of the Gods.

31 May 1987.   Foreign Travel An Indian Summer.

31 May 1987.   The House of Horror.

15 June 1987.   The Agony of Meerut.

30 June 1987.   Tribal Godman.

31 Oct. 1987.   The New Millionaires and How They Made It.

31 Oct. 1987.   Urban Housewife Conforming to Type.

15 Nov. 1987.   Unusual Endeavour A Show to Demystify Science.

15 Nov. 1987.   Divisive Move.

31 Dec. 1987.   Computers A Quiet Revolution.

31 Dec. 1987.   The Swami Scandal.

31 Dec. 1987.   Dowry Death Public Outcry.

15 Feb. 1988.   Godman's Gaffe.

Maya

Nov. 1987.   The Battle Cry of Hindu Extremism.

Dec. 1987.   Is Chandraswamy a Double Agent?

Probe India

Nov. 1987.   Will the Hindus Survive?

Raviwar

6 Sept. 1987.   The Hindu Psyche: Why Is It So Agitated Today?

Statesman

6 April 1987.   Internecine Feud at Tumkur Mutt.

Sunday

23 Aug. 1987.   Spreading Communalism.

25 Oct. 1987.   The Angry Hindu.

8 Nov. 1987.   The Power and the Glory.

13 Dec. 1987.   The New Gold Rush.

13 Dec. 1987.   Khashoggi and the Swami.

10 Jan. 1988.   Worship of the Ganga. (Khushwant Singh).

Sunday Mail

26 Sept. 1987.   Sati.

Surya India

Aug. 1987.   Chandra Swamy on Rajiv's Future.

Swagat

Oct. 1987.   Managing for Effectiveness.

Times of India
26 July 1987.   Which Way to the Jobs?
26 Aug. 1987.   District News in Brief.
10 Sept. 1987.   District News in Brief.
21 Sept. 1987.   Sati Information Was Received Late.
21 Sept. 1987.   Transfers not Related to Sati Only.
27 Sept. 1987.   Gateway of the Gods. (Travel Supplement).
2 Oct. 1987.   Mahabodhi Vihar. (Letter to the editor).
12 Oct. 1987.   Sadhu Mohan Flays Communalism.
26 Oct. 1987.   Radha-Krishna Idols Worth over Rs 3 cr Recovered.
30 Oct. 1987.   Sant Nirankari Mission.
11 Nov. 1987.   Political Will to Fight Sati Urged.
13 Nov. 1987.   HC Orders Return of Passport.
16 Nov. 1987.   Acharya Sharma Hits Back at Disciple.
18 Nov. 1987.   Correct Stand. (Letter to the editor).
2 Dec. 1987.   Six-year-old Sacrificed Near Ghaziabad.
3 Dec. 1987.   Shame for Hindus. (Editorial).
6 Dec. 1987.   Joshi Offers to Help in Anti-sati Campaign.
14 Dec. 1987.   Grinding Machine for the Lord.
14 Dec. 1987.   Four Idols Stolen in Ujjain.
5 Jan. 1988.   Rich Poor Told to Sink Differences.
15 Jan. 1988.   Shrimad Bhagavad Gita Pathshala. (photograph).
16 Jan. 1988.   Post Women Police at Puri temple.
17 Jan. 1988.   Rajiv Gandhi in Hardwar. (photograph).
6 Feb. 1988.   Dowry Drives Them to Death.
7 Feb. 1988.   District News in Brief.
21 Feb. 1988.   District News in Brief.
3 Mar. 1988.   Ideology and Economics The Case of India. (Achin Vanaik).
24 Mar. 1988.   Five Arrested for Sacrificing Girl.
27 Mar. 1988.   District News in Brief.
27 Mar. 1988.   "Baba" Commits Suicide.
28 Mar. 1988.   Barbaric Practice. (Editorial).
4 April 1988.   Boys Being Forcibly Emasculated.

Wall Street Journal
19 May 1988.   A Thriving Middle Class is Changing the Face of India.

ADVERTISEMENTS IN MAGAZINES AND NEWSPAPERS

The Hindu
17 Mar. 1987.   G. Parameswaram.

Hindustan Times
18 May 1987.   Jay Pee Exports.
22 May 1987.   Arsha Vidya Mandir.
5 June 1987.   L. Ramlal Chadhok.
3 July 1987.   Bharat Co-operative Group Housing Society.
5 July 1987.   Sohna Rice.

17 Aug. 1987.   Margdarshan Ganapati Puja Video Cassette.
1 Nov. 1987.   Shalimar Chemical Works.
23 Nov. 1987.   Government of India Central Cottage Industries Emporium.

India Today
30 Sept. 1987.   Himachal Pradesh Tourism Department.
1 Nov. 1987.   Garcoat Paints.
31 Nov. 1987.   Raymond's Textiles.
31 Dec. 1987.   Siddhi Cement.

India West
12 Feb. 1993.   Concerned NRIs of Southern California.

Indian Express
14 Aug. 1987.   Tamil Nadu Tourism Development Corporation.
27 Dec. 1987.   Chandulal Bahl.
13 Jan. 1988.   Hindustan Computer, Ltd.

Nav Bharat Times
8 Sept. 1987.   Divine Life Society Sivananda Centenary Advertising Supplement
    (six pages).

Times of India
18 Mar. 1987.   Wazir Chand Kawatra.
18 Mar. 1987.   Gopal Chandrajee.
18 Mar. 1987.   Suresh Kumar Mittal.
22 Mar. 1987.   Jayantilal Chauhan.
4 July 1987.   Dada Ishwar Balvani.
26 Aug. 1987.   Vishnudevananda International Sivananda Yoga Vedanta Centers.
10 Sept. 1987.   Raja Rattan Amol Singh.
13 Sept. 1987.   Aurobindo Society.
28 Sept. 1987.   Uttar Pradesh Department of Cultural Affairs.
12 Oct. 1987.   Bharat Vikas Parishad.
21 Oct. 1987.   Indrajal Comics.
21 Nov. 1987.   Army Welfare Housing Organisation.
24 Nov. 1987.   Uttar Pradesh Department of Cultural Affairs.
27 Nov. 1987.   Siddhi Cement.
29 Nov. 1987.   FICCI Ladies Organisation (Say No to Dowry).
4 Dec. 1987.   Balyogeshwar Shri Sant Maharaj.
18 Dec. 1987.   Gurdev Siddha Peeth.
27 Dec. 1987.   Guru Ramdas Naturopathy Clinic/Texla TV.
16 Jan. 1988.   Government of India Department of Cultural Affairs.
17 Jan. 1988.   Lawrence Food Industries.
13 Feb. 1988.   Vishva Hindu Parishad.
12 Mar. 1988.   Tamil Nadu Development Corporation.
15 Mar. 1988.   Uttar Pradesh Department of Cultural Affairs.
11 Sept. 1988.   Savitri Market.
12 Sept. 1988.   Computer Training.

INDEX